Audi A4 Diesel
Owners Workshop Manual

John S. Mead

(6300 - 256)

Models covered

Saloon & Estate (Avant) with 2.0 litre (1968cc) turbo-diesel engines

Does NOT cover 2.7 or 3.0 litre diesel engines, 7-speed 'S-tronic' automatic transmission, petrol models, Quattro, Allroad, Cabiolet, S4 or RS4 models
Does NOT cover new A4 range introduced November 2015

A book in the **Haynes Owners Workshop Manual Series**

ISBN **978 1 78521 300 7**

British Library Cataloguing in Publication Data
A catalogue record for this book is available from the British Library.

Haynes Group Limited
Haynes North America, Inc

www.haynes.com

The manufacturer's authorised representative in the EU for product safety is:

HaynesPro BV
Stationsstraat 79 F, 3811MH Amersfoort, The Netherlands
gpsr@haynes.co.uk

Disclaimer

There are risks associated with automotive repairs. The ability to make repairs depends on the individual's skill, experience and proper tools. Individuals should act with due care and acknowledge and assume the risk of performing automotive repairs.

The purpose of this manual is to provide comprehensive, useful and accessible automotive repair information, to help you get the best value from your vehicle. However, this manual is not a substitute for a professional certified technician or mechanic.

This repair manual is produced by a third party and is not associated with an individual vehicle manufacturer. If there is any doubt or discrepancy between this manual and the owner's manual or the factory service manual, please refer to the factory service manual or seek assistance from a professional certified technician or mechanic.

Even though we have prepared this manual with extreme care and every attempt is made to ensure that the information in this manual is correct, neither the publisher nor the author can accept responsibility for loss, damage or injury caused by any errors in, or omissions from, the information given.

Contents

LIVING WITH YOUR AUDI A4

Roadside repairs

Weekly checks

Lubricants and fluids

Tyre pressures

MAINTENANCE

Routine maintenance and servicing

Contents

The Audi A4 (B8) model was launched in March 2008, and is a further development of the existing A4 model. The A4 is available as a 4-door Saloon or 5-door Estate (Avant), with a wide range of petrol and diesel engines. The engine we will be covering in this manual is the 2.0 litre turbo diesel unit which features excellent performance with industry leading standards of fuel consumption and emissions. The body shape has been developed to further reduce consumption and emissions by having a Coefficient of Drag (CD) of 0.28, made possible by the fitment of underbody panels to smooth the flow of air under the vehicle. All models are equipped with independent front and rear suspension.

High standards of safety are achieved by the standard fitment of driver's airbag, passenger's airbag, side airbags, head airbags, and seat belt pretensioners. Safety levels are further enhanced by features such as, Traction control, ABS, Emergency brake assist, Electronic stability program, and Electronic differential lock. All models are fitted with an immobiliser, alarm, remote control central locking and air conditioning.

For the home mechanic, the Audi A4 is a straightforward vehicle to maintain and most of the items requiring frequent attention are easily accessible.

Your Audi A4 manual

The aim of this Manual is to help you get the best value from your vehicle. It can do so in several ways. It can help you decide what work must be done (even should you choose to get it done by a garage). It will also provide information on routine maintenance and servicing, and give a logical course of action and diagnosis when random faults occur. However, it is hoped that you will use the manual by tackling the work yourself. On simpler jobs it may even be quicker than booking the car into a garage and going there twice, to leave and collect it. Perhaps most important, a lot of money can be saved by avoiding the costs a garage must charge to cover its labour and overheads.

The manual has drawings and descriptions to show the function of the various components so that their layout can be understood. Tasks are described and photographed in a clear step-by-step sequence. The illustrations are numbered by the Section number and paragraph number to which they relate – if there is more than one illustration per paragraph, the sequence is denoted alphabetically.

References to the 'left' or 'right' of the vehicle are in the sense of a person in the driver's seat, facing forwards.

Acknowledgements

Thanks are due to Draper Tools, who provided some of the workshop tools, and to all those people at Sparkford who helped in the production of this manual.

This manual is not a direct reproduction of the vehicle manufacturer's data, and its publication should not be taken as implying any technical approval by the vehicle manufacturers or importers.

We take great pride in the accuracy of information given in this manual, but vehicle manufacturers make alterations and design changes during the production run of a particular vehicle of which they do not inform us. No liability can be accepted by the authors or publishers for loss, damage or injury caused by any errors in, or omissions from, the information given.

Project vehicles

The main vehicle used in the preparation of this manual, and which appears in many of the photographic sequences, was an Audi A4 2.0 litre TDI Estate (Avant).

Audi A4 Avant

Working on your car can be dangerous. This page shows just some of the potential risks and hazards, with the aim of creating a safety-conscious attitude.

General hazards

Scalding

• Don't remove the radiator or expansion tank cap while the engine is hot.
• Engine oil, transmission fluid or power steering fluid may also be dangerously hot if the engine has recently been running.

Burning

• Beware of burns from the exhaust system and from any part of the engine. Brake discs and drums can also be extremely hot immediately after use.

Crushing

• When working under or near a raised vehicle, always supplement the jack with axle stands, or use drive-on ramps.
Never venture under a car which is only supported by a jack.
• Take care if loosening or tightening high-torque nuts when the vehicle is on stands. Initial loosening and final tightening should be done with the wheels on the ground.

Fire

• Fuel is highly flammable; fuel vapour is explosive.
• Don't let fuel spill onto a hot engine.
• Do not smoke or allow naked lights (including pilot lights) anywhere near a vehicle being worked on. Also beware of creating sparks (electrically or by use of tools).
• Fuel vapour is heavier than air, so don't work on the fuel system with the vehicle over an inspection pit.
• Another cause of fire is an electrical overload or short-circuit. Take care when repairing or modifying the vehicle wiring.
• Keep a fire extinguisher handy, of a type suitable for use on fuel and electrical fires.

Electric shock

• Ignition HT and Xenon headlight voltages can be dangerous, especially to people with heart problems or a pacemaker. Don't work on or near these systems with the engine running or the ignition switched on.

• Mains voltage is also dangerous. Make sure that any mains-operated equipment is correctly earthed. Mains power points should be protected by a residual current device (RCD) circuit breaker.

Fume or gas intoxication

• Exhaust fumes are poisonous; they can contain carbon monoxide, which is rapidly fatal if inhaled. Never run the engine in a confined space such as a garage with the doors shut.
• Fuel vapour is also poisonous, as are the vapours from some cleaning solvents and paint thinners.

Poisonous or irritant substances

• Avoid skin contact with battery acid and with any fuel, fluid or lubricant, especially antifreeze, brake hydraulic fluid and Diesel fuel. Don't syphon them by mouth. If such a substance is swallowed or gets into the eyes, seek medical advice.
• Prolonged contact with used engine oil can cause skin cancer. Wear gloves or use a barrier cream if necessary. Change out of oil-soaked clothes and do not keep oily rags in your pocket.
• Air conditioning refrigerant forms a poisonous gas if exposed to a naked flame (including a cigarette). It can also cause skin burns on contact.

Asbestos

• Asbestos dust can cause cancer if inhaled or swallowed. Asbestos may be found in gaskets and in brake and clutch linings. When dealing with such components it is safest to assume that they contain asbestos.

Special hazards

Hydrofluoric acid

• This extremely corrosive acid is formed when certain types of synthetic rubber, found in some O-rings, oil seals, fuel hoses etc, are exposed to temperatures above 4000C. The rubber changes into a charred or sticky substance containing the acid. *Once formed, the acid remains dangerous for years. If it gets onto the skin, it may be necessary to amputate the limb concerned.*
• When dealing with a vehicle which has suffered a fire, or with components salvaged from such a vehicle, wear protective gloves and discard them after use.

The battery

• Batteries contain sulphuric acid, which attacks clothing, eyes and skin. Take care when topping-up or carrying the battery.
• The hydrogen gas given off by the battery is highly explosive. Never cause a spark or allow a naked light nearby. Be careful when connecting and disconnecting battery chargers or jump leads.

Air bags

• Air bags can cause injury if they go off accidentally. Take care when removing the steering wheel and trim panels. Special storage instructions may apply.

Diesel injection equipment

• Diesel injection pumps supply fuel at very high pressure. Take care when working on the fuel injectors and fuel pipes.

 Warning: Never expose the hands, face or any other part of the body to injector spray; the fuel can penetrate the skin with potentially fatal results.

Remember...

DO

• Do use eye protection when using power tools, and when working under the vehicle.
• Do wear gloves or use barrier cream to protect your hands when necessary.
• Do get someone to check periodically that all is well when working alone on the vehicle.
• Do keep loose clothing and long hair well out of the way of moving mechanical parts.
• Do remove rings, wristwatch etc, before working on the vehicle – especially the electrical system.
• Do ensure that any lifting or jacking equipment has a safe working load rating adequate for the job.

DON'T

• Don't attempt to lift a heavy component which may be beyond your capability – get assistance.
• Don't rush to finish a job, or take unverified short cuts.
• Don't use ill-fitting tools which may slip and cause injury.
• Don't leave tools or parts lying around where someone can trip over them. Mop up oil and fuel spills at once.
• Don't allow children or pets to play in or near a vehicle being worked on.

The following pages are intended to help in dealing with common roadside emergencies and breakdowns. You will find more detailed fault finding information at the back of the manual, and repair information in the main chapters.

If your car won't start and the starter motor doesn't turn

☐ If it's a model with Multitronic transmission, make sure the selector is in P or N.
☐ Gain access to the battery in the luggage compartment and make sure that the battery terminals are clean and tight.
☐ Switch on the headlights and try to start the engine. If the headlights go very dim when you're trying to start, the battery is probably flat. Get out of trouble by jump starting (see next page) using a friend's car.

If your car won't start even though the starter motor turns as normal

☐ Is there fuel in the tank?
☐ Is there moisture on electrical components under the bonnet? Switch off the ignition, then wipe off any obvious dampness with a dry cloth. Spray a water-repellent aerosol product (WD-40 or equivalent) on fuel system electrical connectors like those shown in the photos. (Note that diesel engines don't normally suffer from damp.)

A From within the luggage compartment check the condition and security of the battery connections.

B Check the fuel injection system air mass meter wiring is secure.

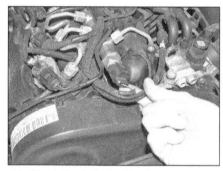

C Check the fuel rail wiring is secure.

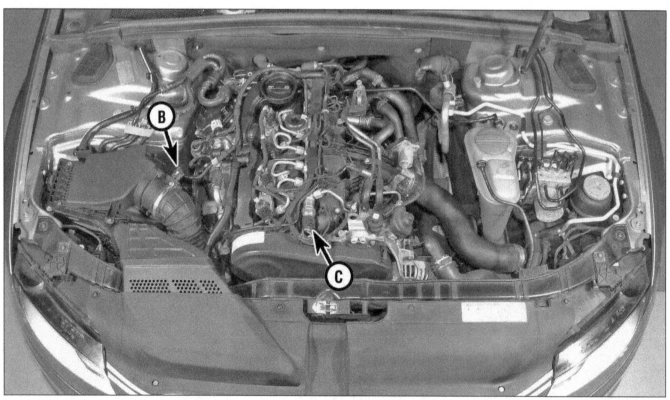

Check that electrical connections are secure (with the ignition switched off) and spray them with a water-dispersant spray like WD-40 if you suspect a problem due to damp.

Jump starting

 HAYNES HiNT *Jump starting will get you out of trouble, but you must correct whatever made the battery go flat in the first place. There are three possibilities:*

1 *The battery has been drained by repeated attempts to start, or by leaving the lights on.*

2 *The charging system is not working properly (alternator drivebelt slack or broken, alternator wiring fault or alternator itself faulty).*

3 *The battery itself is at fault (electrolyte low, or battery worn out).*

When jump-starting a car, observe the following precautions:

Note: *Remove the key in case the central locking engages when the jump leads are connected*

✓ Before connecting the booster battery, make sure that the ignition is switched off.
✓ Ensure that all electrical equipment (lights, heater, wipers, etc) is switched off.
✓ Take note of any special precautions printed on the battery case.
✓ Make sure that the booster battery is the same voltage as the discharged one in the vehicle.

✓ If the battery is being jump-started from the battery in another vehicle, the two vehicles MUST NOT TOUCH each other.
✓ Make sure that the transmission is in neutral (or PARK, in the case of Multitronic transmission).

 HAYNES HiNT *Budget jump leads can be a false economy, as they often do not pass enough current to start large capacity or diesel engines. They can also get hot.*

1 Lift up the flap and connect one end of the red jump lead to the positive (+) jump start terminal of the flat battery, located under the plenum chamber cover.

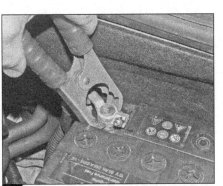

2 Connect the other end of the red lead to the positive (+) terminal of the booster battery.

3 Connect one end of the black jump lead to the negative (-) terminal of the booster battery

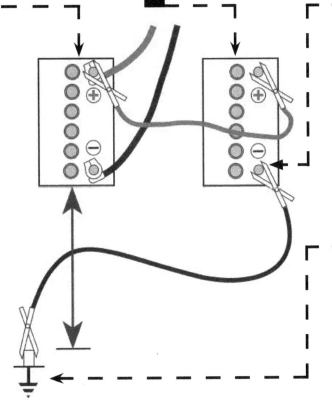

4 Connect the other end of the black jump lead to the earthing point in the engine compartment on the vehicle to be started.

5 Make sure that the jump leads will not come into contact with the fan, drive-belts or other moving parts of the engine.

6 Start the engine using the booster battery and run it at idle speed. Switch on the lights, rear window demister and heater blower motor, then disconnect the jump leads in the reverse order of connection. Turn off the lights etc.

Identifying leaks

Puddles on the garage floor or drive, or obvious wetness under the bonnet or underneath the car, suggest a leak that needs investigating. It can sometimes be difficult to decide where the leak is coming from, especially if an engine undershield is fitted. Leaking oil or fluid can also be blown rearwards by the passage of air under the car, giving a false impression of where the problem lies.

 Warning: Most automotive oils and fluids are poisonous. Wash them off skin, and change out of contaminated clothing, without delay.

 The smell of a fluid leaking from the car may provide a clue to what's leaking. Some fluids are distinctively coloured. It may help to remove the engine undershield, clean the car carefully and to park it over some clean paper overnight as an aid to locating the source of the leak. Remember that some leaks may only occur while the engine is running.

Sump oil

Engine oil may leak from the drain plug...

Oil from filter

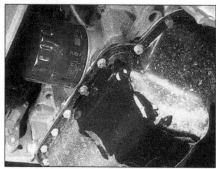

...or from the base of the oil filter.

Gearbox oil

Gearbox oil can leak from the seals at the inboard ends of the driveshafts.

Antifreeze

Leaking antifreeze often leaves a crystalline deposit like this.

Brake fluid

A leak occurring at a wheel is almost certainly brake fluid.

Power steering fluid

Power steering fluid may leak from the pipe connectors on the steering rack.

Towing

When all else fails, you may find yourself having to get a tow home – or of course you may be helping somebody else. Long-distance recovery should only be done by a garage or breakdown service. For shorter distances, DIY towing using another car is easy enough, but observe the following points:

☐ Use a proper tow-rope – they are not expensive. The vehicle being towed must display an ON TOW sign in its rear window.
☐ Always turn the ignition key to the 'On' position when the vehicle is being towed, so that the steering lock is released, and

the direction indicator and brake lights work.
☐ Lashing eyes are provided at the front and rear of the vehicle as a means of securing the vehicle onto a breakdown truck.
☐ Towing eyes are provided front and rear.
☐ Audi state that the towing distance should not exceed 50 miles, and the towing speed should be limited to 30 mph.
☐ On Multitronic transmission models, if it is necessary to tow the vehicle on two wheels (suspended from a recovery vehicle), then it is essential that it is suspended at the front to prevent damage to the final drive assembly.
☐ Before being towed, release the

handbrake and select neutral on the transmission.
☐ Note that greater-than-usual pedal pressure will be required to operate the brakes, since the vacuum servo unit is only operational with the engine running.
☐ Greater-than-usual steering effort will also be required.
☐ The driver of the car being towed must keep the tow-rope taut at all times to avoid snatching.
☐ Make sure that both drivers know the route before setting off.
☐ Only drive at moderate speeds and keep the distance towed to a minimum. Drive smoothly and allow plenty of time for slowing down at junctions.

Wheel changing

⚠️ *Warning: Do not change a wheel in a situation where you risk being hit by other traffic. On busy roads, try to stop in a lay-by or a gateway. Be wary of passing traffic while changing the wheel – it is easy to become distracted by the job in hand.*

Preparation

- ☐ When a puncture occurs, stop as soon as it is safe to do so.
- ☐ Park on firm level ground, if possible, and well out of the way of other traffic.
- ☐ Apply the handbrake and engage first or reverse gear (or Park on models with Multitronic transmission).
- ☐ Use hazard warning lights if necessary, and display the warning triangle supplied.
- ☐ Chock the wheel diagonally opposite the one being removed – a couple of large stones will do for this.
- ☐ If the ground is soft, use a flat piece of wood to spread the load under the jack.

Note: *Many A4 models are equipped with a puncture repair kit and do not have a spare wheel and jack. If your car has a puncture repair kit, refer to the information contained in the vehicle handbook.*

5 Use the wheel brace to slacken each wheel bolt half a turn. Use the special adapter when slackening the locking wheel bolt.

8 Fit the sparewheel and lightly tighten the bolts with the wheel brace.

Changing the wheel

1 The spare wheel and tools are located under the floor in the luggage compartment. Where fitted, undo the retaining bolt and lift out the spare wheel.

3 On Avant models, the tool kit is located in a separate compartment in front of the spare wheel.

6 Position the jack with the base directly under the jacking point. Turn the jack handle clockwise until the head ofthe jack fits snugly around the centre of the jacking point, then raise the car until the wheel is clear of the ground.

9 Lower the vehicle to the ground and tighten the wheel bolts in a diagonal sequence. Refit the wheel bolt cover.

2 Take out the jack from its location in front of the battery.

4 Use the hook provided to remove the wheel bolt covers.

7 Remove the wheel bolt nearest the top, and screw-in the mounting pin provided in the tool kit. Unscrew the remaining wheel bolts and remove the wheel.

Finally . . .

- ☐ Stow the jack and tools in the correct locations in the car.
- ☐ Check the tyre pressure on the wheel just fitted. If it is low, or if you don't have a pressure gauge with you, drive slowly to the nearest garage and inflate the tyre to the right pressure.
- ☐ Have the damaged tyre or wheel repaired as soon as possible.
- ☐ Have the wheel bolts tightened to the specified torque at the earliest opportunity.

Note: *If a temporary 'space-saver' spare wheel has been fitted, special conditions apply to its use. This type of spare wheel is only intended for use in an emergency, and should not remain fitted any longer than it takes to get the punctured wheel repaired. While the temporary wheel is in use, ensure it is inflated to the correct pressure, do not exceed 50 mph (80 kph), and avoid harsh acceleration, braking or cornering.*

Introduction

There are some very simple checks which need only take a few minutes to carry out, but which could save you a lot of inconvenience and expense.

These checks require no great skill or special tools, and the small amount of time they take to perform could prove to be very well spent, for example:

☐ Keeping an eye on tyre condition and pressures, will not only help to stop them wearing out prematurely, but could also save your life.

☐ Many breakdowns are caused by electrical problems. Battery-related faults are particularly common, and a quick check on a regular basis will often prevent the majority of these.

☐ If your car develops a brake fluid leak, the first time you might know about it is when your brakes don't work properly. Checking the level regularly will give advance warning of this kind of problem.

☐ If your car develops a brake fluid leak, the first time you might know about it is when your brakes don't work properly. Checking the level regularly will give advance warning of this kind of problem.

☐ If the oil or coolant levels run low, the cost of repairing any engine damage will be far greater than fixing the leak, for example.

Underbonnet check points

▲ **2.0 litre diesel engine**

A *Engine oil filler cap*
B *Coolant expansion tank*
C *Brake (and clutch) fluid reservoir*
D *Screen washer fluid reservoir*
E *Power steering fluid reservoir*

Engine oil level

Before you start
✔ Make sure that the car is on level ground.
✔ Switch off the warm engine.
✔ Wait approximately two minutes before checking the oil level.

 HAYNES HiNT *If the oil is checked immediately after driving the vehicle, some of the oil will remain in the upper engine components, resulting in an inaccurate reading.*

The correct oil
Modern engines place great demands on their oil. It is very important that the correct oil for your car is used (see *Lubricants and fluids*).

Car care
● If you have to add oil frequently, you should check whether you have any oil leaks. Place some clean paper under the car overnight, and check for stains in the morning. If there are no leaks, then the engine may be burning oil.
● Not all engines are equipped with a dipstick. Where a dipstick is not provided, the oil level is checked via the sound system or multi-media interface (MMI).
● To check the oil level via the MMI, use the function selector button and select CAR > Oil level. A digital dipstick will appear on the display, showing the oil level. A message will also appear stating the oil level situation.

1 If a dipstick is provided it will be located on the left-hand side of the engine. It is brightly coloured for ease of location.

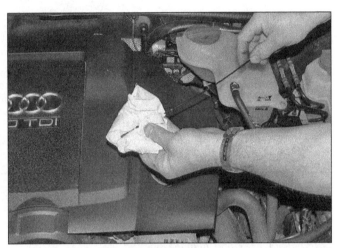

2 Withdraw the dipstick. Using a clean rag or paper towel, wipe all the oil from the dipstick. Insert the clean dipstick into the tube as far as it will go, then withdraw it again.

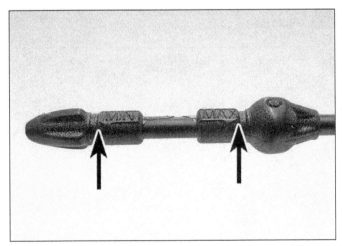

3 Note the oil level on the end of the dipstick which should be between the upper (MAX) and lower (MIN) marks. Approximately 1.0 litre of oil will raise the level from the lower mark to the upper mark.

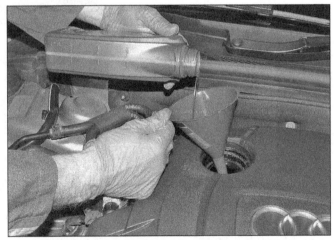

4 If topping up is necessary, oil is added through the filler cap on the top of the engine. Rotate the cap through a quarter-turn anti-clockwise and withdraw it. A funnel may help to reduce spillage. Add the oil slowly, 0.5 litres at a time. Wait 2 minutes then check the level again using the dipstick, sound system or MMI. Do not overfill.

Coolant level

Warning: Do not attempt to remove the expansion tank pressure cap when the engine is hot, as there is a very great risk of scalding. Do not leave open containers of coolant about, as it is poisonous.

Car care

● With a sealed-type cooling system, adding coolant should not be necessary on a regular basis. If frequent topping-up is required, it is likely there is a leak. Check the radiator, all hoses and joint faces for signs of staining or wetness, and rectify as necessary.

● It is important that antifreeze is used in the cooling system all year round, not just during the winter months. Don't top up with water alone, as the antifreeze will become diluted.

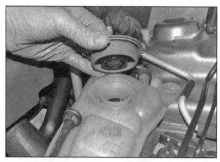

1 The coolant level varies with the temperature of the engine. When the engine is cold, the coolant level should be between the MIN and MAX mark on the side of the expansion tank located on the left-hand side of the engine compartment. When the engine is hot, the level will rise slightly.

2 If topping-up is necessary, wait until the engine is cold, then slowly unscrew the expansion tank filler cap anti-clockwise, to release any pressure in the system, and remove it.

3 Add a mixture of water and antifreeze through the expansion tank filler neck, until the coolant is at the correct level. Refit the cap, turning it clockwise as far as it will go until it is secure.

Brake (and clutch) fluid level

Warning: Brake fluid can harm your eyes and damage painted surfaces, so use extreme caution when handling and pouring it.

Warning: Do not use fluid that has been standing open for some time, as it absorbs moisture from the air, which can cause a dangerous loss of braking effectiveness.

Safety first!

● If the reservoir requires repeated topping-up this is an indication of a fluid leak somewhere in the system, which should be investigated immediately.

● If a leak is suspected, the car should not be driven until the braking system has been checked. Never take any risks where brakes are concerned.

 HAYNES HiNT *Checking the fluid level in the master cylinder reservoir is easier if the plenum chamber cover is removed*

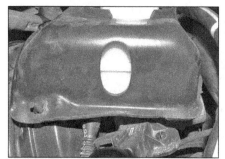

1 The brake master cylinder and fluid reservoir are mounted on the vacuum servo unit in the engine compartment on the right-hand side of the bulkhead. With the plenum chamber cover removed, the MAX and MIN marks are visible through the window in the reservoir metal cover. The fluid level should be maintained between these marks at all times.

2 If topping-up is necessary, wipe the area around the filler cap with a clean rag before removing the cap. It's a good idea to inspect the reservoir. The fluid should be changed if dirt is visible.

3 Carefully add fluid, avoiding spilling it on surrounding paintwork. Use only the specified hydraulic fluid; mixing different types of fluid can cause damage to the system and/or a loss of braking effectiveness. After filling to the correct level, refit the cap securely. Wipe off any spilt fluid.

Battery

Caution: Before carrying out any work on the vehicle battery, read the precautions given in Safety First! at the start of this manual.

✔ Make sure that the battery tray is in good condition, and that the clamp is tight. Corrosion on the tray, retaining clamp and the battery itself can be removed with a solution of water and baking soda, after removing the affected components from the car (see Chapter 5, Section 3). Thoroughly rinse all cleaned areas with water. Any metal parts damaged by corrosion should be covered with a zinc-based primer, then painted.

✔ Periodically (approximately every three months), check the charge condition of the battery as described in Chapter 5, Section 2. A 'magic eye' charge indicator is fitted to the standard battery – if the indicator is green in colour, the battery is fully charged, however, if it is colourless, it should be recharged. If it is yellow in colour, the battery should be renewed.

✔ If the battery is flat, and you need to jump start your vehicle, see *Roadside Repairs.*

1 The battery is located under the floor in the luggage compartment. To gain access it is necessary to remove the spare wheel (where applicable), tool kit, spare wheel or tool kit carrier and battery cover. Refer to Chapter 5, Section 3 for details. The exterior of the battery should be inspected periodically for damage such as a cracked case or cover.

2 Check the tightness of the battery cable clamps to ensure good electrical connections. You should not be able to move them. Also check each cable for cracks and frayed conductors.

3 If corrosion (white, fluffy deposits) is evident, remove the cables from the battery terminals, clean them with a small wire brush, then refit them. Automotive stores sell a tool for cleaning the battery post...

4 ...as well as the battery cable clamps. Note: Audi state that the terminals should not be greased.

Washer fluid level

* The underbonnet reservoir also serves the tailgate washer.

● Screenwash additives not only keep the windscreen clean during bad weather, they also prevent the washer system freezing in cold weather which is when you are likely to need it most. Don't top-up using plain water, as the screenwash will become diluted, and will freeze in cold weather.

 Warning: On no account use coolant antifreeze in the washer system – this could discolour or damage paintwork.

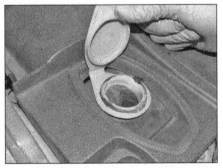

1 The reservoir for the windscreen and rear window (where applicable) washer systems is located in the rear left-hand corner of the engine compartment. If topping-up is necessary, open the cap.

2 When topping-up the reservoir a screenwash additive should be added in the quantities recommended on the bottle.

Tyre condition and pressure

It is very important that tyres are in good condition, and at the correct pressure – having a tyre failure at any speed is highly dangerous.

Tyre wear is influenced by driving style – harsh braking and acceleration, or fast cornering, will all produce more rapid tyre wear. As a general rule, the front tyres wear out faster than the rears. Interchanging the tyres from front to rear ("rotating" the tyres) may result in more even wear. However, if this is completely effective, you may have the expense of replacing all four tyres at once!

Remove any nails or stones embedded in the tread before they penetrate the tyre to cause deflation. If removal of a nail does reveal that the tyre has been punctured, refit the nail so that its point of penetration is marked. Then immediately change the wheel, and have the tyre repaired by a tyre dealer.

Regularly check the tyres for damage in the form of cuts or bulges, especially in the sidewalls. Periodically remove the wheels, and clean any dirt or mud from the inside and outside surfaces. Examine the wheel rims for signs of rusting, corrosion or other damage. Light alloy wheels are easily damaged by "kerbing" whilst parking; steel wheels may also become dented or buckled. A new wheel is very often the only way to overcome severe damage.

New tyres should be balanced when they are fitted, but it may become necessary to re-balance them as they wear, or if the balance weights fitted to the wheel rim should fall off. Unbalanced tyres will wear more quickly, as will the steering and suspension components. Wheel imbalance is normally signified by vibration, particularly at a certain speed (typically around 50 mph). If this vibration is felt only through the steering, then it is likely that just the front wheels need balancing. If, however, the vibration is felt through the whole car, the rear wheels could be out of balance. Wheel balancing should be carried out by a tyre dealer or garage.

1 Tread Depth - visual check
The original tyres have tread wear safety bands (B), which will appear when the tread depth reaches approximately 1.6 mm. The band positions are indicated by a triangular mark on the tyre sidewall (A).

2 Tread Depth - manual check
Alternatively, tread wear can be monitored with a simple, inexpensive device known as a tread depth indicator gauge.

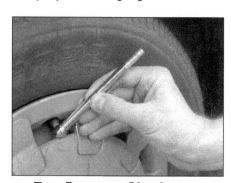

3 Tyre Pressure Check
Check the tyre pressures regularly with the tyres cold. Do not adjust the tyre pressures immediately after the vehicle has been used, or an inaccurate setting will result.

Tyre tread wear patterns

Shoulder Wear

Underinflation (wear on both sides)
Under-inflation will cause overheating of the tyre, because the tyre will flex too much, and the tread will not sit correctly on the road surface. This will cause a loss of grip and excessive wear, not to mention the danger of sudden tyre failure due to heat build-up.
Check and adjust pressures
Incorrect wheel camber (wear on one side)
Repair or renew suspension parts
Hard cornering
Reduce speed!

Centre Wear

Overinflation
Over-inflation will cause rapid wear of the centre part of the tyre tread, coupled with reduced grip, harsher ride, and the danger of shock damage occurring in the tyre casing.
Check and adjust pressures

If you sometimes have to inflate your car's tyres to the higher pressures specified for maximum load or sustained high speed, don't forget to reduce the pressures to normal afterwards.

Uneven Wear

Front tyres may wear unevenly as a result of wheel misalignment. Most tyre dealers and garages can check and adjust the wheel alignment (or "tracking") for a modest charge.
Incorrect camber or castor
Repair or renew suspension parts
Malfunctioning suspension
Repair or renew suspension parts
Unbalanced wheel
Balance tyres
Incorrect toe setting
Adjust front wheel alignment
Note: *The feathered edge of the tread which typifies toe wear is best checked by feel.*

Electrical systems

✔ Check all external lights and the horn. Refer to the appropriate Sections of Chapter 12 for details if any of the circuits are found to be inoperative.

✔ Visually check all accessible wiring connectors, harnesses and retaining clips for security, and for signs of chafing or damage.

 HAYNES HiNT *If you need to check your brake lights and indicators unaided, back up to a wall or garage door and operate the lights. The reflected light should show if they are working properly.*

1 If a single indicator light, brake light or headlight has failed, it is likely that a bulb has blown and will need to be renewed. Refer to Chapter 12 for details. If both brake lights have failed, it is possible that the stop-light switch operated by the brake pedal has failed. Refer to Chapter 9 for details.

2 If more than one indicator light or headlight has failed, it is likely that either a fuse has blown or that there is a fault in the circuit (see Chapter 12). The main fuseboxes are located behind a panel at each end of the facia and behind the trim panel on the right-hand side of the luggage compartment. To access a facia fusebox pull the panel from the end of the facia after releasing it using a plastic spatula or similar in the slot provided.

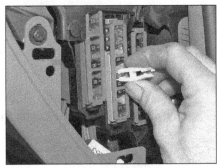

3 To renew a blown fuse, pull it out directly from the fusebox using the pliers provided (located on the inside of the facia end panel). Fit a new fuse of the same rating, available from car accessory shops. It is important that you find the reason that the fuse blew (see Electrical fault finding in Chapter 12).

Wiper blades

 HAYNES HiNT *The windscreen wipers should be in the service position before removing the wiper blades. To move the wipers to the service position using the MMI, use the function selector button to select CAR > Windscreen wipers > Service position > on. The wipers will move into the service position.*

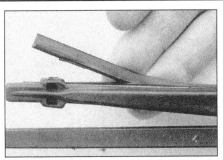

1 Check the condition of the wiper blades. If they are cracked or show any signs of deterioration, or if the glass swept area is smeared, renew them. For maximum clarity of vision, wiper blades should be renewed annually, as a matter of course.

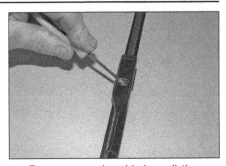

2 To remove a wiper blade, pull the arm fully away from the glass until it locks, then using a small screwdriver, depress the retaining tab.

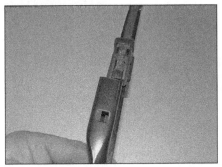

3 Pull the blade off the arm to remove. When fitting the blade, make sure that the retaining tab fully engages with the arm.

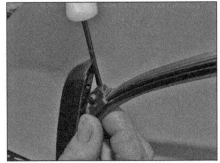

4 To remove the tailgate wiper blade, use a screwdriver to prise the blade free of the arm. Push the blade fully into engagement when refitting.

Lubricants and fluids

Note: *Using lubricants and fluids which do not meet the VAG standard may invalidate the warranty*

Engine
Models fitted with a particulate filter . . . . LongLife oil VW 507 00 only‡
Models without a particulate filter:
   Standard (distance/time) service interval . . . . Multigrade oil viscosity 5W/30 to 20W/50, VW 505 01 or VW 507 00
   LongLife (variable) service interval . . . . LongLife oil VW 507 00*

Cooling system . . . . VW G12+ Anti-freeze

Manual transmission. . . . . VW G 052 911 A1 SAE 75W 90 synthetic oil

Multitronic transmission . . . . VW G 052 180 A2 CVT fluid

Brake and clutch hydraulic systems . . . . Hydraulic fluid to DOT 4

Power steering system . . . . VW Hydraulic fluid G002 000

Air conditioning system. R134a

* *A maximum of 0.5 litres of standard VW oil may be used for topping-up when LongLife oil is unobtainable*
‡ *In an emergency, a maximum of 0.5 litres of VW 506 00/506 01 or VW 505 00/505 01 may be used for topping-up*

Tyre pressures

The recommended tyre pressures are shown on a sticker attached to the edge of the driver's side front door.

Chapter 1
Routine maintenance and servicing

Contents

Degrees of difficulty

Easy, suitable for novice with little experience	**Fairly easy,** suitable for beginner with some experience	**Fairly difficult,** suitable for competent DIY mechanic	**Difficult,** suitable for experienced DIY mechanic	**Very difficult,** suitable for expert DIY or professional

Lubricants and fluids . . . .   Refer to Lubricants, fluids and tyre pressures in *Weekly checks*

Capacities

Engine oil (including filter) . . . .   5.0 litres (approx)
Cooling system . . . .   6.0 litres (approx)
Fuel tank . . . .   65 litres
Washer reservoirs . . . .   4.5 litres

Cooling system

Antifreeze mixture:
   40% antifreeze . . . .   Protection down to -25°C
   50% antifreeze . . . .   Protection down to -35°C
Note: *Refer to antifreeze manufacturer for latest recommendations.*

Brakes

Brake pad minimum thickness (including backing plate) . . . .   10.0 mm

Torque wrench settings

	Nm	lbf ft
Manual transmission filler/level plug	45	33
Oil filter cap	25	18
Roadwheel bolts	120	89
Sump drain plug	30	22

Front underbonnet view

1 Engine oil filter cap
2 Air cleaner housing
3 Brake/clutch fluid reservoir
4 Power steering fluid reservoir
5 Coolant expansion tank
6 Alternator
7 ABS modulator
8 Screen washer reservoir

Front underbody view

1 Brake caliper
2 Guide link
3 Engine oil drain plug
4 Anti-roll bar
5 Track control link
6 Driveshaft
7 Air conditioning compressor
8 Steering gear
9 Charge air duct
10 Track rod balljoint
11 Oil level sender
12 Transmission undertray

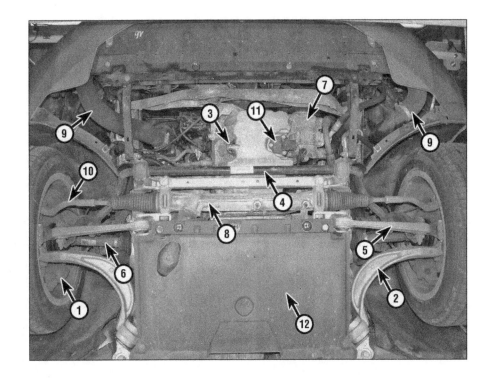

Rear underbody view

1 Lower transverse link
2 Hub carrier
3 Fuel tank
4 Rear silencer
5 Subframe
6 Anti-roll bar
7 Shock absorber lower mounting
8 Underbody cover trim
9 Rear lower link arm (track rod)
10 Coil spring
11 Subframe rear mounting

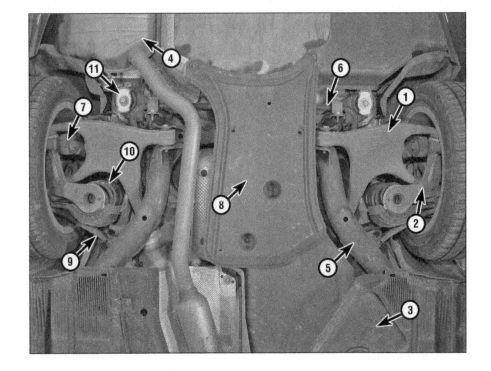

The maintenance intervals in this manual are provided with the assumption that you, not the dealer, will be carrying out the work. These are the minimum intervals recommended by us for vehicles driven daily. If you wish to keep your vehicle in peak condition at all times, you may wish to perform some of these procedures more often. We encourage frequent maintenance, since it enhances the efficiency, performance and resale value of your vehicle.

When the vehicle is new, it should be serviced by a dealer service department (or other workshop recognised by the vehicle manufacturer as providing the same standard of service) in order to preserve the warranty. The vehicle manufacturer may reject warranty claims if you are unable to prove that servicing has been carried out as and when specified, using only original equipment parts or parts certified to be of equivalent quality.

All models are equipped with a service interval display indicator in the instrument panel. Every time the engine is started the panel will illuminate briefly with service information. With the standard non-variable display, the service intervals are in accordance with specific distances and time periods. With the LongLife display, the service interval is variable according to the number of starts, length of journeys, vehicle speeds, brake pad wear, bonnet opening frequency, fuel consumption, oil level and oil temperature, however the vehicle must be serviced at least every two years. At a certain distance before the next service is due, 'Service in XXXX miles, XXX days' will appear in the instrument cluster display, and this figure will reduce as the vehicle is used. Once the service interval has been reached, the display will flash SERVICE DUE! Note that if the variable (LongLife) service interval is being used, the engine must only be filled with the recommended LongLife engine oil (see Lubricants and fluids in *Weekly checks*).

After completing a service, Audi technicians use a special instrument to reset the service display to the next service interval, and a print-out is put in the vehicle service record. The display can be reset by the owner as described in Section 5, but note that for models using the 'LongLife' interval, the procedure will automatically reset the display to the 10 000 miles 'distance' interval. To have the display reset to the 'variable' (LongLife) interval, it is necessary to take the vehicle to an Audi dealer or suitably-equipped specialist who will use a special instrument to encode the on-board computer.

Every 250 miles or weekly

☐ Refer to Weekly checks.

SERVICE DUE! on display

☐ Renew the engine oil and filter (Section 3)
Note: *Frequent oil and filter changes are good for the engine. We recommend changing the oil at least once a year.*
☐ Check the brake pad thicknesses (Section 4)
☐ Reset the service interval display (Section 5)
☐ Check the condition of the exhaust system and its mountings (Section 6)
☐ Check all underbonnet components and hoses for fluid and oil leaks (Section 7)
☐ Check the condition of the auxiliary drivebelt (Section 8)
☐ Check the coolant antifreeze concentration (Section 9)
☐ Check the brake hydraulic circuit for leaks and damage (Section 10)
☐ Check the headlight beam adjustment (Section 11)
☐ Renew the pollen filter element (Section 12)
☐ Check the manual transmission oil level (Section 13)
☐ Check the underbody protection for damage (Section 14)
☐ Check the condition of the driveshaft gaiters (Section 15)
☐ Check the steering and suspension components for condition and security (Section 16)
☐ Check the battery condition, security and electrolyte level (Section 17)
☐ Lubricate all hinges and locks (Section 18)
☐ Check the condition of the airbag unit(s) (Section 19)
☐ Check the operation of the windscreen/tailgate/head- light washer system(s) (as applicable) (Section 20)
☐ Check the engine management self-diagnosis memory for faults (Section 21)
☐ Check the operation of the sunroof and lubricate the guide rails (Section 22)
☐ Carry out a road test and check exhaust emissions (Section 23)

Every 40 000 miles or 4 years, whichever comes first

☐ Renew the fuel filter (Section 24)
☐ Check the power steering hydraulic fluid level (Section 25)
☐ Renew the Multitronic transmission fluid (Section 26)

Every 60 000 miles

☐ Renew the air filter element (Section 27)

Every 75 000 miles

☐ Renew the timing belt and tensioning roller (Section 28)
Note: *Audi specify a timing belt renewal interval of 95 000 miles and a tensioner roller renewal interval of 190 000 miles. However, if the vehicle is used mainly for short journeys, we recommend that this shorter renewal interval be adhered to. The belt and tensioner renewal interval is very much up to the individual owner but, bearing in mind that severe engine damage will result if the belt breaks in use, we recommend the shorter interval.*

At 95 000 miles then every 19 000 miles

☐ Check the particulate filter ash deposit mass (Section 29)

Every 2 years

☐ Renew the brake (and clutch) fluid (Section 30)
☐ Renew the coolant* (Section 31)
Note: **This work is not included in the Audi schedule and should not be required if the recommended Audi G12+ LongLife coolant antifreeze/inhibitor is used.*

1 Introduction

1 This Chapter is designed to help the home mechanic maintain his/her vehicle for safety, economy, long life and peak performance.

2 The Chapter contains a master maintenance schedule, followed by Sections dealing specifically with each task in the schedule. Visual checks, adjustments, component renewal and other helpful items are included. Refer to the accompanying illustrations of the engine compartment and the underside of the vehicle for the locations of the various components.

3 Servicing your vehicle will provide a planned maintenance programme, which should result in a long and reliable service life. This is a comprehensive plan, so maintaining some items but not others will not produce the same results.

4 As you service your vehicle, you will discover that many of the procedures can – and should – be grouped together, because of the particular procedure being performed, or because of the proximity of two otherwise unrelated components to one another. For example, if the vehicle is raised for any reason, the exhaust can be inspected at the same time as the suspension and steering components.

5 The first step in this maintenance programme is to prepare yourself before the actual work begins. Read through all the Sections relevant to the work to be carried out, then make a list and gather all the parts and tools required. If a problem is encountered, seek advice from a parts specialist, or a dealer service department.

2 Regular maintenance

1 If, from the time the vehicle is new, the routine maintenance schedule is followed closely, and frequent checks are made of fluid levels and high-wear items, as suggested throughout this manual, the engine will be kept in relatively good running condition, and the need for additional work will be minimised.

2 It is possible that there will be times when the engine is running poorly due to the lack of regular maintenance. This is even more likely if a used vehicle, which has not received regular and frequent maintenance checks, is purchased. In such cases, additional work may need to be carried out, outside of the regular maintenance intervals.

3 If engine wear is suspected, a compression test (see Chapter 2A) will provide valuable information regarding the overall performance of the main internal components. Such a test can be used as a basis to decide on the extent of the work to be carried out. If, for example, a compression test indicates serious internal engine wear, conventional maintenance as described in this Chapter will not greatly improve the performance of the engine, and may prove a waste of time and money, unless extensive overhaul work is carried out first.

4 The following series of operations are those most often required to improve the performance of a generally poor-running engine:

Primary operations

a) Clean, inspect and test the battery (See Weekly checks).
b) Check all the engine-related fluids (See Weekly checks).
c) Check the condition and tension of the auxiliary drivebelt (Section 8).
d) Check the condition of the air filter, and renew if necessary (Section 27).
e) Check the condition of all hoses, and check for fluid leaks (Section 7).

5 If the above operations do not prove fully effective, carry out the following secondary operations:

Secondary operations

6 All items listed under Primary operations, plus the following:
a) Check the charging system (see Chapter 5).
b) Check the preheating system (see Chapter 5).
c) Renew the fuel filter (Section 24) and check the fuel system (see Chapter 4A).

3 Engine oil and filter renewal

1 Frequent oil and filter changes are the most important preventative maintenance procedures, which can be undertaken by the DIY owner. As engine oil ages, it becomes diluted and contaminated, which leads to premature engine wear.

2 Before starting this procedure, gather all the necessary tools and materials. Also make sure that you have plenty of clean rags and newspapers handy, to mop-up any spills. Ideally, the engine oil should be warm, as it will drain better, and more built-up sludge will be removed with it. Take care, however, not to touch the exhaust or any other hot parts of the engine when working under the vehicle. To avoid any possibility of scalding, and to protect yourself from possible skin irritants and other harmful contaminants in used engine oils, it is advisable to wear gloves when carrying out this work. Access to the underside of the vehicle will be greatly improved if it can be raised on a lift, driven onto ramps, or jacked up and supported on axle stands (see *Jacking and vehicle support*). Whichever method is chosen, make sure that the vehicle remains level, or if it is at an angle, that the drain plug is at the lowest point. Undo the retaining screws and remove the engine undertray, then also remove the engine top cover.

3 Slacken the sump drain plug about half a turn. Position the draining container under the drain plug, then remove the plug completely **(see illustration)**. Recover the sealing ring from the drain plug. To drain all oil from the engine, loosen the cap from the top of the oil filter housing using a socket or spanner – this will allow the oil to drain from the filter housing into the sump.

> **HAYNES HiNT** *Keep the drain plug pressed into the sump while unscrewing it by hand the last couple of turns. As the plug releases, move it away sharply so the stream of oil issuing from the sump runs into the container, not up your sleeve.*

4 Allow some time for the old oil to drain, noting that it may be necessary to reposition the container as the oil flow slows to a trickle.

5 After all the oil has drained, wipe off the drain plug with a clean rag, and fit a new sealing washer. Clean the area around the drain plug opening, and refit the plug. Tighten the plug to the specified torque.

Note: *On some engines, the sealing washer is integral with the drain plug. On these engines, the drain plug must be renewed.*

6 Place absorbent cloths around the oil filter housing to catch any spilt oil. Where necessary, unbolt the bracket and unclip the wiring loom from over the oil filter, or unclip the solenoid valve from above the filter **(see illustration)**.

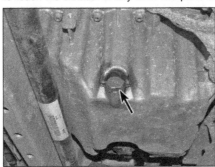

3.3 Sump drain plug

3.6 Where necessary, unclip the solenoid valve for access to the filter

3.7a Use a 32 mm socket to unscrew the filter cap...

3.7b ...withdraw the filter and cap...

3.7c ...then slide the old filter from the cap

7 Fully unscrew the cap from the top of the oil filter and remove it together with the filter element. Recover the large sealing ring from the cap, and the small sealing ring(s) from the centre rod (where applicable). Unclip the filter element from the cap and dispose of it **(see illustrations)**.

8 Using a clean rag, wipe all oil and sludge from the inside of the filter housing and cap.

9 Fit new sealing rings, then refit the assembly and tighten to the specified torque. Make sure the filter element is engaged with the cap and the correct way up **(see illustrations)**. Wipe up any spilt oil before refitting the engine top cover.

Note: *The following photos depict one type of filter assembly. A filter assembly with only one small O-ring, or no small O-ring at all, may be encountered.*

10 Remove the old oil and all tools from under the car then refit the undertray and lower the car to the ground. Also refit the engine top cover.

11 Unscrew the oil filler cap from the cylinder head cover. Fill the engine, using the correct grade and type of oil (see *Lubricants and fluids* in *Weekly checks*). An oil can spout or funnel may help to reduce spillage. Pour in two litres of oil first, and then wait a few minutes for the oil to run to the sump. Pour in another two litres, then refit the filler cap.

12 Start the engine and run it until it reaches normal operating temperature; check for leaks around the oil filter cap and the sump drain plug. Note that there may be a few seconds delay before the oil pressure warning light goes out when the engine is started, as the oil circulates through the engine oil galleries

and the new oil filter before the pressure builds-up.

⚠️ **Warning: Do not increase the engine speed above idling while the oil pressure light is illuminated, as considerable damage can be caused to the turbocharger.**

13 Switch off the engine, and wait a few minutes for the oil to settle in the sump once more.

14 Not all engines are provided with a dipstick, and in this case the oil level is checked via the sound system or multi-media interface (MMI). On engines with or without dipsticks, refer to the engine oil level checking procedures in *Weekly checks*.

15 Dispose of the used engine oil safely, with reference to *General repair procedures*.

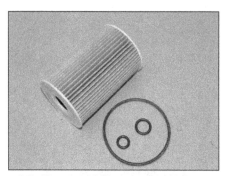

3.9a The new oil filter comes with large and small O-ring seals

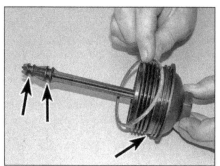

3.9b Fit the three seals to the oil filter cap in the positions shown...

3.9c ...then slide the new filter to the cap...

3.9d ...noting 'TOP' on the filter for correct fitting

3.9e Lubricate the O-ring seals with clean engine oil...

3.9f ...then refit to the filter housing

4 Brake pad check

1 On some models, the outer brake pads can be checked without removing the wheels by observing the brake pads through the holes in the wheels **(see illustration)**. If necessary, remove the wheel trim. The thickness of the pad (including backing plate) must not be less than the dimension given in the Specifications.

2 If the outer pads are worn near their limits, it is worthwhile checking the inner pads as well. Apply the handbrake then jack up vehicle and support it on axle stands (see *Jacking and vehicle support*). Remove the roadwheels.

3 Use a steel rule to check the thickness of the brake pads (including the backing plate), and compare with the minimum thickness given in the Specifications.

4 For a comprehensive check, the brake pads should be removed and cleaned. The operation of the caliper can then also be checked, and the condition of the brake disc itself can be fully examined on both sides. Refer to Chapter 9, Section 4 or 6.

5 If any pad's are worn to the specified minimum thickness or less, all four pads at the front or rear, as applicable, must be renewed as a set.

6 On completion of the check, refit the roadwheels and lower the vehicle to the ground.

5 Resetting the service interval display

1 After all necessary maintenance work has been completed, the service interval display must be reset. Audi technicians use a special dedicated instrument to do this, and a print-out is then put in the vehicle service record. It is possible for the owner to reset the display as described in the following paragraphs, but note that the procedure will automatically reset the display to a 10 000 mile interval. To continue with the 'variable' intervals which take into consideration the number of starts, length of journeys, vehicle speeds, brake pad wear, bonnet opening frequency, fuel consumption, oil level and oil temperature, the display must be reset by an Audi dealership using the special dedicated instrument.

2 To reset the standard display manually, use the function selector button CAR > Service interval display > Reset oil change interval.

6 Exhaust system check

1 With the engine cold (at least an hour after the vehicle has been driven), check the complete exhaust system from the engine to the end of the tailpipe. The exhaust system is

4.1 The outer brake pads can be observed through the holes in the wheels

most easily checked with the vehicle raised on a hoist, or suitably-supported on axle stands, so that the exhaust components are readily visible and accessible (see *Jacking and vehicle support*).

2 Check the exhaust pipes and connections for evidence of leaks, severe corrosion and damage. Make sure that all brackets and mountings are in good condition, and that all relevant nuts and bolts are tight **(see illustration)**. Leakage at any of the joints or in other parts of the system will usually show up as a black sooty stain in the vicinity of the leak.

3 Rattles and other noises can often be traced to the exhaust system, especially the brackets and mountings. Try to move the pipes and silencers. If the components are able to come into contact with the body or suspension parts, secure the system with new mountings. Otherwise separate the joints (if possible) and twist the pipes as necessary to provide additional clearance.

7 Hose and fluid leak check

1 Visually inspect the engine joint faces, gaskets and seals for any signs of water or oil leaks. Pay particular attention to the areas around the camshaft cover, cylinder head, oil filter and sump joint faces. Bear in mind that, over a period of time, some very slight seepage from these areas is to be expected – what you are really looking for is any indication of a serious leak. Should a leak be found, renew the offending gasket or oil seal by referring to the appropriate Chapters in this manual.

2 Also check the security and condition of all the engine-related pipes and hoses. Ensure that all cable-ties or securing clips are in place and in good condition. Clips which are broken or missing can lead to chafing of the hoses, pipes or wiring, which could cause more serious problems in the future.

3 Carefully check the radiator hoses and heater hoses along their entire length. Renew any hose which is cracked, swollen or deteriorated. Cracks will show up better if the hose is squeezed. Pay close attention to the hose clips that secure the hoses to the

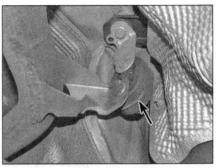

6.2 Check the condition of the exhaust rubber mountings

cooling system components. Hose clips can pinch and puncture hoses, resulting in cooling system leaks.

4 Inspect all the cooling system components (hoses, joint faces, etc) for leaks (see **Haynes Hint**). Where any problems of this nature are found on system components, renew the component or gasket with reference to Chapter.

5 With the vehicle raised, inspect the fuel tank and filler neck for punctures, cracks and other damage. The connection between the filler neck and tank is especially critical. Sometimes a rubber filler neck or connecting hose will leak due to loose retaining clamps or deteriorated rubber.

6 Carefully check all rubber hoses and metal fuel lines leading away from the fuel tank. Check for loose connections, deteriorated hoses, crimped lines, and other damage. Pay particular attention to the vent pipes and hoses, which often loop up around the filler neck and can become blocked or crimped. Follow the lines to the front of the vehicle, carefully inspecting them all the way. Renew damaged sections as necessary.

7 From within the engine compartment, check the security of all fuel hose attachments and pipe unions, and inspect the fuel hoses and vacuum hoses for kinks, chafing and deterioration.

8 Where applicable, check the condition of the power steering fluid hoses and pipes.

HAYNES HiNT

A leak in the cooling system will usually show up as white- or antifreeze-coloured deposits on the area adjoining the leak.

8.9a Turn the tensioner clockwise...

8.9b...and lock the tensioner in position

8 Auxiliary drivebelt check and renewal

Check

1 The auxiliary drivebelt drives the alternator, air conditioning compressor and, where applicable, the power steering pump.

2 For access to the drivebelt, apply the hand brake, then jack up the front of the vehicle and support it on axle stands (see *Jacking and vehicle support*). Remove the engine undertray, and remove the engine top cover as well.

3 Remove the timing belt upper outer cover as described in Chapter 2A, Section 6.

4 Examine the auxiliary drivebelt along its entire length for damage and wear in the form of cuts and abrasions, fraying and cracking. The use of a mirror and possibly an electric torch will help, and the engine may be turned with a spanner on the crankshaft pulley in order to observe all areas of the belt.

5 The drivebelt tension is adjusted automatically by a spring-loaded tensioner.

6 If a drivebelt requires renewal, proceed as follows:

Renewal

7 Apply the hand brake, then jack up the front of the vehicle and support it on axle stands (see *Jacking and vehicle support*). Remove the engine undertray, and remove the engine top cover as well.

8 Remove the timing belt upper outer cover as described in Chapter 2A, Section 6.

9 Use a spanner on the centre bolt and turn the tensioner clockwise. Lock the tensioner in its released position by inserting a locking pin (Allen key or similar) through the lug into the tensioner body **(see illustrations)**.

Note: *On certain later engines a modified tensioner is fitted and it is necessary to turn the tensioner anti-clockwise to release it.*

10 Note how the drivebelt is routed, then

remove it from the crankshaft pulley, alternator pulley, air conditioning compressor pulley and, where applicable, power steering pump pulley..

11 Locate the new drivebelt on the pulleys, then by holding the pressure of the tensioner with a spanner, remove the locking pin. Slowly release the pressure on the spanner so that the tensioner takes up the slack in the belt. Check that the belt is located correctly in the multi-grooves in the pulleys.

12 Start the engine and check that the drivebelt runs, as it should over the pulleys. Make sure that all tools and hands are kept clear of the drivebelt with the engine running.

13 With the engine stopped, refit the components removed for access.

9 Antifreeze check

1 The cooling system should be filled with the recommended G12+ antifreeze and corrosion protection fluid, which is designed to last the life of the vehicle. Do not mix this antifreeze with any other type apart from G11 or G12. However, if it is mixed with these other types, G12+ loses its 'filled for life' quality. Over a period of time, the concentration of fluid may be reduced due to topping-up (this can be avoided by topping-up with the correct antifreeze mixture – see Specifications) or fluid loss. If loss of coolant has been evident, it is important to make the necessary repair before adding fresh fluid.

2 With the engine cold, carefully remove the cap from the expansion tank. If the engine is not completely cold, place a cloth rag over the cap before removing it, and remove it slowly to allow any pressure to escape.

3 Antifreeze checkers (hydrometers) are available from car accessory shops. Draw some coolant from the expansion tank into the hydrometer and follow the manufacturer's instructions.

4 If the concentration is incorrect, it will be necessary to either withdraw some coolant and add antifreeze, or alternatively drain the old coolant and add fresh coolant of the correct concentration (see Section 33).

10 Brake hydraulic circuit check

1 Check the entire brake hydraulic circuit for leaks and damage. Start by checking the master cylinder in the engine compartment. At the same time, check the vacuum servo unit and ABS units for signs of fluid leakage.

2 Raise the front and rear of the vehicle and support it securely on axle stands (see *Jacking and vehicle support*). Check the rigid hydraulic brake lines for corrosion and damage.

3 At the front of the vehicle, check that the flexible hydraulic hoses to the calipers are not twisted or chafing on any of the surrounding suspension components. Turn the steering on full lock to make this check. Also check that the hoses are not brittle or cracked.

4 Lower the vehicle to the ground after making the checks.

11 Headlight beam adjustment

Halogen headlamps

1 Accurate adjustment of the headlight beam is only possible using optical beam setting equipment, and this work should therefore be carried out by an Audi dealer or suitably-equipped workshop.

2 For reference, the headlights can be adjusted using the adjuster bolts, accessible at the top of each light unit.

3 Some models are equipped with an

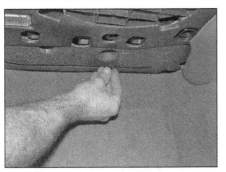

12.2a Undo the three fasteners...

12.2b...and remove the insulation panel

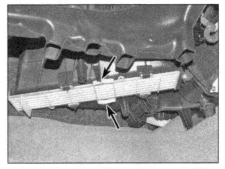

12.3 Release the retaining tabs and slide out the access cover

electrically-operated headlight beam adjustment system which is controlled through the switch in the facia. On these models, ensure that the switch is set to the basic 0 position before adjusting the headlight aim.

Gas discharge headlights

4 The headlamp range is controlled dynamically by an electronic control unit which monitors the ride height of the vehicle by sensors fitted to the front and rear suspension. Beam adjustment can only be carried out using Audi test equipment.

12 Pollen filter element renewal

1 The pollen filter is located in the heater unit and is accessed from inside the car on the passenger's side.
2 Undo the three fasteners and remove the insulation panel from beneath the glovebox **(see illustrations)**.
3 Release the two retaining tabs and slide the access cover to the left to remove it **(see illustration)**.
4 Slide the pollen filter element downward from the heater unit **(see illustration)**.
5 Fit the new element with its angled side towards the heater blower motor.
6 Refit the access cover followed by the insulation panel.

13 Manual transmission oil level check

1 The oil filler/level plug is located on the left-hand side of the manual transmission, below the clutch slave cylinder **(see illustration)**.
2 Apply the handbrake, then jack up the front and rear of the vehicle and support it on axle stands (see *Jacking and vehicle support*). To ensure an accurate check, make sure that the vehicle is level.
3 Remove the relevant engine/transmission undertrays.
4 Unscrew and remove the filler/level plug. The fluid must be level with the bottom of the hole.
5 If necessary, add the specified oil through the filler/level hole. If the level requires constant topping-up, check for leaks and repair.
6 Refit the plug and tighten to the specified torque. Refit the undertrays, then lower the vehicle to the ground.

14 Underbody protection check

1 Raise and support the vehicle on axle stands (see *Jacking and vehicle support*). Using an electric torch or lead light, inspect the entire underside of the vehicle, paying particular attention to the wheel arches. Look for any damage to the flexible underbody

coating, which may crack or flake off with age, leading to corrosion. Also check that the wheel arch liners are securely attached with any clips provided – if they come loose, dirt may get in behind the liners and defeat their purpose. If there is any damage to the underseal, or any corrosion, it should be repaired before the damage gets too serious.

15 Driveshaft gaiter check

1 With the vehicle raised and securely supported on stands, slowly rotate the roadwheel. Inspect the condition of the outer constant velocity (CV) joint rubber gaiters, squeezing the gaiters to open out the folds. Check for signs of cracking, splits or deterioration of the rubber, which may allow the grease to escape, and lead to water and grit entry into the joint. Also check the security and condition of the retaining clips. Repeat these checks on the inner joints **(see illustration)**. If any damage or deterioration is found, the gaiters should be renewed (see Chapter 8, Section 3).
2 At the same time, check the general condition of the CV joints themselves by first holding the driveshaft and attempting to rotate the wheel. Repeat this check by holding the inner joint and attempting to rotate the driveshaft. Any appreciable movement indicates wear in the joints, wear in the driveshaft splines, or a loose driveshaft retaining bolt.

12.4 Slide the filter element downward from the heater unit

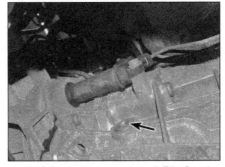

13.1 Manual transmission oil filler/level plug

15.1 Check the condition of the rubber driveshaft gaiters

16 Steering and suspension check

1 Raise the front and rear of the vehicle, and securely support it on axle stands (see *Jacking and vehicle support*).
2 Visually inspect the track rod end balljoint dust cover, the lower front suspension balljoint dust cover, and the steering rack-and-pinion gaiters for splits, chafing or deterioration. Any wear of these components will cause loss of lubricant, together with dirt and water entry, resulting in rapid deterioration of the balljoints or steering gear.
3 Where applicable, check the power steering fluid hoses for chafing or deterioration, and the pipe and hose unions for fluid leaks. Also check for signs of fluid leakage under pressure from the steering gear rubber gaiters, which would indicate failed fluid seals within the steering gear.
4 Grasp the roadwheel at the 12 o'clock and 6 o'clock positions, and try to rock it **(see illustration)**. Very slight free play may be felt, but if the movement is appreciable, further investigation is necessary to determine the source. Continue rocking the wheel while an assistant depresses the footbrake. If the movement is now eliminated or significantly reduced, it is likely that the hub bearings are at fault. If the free play is still evident with the footbrake depressed, then there is wear in the suspension joints or mountings.
5 Now grasp the wheel at the 9 o'clock and 3 o'clock positions, and try to rock it as before. Any movement felt now may again be caused by wear in the hub bearings or the steering track rod balljoints. If the inner or outer balljoint is worn, the visual movement will be obvious.
6 Using a large screwdriver or flat bar, check for wear in the suspension mounting bushes by levering between the relevant suspension component and its attachment point. Some movement is to be expected as the mountings are made of rubber, but excessive wear should be obvious. Also check the condition of any visible rubber bushes, looking for splits, cracks or contamination of the rubber.
7 With the car standing on its wheels, have an assistant turn the steering wheel back-

16.4 Check for wear in the hub bearings by grasping the wheel and trying to rock it

and-forth about an eighth of a turn each way. There should be very little, if any, lost movement between the steering wheel and roadwheels. If this is not the case, closely observe the joints and mountings previously described, but in addition, check the steering column universal joints for wear, and the rack-and-pinion steering gear itself.
8 Check for any signs of fluid leakage around the front suspension struts and rear shock absorber. Should any fluid be noticed, the suspension strut or shock absorber is defective internally, and should be renewed. **Note:** *Suspension struts/shock absorbers should always be renewed in pairs on the same axle to ensure correct vehicle handling.*
9 The efficiency of the suspension strut/shock absorber may be checked by bouncing the vehicle at each corner. Generally speaking, the body will return to its normal position and stop after being depressed. If it rises and returns on a rebound, the suspension strut/shock absorber is probably suspect. Examine also the suspension strut/shock absorber upper and lower mountings for any signs of wear.

17 Battery check

1 Refer to the information contained in *Weekly checks*.

18 Hinge and lock lubrication

1 Lubricate the hinges of the bonnet, doors and tailgate with a light general-purpose oil. Similarly, lubricate all latches, locks and lock strikers. At the same time, check the security and operation of all the locks, adjusting them if necessary (see Chapter 11).
2 Lightly lubricate the bonnet release mechanism and cable with a suitable grease.

19 Airbag unit check

1 Inspect the exterior condition of the airbag(s) for signs of damage or deterioration. If an airbag shows signs of damage, it must be renewed (see Chapter 12). Note that it is not permissible to attach any stickers to the surface of the airbag, as this may affect the deployment of the unit.

20 Windscreen/tailgate/ headlight washer system check

1 Check that each of the washer jet nozzles are clear and that each nozzle provides a strong jet of washer fluid.

2 The tailgate jet should be aimed to spray at the centre of the screen, using a pin.
3 The inner windscreen washer nozzles should be aimed slightly above the centre of the screen, and the outer nozzles slightly below the centre of the screen and towards the outside. Use a pin to adjust the nozzle aim.
4 The aim of the headlight jets is set in the factory and there is no provision for adjustment.
5 Especially during the winter months, make sure that the washer fluid frost concentration is sufficient.

21 Engine management self-diagnosis memory fault check

1 This work should be carried out by an Audi dealer or diagnostic specialist using special equipment. The diagnostic socket is located beneath the driver's side of the facia.

22 Sunroof check and lubrication

1 Check the operation of the sunroof, and leave it in the fully open position.
2 Wipe clean the guide rails on each side of the sunroof opening, then apply lubricant to them. Audi recommend lubricant spray G 052 778 A2.

23 Road test and exhaust emissions check

Instruments and electrical equipment

1 Check the operation of all instruments and electrical equipment.
2 Make sure that all instruments read correctly, and switch on all electrical equipment in turn, to check that it functions properly.

Steering and suspension

3 Check for any abnormalities in the steering, suspension, handling or road feel.
4 Drive the vehicle, and check that there are no unusual vibrations or noises which may indicate wear in the driveshafts, wheel bearings, etc.
5 Check that the steering feels positive, with no excessive sloppiness, or roughness, and check for any suspension noises when cornering and driving over bumps.

Drivetrain

6 Check the performance of the engine, clutch (where applicable), gearbox/transmission and driveshafts.
7 Listen for any unusual noises from the engine, clutch and gearbox/transmission.

24.1 Remove the right-hand underbody panel for access to the fuel filter

24.3 Undo the nuts and remove the filter bracket

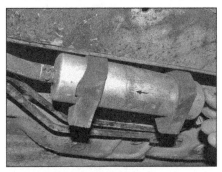

24.5 Withdraw the filter and disconnect the fuel hoses

8 Make sure that the engine runs smoothly when idling, and that there is no hesitation when accelerating.

9 Check that, where applicable, the clutch action is smooth and progressive, that the drive is taken up smoothly, and that the pedal travel is not excessive. Also listen for any noises when the clutch pedal is depressed.

10 On manual gearbox models, check that all gears can be engaged smoothly without noise, and that the gear lever action is smooth and not abnormally vague or notchy.

11 Listen for a metallic clicking sound from the front of the vehicle, as the vehicle is driven slowly in a circle with the steering on full-lock. Carry out this check in both directions. If a clicking noise is heard, this indicates wear in a driveshaft joint, in which case renew the joint if necessary.

Braking system

12 Make sure that the vehicle does not pull to one side when braking, and that the wheels do not lock when braking hard.

13 Check that there is no vibration through the steering when braking.

14 Check that the handbrake operates correctly and that it holds the vehicle stationary on a slope.

15 Test the operation of the brake servo unit as follows. With the engine off, depress the footbrake four or five times to exhaust the vacuum. Hold the brake pedal depressed, then start the engine. As the engine starts, there should be a noticeable 'give' in the brake pedal as vacuum builds-up. Allow the engine to run for at least two minutes, and then switch it off. If the brake pedal is depressed now, it should be possible to detect a hiss from the servo as the pedal is depressed. After about four or five applications, no further hissing should be heard, and the pedal should feel considerably harder.

16 Under controlled emergency braking, the pulsing of the ABS unit must be felt at the footbrake pedal.

Exhaust emissions check

17 Although not part of the manufacturer's maintenance schedule, this check will normally be carried out on a regular basis according to the country the vehicle is operated in.

Currently in the UK, exhaust emissions testing is included as part of the annual MOT test after the vehicle is 3 years old. In Germany the test is made when the vehicle is 3 years old, then repeated every 2 years.

24 Fuel filter renewal

1 The fuel filter is located under the car, approximately half way along on the right-hand side. To gain access, remove the large right-hand underbody panel **(see illustration)**.

2 Position a container underneath the filter and have rags handy to absorb any fuel that may be spilt.

3 Undo the filter bracket retaining nuts, then disengage and remove the bracket **(see illustration)**.

4 Disengage the fuel return line from the filter rubber mountings.

5 Withdraw the filter from its location, then release the retaining clips and disconnect the fuel hoses from each end of the filter **(see illustration)**. Remove the filter from under the car.

6 Fill the new filter with clean diesel to aid restarting.

7 Connect the two fuel hoses then locate the filter in position. Note that the arrows on the filter point in the direction of fuel flow.

8 Locate the fuel return line in the filter rubber mountings.

27.1 Slacken the clamp and detach the air outlet duct

9 Refit the filter bracket and secure with the retaining nuts.

10 Refit the underbody panel then lower the vehicle to the ground.

25 Power steering hydraulic fluid level check

1 Refer to Chapter 10, Section 17.

26 Multitronic transmission fluid renewal

1 The refilling of this transmission requires specialist equipment to overfill the casing and purge any air from the internals. Running the engine without purging the system could cause severe damage to the transmission. For this reason, we recommend entrusting this task to an Audi dealer or suitably-equipped repairer.

27 Air filter element renewal

1 Slacken the retaining clamp and detach the air outlet duct from the air cleaner cover **(see illustration)**.

2 Unclip the air intake duct from the lock carrier panel, then pull the ducting from the top of the air cleaner cover **(see illustration)**.

27.2 Unclip the air intake duct and remove it from the lock carrier panel and air cleaner cover.

27.3a Undo the retaining screws...

27.3b...and lift off the air cleaner cover

27.4 Note which way around the filter element is fitted

3 Undo the retaining screws and lift off the air cleaner cover (see illustrations). If necessary, disconnect the wiring connector from the air mass meter in the air cleaner cover.

4 Remove the air filter element, noting which way round it is fitted (see illustration).

5 Wipe clean the main body, if necessary use a vacuum cleaner to remove any debris, then fit the new air filter, making sure it is the correct way round.

6 The remainder of refitting is a reversal of removal.

28 Timing belt and tensioning roller renewal

1 Refer to Chapter 2A, Section 7 for details of renewing the timing belt and Chapter 2A, Section 8 for details of renewing the tensioning roller.

29 Particulate filter ash deposit mass check

1 Eventually, the amount of ash deposited in the particulate filter by the filtration process will cause a blockage, and engine running problems.

2 Audi state that the maximum amount of ash is 60 g. At this point, the particulate filter must be renewed.

3 Unfortunately, the mass of the ash can only be established using dedicated Audi diagnostic equipment, connected to the vehicle through the diagnostic plug under the driver's side of the facia. Consequently, we recommend this task is entrusted to an Audi dealer or suitably-equipped specialist.

30 Brake (and clutch) fluid renewal

⚠ *Warning: Brake hydraulic fluid can harm your eyes and damage painted surfaces, so use extreme caution when handling and pouring it. Do not use fluid that has been standing open*

for some time, as it absorbs moisture from the air. Excess moisture can cause a dangerous loss of braking effectiveness.

1 The procedure is similar to that for the bleeding of the hydraulic system as described in Chapter 9, Section 2, except that the brake fluid reservoir should be emptied by siphoning, using a clean poultry baster or similar before starting, and allowance should be made for the old fluid to be expelled when bleeding a section of the circuit. Since the clutch hydraulic system on manual gearbox models also uses fluid from the brake system reservoir, it should also be bled at the same time by referring to Chapter 6, Section 2.

2 Working as described in Chapter 9, open the first bleed screw in the sequence, and pump the brake pedal gently until nearly all the old fluid has been emptied from the master cylinder reservoir.

3 Top-up to the MAX level with new fluid, and continue pumping until only the new fluid remains in the reservoir, and new fluid can be seen emerging from the bleed screw. Tighten the screw, and top the reservoir level up to the MAX level line.

4 Work through all the remaining bleed screws in the sequence until new fluid can be seen at all of them. Be careful to keep the master cylinder reservoir topped-up to above the MIN level at all times, or air may enter the system and greatly increase the length of the task.

5 When the operation is complete, check that all bleed screws are securely tightened, and that their dust caps are refitted. Wash off all traces of spilt fluid, and recheck the master cylinder reservoir fluid level.

6 On models with a manual transmission unit, once the brake fluid has been changed the clutch fluid should also be renewed. Referring to Chapter 6, bleed the clutch until new fluid is seen to be emerging from the slave cylinder bleed screw, keeping the master cylinder fluid level above the MIN level line at all times to prevent air entering the system. Once the new fluid emerges, securely tighten the bleed screw then disconnect and remove the bleeding equipment. Securely refit the dust cap then wash off all traces of spilt fluid.

7 On all models, ensure the master cylinder fluid level is correct (see *Weekly checks.*) and

thoroughly check the operation of the brakes and (where necessary) clutch before taking the car on the road.

31 Coolant renewal

Note: *This work is not included in the Audi schedule and should not be required if the recommended Audi G12+ LongLife coolant antifreeze/inhibitor is used. However, if standard antifreeze/inhibitor is used, the work should be carried out at the recommended interval.*

⚠ *Warning: Wait until the engine is cold before starting this procedure. Do not allow antifreeze to come in contact with your skin, or with the painted surfaces of the vehicle. Rinse off spills immediately with plenty of water. Never leave antifreeze lying around in an open container, or in a puddle in the driveway or on the garage floor. Children and pets are attracted by its sweet smell, but antifreeze can be fatal if ingested.*

Cooling system draining

1 With the engine completely cold, cover the expansion tank cap with a wad of rag, and slowly turn the cap anti-clockwise to relieve the pressure in the cooling system (a hissing sound will normally be heard). Wait until any pressure remaining in the system is released, then continue to turn the cap until it can be removed.

2 Release the fasteners and remove the engine undertray. Position a suitable container beneath the radiator bottom hose, then undo the drain tap in the radiator bottom hose and allow the coolant to drain into the container.

3 If the coolant has been drained for a reason other than renewal, then provided it is clean, it can be re-used, but this is not recommended.

4 Once all the coolant has drained, tighten the drain tap.

Cooling system flushing

5 If coolant renewal has been neglected, or if the antifreeze mixture has become diluted, then in time, the cooling system may gradually lose efficiency, as the coolant passages become restricted due to rust, scale deposits, and other sediment. Flushing the system clean can restore the cooling system efficiency.

6 The radiator should be flushed independently of the engine, to avoid unnecessary contamination.

Radiator flushing

7 To flush the radiator, disconnect the top and bottom hoses and any other relevant hoses from the radiator, with reference to Chapter 3.

8 Insert a garden hose into the radiator top inlet. Direct a flow of clean water through the radiator, and continue flushing until clean water emerges from the radiator bottom outlet.

9 If after a reasonable period, the water still does not run clear, the radiator can be flushed with a good proprietary cooling system cleaning agent. It is important that their manufacturer's instructions are followed carefully. If the contamination is particularly bad, insert the hose in the radiator bottom outlet, and reverse-flush the radiator.

Engine flushing

10 To flush the engine, remove the thermostat as described in Chapter 3, Section 4, then temporarily refit the thermostat cover.

11 With the top and bottom hoses disconnected from the radiator, insert a garden hose into the radiator top hose. Direct a clean flow of water through the engine, and continue flushing until clean water emerges from the radiator bottom hose.

12 On completion of flushing, refit the thermostat and reconnect the hoses with reference to Chapter 3.

Cooling system filling

13 Before attempting to fill the cooling system, ensure the drain plug is securely closed and make sure that all hoses are connected and are securely retained by their clips. If the recommended Audi coolant is not being used, ensure that a suitable antifreeze mixture is used all year round, to prevent corrosion of the engine components (see following sub-Section).

14 Remove the expansion tank filler cap and slowly fill the system with the coolant. Continue to fill the cooling system until bubbles stop appearing in the expansion tank. Help to bleed the air from the system by repeatedly squeezing the radiator bottom hose.

15 When no more bubbles appear, top the coolant level up to the MAX level mark then securely refit the cap to the expansion tank.

16 Run the engine at a fast idle speed until the cooling fan cuts in. Wait for the fan to stop then switch the engine off and allow the engine to cool.

17 When the engine has cooled, check the coolant level with reference to *Weekly checks*. Top-up the level if necessary, and refit the expansion tank cap.

Antifreeze mixture

Caution: Audi specify the use of G12+ antifreeze (purple in colour). DO NOT mix this with any other type of antifreeze, as severe engine damage may result. If the coolant visible in the expansion tank is brown in colour, then the cooling system may have been topped-up with coolant containing the wrong type of antifreeze. If you are unsure of the type of antifreeze used, or if you suspect that mixing may have occurred, the best course of action is to drain, flush and refill the cooling system.

18 If the recommended Audi coolant is not being used, the antifreeze should always be renewed at the specified intervals. This is necessary not only to maintain the antifreeze properties, but also to prevent corrosion which would otherwise occur as the corrosion inhibitors become progressively less effective.

19 The quantity of antifreeze and levels of protection are indicated in the Specifications.

20 Before adding antifreeze, the cooling system should be completely drained, preferably flushed, and all hoses checked for condition and security.

21 After filling with antifreeze, a label should be attached to the expansion tank, stating the type and concentration of antifreeze used, and the date installed. Any subsequent topping-up should be made with the same type and concentration of antifreeze.

Caution: Do not use engine antifreeze in the windscreen/tailgate/headlight washer system, as it will cause damage to the vehicle paintwork.

Chapter 2 Part A
Engine in-car repair procedures

Contents

Degrees of difficulty

Easy, suitable for novice with little experience	**Fairly easy,** suitable for beginner with some experience	**Fairly difficult,** suitable for competent DIY mechanic	**Difficult,** suitable for experienced DIY mechanic	**Very difficult,** suitable for expert DIY or professional

Specifications

General

Manufacturer's engine codes:
Up to model year 2012:
    1968 cc (2.0 litre), 16-valve, DOHC .... CAGA, CAGB, CAGC, CAHA, CAHB and CMEA
From approximately model year 2012 onward:
    1968 cc (2.0 litre), 16-valve, DOHC .... CGLC, CGLD, CJCA, CJCB, CJCC, CJCD, CMBG, CMFA, CMFB and CMGB

Maximum outputs:	Power	Torque
Engine code CAGA, CMEA, CJCA and CMFA.................	105 kW @ 4200 rpm	320 Nm @ 1750 to 2500 rpm
Engine code CAGB and CJCB............................	100 kW @ 4200 rpm	320 Nm @ 1750 to 2500 rpm
Engine code CAGC and CJCC...........................	88 kW @ 4200 rpm	300 Nm @ 1750 to 2500 rpm
Engine code CAHA....................................	125 kW @ 4200 rpm	350 Nm @ 1750 to 2500 rpm
Engine code CAHB and CGLD...........................	120 kW @ 4200 rpm	350 Nm @ 1750 to 2500 rpm
Engine code CGLC....................................	130 kW @ 4200 rpm	380 Nm @ 1750 to 2500 rpm
Engine code CJCD and CMFB...........................	110 kW @ 4200 rpm	320 Nm @ 1750 to 2500 rpm
Engine code CMBG	130 kW @ 4200 rpm	380 Nm @ 1750 to 2500 rpm

Bore .... 81.0 mm
Stroke .... 95.5 mm
Compression ratio:
  Engine codes CAGA, CAGB, CAGC and CMEA .... 18.5 : 1
  All other engines...................................... 16.5 : 1
Compression pressures:
  Minimum compression pressure .... Approximately 19.0 bar
  Maximum difference between cylinders..................... Approximately 5.0 bar
Firing order... 1 – 3 – 4 – 2
No 1 cylinder location.. Timing belt end
Note: See 'Vehicle identification' in Reference chapter for the location of engine code markings.

Lubrication system

Oil pump type... Gear type, driven by front balance shaft
Oil pressure switch (green cap) .... 0.5 bar
Oil pressure switch (brown cap)............................... 0.7 bar
Oil pressure (oil temperature 80°C):
  Minimum @ idling .... 0.8 bar
  Minimum @ 2000 rpm................................... 1.4 bar

Torque wrench settings

	Nm	lbf ft
Ancillary (alternator, etc) bracket mounting bolts: *		
Stage 1 (all six bolts)	40	30
Stage 2 (for two lower bolts)	Angle-tighten a further 180°	
Stage 2 (for four upper bolts)	Angle-tighten a further 60°	
Auxiliary drivebelt tensioner securing bolt: *		
Stage 1	20	15
Stage 2	Angle-tighten a further 180°	
Balance shaft drivegear bolts: *		
Stage 1	20	15
Stage 2	Angle-tighten a further 90°	
Balance shaft housing to cylinder block: *		
M7:		
Stage 1	13	10
Stage 2	Angle-tighten a further 90°	
M8:		
Stage 1	20	15
Stage 2	Angle-tighten a further 90°	
Balance shaft idler gear: *		
Stage 1	90	66
Stage 2	Angle-tighten a further 90°	
Big-end bearing caps bolts: *		
Stage 1	30	22
Stage 2	Angle-tighten a further 90°	
Camshaft bearing frame bolts/nut	10	7
Camshaft cover bolts	10	7
Camshaft sprocket hub centre bolt	100	74
Camshaft sprocket-to-hub bolts: *		
Stage 1	20	15
Stage 2	Angle-tighten a further 45°	
Crankshaft oil seal housing bolts	15	11
Crankshaft pulley-to-sprocket bolts: *		
Stage 1	10	7
Stage 2	Angle-tighten a further 90°	
Crankshaft sprocket bolt: *		
Stage 1	180	133
Stage 2	Angle-tighten a further 90°	
Stage 3	Angle-tighten a further 45°	
Cylinder head bolts: *		
Stage 1	30	22
Stage 2	50	37
Stage 3	Angle-tighten a further 90°	
Stage 4	Angle-tighten a further 90°	
Driveplate bolts: *		
Stage 1	60	44
Stage 2	Angle-tighten a further 90°	
Engine/transmission mountings: *		
Left- and right-hand engine mountings:		
Mounting bracket-to-engine	40	30
Mounting-to-mounting bracket:	90	66
Stage 1	40	30
Stage 2	Angle-tighten a further 90°	
Mounting-to-subframe	55	41
Retaining plate bolts	20	15
Torque reaction support:		
Support-to-cylinder block	40	30
Torque reaction support crossmember bolts	25	18
Transmission mounting:		
Transmission crossmember-to-underbody	70	52
Transmission mounting bracket-to-transmission	40	30
Transmission mounting-to-bracket	20	15
Transmission mounting-to-crossmember	20	15
Fuel pump hub nut	95	70
Fuel pump sprocket bolts*	20	15
Intermediate gear bolt: *		
Stage 1	90	66
Stage 2	Angle-tighten a further 90°	

Torque wrench settings (continued)

	Nm	lbf ft
Main bearing cap bolts: *		
Stage 1	65	48
Stage 2	Angle-tighten a further 90°	
Oil cooler screws	11	7
Oil cooler centre bolt	25	18
Oil drain plug*	30	22
Oil filter housing-to-cylinder block bolts: *		
Stage 1	15	11
Stage 2	Angle-tighten a further 90°	
Oil filter cover	25	18
Oil level/temperature sensor-to-sump bolts	10	7
Oil pick-up pipe securing bolts	10	7
Oil pressure warning light switch	20	15
Oil pump to balance shaft securing bolts	9	6
Piston oil spray jet bolt	25	18
Subframe mounting bolts: *		
Stage 1	115	85
Stage 2	Angle-tighten a further 90°	
Sump:		
Sump-to-cylinder block bolts	15	11
Sump-to-transmission bolts	45	33
Timing belt outer cover bolts	10	7
Timing belt tensioner roller securing nut: *		
Stage 1	20	15
Stage 2	Angle-tighten a further 45°	
Timing belt idler pulleys:		
Lower idler roller nut	20	15
Upper idler roller (small) bolt	20	15
Upper idler roller (large) bolt: *		
Stage 1	50	37
Stage 2	Angle-tighten a further 90°	

*Use new fasteners

1 General Information

How to use this Chapter

1 This Part of Chapter 2 describes those repair procedures that can reasonably be carried out on the engine while it remains in the vehicle. If the engine has been removed from the vehicle and is being dismantled as described in Part B, any preliminary dismantling procedures can be ignored.

2 Note that while it may be possible physically to remove certain items while the engine is in the vehicle, such tasks are not usually carried out as separate operations, and usually require the execution of several additional procedures (not to mention the cleaning of components and of oilways); for this reason, all such tasks are classed as major overhaul procedures, and are described in Part B of this Chapter.

Engine description

3 Throughout this Chapter, engines are referred to by type, and are identified and referred to by the manufacturer's code letters. A listing of all engines covered, together with their code letters, is given in the Specifications at the start of this Chapter.

4 The engines are water-cooled, double overhead camshafts (DOHC), in-line four-cylinder units, with cast-iron cylinder blocks and aluminium-silicon alloy cylinder heads. All are mounted in-line at the front of the vehicle, with the transmission bolted to the rear of the engine.

5 The crankshaft is of five-bearing type, and thrustwashers are fitted to the centre main bearing to control crankshaft endfloat.

6 Drive for the exhaust camshaft is by a toothed timing belt from the crankshaft, with the intake camshaft driven by interlocking gears at the left-hand end of both camshafts. The gears incorporate a toothed backlash compensator element. Each camshaft is mounted at the top of the cylinder head, and is secured by a bearing frame/ladder.

7 The valves are closed by coil springs, and run in guides pressed into the cylinder head. The valves are operated by roller rocker arms incorporating hydraulic tappets.

8 A twin, counter-rotating balance shaft assembly is fitted to the base of the cylinder block. The rearmost balance shaft is driven by a gear on the crankshaft, via an intermediate gear bolted to the balance shaft housing. The two balance shafts are geared together.

9 The oil pump is driven by the front balance shaft. Oil is drawn from the sump through a strainer, and then forced through an externally-mounted, renewable filter. From there, it is distributed to the cylinder head, where it lubricates the camshaft journals and hydraulic tappets, and also to the crankcase, where it lubricates the main bearings, connecting rod big-ends, gudgeon pins and cylinder bores. A coolant-fed oil cooler is fitted to the oil filter housing on all engines. Oil jets are fitted to the base of each cylinder – these spray oil onto the underside of the pistons, to improve cooling.

10 All engines are fitted with a brake servo vacuum pump driven by the camshaft on the transmission end of the cylinder head.

11 On all engines, engine coolant is circulated by a pump, driven by the timing belt. For details of the cooling system, refer to Chapter 3.

Operations with engine in car

12 The following operations can be performed without removing the engine:
a) Compression pressure – testing.
b) Camshaft cover – removal and refitting.
c) Crankshaft pulley – removal and refitting.
d) Timing belt covers – removal and refitting.
e) Timing belt – removal, refitting and adjustment.
f) Timing belt tensioner and sprockets – removal and refitting.
g) Camshaft oil seals – renewal.
h) Camshafts and hydraulic tappets – removal, inspection and refitting.
i) Cylinder head – removal and refitting.
j) Cylinder head and pistons – decarbonising.
k) Crankshaft oil seals – renewal.
l) Engine/transmission mountings – inspection and renewal.

Note: *Removal of the sump for access to the oil pump and the pistons and connecting rods entails removal of the front subframe. This is an extremely complicated and involved operation, requiring numerous Audi special tools and support jigs and a well equipped workshop with vehicle jacking and lifting facilities. For this reason, removal of the engine bottom end components can realistically only be carried out with the engine removed from the vehicle. Refer to the procedures contained in Chapter 2B.*

2 Compression and leakdown tests – description and interpretation

Compression test

Note: *A compression tester suitable for use with diesel engines will be required for this test.*
1 When engine performance is down, or if misfiring occurs which cannot be attributed to the ignition or fuel systems, a compression test can provide diagnostic clues as to the engine's condition. If the test is performed regularly, it can give warning of trouble before any other symptoms become apparent.
2 The engine must be fully warmed-up to normal operating temperature, the battery must be fully charged, and you will require the aid of an assistant.
3 Remove the glow plugs as described in Chapter 5, Section 10, and then fit a compression tester to the No 1 cylinder glow plug hole. The type of tester that bolts into the plug thread is preferred.

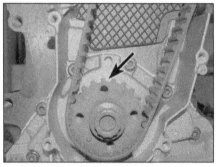

3.7 The alignment mark on the crankshaft sprocket should be almost vertical

3.8b ...so the marks on the tool and sprocket align

Note: *As a result of the glow plug wiring connectors being disconnected and the engine cranked, faults will be stored in the ECU memory. These must be erased after the compression test.*
4 Have your assistant crank the engine for several seconds on the starter motor. After one or two revolutions, the compression pressure should build-up to a maximum figure and then stabilise. Record the highest reading obtained.
5 Repeat the test on the remaining cylinders, recording the pressure in each.
6 The cause of poor compression is less easy to establish on a diesel engine than on a petrol engine. The effect of introducing oil into the cylinders (wet testing) is not conclusive, because there is a risk that the oil will sit in the recess on the piston crown, instead of passing to the rings. However, the following can be used as a rough guide to diagnosis.
7 All cylinders should produce very similar pressures. Any difference greater than that specified indicates the existence of a fault. Note that the compression should build-up quickly in a healthy engine. Low compression on the first stroke, followed by gradually increasing pressure on successive strokes, indicates worn piston rings. A low compression reading on the first stroke, which does not build-up during successive strokes, indicates leaking valves or a blown head gasket (a cracked head could also be the cause).
8 A low reading from two adjacent cylinders is almost certainly due to the head gasket having blown between them and the presence of coolant in the engine oil will confirm this.
9 On completion, remove the compression

3.8a Fit the tool to the hole in the oil seal housing...

3.8c Insert a 6 mm drill bit/rod to lock the camshaft hub

tester, and refit the glow plugs, with reference to Chapter 5 Section 10.
10 Reconnect the wiring to the injector solenoids. Finally, have an Audi dealer or suitably equipped specialist erase the fault codes from the ECU memory.

Leakdown test

11 A leakdown test measures the rate at which compressed air fed into the cylinder is lost. It is an alternative to a compression test, and in many ways it is better, since the escaping air provides easy identification of where pressure loss is occurring (piston rings, valves or head gasket).
12 The equipment required for leakdown testing is unlikely to be available to the home mechanic. If poor compression is suspected, have the test performed by a suitably equipped garage.

3 Engine assembly and valve timing marks – general information and usage

General information

1 TDC is the highest point in the cylinder that each piston reaches as it travels up-and-down when the crankshaft turns. Each piston reaches TDC at the end of the compression stroke and again at the end of the exhaust stroke, but TDC generally refers to piston position on the compression stroke. No 1 piston is at the timing belt end of the engine.
2 Positioning No 1 piston at TDC is an essential part of many procedures, such as timing belt removal and camshaft removal.
3 The design of the engines covered in this Chapter is such that piston-to-valve contact may occur if the camshaft or crankshaft is turned with the timing belt removed. For this reason, it is important to ensure that the camshaft and crankshaft do not move in relation to each other once the timing belt has been removed from the engine.

Setting TDC on No 1 cylinder

Note: *VAG special tool T10050 is required to lock the crankshaft sprocket in the TDC position. Alternatively obtain a tool from automotive tool specialists.*
4 Remove the auxiliary drivebelt as described in Chapter 1, Section 8.
5 Remove the crankshaft pulley as described in Section 5.
6 Remove the timing belt outer covers as described in Section 6.
7 Using a spanner or socket on the crankshaft sprocket bolt, turn the crankshaft in the normal direction of rotation (clockwise) until the alignment mark on the face of the sprocket is almost vertical, and the hole in the camshaft sprocket hub aligns with the hole in the cylinder head **(see illustration)**.
8 While in this position it should be possible to insert the VAG tool T10050 to lock the crankshaft, and a 6 mm diameter rod/drill bit to lock the camshafts **(see illustrations)**.

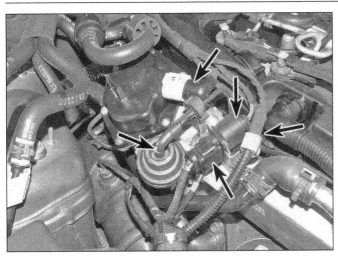

4.3 Disconnect the vacuum hose and wiring connectors at the right-hand side of the cover

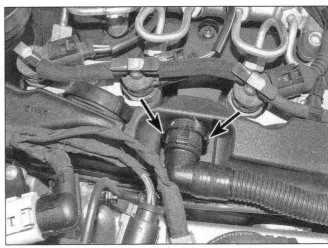

4.4 Squeeze together the sides of the collar and disconnect the breather hose

Note: *The mark on the crankshaft sprocket and the mark on the VAG tool must align, whilst at the same time the shaft of tool must engage in the drilling in the crankshaft oil seal housing.*
9 The engine is now set to TDC on No 1 cylinder.

4 Camshaft cover – removal and refitting

Removal

1 Remove the fuel injectors as described in Chapter 4A, Section 4 and the fuel rail as described in Chapter 4A, Section 11.
2 Remove the timing belt upper cover as described in Section 6.
3 On later engines, disconnect the vacuum hose and the wiring connectors at the right-hand side of the camshaft cover **(see illustration)**.
4 Squeeze together the sides of the collar, and disconnect the breather hose from the camshaft cover **(see illustration)**.
5 Remove the diesel particulate filter pressure sensor from the bracket on the vacuum pump. at the rear of the cylinder head

6 Unclip the pressure sensor pipe and carefully move it to one side.
7 Remove the pressure sensor bracket from the vacuum pump.
8 Undo the bolt securing the fuel return hose to the front of the camshaft cover
9 Undo the two bolts securing the fuel pipes to the inlet manifold **(see illustration)**.
10 Release the clips and disconnect the two fuel hoses from the top of the fuel pump. Suitably plug or cover the disconnected hoses and unions.
11 Move the fuel pipes to one side, clear of the camshaft cover.
12 Disconnect the vacuum line at the front of the camshaft cover, then detach the support bracket and move it to one side.
13 Unscrew the camshaft cover retaining bolts and lift the cover away. If the cover sticks, do not attempt to lever it off – instead free it by working around the cover and tapping it lightly with a soft-faced mallet.
14 Recover the camshaft cover gasket. Inspect the gasket carefully, and renew it if damage or deterioration is evident – note that the retaining bolts and seals must be pushed fully through the cover **(see illustrations)**.
15 Clean the mating surfaces of the cylinder head and camshaft cover thoroughly,

removing all traces of oil – take care to avoid damaging the surfaces as you do this.

Refitting

16 Refit the camshaft cover by following the removal procedure in reverse, tightening the cover retaining bolts to the specified torque starting with the centre bolts and working outwards.

5 Crankshaft pulley – removal and refitting

Removal

1 Switch off the ignition and all electrical consumers and remove the ignition key.
2 Chock the front wheels, raise the front of the vehicle, and support securely on axle stands (see *Jacking and vehicle support*).
3 Release the securing fasteners and remove the engine undertray.
4 Remove the engine torque reaction support cross member as described in Section 14.
5 Disconnect the wiring connectors, undo the retaining bolt and remove the electric cooling fan control unit from the fan shroud.

4.9 Undo the two bolts securing the fuel pipes to the manifold

4.14a Renew the cover seal if necessary

4.14b Bolts and seals must be pushed fully through the cover before fitting the gasket

5.7 Undo the pulley bolts, counterholding it with a socket on the centre sprocket bolt

6 Detach the cap from the front of the crankshaft pulley.

7 Slacken the bolts securing the crankshaft pulley to the sprocket **(see illustration)**. If necessary, the pulley can be prevented from turning by counterholding with a spanner or socket on the crankshaft sprocket bolt.

8 Remove the auxiliary drivebelt, as described in Chapter 1, Section 8.

9 Unscrew the bolts securing the pulley to the sprocket, and remove the pulley. Discard the bolts – new ones must be fitted.

Refitting

10 Refitting is the reverse of removal bearing in mind the following points:

a) *Fit the pulley using new retaining bolts tightened to the specified torque.*

b) *Refit the auxiliary drivebelt as described in Chapter 1, Section 8.*

c) *Refit the engine torque reaction support cross member as described in Section 14.*

6 Timing belt covers – removal and refitting

Upper outer cover

1 Pull the engine top cover upwards to release the mountings.

2 Release the three clips and remove the timing belt upper cover **(see illustration)**.

3 Refitting is a reversal of removal, noting that the lower edge of the upper cover engages with the cover below.

Lower outer cover

Note: *On some engines, the lower outer cover is in two parts.*

4 Remove the upper cover as described previously.

5 If not already done, remove the crankshaft pulley as described in Section 5.

6 Unscrew the five bolts securing the lower cover, and remove it **(see illustrations)**.

7 Refitting is a reversal of removal; noting that the upper edge of the lower cover engages with the upper cover.

Rear cover

8 Remove the timing belt, tensioner and sprockets as described in Section 7 and Section 8.

9 Undo the retaining bolt and remove the rear hub cover from the end of the camshaft.

10 Slacken and withdraw the retaining bolts and lift the timing belt inner cover from the studs on the end of the engine, and remove it from the engine compartment **(see illustrations)**. It may be required to remove the coolant pump (Chapter 3, Section 7), before the rear cover can be removed.

11 Refitting is a reversal of removal.

7 Timing belt – removal, inspection and refitting

Removal

1 The primary function of the toothed timing belt is to drive the camshaft, but it also drives the coolant pump and high-pressure fuel pump. Should the belt slip or break in service, the valve timing will be disturbed and piston-to-valve contact may occur, resulting in serious engine damage. For this reason, it is important that the timing belt is tensioned correctly, and inspected regularly for signs of wear or deterioration.

2 Switch off the ignition and all electrical consumers and remove the ignition key.

3 Set the engine to TDC on No. 1 cylinder as described in Section 3.

4 Slacken the three bolts securing the sprocket to the camshaft hub by 90° **(see illustration)**.

5 Slacken the three bolts securing the

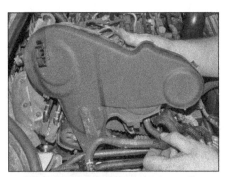

6.2 Release the clips and remove the timing belt upper cover

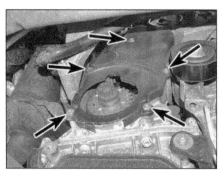

6.6a Undo the lower cover retaining bolts...

6.6b ...and manoeuvre the lower cover from place

6.10a Remove the retaining bolts...

6.10b ...and remove the rear cover

7.4 Slacken the sprocket-to-hub bolts

7.5 Slacken the high-pressure fuel pump sprocket bolts

7.6 Insert an Allen key, slacken the nut, and rotate the hub anti-clockwise until a 2 mm rod/drill bit can be inserted to lock the hub to the pulley

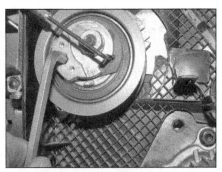

7.7 Rotate the tensioner hub clockwise until it hits the stop

sprocket to the high-pressure fuel pump by 90° **(see illustration)**.

6 Insert a suitable Allen key into the tensioner hub, then slacken the retaining nut and rotate the tensioner hub anti-clockwise until it can be locked in place using a 2.0 mm pin/drill bit **(see illustration)**.

7 Leaving the pin in place, now rotate the tensioner hub clockwise to the stop, and hand-tighten the retaining nut **(see illustration)**.

8 If the original timing belt is to be refitted, mark the running direction of the belt, to ensure correct refitting.

Caution: If the belt appears to be in good condition and can be re-used, it is essential that it is refitted the same way around, otherwise accelerated wear will result, leading to premature failure.

9 Slide the belt from the sprockets, taking care not to twist or kink the belt excessively if it is to be re-used.

Inspection

10 Examine the belt for evidence of contamination by coolant or lubricant. If this is the case, find the source of the contamination

before progressing any further. Check the belt for signs of wear or damage, particularly around the leading edges of the belt teeth. Renew the belt if its condition is in doubt; the cost of belt renewal is negligible compared with potential cost of the engine repairs, should the belt fail in service. The belt must be renewed if it has covered the mileage given in Chapter 1 Specifications, however, if it has covered less, it is prudent to renew it regardless of condition, as a precautionary measure.

11 If the timing belt is not going to be refitted for some time, it is a wise precaution to hang a warning label on the steering wheel, to remind yourself (and others) not to attempt to start the engine. Have the battery disconnected to prevent any engine damage.

Refitting

12 Ensure that the crankshaft and camshaft are still set to TDC on No 1 cylinder, as described in Section 3. The camshaft sprocket bolts should be renewed, and slackened at this point.

13 Renew the high-pressure fuel pump sprocket bolts one at a time. They should also be slackened.

7.14 Rotate the high-pressure fuel pump clockwise until a 6 mm drill bit/rod can be inserted into the housing and hub

14 Using a screwdriver on the bolts heads, rotate the high-pressure fuel pump clockwise until a 6.0 mm locking pin/drill bit can be inserted into the housing adjacent to the sprocket, locking the pump in place **(see illustration)**.

15 Rotate the camshaft sprocket and high-pressure fuel pump sprocket fully clockwise so that the securing bolts are at the end of the elongated holes **(see illustrations)**.

7.15a Rotate the sprockets fully clockwise until the fuel pump sprocket...

7.15b ...and camshaft sprocket bolts are at the end of the elongated holes

7.18 Timing belt routing

7.19a Rotate the tensioner clockwise...

7.19b ...until the pointer (arrowed) is just past the gap in the base plate

7.20a Counterhold the camshaft sprocket...

7.20b ...and the pump sprocket, while the bolts are tightened

16 Loop the timing belt loosely under the crankshaft sprocket.

Note: *Observe any direction of rotation markings on the belt.*

17 Fit the belt around the tensioner pulley, engage the timing belt teeth with the camshaft sprockets, then manoeuvre it into position around the coolant pump sprocket and the fuel pump sprocket. Make sure that the belt teeth seat correctly on the sprockets.

Note: *Slight adjustment to the position of the camshaft sprocket may be necessary to achieve this. Avoid bending the belt back on itself or twisting it excessively as you do this.*

18 Finally, fit the belt around the idler roller **(see illustration)**. Ensure that any slack in the belt is in the section of belt that passes over the tensioner roller.

19 Loosen the timing belt tensioner securing nut, and pull out the tensioner locking pin. Turn the tensioner clockwise with an Allen key until the pointer is just past the middle of the gap in the tensioner base plate **(see illustrations)**. With the tensioner held in this position, tighten the securing nut to the specified torque and angle.

20 Counterhold the camshaft sprocket and fuel pump sprocket with a home made tool to prevent any rotation, and then tighten the

camshaft sprocket and fuel pump sprocket bolts to 20 Nm **(see illustrations)**.

21 Remove the sprockets' locking tools and the crankshaft locking tool **(see illustrations)**.

22 Using a spanner or wrench and socket on the crankshaft pulley centre bolt, rotate the crankshaft clockwise through two complete revolutions. Reset the engine to TDC on No.1 cylinder, with reference to Section 3 and refit the crankshaft locking tool.

23 Check that the tensioner roller indicator arm is centred, or within a maximum of 5 mm to the right of the notch in the base plate **(see illustration)**. If not, hold the tensioner

7.21a Remove the upper locking pins...

7.21b ...and crankshaft locking tool

7.23 Check the pointer is centred or within 5mm to the right of the gap in the base plate

7.24 Slight misalignment of the pump sprocket timing hole is acceptable

8.3 Ensure the lug on the backplate engages with the cut-out in the timing belt cover

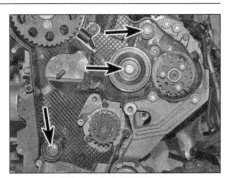

8.6 Timing belt idler pulleys

hub stationary with an Allen key, slacken the retaining nut and position the arm in the centre of the notch. Tighten the retaining nut to the specified torque. Remove the Allen key.
24 Check that the camshaft sprocket locking pin can still be inserted. **Note:** *It's very difficult to align the locking point of the fuel pump hub again* **(see illustration).** *However, a slight misalignment of holes will not affect engine performance.*
25 If the camshaft sprocket locking pin cannot be inserted, pull the crankshaft locking tool slight away from the engine, and rotate the crankshaft anti-clockwise slightly past TDC. Now slowly rotate the crankshaft clockwise until the camshaft sprocket locking tool can be inserted.
26 If the locating pin of the crankshaft locking tool is to the left of the corresponding hole, slacken the camshaft sprocket bolts, slowly rotate the crankshaft clockwise until the locking tool can be fully inserted. Tighten the camshaft sprocket bolts to 20 Nm.
27 If the locating pin of the crankshaft locking tool is to the right of the corresponding hole, slacken the camshaft sprocket bolts, rotate the crankshaft anti-clockwise slightly until the pin is to the left of the hole, then slowly rotate it clockwise until the lock tool can be fully inserted. Tighten the camshaft sprocket bolts to 20 Nm.
28 Remove the crankshaft and camshaft locking tools, then rotate the crankshaft 2 complete revolutions clockwise and check the locking tools can be reinserted. If necessary, repeat the adjustment procedure described previously.
29 Tighten the camshaft and fuel pump sprocket bolts to the specified torque.
30 The remainder of refitting is a reversal of removal.

8 Timing belt tensioner and sprockets – removal and refitting

Timing belt tensioner
Removal
1 Remove the timing belt as described in Section 7.
2 Unscrew the timing belt tensioner nut, and remove the tensioner from the engine.

Refitting
3 When refitting the tensioner to the engine, ensure that the lug on the tensioner backplate engages with the corresponding cut-out in the rear timing belt cover, then refit the tensioner nut **(see illustration).**
4 Refit the timing belt as described in Section 7.

Idler pulleys
Removal
5 Remove the timing belt as described in Section 7.
6 Unscrew the relevant idler pulley/roller securing bolt/nut, and then withdraw the pulley **(see illustration).**

Refitting
7 Refit the pulley and tighten the securing bolt or nut to the specified torque.
Note: *Renew the large roller/pulley retaining bolt (where applicable).*
8 Refit and tension the timing belt as described in Section 7.

Crankshaft sprocket
Note: *A new crankshaft sprocket securing bolt must be used on refitting.*
Removal
9 Remove the timing belt as described in Section 7.
10 The sprocket securing bolt must now be slackened, and the crankshaft must be prevented from turning as the sprocket bolt is unscrewed. To hold the sprocket, make up a suitable tool, and bolt it to the sprocket using two bolts bolted into two of the crankshaft pulley bolt holes.
11 Hold the sprocket using the tool, then slacken the sprocket securing bolt. Take care, as the bolt is very tight. Do not allow the crankshaft to turn as the bolt is slackened.
12 Unscrew the bolt, and slide the sprocket from the end of the crankshaft, noting which way round the sprocket's raised boss is fitted.

Refitting
13 Commence refitting by positioning the sprocket on the end of the crankshaft.
14 Fit a new sprocket securing bolt, then counter hold the sprocket using the method employed on removal, and tighten the bolt to the specified torque in the two stages given in the Specifications.

15 Refit the timing belt as described in Section 7.

Camshaft sprocket
Removal
16 Remove the timing belt as described in Section 7, then rotate the crankshaft 90° anti-clockwise to prevent any accidental piston-to-valve contact.
17 Unscrew and remove the three retaining bolts and remove the camshaft sprocket from the camshaft hub.

Refitting
18 Refit the sprocket ensuring that it is fitted the correct way round, as noted before removal, then insert the new sprocket bolts, and tighten by hand only at this stage.
19 If the crankshaft has been turned, turn the crankshaft clockwise 90° back to TDC.
20 Refit and tension the timing belt as described in Section 7.

Camshaft hub
Note: *VAG technicians use special tool T10051 to counter hold the hub, however it is possible to fabricate a suitable alternative.*
Removal
21 Remove the camshaft sprocket as described previously in this Section.
22 Engage special tool T10051 with the three locating holes in the face of the hub to prevent the hub from turning. If this tool is not available, fabricate a suitable alternative. Whilst holding the tool, undo the central hub retaining bolt about two turns **(see illustration).**

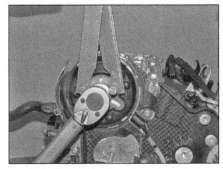

8.22 Fabricate a home-made tool to counterhold the hub. Undo the bolt...

23 Slide the hub from the camshaft. If necessary, attach Audi tool T10052 (or a similar three-legged puller) to the hub, and evenly tighten the puller until the hub is free of the camshaft taper (see illustration).

Refitting

24 Ensure that the camshaft taper and the hub centre are clean and dry, locate the hub on the taper, noting that the built-in key in the hub taper must align with the keyway in the camshaft taper (see illustration).
25 Hold the hub in this position with tool T10051 (or similar home-made tool), and tighten the central bolt to the specified torque.
26 Refit the camshaft sprocket as described previously in this Section.

Coolant pump sprocket

27 The coolant pump sprocket is integral with the coolant pump. Refer to Chapter 3, Section 7 for details of coolant pump removal and refitting.

9 Camshaft and hydraulic tappets – removal, inspection and refitting

Note: *A new camshaft oil seal(s) will be required on refitting. VAG removal tool T40094 (or similar tool) will be required to refit the camshafts – this is necessary to prevent damage to the retaining frame and cylinder head as the camshafts are refitted.*

Removal

1 Remove the camshaft hub as described in Section 8.
2 Remove the camshaft cover as described in Section 4.
3 Remove the brake vacuum pump as described in Chapter 9, Section 18.
4 Progressively unscrew the camshaft retaining frame bolts in the reverse of the sequence shown in illustration 9.20, and carefully remove the retaining frame.

8.23...and slide the hub from the camshaft

5 Carefully lift the camshafts from the cylinder head, keeping them identified for location. Remove the oil seal from the end of the camshaft and discard it – a new one will be required for refitting.
6 Lift the rocker arms and hydraulic tappets from place. Store the rockers and tappets in a container with numbered compartments to ensure they are refitted to their correct locations. It is recommended that the tappets are kept immersed in oil for the period they are removed from the cylinder head.

Inspection

7 With the camshafts removed, examine the retaining frame and the bearing locations in the cylinder head for signs of obvious wear or pitting. If evident, a new cylinder head will probably be required. Also check that the oil supply holes in the cylinder head are free from obstructions.
8 Visually inspect the camshafts for evidence of wear on the surfaces of the lobes and journals. Normally their surfaces should be smooth and have a dull shine; look for scoring, erosion or pitting and areas that appear highly polished, indicating excessive wear. Accelerated wear will occur once the hardened exterior of the camshaft has been damaged, so always renew worn items.
Note: *If these symptoms are visible on*

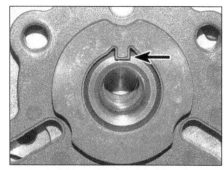

8.24 Ensure the integral key aligns with the keyway in the camshaft (arrowed)

the tips of the camshaft lobes, check the corresponding rocker arm, as it will probably be worn as well.
9 If the machined surfaces of the camshaft appear discoloured or blued, it is likely that it has been overheated at some point, probably due to inadequate lubrication. This may have distorted the shaft, so have the camshaft runout and endfloat checked by an automotive engine reconditioning specialist.
10 Inspect the hydraulic tappets for obvious signs of wear or damage, and renew if necessary. Check that the oil holes in the tappets are free from obstructions.

Refitting

11 Oil the rocker arms and hydraulic tappets, and then refit them to their original positions.

⚠️ *Warning: After fitting hydraulic tappets, wait a minimum of 30 minutes (or preferably, leave overnight) before starting the engine, to allow the tappets time to settle, otherwise the valve heads will strike the pistons.*

12 To set up the tool, remove the supports number 3, 4 and 5, then install the supports number 1, 2, 9 and 10 as shown (see illustrations).
13 Position the inlet camshaft as shown with the cylinder head bolt indent facing outwards,

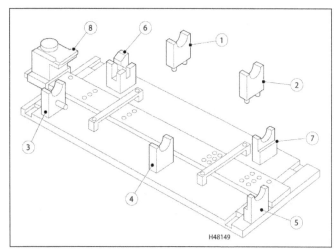

9.12a The different elements of tool No T40094

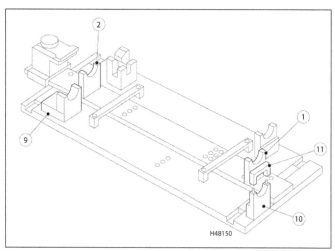

9.12b Position tools No 1, 2, 9 and 10 as shown

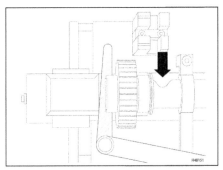

9.13 Position the inlet camshaft on the tool with the bolt indent (arrowed) facing outwards, then slide tool No 8 in to the slot in the end of the camshaft and use a 0.50 mm feeler gauge to remove any free play

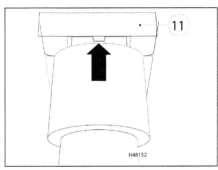

9.14 Fit tool No 11 into the slot (arrowed) in the end of the exhaust camshaft

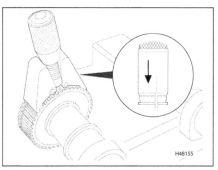

9.15 Tighten the thumbwheel to align the gear teeth. Ensure the clamping jaw with the arrow in seated on the wider gear

then slide the support number 8 into the slot in the end of the camshaft and remove any free play with a 0.50 mm feeler gauge (see illustration).

14 Position the exhaust camshaft on supports numbers 9 and 10, and fit the tool No 11 into the slot in the end of the camshaft (see illustration).

15 Fit the clamping tool No T40096 to the gear on the exhaust camshaft, tightening the knurled thumb wheel until the faces of the gear teeth are in alignment. If necessary, use a 13 mm spanner (see illustration).

16 Slide the exhaust camshaft towards the inlet camshaft until the gear teeth engage.

17 Ensure the gasket faces of the retaining frame are clean, then apply a smear of clean engine oil to the bearing surfaces and lower the frame into position over the camshafts. Ensure the bearing surfaces locate correctly on the camshafts.

18 Fit the clamping tool No T40095 over the camshafts and frame, and tighten the thumbwheels to hold the camshafts in position in the frame (see illustration).

19 Ensure the sealing surfaces of the cylinder head are clean, and then apply a 2.0 mm wide bead of sealant (D 176 501 A1 or equivalent) as shown. Take care not to apply too much sealant, ensuring the oil holes supply holes are not blocked (see illustration).

20 Slide out tool No's 8 and 11, then lift the camshafts, retaining frame and clamping tool from the tool No T40094. Place the camshafts, frame and tool in place on the cylinder head. Progressively and carefully, hand-tighten the frame retaining bolts in the sequence shown, until the retaining frame makes contact with the cylinder head over the complete surface, then tighten the bolts to the specified torque, again in the correct sequence (see illustration).

21 Remove the gear aligning tool (T40096) and the clamping tool (T40095).

22 Renew the camshaft oil seal (Section 10), then drive in a new sealing cap.

23 The remainder of refitting is a reversal of removal.

10 Camshaft oil seals – renewal

Front oil seal

1 Remove the camshaft sprocket and hub, as described in Section 8.

2 Drill two small holes into the existing oil seal, diagonally opposite each other. Take great care to avoid drilling through into the seal housing or camshaft sealing surface.

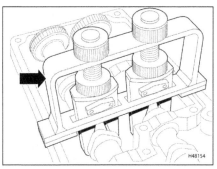

9.18 Secure the camshafts in place in the frame using tool No T40095

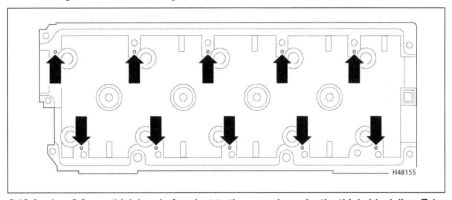

9.19 Apply a 2.0 mm thick bead of sealant to the area shown by the thick, black line. Take care not to block the oil holes

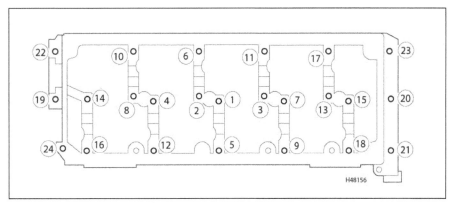

9.20 Camshaft retaining frame bolt tightening sequence

Thread two self-tapping screws into the holes, and using a pair of pliers, pull on the heads of the screws to extract the oil seal **(see illustration)**.

3 Clean out the seal housing and the sealing surface of the camshaft by wiping it with a lint-free cloth. Remove any swarf or burrs that may cause the seal to leak.

4 Do not lubricate the lip and outer edge of the new oil seal, push it over the camshaft until it is positioned in place above its housing. To prevent damage to the sealing lips, wrap some adhesive tape around the end of the camshaft.

5 Using a hammer and a socket of suitable diameter, drive the seal squarely into its housing.

Note: *Select a socket that bears only on the hard outer surface of the seal, not the inner lip that can easily be damaged.*

6 Refit the camshaft sprocket and its hub, as described in Section 8.

Rear oil seal

7 The rear camshaft oil seal is formed by the brake vacuum pump seal, which is fitted to the cylinder head. Refer to Chapter 9, Section 18 for details of brake vacuum pump removal and refitting.

---

11 Cylinder head – removal, inspection and refitting

Note: *The cylinder head must be removed with the engine cold. New cylinder head bolts and a new cylinder head gasket will be required on refitting.*

Removal

1 Disconnect the battery negative lead as described in Chapter 5, Section 3.

2 Drain the cooling system (Chapter 1, Section 31) and engine oil (Chapter 1, Section 3).

3 Pull the plastic cover on the top of the engine upwards from its mountings.

4 Remove the plenum chamber partition panel as described in Chapter 11 Section 21.

5 Remove the air cleaner assembly as described in Chapter 4A, Section 2.

10.2 Bolt in a self-tapping screw, then pull the bolt and seal from place

6 Remove the EGR cooler as described in Chapter 4B, Section 3.

7 Remove the turbocharger as described in chapter 4B, Section 5.

8 Remove the exhaust system front pipe as described in Chapter 4B, Section 8.

9 Remove the camshaft cover as described in Section 4.

10 Remove the camshaft sprocket and hub as described in Section 8.

11 Slacken the hose clips and disconnect the air hose from the throttle valve housing/module and intercooler air duct **(see illustration)**.

12 Detach the oil level dipstick guide tube from the throttle valve housing/module.

13 Slacken the retaining clips and disconnect the coolant hoses at the rear of the cylinder head.

14 Undo the two bolts securing the EGR pipe to the EGR valve. Undo the EGR pipe retaining nut at the rear of the engine and move the EGR pipe clear.

15 Release the retaining clips and disconnect the fuel supply and return hoses at the right-hand side of the engine compartment.

16 Disconnect the wiring plugs from the EGR valve and throttle body/intake manifold flap.

17 Remove the vacuum pump as described in Chapter 9, Section 18.

18 Disconnect the coolant temperature sensor wiring plug at the rear of the cylinder head, and release the wiring loom from any retaining clips.

19 Note their fitted locations, then release the

clamps and disconnect the various coolant hoses from the cylinder head.

20 Undo the bolt securing the timing belt guard adjacent to the timing belt tensioner, and the bolt securing the camshaft position sensor, then remove the tensioner retaining nut **(see illustration)**.

21 Make a final check to ensure all relevant wiring and vacuum hoses have been disconnected. Note the loom/hose routing to aid refitting.

22 Using an M12 multi-splined tool (12-pointed star), undo the cylinder head bolts, working from the outside-in, evenly and gradually. Remove the bolts and recover the washers. Check that nothing remains connected, and starting at the transmission end, lift the cylinder head from the engine block, sliding the belt tensioner from the mounting stud as the cylinder head is removed. Seek assistance if possible, as it is a heavy assembly.

23 Remove the gasket from the top of the block, noting the locating dowels. If the dowels are a loose fit, remove them and store them with the head for safekeeping. Do not discard the gasket yet – it will be needed for identification purposes. If desired, the manifolds can be removed from the cylinder head with reference to Chapter 4A, Section 5 (inlet manifold) or Chapter 4B, Section 7 (exhaust manifold).

Inspection

24 Dismantling and inspection of the cylinder head is covered in Chapter 2B.

Cylinder head gasket selection

Note: *A dial test indicator (DTI) will be required for this operation.*

25 Examine the old cylinder head gasket for manufacturer's identification markings **(see illustration)**. These will be in the form of holes, and a part number on the edge of the gasket. Unless new pistons have been fitted, the new cylinder head gasket must be of the same type as the old one.

26 If new piston assemblies have been fitted as part of an engine overhaul, or if a new short engine is to be fitted, the projection of the piston crowns above the cylinder head mating face of the cylinder block at TDC must

11.11 Slacken the upper and lower clips and disconnect the air hose

11.20 Undo the bolt securing the timing belt guard

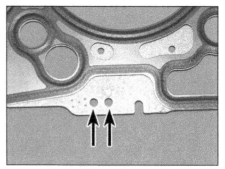

11.25 The holes identify the thickness of the cylinder head gasket

be measured. This measurement is used to determine the thickness of the new cylinder head gasket required.

27 Anchor a dial test indicator (DTI) to the top face (cylinder head gasket mating face) of the cylinder block, and zero the gauge on the gasket mating face.

28 Rest the gauge probe on No 1 piston crown, and turn the crankshaft slowly by hand until the piston reaches TDC. Measure and record the maximum piston projection at TDC **(see illustration)**.

29 Repeat the measurement for the remaining pistons, and record the results.

30 If the measurements differ from piston-to-piston, take the highest figure, and use this to determine the thickness of the head gasket required as follows.

Piston projection	Gasket identification (number of holes)
0.91 to 1.00 mm	1
1.01 to 1.10 mm	2
1.11 to 1.20 mm	3

31 Purchase a new gasket according to the results of the measurements.

Refitting

32 The mating faces of the cylinder head and block must be perfectly clean before refitting the head. Use a scraper to remove all traces of gasket and carbon, also clean the tops of the pistons. Take particular care with the aluminium surfaces, as the soft metal is easily damaged.

33 Make sure that debris is not allowed to enter the oil and water passages – this is particularly important for the oil circuit, as carbon could block the oil supply to the camshaft and crankshaft bearings. Using adhesive tape and paper, seal the water, oil and bolt holes in the cylinder block.

34 To prevent carbon entering the gap between the pistons and bores, smear a little grease in the gap. After cleaning a piston, rotate the crankshaft to that the piston moves down the bore, and then wipe out the grease and carbon with a cloth rag. Clean the other piston crowns in the same way.

35 Check the head and block for nicks, deep scratches and other damage. If slight, they may be removed carefully with a file.

11.28 Measure the piston protrusion using a DTI guage

More serious damage may be repaired by machining, but this is a specialist job.

36 If warpage of the cylinder head is suspected, use a straight-edge to check it for distortion, as described in Chapter 2B, Section 7.

37 Ensure that the cylinder head bolt holes in the crankcase are clean and free of oil. Syringe or soak up any oil left in the bolt holes. This is most important in order that the correct bolt tightening torque can be applied, and to prevent the possibility of the block being cracked by hydraulic pressure when the bolts are tightened.

38 Turn the crankshaft anti-clockwise all the pistons at an equal height, approximately halfway down their bores from the TDC position (see Section 3). This will eliminate any risk of piston-to-valve contact as the cylinder head is refitted.

39 Where applicable, refit the manifolds with reference to Chapter 4A, Section 5 (inlet manifold) or Chapter 4B, Section 7 (exhaust manifold).

40 Ensure that the cylinder head locating dowels are in place in the cylinder block, and then fit the new cylinder head gasket over the dowels, ensuring that the part number is uppermost **(see illustration)**. Note that Audi recommend that the gasket is only removed from its packaging immediately prior to fitting.

41 Lower the cylinder head into position on the gasket, ensuring that it engages correctly over the dowels. Refit the timing belt tensioner as the cylinder head is refitted.

42 Fit the washers in place then fit the new cylinder head bolts to the locations, and bolt

11.40 Ensure the dowels are in place, then fit the new gasket with the part number uppermost

them in as far as possible by hand. Do not oil the bolt threads.

43 Working progressively, in sequence, tighten all the cylinder head bolts to the specified Stage 1 torque **(see illustrations)**.

44 Again working progressively, in sequence, tighten all the cylinder head bolts to the specified Stage 2 torque.

45 Tighten all the cylinder head bolts, in sequence, through the specified Stage 3 angle **(see illustration)**.

46 Finally, tighten all the cylinder head bolts, in sequence, through the specified Stage 4 angle.

47 The remainder of the refitting procedure is a reversal of the removal procedure, noting the following points:

a) *Tighten all fasteners to their specified torque where given.*
b) *Renew all seals and gaskets.*
c) *Refill the cooling system, as described in Chapter 1, Section 31.*
d) *Refill the engine oil, as described in Chapter 1 Section 3.*
e) *Ensure all wiring is correctly routed.*

12 Driveplate – removal and refitting

Removal

1 On manual transmission models, remove the transmission as described in Chapter 7A, Section 3.

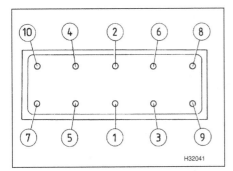

11.43a Cylinder head bolt tightening sequence

11.43b Tighten the cylinder head bolts to the Stage 1 torque

11.45 Use an angle-tightening gauge

13.2 Pull the screw and seal from place using pliers

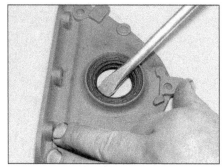

13.3a Prise the oil seal from the crankshaft oil seal housing

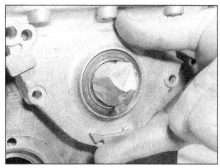

13.9 Slide the oil seal housing over the end of the crankshaft

2 On multitronic transmission models, remove the transmission as described in Chapter 7B, Section 2.

3 Undo the retaining bolts and remove the driveplate from the end of the crankshaft. Discard the bolts as new ones must be fitted.

Refitting

4 Refitting is a reversal of removal, using new bolts tightened to the specified torque, then through the specified angle.

13 Crankshaft oil seals – renewal

Note: *The oil seals are a PTFE (Teflon) type and are fitted dry, without using any grease or oil. These have a wider sealing lip and have been introduced instead of the coil spring type oil seal.*

Timing belt end oil seal

1 Remove the timing belt as described in Section 7, and the crankshaft sprocket with reference to Section 8.

2 To remove the seal without removing the housing, drill two small holes diagonally opposite each other, insert self-tapping screws, and pull on the heads of the screws with pliers **(see illustration)**.

3 Alternatively, to remove the oil seal complete with its housing, proceed as follows.

a) *Remove the sump as described in Chapter 2B Section 9. This is necessary to ensure a satisfactory seal between the sump and oil seal housing on refitting.*

b) *Unscrew and remove the oil seal housing.*

c) *Working on the bench, lever the oil seal from the housing using a suitable screwdriver. Take care not to damage the seal seating in the housing* **(see illustration)**.

4 Thoroughly clean the oil seal seating in the housing.

5 Wind a length of tape around the end of the crankshaft to protect the oil seal lips as the seal (and housing, where applicable) is fitted.

6 Fit a new oil seal to the housing, pressing or driving it into position using a socket or tube

of suitable diameter. Ensure that the socket or tube bears only on the hard outer ring of the seal, and take care not to damage the seal lips. Press or drive the seal into position until it is seated on the shoulder in the housing. Make sure that the closed end of the seal is facing outwards.

7 If the oil seal housing has been removed, proceed as follows, otherwise proceed to paragraph 11.

8 Clean all traces of old sealant from the crankshaft oil seal housing and the cylinder block, then coat the cylinder block mating faces of the oil seal housing with a 2.0 to 3.0 mm thick bead of silicone sealant (VW D 176 404 A2, or equivalent). Note that the seal housing must be refitted within 5 minutes of applying the sealant.

Caution: DO NOT put excessive amounts of sealant onto the housing as it may get into the sump and block the oil pick-up pipe.

9 Refit the oil seal housing, and tighten the bolts progressively to the specified torque **(see illustration)**.

10 Refit the sump as described in Chapter 2B Section 9.

11 Refit the crankshaft sprocket with reference to Section 8, and the timing belt as described in Section 7.

Driveplate end oil seal

Note: *In these engines, the seal, sealing flange and sender wheel are a complete unit. Special*

tools are required to refit the sealing flange, and press the sender wheel onto the end of the crankshaft. It is not possible to accurately fit these parts without the tools, which may be available from Audi (part No T10134) and are available from aftermarket automotive tool specialists.

12 Remove the driveplate as described in Section 12, then prise the intermediate plate from the locating dowels on the cylinder block.

13 Undo the bolts securing the sealing flange to the cylinder block **(see illustration)**.

14 Insert three 6 x 35 mm bolts into the threaded holes in the sealing flange. Tighten the bolts gradually and evenly, and press the sealing flange and sender wheel from the crankshaft/cylinder block **(see illustration)**. The seal, sender wheel and sealing flange are supplied as a complete unit.

15 Ensure the mating face of the cylinder block is clean and free from debris. The new sealing flange/seal/sender wheel assembly is supplied with a sealing lip support ring, which serves as a fitting sleeve, and must not be removed prior to installation. Equally, the sender wheel must not be separated from the assembly.

16 If using the Audi tool, proceed as follows. If using an aftermarket tool specialist's product, follow the instructions supplied with the tool. Rotate the large spindle nut until it's level with the end of the clamping surface of

13.13 Sealing flange bolts

13.14 Bolt in three 6 x 35 mm bolts and draw the sealing flange and sender wheel from place

13.16a Rotate the nut until it is level with the end of the clamping surface...

13.16b...then clamp it in a vice

13.17 Rotate the nut until the inner part of the tool is flush with the housing

the spindle, then clamp the spindle in a vice **(see illustrations)**.

17 Press the tool housing downwards until it rests on the nut and washer. Rotate the nut until the inner part of the tool is at the same height as the housing **(see illustration)**.

18 Remove the seal securing clip. The hole on the sender wheel must align with the marking on the sealing flange **(see illustrations)**.

19 Place the flange outer side down on a clean, flat surface, then press the seal guide fitting sleeve (supplied ready fitted), housing, and sender wheel downwards until all the components are flat on the surface. In this position the upper edge of the sender wheel should be level with the edge of the sealing flange **(see illustrations)**.

20 Place the sealing flange on the assembly tool, so the pin locates in the hole in the sender wheel **(see illustration)**.

21 Push the sealing flange and guide fitting sleeve against the tool whilst tightening the 3 knurled bolts. Ensure the pin is still located in the sender wheel **(see illustration)**.

22 Ensure the end of the crankshaft is clean, and is locked at TDC on No 1 cylinder as described in Section 3.

23 Unscrew the large nut to the end of the spindle threads, then press the spindle inwards as far as possible **(see illustration)**.

24 Align the flat side of the assembly with the sump flange, then secure the tool to

13.18a Remove the securing clip...

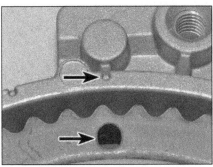

13.18b...the hole in the sender wheel should align with the marking on the flange

13.19a Press the assembly downwards on a clean, flat surface...

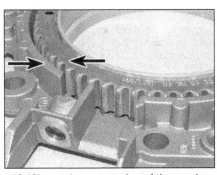

13.19b...so the upper edge of the sender wheel is level with the edge of the flange

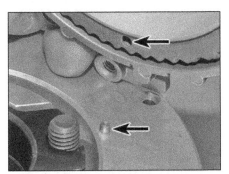

13.20 Fit the flange to the tool, ensuring the pin locates in the hole

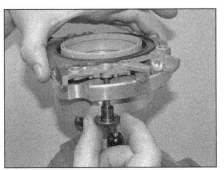

13.21 With the pin engaged in the hole, tighten the 3 knurled bolts to secure the flange to the tool

13.23 Unscrew the nut to the end of the thread, and push the spindle in as far as possible

13.24 Hand-tighten the Allen bolts to secure the tool to the crankshaft

13.25 Use 2 M7 x 35 mm bolts to guide the sealing flange

13.26 Push the black knob into the hole in the crankshaft

the crankshaft using the integral Allen bolts **(see illustration)**. Only hand-tighten the bolts.

25 Insert two M7 x 35 mm bolts to guide the sealing flange to the cylinder block **(see illustration)**.

26 Using hand-pressure alone, push the tool assembly onto the crankshaft until the seal guide fitting sleeve contacts the crankshaft flange, then push the guide pin (black knob) into the hole in the crankshaft. This is to ensure the sender wheel reaches its correct installation position **(see illustration)**.

27 Rotate the large nut until it makes contact with the tool housing, then tighten it to 35 Nm (26 lbf ft). After tightening this nut, a small air gap must still be present between the sealing flange and cylinder block **(see illustration)**.

28 Unscrew the large nut; the two M7 x 35 mm bolts, the three knurled bolts and the Allen bolts securing the tool to the crankshaft. Remove the tool, and pull the seal guide fitting sleeve from place (if it didn't come out with the tool).

29 Use a vernier caliper or feeler gauge to measure the fitted depth of the sender wheel in relation to the crankshaft flange **(see illustration)**. The correct depth is 0.5 mm.

30 If the gap is correct, fit the sealing flange bolts and tighten them to the specified torque.

31 If the gap is too small, re-attach the tool to the sealing flange and crankshaft, then refit the two M7 x 35 mm guide bolts to the flange. Tighten the large spindle nut to 40 Nm

(30 lbf ft), remove the tool and measure the air gap. If the gap is still too small, re-attach the tool and tighten the spindle nut to 45 Nm (33 lbf ft). Measure the gap again. When the gap is correct, refit the flange retaining bolts, and tighten them to the specified torque.

32 The remainder of refitting is a reversal of removal.

14 Engine/transmission mountings – inspection and renewal

Inspection

1 If improved access is required, jack up the front of the vehicle, and support it securely on axle stands (see *Jacking and vehicle support*). Remove the engine top cover, then remove the engine undertray(s).

2 Check the mounting rubbers to see if they are cracked, hardened or separated from the metal at any point; renew the mounting if any such damage or deterioration is evident.

3 Check that all the mountings are securely tightened; use a torque wrench to check if possible.

4 Using a large screwdriver or a crowbar, check for wear in the mounting by carefully levering against it to check for free play. Where this is not possible, enlist the aid of an assistant to move the engine/transmission back-and-forth, or from side-to-side, whilst you observe the mounting. While some free play is to be expected, even from new

components, excessive wear should be obvious. If excessive free play is found, check first that the fasteners are correctly secured, and then renew any worn components as described in the following paragraphs.

Renewal

Note: *New mounting retaining bolts will be required for refitting.*

Right- or left hand engine mounting

5 Apply the handbrake, then jack up the front of the vehicle and support it on axle stands (see *Jacking and vehicle support*). Remove the relevant roadwheel.

6 Remove the engine undertray, then remove the wheel arch liner as described in Chapter 11 Section 21.

7 Attach a hoist and lifting tackle to the engine lifting brackets on the cylinder head, and raise the hoist to just take the weight of the engine. Alternatively the engine can be supported on a trolley jack under the engine. Use a block of wood between the sump and the head of the jack, to prevent any damage to the sump.

8 Where applicable, disconnect the wiring connector from the electro-hydraulic engine mounting solenoid valve.

9 Undo the retaining plate mounting bolts, then undo the two bolts securing the mounting to the subframe and the single bolt securing the mounting to the engine bracket. Move the retaining plate to one side then detach the mounting.

10 Refitting is a reversal of removal, using new retaining bolts tightened to the specified torque.

Torque reaction support

11 Apply the handbrake, then jack up the front of the vehicle and support it on axle stands (see *Jacking and vehicle support*). Remove the engine undertray.

12 Undo the three retaining bolts and remove the torque reaction support from the engine and crossmember **(see illustration)**.

13 Refitting is a reversal of removal, bearing in mind the following points:

a) *Tighten all retaining bolts to the specified torque, where given.*

b) *Before tightening the torque reaction support retaining bolts, push the support*

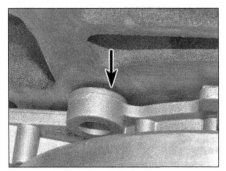

13.27 After tightening the spindle nut there should be an air gap between the sealing flange and the cylinder block

13.29 Measure the fitted depth of the sender wheel in relation to the end of the crankshaft

14.12 Torque reaction support retaining bolts

upwards until it makes contact with the crossmember. The buffer stop must be free of stress and must lie against the crossmember without play.

Torque reaction support crossmember

14 Remove the torque reaction support as described previously in this Section.
15 Undo the nut and bolt and remove the lock carrier support strut on the left-hand side.
16 Move the crossmember wiring harness to one side.
17 Undo the two bolts each side securing the crossmember to the subframe.
18 Slacken the two subframe mounting bolts on each side just enough to enable the crossmember to be moved to the left.

 Warning: DO NOT remove the subframe mounting bolts. Only slacken them very slightly.

15.9a Undo the engine oil cooler retaining screws

15.10a Disconnect the coolant hoses...

19 Move the crossmember to the left, lower it on the right-hand side and remove it from under the vehicle.
20 Refitting is a reversal of removal, bearing in mind the following points:
a) Tighten all retaining bolts to the specified torque and, where applicable, through the specified angle.
b) Remove and renew the subframe mounting bolts one after the other.
c) Refit the torque reaction support as described previously in this Section.

Transmission mounting

21 Apply the handbrake, then jack up the front of the vehicle and support it on axle stands (see *Jacking and vehicle support*). Remove the transmission undertray.
22 Position a trolley jack under the transmission and take the weight. With the transmission securely supported, undo the four bolts securing the transmission crossmember to the vehicle underbody.
23 Suitably support the transmission crossmember. Undo the three nuts securing the transmission crossmember to the transmission mounting and remove the crossmember.
24 Undo the three bolts and remove the tramsmission mounting bracket, together with the mounting, from the transmission.
25 Undo the two bolts and detach the stop plate, then undo the retaining nut and separate the mounting from the mounting bracket.
26 Refitting is a reversal of removal, using new retaining bolts tightened to the specified

15.9b Renew the seals/gaskets

15.10b...release the oil dipstick guide tube retaining clip...

torque and, where applicable, through the specified angle.

15 Engine oil cooler/filter housing – removal and refitting

Removal

Engine codes CAGA, CAGB, CAGC, CAHA, CAHB and CMEA

1 The oil cooler is mounted on the lower part of the oil filter housing on the left-hand side of the cylinder block.
2 Position a container beneath the oil filter housing to catch escaping oil and coolant.
3 Clamp the oil cooler coolant hoses to minimise coolant spillage, and disconnect them from the top of the cooler. If required, drain the cooling system as described in Chapter 1, Section 31.
4 Unscrew the oil cooler centre bolt and lower the oil cooler from oil filter housing. Recover the O-rings from between the cooler and the oil filter housing, new ones will be required for refitting.
5 If required, undo the retaining bolts and remove the oil filter housing from the cylinder block.

Engine codes CGLC, CGLD, CJCA, CJCB, CJCC, CJCD, CMBG, CMFA, CMFB and CMGB

6 The oil cooler is mounted on the oil filter housing on the left-hand side of the cylinder block.
7 Position a container beneath the oil filter housing to catch escaping oil and coolant.
8 Clamp the oil cooler coolant hoses to minimise coolant spillage, or drain the cooling system as described in Chapter 1, Section 31.
9 Unscrew the oil cooler retaining screws and remove the oil cooler from the front of the oil filter housing **(see illustrations)**. Recover the O-rings from between the cooler and filter housing, new ones will be required for refitting.
10 If required, disconnect the coolant hose, unclip the dipstick from the side of the housing, then undo the retaining bolts and remove the oil filter housing from the cylinder block **(see illustrations)**.

15.10c...and undo the filter housing retaining bolts

Refitting

11 Refitting is a reversal of removal, bearing in mind the following points:
a) *Use new oil cooler and housing O-rings.*
b) *Tighten the oil cooler and filter housing bolts to the correct torque.*
c) *On completion, check and if necessary top-up the oil and coolant levels.*

16 Oil pressure warning light switch – removal and refitting

Removal

Engine codes CAGA, CAGB, CAGC, CAHA, CAHB and CMEA

1 The oil pressure warning light switch is fitted to the oil filter housing **(see illustration)**. Remove the engine top cover to gain access to the switch.
2 Disconnect the wiring connector and wipe clean the area around the switch.
3 Unscrew the switch from the filter housing and remove it, along with its sealing washer. If the switch is to be left removed from the engine for any length of time, plug the oil filter housing aperture.

Engine codes CGLC, CGLD, CJCA, CJCB, CJCC, CJCD, CMBG, CMFA, CMFB and CMGB

4 The oil pressure warning light switch

16.1 Oil pressure warning light switch on filter housing

is fitted to the rear of the cylinder head.
5 Remove the air cleaner assembly as described in Chapter 4A, Section 2.
6 Undo the two bolts and detach the engine lifting eye.
7 Disconnect the wiring connector and wipe clean the area around the switch.
8 Unscrew the switch from its location and remove it, along with its sealing washer (if fitted). If the switch is to be left removed from the engine for any length of time, plug the switch aperture.

Refitting

9 Examine the sealing washer for signs of damage or deterioration and if necessary renew.

10 Refit the switch, complete with washer, and tighten it to the specified torque.
11 Securely reconnect the wiring connector then check and, if necessary, top-up the engine oil as described in *Weekly checks*. On completion, refit the engine top cover.

17 Oil level/temperature sender – removal and refitting

Removal

1 The oil level/temperature sender is fitted to bottom of the sump.
2 Drain the engine oil as described in Chapter 1, Section 3.
3 Disconnect the wiring connector from the sender.
4 Undo the retaining bolts and remove the sender from the sump.

Refitting

5 Refitting is the reverse sequence to removal, bearing in mind the following points:
a) *Renew the sender unit O-ring seal.*
b) *Tighten the switch retaining bolts to the specified torque.*
c) *Refill the engine with fresh oil.*

Chapter 2 Part B
Engine removal and overhaul procedures

Contents

Degrees of difficulty

Easy, suitable for novice with little experience	**Fairly easy,** suitable for beginner with some experience	**Fairly difficult,** suitable for competent DIY mechanic	**Difficult,** suitable for experienced DIY mechanic	**Very difficult,** suitable for expert DIY or professional

Specifications

Piston rings

	New	Wear limit
End gaps:		
Compression rings	0.25 to 0.50 mm	1.0 mm
Oil scraper ring	0.25 to 0.50 mm	1.0 mm
Ring-to-groove clearance:		
1st compression ring	0.06 to 0.09 mm	0.25 mm
2nd compression ring	0.05 to 0.08 mm	0.25 mm
Oil scraper ring	0.03 to 0.06 mm	0.15 mm

Crankshaft

	New	Wear limit
Endfloat	0.07 to 0.17 mm	0.37 mm

Cylinder head

Minimum permissible dimension between top of valve stem and top surface of cylinder head	No reworking permitted
Minimum cylinder head height	No reworking permitted
Maximum cylinder head gasket face distortion	0.1 mm

Valves

	Inlet valves	Exhaust valves
Valve stem diameter	5.968 to 5.982 mm	5.958 to 5.972 mm
Valve seat angle	45°	45°

Torque wrench settings

Refer to Chapter 2A

1 General Information

How to use this Chapter

1 Included in this Part of Chapter 2 are details of removing the engine from the car and general overhaul procedures for the cylinder head, cylinder block and all other engine internal components.

2 The information given ranges from advice concerning preparation for an overhaul and the purchase of new parts, to detailed step-by-step procedures covering removal, inspection, renovation and refitting of engine internal components.

3 After Section 10, all instructions are based on the assumption that the engine has been removed from the car. For information concerning in-car engine repair, as well as the removal and refitting of those external components necessary for full overhaul, refer to the relevant in-car repair procedure section (Chapter 2A) and to Section 2 of this Chapter. Ignore any preliminary dismantling operations described in the relevant in-car repair sections that are no longer relevant once the engine has been removed from the car.

4 Apart from torque wrench settings, which are given at the beginning of the in-car repair procedures in Chapter 2A, all specifications relating to engine overhaul are given at the beginning of this Part of Chapter 2.

2 Engine overhaul – general information

1 It is not always easy to determine when, or if, an engine should be completely overhauled, as a number of factors must be considered.

2 High mileage is not necessarily an indication that an overhaul is needed, while low mileage does not preclude the need for an overhaul. Frequency of servicing is probably the most important consideration. An engine, which has had regular and frequent oil and filter changes, as well as other required maintenance, should give many thousands of miles of reliable service. Conversely, a neglected engine may require an overhaul very early in its life.

3 Excessive oil consumption is an indication that piston rings, valve seals and/or valve guides are in need of attention. Make sure that oil leaks are not responsible before deciding that the rings and/or guides are worn. Perform a compression (or leakdown) test to determine the likely cause of the problem.

4 Check the oil pressure with a gauge fitted in place of the oil pressure switch, and then compare it with that specified (see Chapter 2A specifications). If it is extremely low, the main and big-end bearings, and/or the oil pump, are probably worn.

5 Loss of power, rough running, knocking or metallic engine noises, excessive valve gear noise, and high fuel consumption may also point to the need for an overhaul, especially if they are all present at the same time. If a complete service does not remedy the situation, major mechanical work is the only solution.

6 An engine overhaul involves restoring all internal parts to the specification of a new engine. During an overhaul, the pistons and the piston rings are renewed. New main and big-end bearings are generally fitted (where possible); if necessary, the crankshaft may be renewed to restore the journals. The valves are also serviced as well, since they are usually in less-than-perfect condition at this point. While the engine is being overhauled, other components, such as the starter and alternator, can be overhauled as well. The end result should be an as-new engine that will give many trouble-free miles.

Note: *Critical cooling system components such as the hoses, thermostat and coolant pump should be renewed when an engine is overhauled. The radiator should be checked carefully, to ensure that it is not clogged or leaking. Also, it is a good idea to renew the oil pump whenever the engine is overhauled.*

7 Before beginning the engine overhaul, read through the entire procedure, to familiarise yourself with the scope and requirements of the job. Overhauling an engine is not difficult if you follow carefully all of the instructions, have the necessary tools and equipment, and pay close attention to all specifications. It can, however, be time-consuming. Plan on the car being off the road for a minimum of two weeks, especially if parts must be taken to an engineering works for repair or reconditioning. Check on the availability of parts and make sure that any necessary special tools and equipment are obtained in advance. Most work can be done with typical hand tools, although a number of precision measuring tools are required for inspecting parts to determine if they must be renewed. Often the engineering works will handle the inspection of parts and offer advice concerning reconditioning and renewal.

Note: *Always wait until the engine has been completely dismantled, and until all components (especially the cylinder block and the crankshaft) have been inspected, before deciding what service and repair operations must be performed by an engineering works. The condition of these components will be the major factor to consider when determining whether to overhaul the original engine, or to buy a reconditioned unit. Do not, therefore, purchase parts or have overhaul work done on other components until they have been thoroughly inspected. As a general rule, time is the primary cost of an overhaul, so it does not pay to fit worn or sub-standard parts.*

8 As a final note, to ensure maximum life and minimum trouble from a reconditioned engine, everything must be assembled with care, in a spotlessly clean environment.

3 Engine removal – preparation and precautions

1 If you have decided that the engine must be removed for overhaul or major repair work, several preliminary steps should be taken.

2 Locating a suitable place to work is extremely important. Adequate workspace, along with storage space for the vehicle, will be needed. If a workshop or garage is not available, at the very least a solid, level, clean work surface is required.

3 If possible, clear some shelving close to the work area and use it to store the engine components and ancillaries as they are removed and dismantled. In this manner, the components stand a better chance of staying clean and undamaged during the overhaul. Laying out components in groups together with their fixings bolts, screws, etc, will save time and avoid confusion when the engine is refitted.

4 Clean the engine compartment and engine before beginning the removal procedure; this will help visibility and help to keep tools clean.

5 The help of an assistant is essential; there are certain instances when one person cannot safely perform all of the operations required to remove the engine from the vehicle. Safety is of primary importance, considering the potential hazards involved in this kind of operation. A second person should always be in attendance to offer help in an emergency. If this is the first time you have removed an engine, advice and aid from someone more experienced would also be beneficial.

6 Plan the operation ahead of time. Before starting work, obtain (or arrange for the hire of) all of the tools and equipment you will need. Access to the following items will allow the task of removing and refitting the engine to be completed safely and with relative ease: a hoist and lifting tackle – rated in excess of the weight of the engine, complete sets of spanners and sockets as described at the rear of this manual, wooden blocks, and plenty of rags and cleaning solvent for mopping-up spilled oil, coolant and fuel. A selection of different-sized plastic storage bins will also prove useful for keeping dismantled components grouped together. If any of the equipment must be hired, make sure that you arrange for it in advance, and perform all of the operations possible without it beforehand; this may save you time and money.

7 Plan on the vehicle being out of use for quite a while, especially if you intend to carry out an engine overhaul. Read through the whole of this Section and work out a strategy based on your own experience, and the tools, time and workspace available to you. Some of the overhaul processes may have to be carried out by an Audi dealer or an engineering works – these establishments often have busy schedules, so it would be prudent to consult them before removing or dismantling the engine, to get an idea of the amount of time required to carry out the work.

8 When removing the engine from the vehicle, be methodical about the disconnection of external components. Labelling cables and hoses as they are removed will greatly assist the refitting process.

9 Always be extremely careful when lifting the engine from the engine compartment. Serious injury can result from careless actions. If help is required, it is better to wait until it is available rather than risk personal injury and/or damage to components by continuing alone. By planning ahead and taking your time, a job of this nature, although major, can be accomplished successfully and without incident.

10 On all models described in this manual, the engine is lifted from the engine compartment, leaving the transmission in the car. Note that the engine should ideally be removed with the car standing on all four roadwheels, but access to the exhaust system and lower bolts will be improved if the car can be temporarily raised onto axle stands.

4 Engine – removal and refitting

Removal

Note: *The engine is lifted from the engine compartment, leaving the transmission in the car.*

1 Disconnect the battery negative lead as described in Chapter 5, Section 3.

2 Apply the hand brake, then jack up the front of the vehicle and support it on axle stands (see *Jacking and vehicle support*). Remove the engine undertrays, and the engine top cover.

3 Remove both front roadwheels, then remove the front wheel arch liner on both sides as described in Chapter 11 Section 21.

4 Remove the exhaust system front pipe and diesel particulate filter as described in Chapter 4B Section 8.

5 Set the lock carrier, located at the front of the engine compartment to the Service Position as described in Chapter 11 Section 21.

4.10a Remove the cover cap...

4.10b ...undo the retaining bolt...

4.10c ...and detach the wiring junction box from the body brace

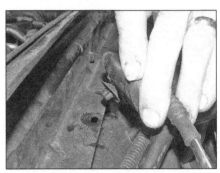
4.11 Release the wiring connector from the body brace and disconnect it

6 Remove the air cleaner assembly as described in Chapter 4A Section 2.

7 Remove the plenum chamber cover as described in Chapter 11 Section 21.

8 Release the catch and open the cover on the wiring junction box located in the plenum chamber.

9 Undo the three nuts and lift off the positive cable and the two adjacent smaller cables from the studs in the wiring junction box.

10 Remove the cover cap then unscrew the wiring junction box retaining bolt. Detach wiring junction box from the body brace **(see illustrations)**.

11 Release the wiring connector, located adjacent to the junction box, from the body brace, then disconnect the connector **(see illustration)**.

12 Working under the right-hand wheel arch release the two catches using a 5.5 mm ring spanner then lift off the wiring harness protector from above.

13 Release the catch and move the wiring harness duct forward to open the duct, then move the wiring harness clear.

14 Undo the retaining nut and swivel the washer fluid reservoir filler neck slightly upward. Pull the filler neck together with the filler pipe out of the reservoir and out through the opening in the body.

15 Remove the bonnet seal from the top of the body brace **(see illustration)**.

16 Undo the body brace retaining nut on the left-hand side, and the two retaining nuts on the right-hand side **(see illustrations)**.

17 Undo the two bolts securing the plenum

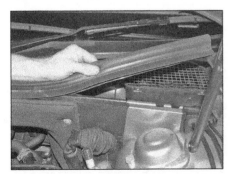
4.15 Remove the rubber seal from the top of the body brace

4.16a Undo the body brace retaining nut on the left-hand side...

4.16b ...and the two nuts on the right-hand side

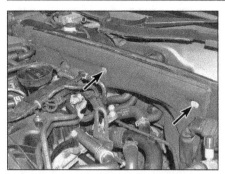

4.17 Undo the two bolts securing the partion panel to the body brace

4.18a Release the wiring harness cable ties...

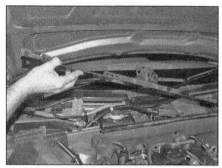

4.18b ...and remove the body brace from the engine compartment

chamber partition panel to the body brace **(see illustration)**.
18 Release the cable ties securing the wiring harness to the body brace, then remove the brace from the engine compartment **(see illustrations)**.
19 Undo the three bolts and lift off the cover from the engine compartment electronics box **(see illustration)**.
20 Release the catch on each side of the engine management ECU and lift the ECU out of the electronics box **(see illustrations)**.
21 Unscrew the retaining nut and disconnect the wiring connectors from the relay carrier and fuse holder inside the engine compartment electronics box.
22 Release the catch on each side and lift the relay carrier and fuse holder out of the electronics box.
23 Release any additional retainers where

necessary and disengage the engine wiring harness from the engine compartment electronics box. Lay the wiring harness and engine management ECU over the top of the engine so it can be removed with the engine.
24 Drain the cooling system as described in Chapter 1, Section 31.
25 Remove the torque reaction support crossmember as described in Chapter 2A, Section 14.
26 Undo the nut and bolt and remove the remaining lock carrier support strut on the right-hand side.
27 Release the retaining clips and disconnect the charge air ducts from the intercooler and engine connections.
28 Undo the retaining nut and disconnect the earth cables from the longitudinal member on the right-hand side of the engine compartment.

29 Disconnect the radiator electric cooling fan wiring harness connector(s) and place the harness over the engine.
30 Disconnect the vacuum hose from the rear of the plenum chamber partition panel, then detach the vacuum connection from the front of the panel **(see illustration)**.
31 Release the retaining clips and disconnect the two coolant hoses from the heater matrix pipe stubs **(see illustration)**.Trace the two hoses back to their connections on the engine, release the retaining clips and disconnect the hoses.
32 Undo the retaining nut on the right-hand side of the plenum chamber partition panel, then remove the partition panel from the engine compartment.
33 Undo the five upper transmission-to-engine retaining bolts which are accessible from within the engine compartment. Note that one of the bolts also secures the starter motor and is fitted with a spacer sleeve. When refitting, ensure that the spacer sleeve is fitted between the starter and transmission.
34 Disconnect the coolant hoses from the coolant expansion tank and move them to one side.
35 On models fitted with the Multitronic transmission, turn the retainer catch anti-clockwise and disconnect the wiring harness connector at the transmission.
36 On models equipped with hydraulic power steering, disconnect the electrical connector on the steering gear. On models with electro-mechanical power steering, disconnect the

4.19 Undo the bolts and remove the electronics box cover

4.20a Release the catch on each side of the ECU...

4.20b ...and lift the ECU out of the electronics box

4.30 Detach the vacuum connection from the plenum chamber partition panel

4.31 Disconnect the two coolant hoses from the heater matrix pipe stubs

electrical connector at the power steering control unit on the steering gear.

37 Remove the auxiliary drivebelt as described in Chapter 1, Section 8.

38 Pull off the cover cap, undo the retaining bolt and remove the auxiliary drivebelt idler roller from the engine.

39 Undo the retaining bolt and remove the auxiliary drivebelt tensioner from the engine.

40 Refer to Chapter 3, Section 10, and unbolt the air conditioning compressor from the the engine, without disconnecting the refrigerant lines. Suspend the compressor to one side of the engine compartment.

41 Remove the alternator as described in Chapter 5, Section 5.

42 On models with hydraulic power steering, refer to Chapter 10, Section 18 and detach the power steering pump from the engine. Leave the power steering fluid pipes connected to the pump and suspend the pump clear of the engine.

43 Position a trolley jack under the transmission and take the weight. With the transmission securely supported, undo the four bolts securing the transmission crossmember to the vehicle underbody.

44 Lower the jack slightly so that the transmission drops by approximately 80 mm.

45 Note their fitted positions and disconnect all wiring plugs and wiring harnesses from the transmission.

46 Raise the transmission on the jack and refit the four transmission crossmember retaining bolts.

47 Pull off the rubber cover from the lower left-hand side of the transmission bellhousing. Using a spanner or socket on the crankshaft sprocket bolt, turn the crankshaft in the normal direction of rotation (clockwise) until one of the three bolts securing the clutch module to the driveplate on the crankshaft becomes accessible through the bellhousing aperture **(see illustrations)**.

48 Undo the first accessible bolt, then turn the crankshaft 120° each time and remove the remaining bolts. Note that new bolts will be required for refitting.

49 Noting their locations, disconnect all remaining wiring, coolant hoses, vacuum hoses and fuel lines from the engine, with reference to the relevant Chapters of this Manual. Tape over or plug fuel lines and unions to prevent entry of dust and dirt.

50 Connect a hoist and lifting tackle to the engine lifting brackets on the cylinder head.

51 Undo the remaining lower bolts securing the transmission to the engine.

52 From under the wheel arch, undo the bolt each side securing the engine mountings to the engine brackets.

53 Make a final check to ensure that all relevant wiring, hoses and pipes have been disconnected, then carefully separate the engine from the transmission and lift the engine out of the engine compartment.

4.47a Pull off the rubber cover from the bellhousing...

4.47b ...then turn the crankshaft until one of the clutch module retaining bolts becomes accessible

Refitting

54 Refitting is a reversal of removal, bearing in mind the following points:
a) Smear the splines of the transmission input shaft with a little high melting-point grease.
b) If the crankshaft driveplate is of the type containing locating pins for the clutch module, ensure that the locating pins engage in the large holes in the clutch module.
c) Hand-tighten the three clutch module-to-driveplate retaining bolts first, then tighten them to the specified torque (see Chapter 7A specifications).
d) Ensure that any brackets noted before removal are in place on the engine-to-transmission bolts.
e) Tighten all fixings to the specified torque, where given.
f) Ensure that all wiring, hoses and pipes are correctly reconnected and routed as noted before removal.
g) Ensure that the fuel lines are correctly reconnected.
h) Refill the cooling system as described in Chapter 1, Section 31.
i) Bleed the fuel system as described in Chapter 4A, Section 10.

5 Engine overhaul – preliminary information

1 It is much easier to dismantle and work on the engine if it is mounted on a portable engine stand. These stands can often be hired from a tool hire shop.

Note: *Do not measure cylinder bore dimensions with the engine mounted on this type of stand.*

2 If a stand is not available, it is possible to dismantle the engine with it blocked up on a sturdy workbench, or on the floor. Be very careful not to tip or drop the engine when working without a stand.

3 If you intend to obtain a reconditioned engine, all ancillaries must be removed first, to be transferred to the new engine (just as they will if you are doing a complete engine overhaul yourself). These components include the following (it may be necessary to transfer additional components, such as the oil level dipstick/tube assembly, oil filter housing, etc, depending on which components are supplied with the reconditioned engine:
a) Alternator (including mounting brackets) and starter motor (Chapter 5).
b) The glow plug/preheating system components (Chapter 5).
c) All fuel system components, including fuel injectors, all sensors and actuators (Chapter 4A or or 4B).
d) The brake vacuum pump (Chapter 9).
e) All electrical switches, actuators and sensors, and the engine wiring harness (Chapter 4A).
f) Inlet and exhaust manifolds and turbocharger (Chapter 4A or 4B).
g) Engine mountings (Chapter 2A).
h) Clutch components (Chapter 6).

Note: *When removing the external components from the engine, pay close attention to details that may be helpful or important during refitting. Note the fitted position of gaskets, seals, spacers, pins, washers, bolts, and other small components.*

4 If you are obtaining a short engine (the engine cylinder block/crankcase, crankshaft, pistons and connecting rods, all fully assembled), then the cylinder head, sump, oil pump, timing belt, (together with tensioner, idler pulleys and timing belt covers), auxiliary drivebelt (together with its tensioner), coolant pump, thermostat housing, coolant outlet elbows, oil filter housing and oil cooler will also have to be removed.

5 If you are planning a full overhaul, the engine can be dismantled in the order given below:
a) Inlet and exhaust manifolds and turbocharger (Chapter 4A or 4B).
b) Timing belt, sprockets and tensioner (Chapter 2A).
c) Cylinder head (Chapter 2A).
d) Driveplate (Chapter 2A).
e) Sump (Section 9).
f) Oil pump (Section 10).
g) Piston/connecting rod assemblies (Section 11).
h) Crankshaft (Section 12).

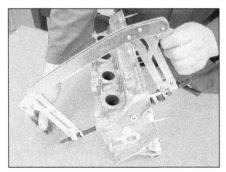

6.9a Compress a valve spring with a compressor tool

6.9b Remove the spring cap...

6.9c ...and valve spring

6 Cylinder head – dismantling

Note: *A valve spring compressor tool will be required for this operation.*

1 With the cylinder head removed, proceed as follows.
2 Remove the inlet and exhaust manifolds and turbocharger as described in Chapter 4A and 4B.
3 Remove the camshaft and hydraulic tappets as described in Chapter 2A, Section 9.
4 Remove the glow plugs as described in Chapter 5, Section 10.
5 Remove the fuel injectors as described in Chapter 4A, Section 4.
6 Unscrew the nut and remove the timing belt tensioner pulley from the stud on the timing belt end of the cylinder head.
7 Unbolt any remaining auxiliary brackets and/or engine lifting brackets from the cylinder head as necessary, noting their locations to aid refitting.
8 Turn the cylinder head over, and rest it on one side.
9 Using a valve spring compressor, compress each valve spring in turn until the split collets can be removed. Release the compressor, and lift off the spring cap and spring. If, when the valve spring compressor is screwed down, the spring cap refuses to free and expose the split collets, gently tap the top of the tool, directly

over the spring cap, with a light hammer. This will free the retainer **(see illustrations)**.
10 Using a pair of pliers, or a removal tool, carefully extract the valve stem oil seal from the top of the valve guide **(see illustrations)**.
11 Withdraw the valve from the gasket side of the cylinder head **(see illustration)**.
12 It is essential that each valve is stored together with its collets, cap, spring and spring seat. The valves should be kept in their correct sequences, unless they are so badly worn that they are to be renewed.

7 Cylinder head and valves – cleaning and inspection

1 Thorough cleaning of the cylinder head and valve components, followed by a detailed inspection, will enable you to decide how much valve service work must be carried out during engine overhaul.
Note: *If the engine has been severely overheated, it is best to assume that the cylinder head is warped. Check carefully for signs of this.*

Cleaning

2 Using a suitable degreasing agent, remove all traces of oil deposits from the cylinder head, paying particular attention to the camshaft bearing surfaces, hydraulic tappet bores, valve guides and oil ways. Scrape off any traces of old gasket from the mating

surfaces, taking care not to score or gouge them. If using emery paper, do not use a grade of less than 100. Turn the head over and, using a blunt blade, scrape any carbon deposits from the combustion chambers and ports. Finally, wash the entire head casting with a suitable solvent to remove the remaining debris.
3 Clean the valve heads and stems using a fine wire brush (or a power-operated wire brush). If the valve is covered with heavy carbon deposits, scrape off the majority of the deposits with a blunt blade first, then use the wire brush.
4 Thoroughly clean the remainder of the components using solvent and allow them to dry completely. Discard the oil seals, as new ones must be fitted when the cylinder head is reassembled.

Inspection

Cylinder head

5 Examine the head casting closely to identify any damage or cracks that may have developed. Cracks can often be identified from evidence of coolant or oil leakage. Pay particular attention to the areas around the valve seats and fuel injector holes. If cracking is discovered in this area, Audi state that the cylinder head may be re-used, provided the cracks are no larger than 0.5 mm wide. More serious damage will mean the renewal of the cylinder head casting.
6 Moderately pitted and scorched valve

6.10a Use a removal tool...

6.10b ...to remove the valve stem oil seals

6.11 Removing a valve

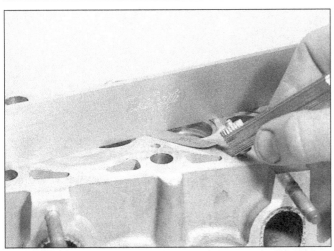

7.7 Measure the distortion of the cylinder head gasket surface

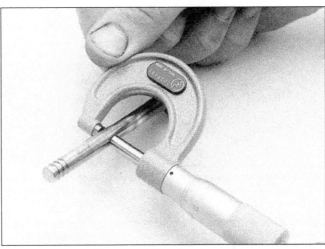

7.10 Measure the diameter of the valve stems using a micrometer

seats can be repaired by lapping the valves in during reassembly, as described later in this Chapter. The valve seats must not be recut.

7 Measure any distortion of the gasket surfaces using a straight-edge and a set of feeler blades. Take one measurement longitudinally on the manifold mating surface(s). Take several measurements across the head gasket surface, to assess the level of distortion in all planes **(see illustration)**. Compare the measurements with the figures in the Specifications.

8 If the head is distorted beyond the specified limit, the head must be renewed.

Camshaft

9 Inspection of the camshaft is covered in Chapter 2A, Section 9.

Valves and associated components

10 Examine each valve closely for signs of wear. Inspect the valve stems for wear ridges, scoring or variations in diameter; measure their diameters at several points along their lengths with a micrometer, and compare with the figures given in the Specifications **(see illustration)**.

11 The valve heads should not be cracked, badly pitted or charred. Note that light pitting of the valve head can be rectified by lapping in

the valves during reassembly, as described in Section 8.

12 Check that the valve stem end face is free from excessive pitting or indentation; this could be caused by defective hydraulic tappets.

13 Using vernier calipers, measure the free length of each of the valve springs. As a manufacturer's figure is not quoted, the only way to check the length of the springs is by comparison with a new component. Note that valve springs are usually renewed during a major engine overhaul **(see illustration)**.

14 Stand each spring on its end on a flat surface, against an engineer's square **(see illustration)**. Check the squareness of the spring visually, and renew it if it appears distorted.

15 Renew the valve stem oil seals regardless of their apparent condition.

8 Cylinder head – reassembly

Note: *A valve spring compressor tool will be required for this operation.*

1 To achieve a gas-tight seal between the valves and their seats, it will be necessary

to lap-in (or grind-in) the valves. To complete this process you will need a quantity of fine/coarse grinding paste and a grinding tool – this can either be of the rubber sucker type, or the automatic type which is driven by a rotary power tool.

2 Smear a small quantity of fine grinding paste on the sealing face of the valve head. Turn the cylinder head over so that the combustion chambers are facing upwards and insert the valve into the correct guide. Attach the grinding tool to the valve head and using a backward/forward rotary action, grind the valve head into its seat. Periodically lift the valve and rotate it to redistribute the grinding paste **(see illustration)**.

3 Continue this process until the contact between valve and seat produces an unbroken, matt grey ring of uniform width, on both faces. Repeat the operation on the remaining valves.

4 If the valves and seats are so badly pitted that coarse grinding paste must be used, bear in mind that there is a maximum protrusion of the end of the valve stem from the valve guide. Refer to an Audi dealer or engine reconditioning specialist. If this minimum dimension is outside the limit due to excessive grinding-in, the hydraulic tappets may not

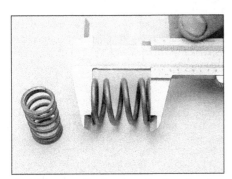

7.13 Measure the free length of each valve spring

7.14 Check the squareness of a valve spring

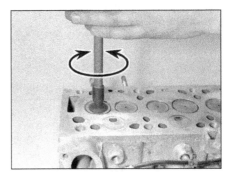

8.2 Grinding-in a valve

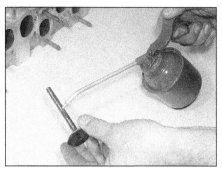
8.8a Lubricate the valve stem with clean engine oil

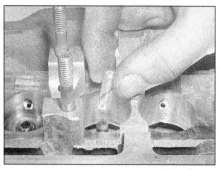
8.8b Fit a protective sleeve over the valve stem before fitting the stem seal

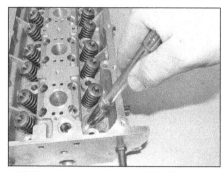
8.9 Use a long-reach socket to fit a valve stem oil seal

operate correctly, and the cylinder head must be renewed.

5 Assuming the repair is feasible, work as described previously, but use coarse grinding paste initially, to achieve a dull finish on the valve face and seat. Wash off the coarse paste with solvent and repeat the process using fine grinding paste to obtain the correct finish.

6 When all the valves have been ground in, remove all traces of grinding paste from the cylinder head and valves using solvent, and allow the head and valves to dry completely.

7 Turn the cylinder head on its side.

8 Working on one valve at a time, lubricate the valve stem with clean engine oil, and insert the valve into its guide. Fit one of the protective plastic sleeves (where supplied) to fit over the end of the valve stem – this will

protect the oil seal as it is being fitted **(see illustrations)**.

9 Dip a new valve stem seal in clean engine oil, and carefully push it over the valve stem and onto the top of the valve guide – take care not to damage the stem seal as it is fitted. Use a suitable long-reach socket or a valve stem seal fitting tool to press the seal firmly into position **(see illustration)**. Remove the protective sleeve from the valve stem.

10 Locate the valve spring over the valve stem, ensuring that the lower end of the spring seats correctly on the cylinder head **(see illustration)**.

11 Fit the upper spring seat over the top of the spring, then using a valve spring compressor, compress the spring until the upper seat is pushed beyond the collet grooves in the valve

stem. Refit the split collets. Gradually release the spring compressor, checking that the collets remain correctly seated as the spring extends. When correctly seated, the upper spring seat should force the collets securely into the grooves in the end of the valve stem **(see illustrations)**.

12 Repeat this process for the remaining sets of valve components, ensuring that all components are refitted to their original locations. To settle the components after installation, strike the end of each valve stem with a mallet, using a block of wood to protect the stem from damage. Check before progressing any further that the split collets remain firmly seated in the grooves in the end of the valve stem.

13 Refit any auxiliary brackets and/or engine lifting brackets to their original locations, as noted before removal.

14 Refit the timing belt tensioner pulley to the stud on the cylinder head, and refit the securing nut.

15 Refit the components removed in Section 6 paragraphs 2 to 5.

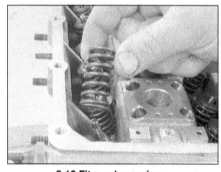
8.10 Fit a valve spring...

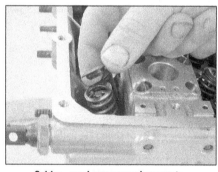
8.11a ...and upper spring seat...

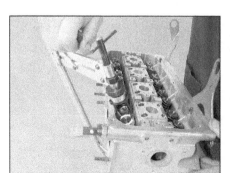
8.11b ...then compress a valve spring using a compressor tool

8.11c Use grease to hold the split collets in the groove

9 Sump – removal and refitting

Removal

1 With the engine removed from the car, drain the engine oil if not already done.

2 Unscrew and remove the bolts securing the sump to the cylinder block, then withdraw the sump. If necessary, release the sump by tapping with a soft-faced hammer.

Refitting

3 Begin refitting by thoroughly cleaning the mating faces of the sump and cylinder block. Ensure that all traces of old sealant are removed.

4 Ensure that the cylinder block mating face of the sump is free from all traces of old sealant, oil and grease, and then apply a 2.0 to 3.0 mm thick bead of silicone sealant (VW D 176 404 A2 or equivalent) to the sump **(see**

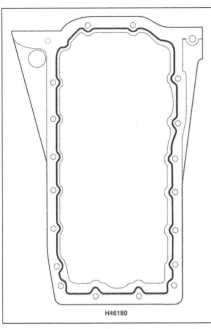

9.4 Apply a bead of sealant around the inside of the bolt holes

illustration). Note that the sealant should be run around the inside of the bolt holes in the sump. The sump must be fitted within 5 minutes of applying the sealant.

5 Offer the sump up to the cylinder block, then refit the sump-to-cylinder block bolts and lightly tighten them by hand. Use a straight-edge to check that the sump is flush with the driveplate end of the cylinder block, then tighten the retaining bolts to the specified torque working progressively in a diagonal sequence.

10 Oil pump and balance shaft assembly – removal, inspection and refitting

Removal

1 Remove the sump as described in Section 9.

Oil pump

2 Remove the retaining circlip, then pull the oil pump shaft out using an M3 bolt **(see illustrations)**.

3 Undo the retaining bolts, and then detach the pick-up pipe from the pump **(see illustration)**.

4 Undo the bolts and detach the oil pump from the balance shaft assembly **(see illustration)**.

Balance shaft assembly

5 Lock the camshafts and crankshaft at TDC on No 1 cylinder as described in Chapter 2A, Section 3.

6 Working gradually and evenly, undo the retaining bolts and detach the balance shaft assembly from the base of the cylinder block.

Inspection

7 At the time of writing, it would appear that no parts are available for the oil pump or balance shaft assembly. If defective, the oil pump or balance shaft assembly must be renewed. Consult an Audi dealer or parts specialist.

Refitting

Oil pump

8 Refit the pump to the balance shaft assembly and tighten the retaining bolts to the specified torque.

10.2a Remove the circlip...

10.2b ...and pull out the oil pump shaft using an M3 bolt

10.3 Oil pump pick-up pipe bolts

10.4 Oil pump mounting bolts

10.9 Renew the pick-up pipe O-ring seal

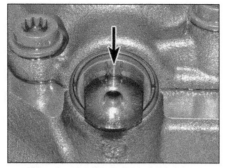

10.12a Rotate the balance shaft until the groove on the end of the rear shaft is vertical...

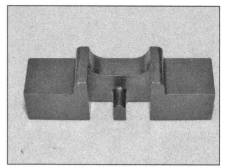

10.12b ...and tool No T10255...

9 Refit the oil pick-up pipe using a new O-ring, then tighten the retaining bolts to the specified torque **(see illustration)**.
10 Push the driveshaft into place, and secure it with the circlip.
11 The remainder of refitting is a reversal of removal.

Balance shaft assembly

Note: *If the original balance shaft assembly is being refitted, it's essential that neither the drivegear on the crankshaft or the crankshaft itself has been renewed, or the idler gear bolt has been slackened. If they have, proceed under the heading for the installation of a new balance shaft assembly.*

Refitting the original assembly

12 Rotate the balance shaft until VAG tool No T10255 can be fitted into the groove on the left-hand end of the rear shaft **(see illustrations)**.
13 Ensure the engine is still locked at TDC for No 1 cylinder, and then position the balance shaft assembly over the locating dowels on the base of the cylinder block. The idler gear must engage with the drivegear of the crankshaft, and there must be noticeable backlash.
14 Fit the new balance shaft assembly retaining bolts, and working from the centre outwards, tighten them to the specified torque. Remove the special tool.
15 The remainder of refitting is a reversal of removal.

Fitting a new balance shaft assembly

16 New balance shaft assemblies are supplied with an idler gear with a special coating. Once fitted, the coating wears down to give the correct backlash between the gears.
17 Ensure the engine is still locked at TDC for No 1 cylinder as described in Chapter 2A, Section 3.
18 Slacken the idler gear retaining bolt 90°.
19 Position the balance shaft assembly over the locating dowels on the base of the cylinder block, ensuring the white mark on the idler gear is centrally aligned with the crankshaft drivegear. Idler gears not marked with a white mark can be installed in any position.
20 Fit the new balance shaft assembly retaining bolts, and working from the centre outwards, tighten them to the specified torque.
21 Rotate the balance shaft until VAG tool No T10255 can be fitted into the groove on the left-hand end of the rear shaft **(see illustration 10.12a, 10.12b and 10.12c)**.
22 Fit the balance shaft drivegear onto the shaft so the holes in the gear align with the holes in the shaft. Tighten the retaining bolts to the specified torque.
23 Have an assistant push the idler gear between the two gears to remove any backlash. At the same time, rotate the balance shaft anti-clockwise slightly, and tighten the idler gear retaining bolt to the specified

torque. Remove the balance shaft locking tool.
24 The remainder of refitting is a reversal of removal.

11 Piston/connecting rod assemblies – removal

1 Remove the cylinder head as described in Chapter 2A, Section 11, and the oil pump and balance shaft assembly as described in Section 10.
2 Inspect the tops of the cylinder bores for ridges at the point where the pistons reach top dead centre. These must be removed otherwise the pistons may be damaged when they are pushed out of their bores. Use a scraper or ridge reamer to remove the ridges. Such a ridge indicates excessive wear of the cylinder bore.
3 Check the connecting rods and big-end caps for identification markings. Both connecting rods and caps should be marked with the cylinder number on one side of each assembly. Note that No 1 cylinder is at the timing belt end of the engine. If no marks are present, using a hammer and centre-punch, paint or similar, mark each connecting rod and big-end bearing cap with its respective cylinder number – note on which side of the connecting rods and caps the marks are made **(see illustration)**.
4 Similarly, check the piston crowns for direction markings. An arrow on each piston crown should point towards the timing belt end of the engine. On some engines, this mark may be obscured by carbon build-up, in which case the piston crown should be cleaned to check for a mark. In some cases, the direction arrow may have worn off, in which case a suitable mark should be made on the piston crown using a scriber – do not deeply score the piston crown, but ensure that the mark is easily visible.
5 Turn the crankshaft to bring No's 1 and 4 pistons to bottom dead centre.
6 Unscrew the bolts from No 1 piston big-end bearing cap. Lift off the cap, and recover the bottom half bearing shell. If the bearing

10.12c ...can be fitted

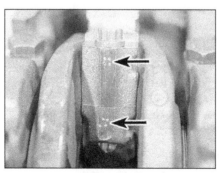

11.3 Mark the big-end caps and connecting rods with their cylinder numbers

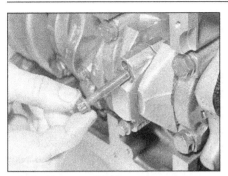

11.6a Unscrew the big-end bearing cap bolts...

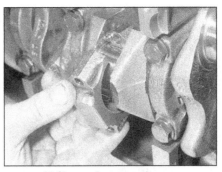

11.6b ...and remove the cap

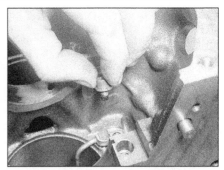

11.11a Remove the securing bolts...

shells are to be re-used, tape the cap and bearing shell together. Note that if the bearing shells are to be re-used, they must be fitted to the original connecting rod and cap **(see illustrations)**.

7 Using a hammer handle, push the piston up through the bore, and remove it from the top of the cylinder block. Take care not to damage the piston cooling oil spray jets in the cylinder block as the piston/connecting rod assembly is removed. Recover the upper bearing shell, and tape it to the connecting rod for safe-keeping.

8 Loosely refit the big-end cap to the connecting rod, and secure with the bolts – this will help to keep the components in their correct order.

9 Remove No.4 piston assembly in the same way.

10 Turn the crankshaft as necessary to bring No's 2 and 3 pistons to bottom dead centre, and remove them in the same way.

11 Remove the securing bolts, and withdraw the piston cooling oil spray jets from the bottom of the cylinder block **(see illustrations)**.

12 Crankshaft – removal

Note: *If no work is to be done on the pistons and connecting rods, there is no need to push the pistons out of the cylinder bores. The pistons should just be pushed far enough up*
the bores so that they are positioned clear of the crankshaft journals.

1 Remove the timing belt and crankshaft sprocket, oil pump and balance shaft assembly, driveplate and the crankshaft oil seal housings.

2 Remove the pistons and connecting rods, or disconnect them from the crankshaft, as described in Section 11 (see Note at the beginning of this Section).

3 Check the crankshaft endfloat as described in Section 15, then proceed as follows.

4 The main bearing caps should be numbered 1 to 5 from the timing belt end of the engine. If the bearing caps are not marked, mark them accordingly using a centre-punch. Note the orientation of the markings to ensure correct refitting.

5 Slacken and remove the main bearing cap bolts, and lift off each cap. If the caps appear to be stuck, tap them with a soft-faced mallet to free them from the cylinder block **(see illustration)**. Recover the lower bearing shells, and tape them to their caps for safekeeping.

6 Recover the lower crankshaft endfloat control thrustwasher halves from either side of the No 3 main bearing cap, noting their orientation.

7 Lift the crankshaft from the cylinder block. Take care, as the crankshaft is heavy.

8 Recover the upper bearing shells from the cylinder block, and tape them to their respective caps for safekeeping. Similarly, recover the upper crankshaft endfloat control thrustwasher halves, noting their orientation.

13 Cylinder block/crankcase – cleaning and inspection

Cleaning

1 Remove all external components and electrical switches/sensors from the block, including mounting brackets, coolant pump, oil filter housing, oil cooler and EGR cooler, etc. For complete cleaning, the core plugs should ideally be removed. Drill a small hole in the plugs, and then insert a self-tapping screw into the hole. Extract the plugs by pulling on the screw with a pair of grips, or by using a slide hammer.

2 Scrape all traces of gasket and sealant from the cylinder block/crankcase, taking care not to damage the sealing surfaces.

3 Remove all oil gallery plugs (where fitted). The plugs are usually very tight – they may have to be drilled out, and the holes re-tapped. Use new plugs when the engine is reassembled.

4 If the casting is extremely dirty, it should be steam-cleaned. After this, clean all oil holes and galleries one more time. Flush all internal passages with warm water until the water runs clear. Dry thoroughly, and apply a light film of oil to all mating surfaces and cylinder bores, to prevent rusting. If you have access to compressed air, use it to speed up the drying process, and to blow out all the oil holes and galleries.

⚠️ *Warning: Wear eye protection when using compressed air.*

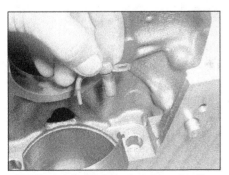

11.11b ...and withdraw the piston cooling oil spray jets

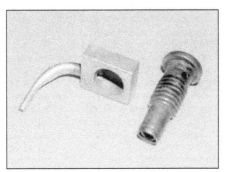

11.11c Piston cooling spray jet and retainer

12.5 Slacken and remove the main bearing cap bolts

5 If the castings are not very dirty, you can do an adequate cleaning job with hot, soapy water and a stiff brush. Take plenty of time, and do a thorough job. Regardless of the cleaning method used, be sure to clean all oil holes and galleries very thoroughly, and to dry all components well. Protect the cylinder bores as described above, to prevent rusting.

6 Where applicable, check the piston cooling oil spray jets for damage, and renew if necessary. Check the oil spray hole and the oil passages for blockage.

7 All threaded holes must be clean, to ensure accurate torque readings during reassembly. To clean the threads, run the correct-size tap into each of the holes to remove rust, corrosion, thread sealant or sludge, and to restore damaged threads **(see illustration)**. If possible, use compressed air to clear the holes free of debris produced by this operation.

Note: *Take extra care to exclude all cleaning liquid from blind tapped holes, as the casting may be cracked by hydraulic action if a bolt is threaded into a hole containing liquid.*

8 After coating the mating surfaces of the new core plugs with suitable sealant, fit them to the cylinder block. Make sure that they are driven in straight and seated correctly, or leakage could result.

9 Apply suitable sealant to the new oil gallery plugs, and insert them into the holes in the block. Tighten them securely.

10 If the engine is not going to be reassembled immediately, cover it with a large plastic bag to keep it clean; protect all mating surfaces and the cylinder bores, to prevent rusting.

Inspection

11 Visually check the castings for cracks and corrosion. Look for stripped threads in the threaded holes. If there has been any history of internal coolant leakage, it may be worthwhile having an engine overhaul specialist check the cylinder block/crankcase for cracks with special equipment. If defects are found, have them repaired, if possible, or renew the assembly.

12 Check each cylinder bore for scuffing and scoring.

13 If in any doubt as the condition of the cylinder block have the block/bores inspected

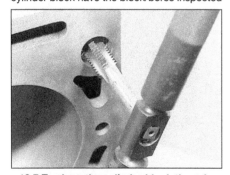

13.7 To clean the cylinder block threads, run a correct-size tap into the holes

and measured by an engine reconditioning specialist. They will be able to advise on whether the block is serviceable, whether a re-bore is necessary, and supply the appropriate pistons and rings.

14 If the bores are in reasonably good condition and not excessively worn, then it may only be necessary to renew the piston rings.

15 If this is the case, the bores should be honed, to allow the new rings to bed-in correctly and provide the best possible seal. Consult an engine reconditioning specialist

16 The cylinder block/crankcase should now be completely clean and dry, with all components checked for wear or damage, and repaired or overhauled as necessary.

17 Apply a light coating of engine oil to the mating surfaces and cylinder bores to prevent rust forming.

18 Refit as many ancillary components as possible, for safekeeping. If reassembly is not to start immediately, cover the block with a large plastic bag to keep it clean, and protect the machined surfaces as described above to prevent rusting.

14 Piston/connecting rod assemblies – cleaning and inspection

Cleaning

1 Before the inspection process can begin, the piston/connecting rod assemblies must be cleaned, and the original piston rings removed from the pistons.

2 The rings should have smooth, polished working surfaces, with no dull or carbon-coated sections (showing that the ring is not sealing correctly against the bore wall, so allowing combustion gases to blow by) and no traces of wear on their top and bottom surfaces. The end gaps should be clear of carbon, but not polished (indicating a too-small end gap), and all the rings (including the elements of the oil control ring) should be free to rotate in their grooves, but without excessive up-and-down movement. If the rings appear to be in good condition, they are probably fit for further use; check the end gaps (in an unworn part of the bore) as described in Section 18.

3 If any of the rings appears to be worn or damaged, or has an end gap significantly different from the specified value, the usual course of action is to renew all of them as a set. **Note:** *While it is usual to renew piston rings when an engine is overhauled, they may be re-used if in acceptable condition. If re-using the rings, make sure that each ring is marked during removal to ensure that it is refitted correctly.*

4 Carefully expand the old rings over the top of the pistons. The use of two or three old feeler blades will be helpful in preventing the rings dropping into empty grooves **(see illustration)**. Be careful not to scratch the piston with the ends of the ring. The rings are

14.4 Old feeler blades can be used to prevent piston rings from dropping into empty grooves

brittle, and will snap if they are spread too far. They are also very sharp – protect your hands and fingers. Note that the third ring incorporates an expander. Keep each set of rings with its piston if the old rings are to be re-used. Note which way up each ring is fitted to ensure correct refitting.

5 Scrape away all traces of carbon from the top of the piston. A hand-held wire brush (or a piece of fine emery cloth) can be used, once the majority of the deposits have been scraped away.

6 Remove the carbon from the ring grooves in the piston, using an old ring. Break the ring in half to do this (be careful not to cut your fingers – piston rings are sharp). Be careful to remove only the carbon deposits – do not remove any metal, and do not nick or scratch the sides of the ring grooves.

7 Once the deposits have been removed, clean the piston/connecting rod assembly with paraffin or a suitable solvent, and dry thoroughly. Make sure that the oil return holes in the ring grooves are clear.

Inspection

8 If the pistons and cylinder bores are not damaged or worn excessively, and if the cylinder block does not need to be re-bored, the original pistons can be refitted.

9 Have the pistons and cylinder bore measure by an engine reconditioning specialist. They will be able to advise on possible repairs, and supply the correct replacement parts.

10 Normal piston wear shows up as even vertical wear on the piston thrust surfaces, and slight looseness of the top ring in its groove. New piston rings should always be used when the engine is reassembled.

11 Carefully inspect each piston for cracks around the skirt, around the gudgeon pin holes, and at the piston ring 'lands' (between the ring grooves).

12 Look for scoring and scuffing on the piston skirt, holes in the piston crown, and burned areas at the edge of the crown. If the skirt is scored or scuffed, the engine may have been suffering from overheating, and/or abnormal combustion, which caused excessively high operating temperatures. The cooling and lubrication systems should be checked thoroughly.

13 Scorch marks on the sides of the pistons

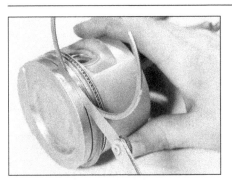

14.17 Measure the piston ring-to-groove clearance using a feeler blade

14.20a Use a small flat-bladed screwdriver to prise out the circlip...

14.20b ...then push out the gudgeon pin and separate the piston and connecting rod

show that blow-by has occurred.

14 A hole in the piston crown, or burned areas at the edge of the piston crown, indicates that abnormal combustion (pre-ignition, knocking, or detonation) has been occurring.

15 If any of the above problems exist, the causes must be investigated and corrected, or the damage will occur again. The causes may include incorrect injection pump timing, inlet air leaks or a faulty fuel injector.

16 Corrosion of the piston, in the form of pitting, indicates that coolant has been leaking into the combustion chamber and/or the crankcase. Again, the cause must be corrected, or the problem may persist in the rebuilt engine.

17 Locate a new piston ring in the appropriate groove and measure the ring-to-groove clearance using a feeler blade **(see illustration)**. Note that the rings are of different widths, so use the correct ring for the groove. Compare the measurements with those listed; if the clearances are outside of the tolerance band, then the piston must be renewed. Confirm this by checking the width of the piston ring with a micrometer.

18 Examine each connecting rod carefully for signs of damage, such as cracks around the big-end and small-end bearings. Check that the rod is not bent or distorted. Damage is highly unlikely, unless the engine has been seized or badly overheated. Detailed checking of the connecting rod assembly can only be carried out by an Audi dealer or engine repair specialist with the necessary equipment.

19 The gudgeon pins are of the floating type, secured in position by two circlips. The

pistons and connecting rods can be separated as follows.

20 Using a small flat-bladed screwdriver, prise out the circlips, and push out the gudgeon pin **(see illustrations)**. Hand pressure should be sufficient to remove the pin. Identify the piston and rod to ensure correct reassembly. Discard the circlips – new ones must be used on refitting. If the gudgeon pin proves difficult to remove, heat the piston to 60°C with hot water – the resulting expansion will then allow the two components to be separated.

21 Examine the gudgeon pin and connecting rod small-end bearing for signs of wear or damage. It should be possible to push the gudgeon pin through the connecting rod bush by hand, without noticeable play. Wear can be cured by renewing both the pin and bush. Bush renewal, however, is a specialist job – press facilities are required, and the new bush must be reamed accurately.

22 Examine all components, and obtain any new parts from your Audi dealer or engine reconditioning specialist. If new pistons are purchased, they will be supplied complete with gudgeon pins and circlips. Circlips can also be purchased individually.

23 The orientation of the piston with respect to the connecting rod must be correct when the two are reassembled. The piston crown is marked with an arrow (which may be obscured by carbon deposits); this must point towards the timing belt end of the engine when the piston is installed. The connecting rod and its bearing cap both have recesses machined into them on one side, close to their mating surfaces –

these recesses must both face the same way as the arrow on the piston crown (ie, towards the timing belt end of the engine) when correctly installed. Reassemble the two components to satisfy this requirement **(see illustrations)**.

24 Apply a smear of clean engine oil to the gudgeon pin. Slide it into the piston and through the connecting rod small-end. Check that the piston pivots freely on the rod, then secure the gudgeon pin in position with two new circlips. Ensure that each circlip is correctly located in its groove in the piston.

25 Repeat the cleaning and inspection process for the remaining pistons and connecting rods.

---

15 Crankshaft – checking endfloat and inspection

Checking endfloat

1 If the crankshaft endfloat is to be checked, this must be done when the crankshaft is still installed in the cylinder block/crankcase, but is free to move (see Section 12).

2 Check the endfloat using a dial gauge in contact with the end of the crankshaft. Push the crankshaft fully one way, and then zero the gauge. Push the crankshaft fully the other way, and check the endfloat. The result can be compared with the specified amount, and will give an indication as to whether new thrustwasher halves are required **(see illustration)**. Note that all thrustwashers must be of the same thickness.

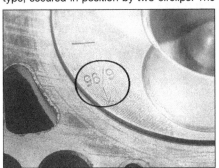

14.23a The piston crown is marked with an arrow which must point towards the timing belt end of the engine

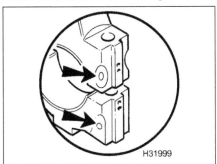

14.23b The recesses in the connecting rod and bearing cap must face the timing belt end of the engine

15.2 Measure crankshaft endfloat using a dial gauge

15.3 Measure crankshaft endfloat using feeler blades

3 If a dial gauge is not available, feeler blades can be used. First push the crankshaft fully towards the flywheel end of the engine, and then use feeler blades to measure the gap between the web of No 3 crankpin and the thrustwasher halves **(see illustration)**.

Inspection

4 Clean the crankshaft using paraffin or a suitable solvent, and dry it, preferably with compressed air if available. Be sure to clean the oil holes with a pipe cleaner or similar probe, to ensure that they are not obstructed.

 Warning: Wear eye protection when using compressed air.

5 Check the main and big-end bearing journals for uneven wear, scoring, pitting and cracking.
6 Big-end bearing wear is accompanied by distinct metallic knocking when the engine is running (particularly noticeable when the engine is pulling from low speed) and some loss of oil pressure.
7 Main bearing wear is accompanied by severe engine vibration and rumble – getting

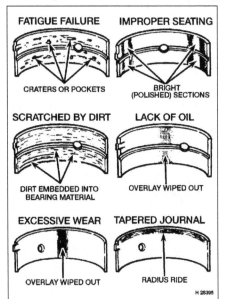

16.1 Typical bearing failures

progressively worse as engine speed increases – and again by loss of oil pressure.
8 Check the bearing journal for roughness by running a finger lightly over the bearing surface. Any roughness (which will be accompanied by obvious bearing wear) indicates that the crankshaft requires regrinding (where possible) or renewal.
9 If the crankshaft has been reground, check for burrs around the crankshaft oil holes (the holes are usually chamfered, so burrs should not be a problem unless regrinding has been carried out carelessly). Remove any burrs with a fine file or scraper, and thoroughly clean the oil holes as described previously.
10 Have the crankshaft measured and inspected by an engine reconditioning specialist. They will be able to advise any possible repairs and supply the correct parts.
11 Check the oil seal contact surfaces at each end of the crankshaft for wear and damage. If the seal has worn a deep groove in the surface of the crankshaft, consult an engine overhaul specialist; repair may be possible, but otherwise a new crankshaft will be required.
12 If the crankshaft journals have not already been reground, it may be possible to have the crankshaft reconditioned, and to fit undersize shells (see Section 19). If no undersize shells are available and the crankshaft has worn beyond the specified limits, it will have to be renewed. Consult your Audi dealer or engine reconditioning specialist for further information on parts availability.

16 Main and big-end bearings – inspection and selection

Inspection

1 Even though the main and big-end bearings should be renewed during the engine overhaul, the old bearings should be retained for close examination, as they may reveal valuable information about the condition of the engine **(see illustration)**.
2 Bearing failure can occur due to lack of lubrication, the presence of dirt or other foreign particles, overloading the engine, or corrosion. Regardless of the cause of bearing failure, the cause must be corrected before the engine is reassembled, to prevent it from happening again.
3 When examining the bearing shells, remove them from the cylinder block/crankcase, the main bearing caps, the connecting rods and the connecting rod big-end bearing caps. Lay them out on a clean surface in the same general position as their location in the engine. This will enable you to match any bearing problems with the corresponding crankshaft journal. Do not touch any shell's internal bearing surface with your fingers while checking it, or the delicate surface may be scratched.

4 Dirt and other foreign matter get into the engine in a variety of ways. It may be left in the engine during assembly, or it may pass through filters or the crankcase ventilation system. It may get into the oil, and from there into the bearings. Metal chips from machining operations and normal engine wear are often present. Abrasives are sometimes left in engine components after reconditioning, especially when parts are not thoroughly cleaned using the proper cleaning methods. Whatever the source, these foreign objects often end up embedded in the soft bearing material, and are easily recognised. Large particles will not embed in the bearing, but will score or gouge the bearing and journal. The best prevention for this cause of bearing failure is to clean all parts thoroughly, and keep everything spotlessly clean during engine assembly. Frequent and regular engine oil and filter changes are also recommended.
5 Lack of lubrication (or lubrication breakdown) has a number of interrelated causes. Excessive heat (which thins the oil), overloading (which squeezes the oil from the bearing face) and oil leakage (from excessive bearing clearances, worn oil pump or high engine speeds) all contribute to lubrication breakdown. Blocked oil passages, which usually are the result of misaligned oil holes in a bearing shell, will also oil-starve a bearing, and destroy it. When lack of lubrication is the cause of bearing failure, the bearing material is wiped or extruded from the steel backing of the bearing. Temperatures may increase to the point where the steel backing turns blue from overheating.
6 Driving habits can have a definite effect on bearing life. Full-throttle, low-speed operation (labouring the engine) puts very high loads on bearings, tending to squeeze out the oil film. These loads cause the bearings to flex, which produces fine cracks in the bearing face (fatigue failure). Eventually, the bearing material will loosen in pieces, and tear away from the steel backing.
7 Short-distance driving leads to corrosion of bearings, because insufficient engine heat is produced to drive off the condensed water and corrosive gases. These products collect in the engine oil, forming acid and sludge. As the oil is carried to the engine bearings, the acid attacks and corrodes the bearing material.
8 Incorrect bearing installation during engine assembly will lead to bearing failure as well. Tight-fitting bearings leave insufficient bearing running clearance, and will result in oil starvation. Dirt or foreign particles trapped behind a bearing shell result in high spots on the bearing, which lead to failure.
9 Do not touch any shell's internal bearing surface with your fingers during re-assembly, as there is a risk of scratching the delicate surface, or of depositing particles of dirt on it.
10 As mentioned at the beginning of this Section, the bearing shells should be renewed as a matter of course during engine overhaul. To do otherwise is false economy.

Selection

11 Main and big-end bearings for the engines described in this Chapter are available in standard sizes and a range of undersizes to suit reground crankshafts.

12 Have the crankshaft measured by an engine reconditioning specialist. They will be able to supply the correctly sized bearings.

17 Engine overhaul – reassembly sequence

1 Before reassembly begins, ensure that all new parts have been obtained, and that all necessary tools are available. Read through the entire procedure to familiarise yourself with the work involved, and to ensure that all items necessary for reassembly of the engine are at hand. In addition to all normal tools and materials, thread-locking compound will be needed. A suitable tube of liquid sealant will also be required for the joint faces that are fitted without gaskets.

2 In order to save time and avoid problems, engine reassembly can be carried out in the following order, referring to Part A of this Chapter unless otherwise stated. Where applicable, use new gaskets and seals when refitting the various components.

a) Crankshaft (Section 19).
b) Piston/connecting rod assemblies (Section 20).
c) Oil pump and balance shaft assembly (Section 10).
d) Sump (Section 9).
e) Driveplate.
f) Cylinder head.
g) Timing belt, tensioner and sprockets.
h) Engine external components.

3 At this stage, all engine components should be absolutely clean and dry, with all faults repaired. The components should be laid out (or in individual containers) on a completely clean work surface.

18 Piston rings – refitting

1 Before fitting new piston rings, the ring end gaps must be checked as follows.

2 Lay out the piston/connecting rod assemblies and the new piston ring sets, so that the ring sets will be matched with the same piston and cylinder during the end gap measurement and subsequent engine reassembly.

3 Insert the top ring into the first cylinder, and push it down the bore using the top of the piston. This will ensure that the ring remains square with the cylinder walls. Position the ring approximately 15.0 mm the bottom of the cylinder bore, at the lower limit of ring travel. Note that the top and second compression rings are different.

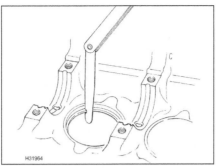

18.4 Check a piston ring end gap using a feeler blade

4 Measure the end gap using feeler blades, and compare the measurements with the figures given in the Specifications **(see illustration)**.

5 If the gap is too small (unlikely if genuine Audi parts are used), it must be enlarged, or the ring ends may contact each other during engine operation, causing serious damage. Ideally, new piston rings providing the correct end gap should be fitted. As a last resort, the end gap can be increased by filing the ring ends very carefully with a fine file. Mount the file in a vice equipped with soft jaws, slip the ring over the file with the ends contacting the file face, and slowly move the ring to remove material from the ends. Take care, as piston rings are sharp, and are easily broken.

6 With new piston rings, it is unlikely that the end gap will be too large. If the gaps are too large, check that you have the correct rings for your engine and for the particular cylinder bore size.

7 Repeat the checking procedure for each ring in the first cylinder, and then for the rings in the remaining cylinders. Remember to keep rings, pistons and cylinders matched up.

8 Once the ring end gaps have been checked and if necessary corrected, the rings can be fitted to the pistons.

9 Fit the piston rings using the same technique as for removal. Fit the bottom (oil control) ring first, and work up. Note that a two- or three-section oil control ring may be fitted; where a two-section ring is fitted, first

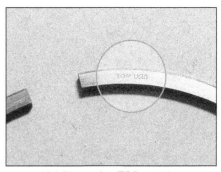

18.9 Piston ring TOP marking

insert the wire expander, then fit the ring. Ensure that the rings are fitted the correct way up – the top surface of the rings is normally marked TOP **(see illustration)**. Offset the piston ring gaps by 120° from each other.

Note: *Always follow any instructions supplied with the new piston ring sets – different manufacturers may specify different procedures. Do not mix up the top and second compression rings, as they have different cross-sections.*

19 Crankshaft – refitting

1 Wipe off the surfaces of the bearing shells in the crankcase and bearing caps.

2 Press the bearing shells into their locations, ensuring that the tab on each shell engages in the notch in the cylinder block or bearing cap, and that the oil holes In the cylinder block and bearing shell are aligned **(see illustration)**. Take care not to touch any shells bearing surface with your fingers.

3 Liberally coat the bearing shells in the crankcase with clean engine oil of the appropriate grade **(see illustration)**. Make sure that the bearing shells are still correctly seated in their locations.

4 Lower the crankshaft into position so that No 1 cylinder crankpin is at BDC, ready for fitting No 1 piston. Ensure that the crankshaft

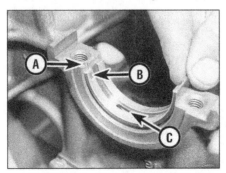

19.2 Bearing shell correctly refitted

A Recess in cylinder block
B Lug on bearing shell
C Oil hole

19.3 Lubricate the upper bearing shells

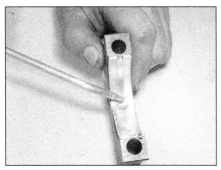

19.5a Lubricate the lower bearing shells...

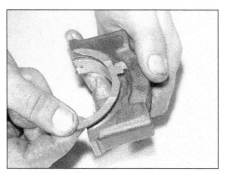

19.5b...and make sure that the thrustwashers are correctly seated

19.6 Fitting No 1 main bearing cap

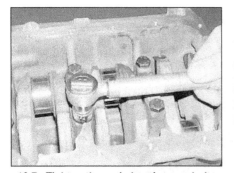

19.7a Tighten the main bearing cap bolts to the specified torque...

19.7b...then through the specified angle

endfloat control thrustwasher halves, either side of the No 3 main bearing location, remain in position.

5 Lubricate the lower bearing shells in the main bearing caps with clean engine oil. Make sure that the crankshaft endfloat control thrustwasher halves are still correctly seated either side of No 3 bearing cap **(see illustrations)**.

6 Fit the main bearing caps in the correct order and orientation – No 1 bearing cap must be at the timing belt end of the engine and the bearing shell tab locating recesses in the crankcase and bearing caps must be adjacent to each other **(see illustration)**. Insert the

bearing cap bolts (using new bolts where necessary), and hand-tighten them only.

7 Working from the centre bearing cap outwards, tighten the bearing cap bolts to the specified Stage 1 torque setting, then go round again, and tighten all bolts through the Stage 2 angle **(see illustrations)**.

8 Check that the crankshaft rotates freely by turning it by hand. If resistance is felt, recheck the bearing running clearances, as described previously.

9 Check the crankshaft endfloat as described at the beginning of Section 15. If the thrust surfaces of the crankshaft have been checked

and new thrustwashers have been fitted, then the endfloat should be within specification.

10 Refit the pistons and connecting rods or reconnect them to the crankshaft as described in Section.

11 Refit the crankshaft oil seal housings, driveplate, oil pump and balance shaft assembly, sump, crankshaft sprocket and timing belt.

20 Piston/connecting rod assemblies – refitting

Note: *A piston ring compressor tool will be required for this operation.*

1 Note that the following procedure assumes that the crankshaft main bearing caps are in place.

2 Where applicable, refit the piston cooling oil spray jets to the bottom of the cylinder block, and tighten the securing bolts to the specified torque.

3 If new bearing shells are being fitted, ensure that all traces of the protective grease are cleaned off using paraffin. Wipe dry the shells and connecting rods with a lint-free cloth.

4 Lubricate the cylinder bores, the pistons, piston rings and upper bearing shells with clean engine oil **(see illustrations)**. Lay out

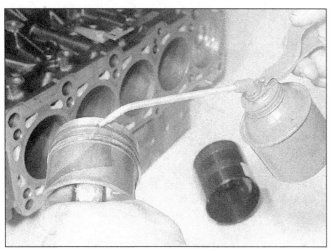

20.4a Lubricate the pistons...

20.4b...and big-end upper bearing shells with clean engine oil

each piston/connecting rod assembly in order on a clean work surface.

5 Start with piston/connecting rod assembly No 1. Make sure that the piston rings are still spaced as described in Section 18, then clamp them in position with a piston ring compressor tool.

6 Insert the piston/connecting rod assembly into the top of cylinder No 1. Lower the big-end in first, guiding it to protect the cylinder bores. Take particular care not to damage the oil spray jets when guiding the connecting rods onto the crankpins.

7 Ensure that the orientation of the piston in its cylinder is correct – the piston crown, connecting rod and big-end bearing cap have markings, which must point towards the timing belt end of the engine when the piston is installed in the bore **(see illustration)** – refer to Section 14 for details.

8 Using a block of wood or hammer handle against the piston crown, tap the assembly into the cylinder until the piston crown is flush with the top of the cylinder **(see illustration)**.

9 Ensure that the bearing shell is still correctly installed in the connecting rod, and then liberally lubricate the crankpin and both bearing shells with clean engine oil.

10 Taking care not to mark the cylinder bores; tap the piston/connecting rod assembly down the bore and onto the crankpin. Oil the bolt threads and the undersides of the bolt heads.

11 Fit the big-end bearing cap, tightening its retaining bolts finger-tight at first. The connecting rod and its bearing cap both have recesses machined into them on one side, close to their mating surfaces – these recesses must both face the same way as the arrow on the piston crown (i.e. towards the timing end of the engine) when correctly installed. Reassemble the two components to satisfy this requirement.

12 Tighten the retaining bolts to the specified torque and angle, in the two stages given in the Specifications **(see illustrations)**.

13 Refit the other three remaining piston/connecting rod assemblies in the same way.

14 Rotate the crankshaft by hand. Check that it turns freely; some stiffness is to be expected if new parts have been fitted, but there should be no binding or tight spots.

15 If new pistons have been fitted, or if a new short engine has been fitted, the projection of the piston crowns above the cylinder head mating face of the cylinder block at TDC must be measured. This measurement is used to determine the thickness of the new cylinder

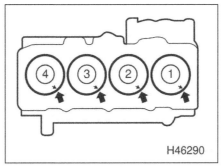

20.7 Piston orientation and coding

20.12a Tighten the big-end bearing cap bolts/nuts to the specified torque...

head gasket required. This procedure is described in Chapter 2A, Section 11.

16 Refit the oil pump and balance shaft assembly, sump and cylinder head.

21 Engine – initial start-up after overhaul and reassembly

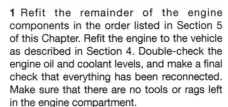

1 Refit the remainder of the engine components in the order listed in Section 5 of this Chapter. Refit the engine to the vehicle as described in Section 4. Double-check the engine oil and coolant levels, and make a final check that everything has been reconnected. Make sure that there are no tools or rags left in the engine compartment.

2 Reconnect the battery negative lead as described in Chapter 5, Section 3.

3 Turn the engine using the starter motor until the oil pressure warning lamp goes out.

4 If the lamp fails to extinguish after several seconds of cranking, check the engine oil level and oil filter security. Assuming these are correct, check the security of the oil pressure

20.8 Using a hammer handle to tap the piston into its bore

20.12b...then through the specified angle

switch cabling – do not progress any further until you are satisfied that oil is being pumped around the engine at sufficient pressure.

5 Bleed the fuel system as described in Chapter 4A, Section 10 then start the engine.

6 While the engine is idling, check for fuel, water and oil leaks. Don't be alarmed if there are some odd smells and the occasional plume of smoke as components heat up and burn off oil deposits.

7 Assuming all is well; keep the engine idling until hot water is felt circulating through the top hose.

8 After a few minutes, recheck the oil and coolant levels, and top-up as necessary.

9 There is no need to retighten the cylinder head bolts once the engine has been run following reassembly.

10 If new pistons, rings or crankshaft bearings have been fitted, the engine must be treated as new, and run-in for the first 600 miles. Do not operate the engine at full-throttle, or allow it to labour at low engine speeds in any gear. It is recommended that the engine oil and filter be changed at the end of this period.

Notes

Chapter 3
Cooling, heating and air conditioning systems

Contents

Degrees of difficulty

Easy, suitable for novice with little experience 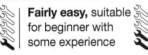	**Fairly easy,** suitable for beginner with some experience	**Fairly difficult,** suitable for competent DIY mechanic	**Difficult,** suitable for experienced DIY mechanic	**Very difficult,** suitable for expert DIY or professional

Specifications

Cooling system pressure cap
Opening pressure . . . . 1.4 to 1.6 bar

Thermostat
Begins to open 85ºC
Fully open 105ºC

Torque wrench settings

	Nm	lbf ft
Air conditioning compressor mounting bolts:		
Steel bolts	25	18
Aluminium bolts: *		
Stage 1	8	6
Stage 2	Angle-tighten a further 90º	
Coolant pump bolts	15	11
Radiator	5	4
Thermostat cover bolts	15	11

Use new fasteners

1 General information and precautions

1 A pressurised cooling system is used, with a pump, an aluminium crossflow radiator, electric cooling fans, a thermostat and a heater matrix, electric coolant circulation pump, engine oil cooler as well as the interconnecting hoses. On models with Multitronic transmission, there is also a separate transmission oil cooler. The thermostat is located on the left-hand side of the cylinder block, in the coolant return from the radiator.

2 The system functions as follows. Coolant is circulated through the cylinder block and head passages by the coolant pump which is driven by the timing belt. The coolant cools the cylinder bores, combustion surfaces and valve seats of the engine.

3 When the engine is cold, the thermostat is closed and the coolant only circulates around the engine and the heater matrix in the passenger compartment, however, when the engine reaches a predetermined temperature, the thermostat opens and the coolant passes through the radiator for additional cooling. The coolant enters the top of the radiator and is cooled, as it circulates down through the cooling tubes, by the inrush of air when the car is in forward motion. Airflow is supplemented by the action of the electric cooling fans when necessary. Upon leaving the bottom of the radiator, the coolant returns to the engine and the cycle is repeated.

4 Refer to Section 10 for information on the air conditioning system.

Precautions

⚠️ **Warning: Do not attempt to remove the expansion tank filler cap or disturb any part of the cooling system while the engine is hot, as there is a high risk of scalding. If the expansion tank filler cap must be removed before the engine and radiator have fully cooled (even though this is not recommended) the pressure in the cooling system must first be relieved. Cover the cap with a thick layer of cloth, to avoid scalding, and slowly unscrew the filler cap until a hissing sound can be heard. When the hissing has stopped, indicating that the pressure has reduced, slowly unscrew the filler cap until it can be removed; if more hissing sounds are heard, wait until they have stopped before unscrewing the cap completely. At all times keep well away from the filler cap opening.**

● *Do not allow antifreeze to come into contact with skin or painted surfaces of the vehicle. Rinse off spills immediately with plenty of water. Never leave antifreeze lying around in an open container or in a puddle in the driveway or on the garage floor. Children and pets are attracted by its sweet smell. Antifreeze can be fatal if ingested.*

● *If the engine is hot, the electric cooling fan may start rotating even if the engine is not running, so be careful to keep hands, hair and loose clothing well clear when working in the engine compartment.*

● *Refer to Section 10 for additional precautions to be observed when working on models with air conditioning.*

2 Cooling system hoses – disconnection and renewal

Note: *Refer to the warnings given in Section 1 of this Chapter before proceeding.*

1 If the checks described in Chapter 1 reveal a faulty hose, it must be renewed as follows.

2 First drain the cooling system as described in Chapter 1, Section 31. If the coolant is not due for renewal, it may be re-used if it is collected in a clean container.

3 To disconnect a hose, release its retaining clips, then move them along the hose, clear of the relevant inlet/outlet union **(see illustrations)**. Carefully work the hose free.

4 In order to disconnect the radiator inlet and outlet hoses, apply pressure to hold the hose on to the relevant union, pull out the spring clip and pull the hose from the union. Note that the radiator inlet and outlet unions are fragile; do not use excessive force when attempting to remove the hoses. If a hose proves to be difficult to remove, try to release it by rotating the hose ends before attempting to free it.

5 When fitting a hose, first slide the clips onto the hose, and then work the hose into position. If clamp type clips were originally fitted, it is a good idea to use screw type clips when refitting the hose. If the hose is stiff, use a little soapy water as a lubricant, or soften the hose by soaking it in hot water.

6 Work the hose into position, checking that it is correctly routed, and then slide each clip along the hose until it passes over the flared end of the relevant union, before securing it in position with the retaining clip.

7 Prior to refitting a radiator inlet or outlet hose, renew the connection O-ring regardless of condition **(see illustration)**. The connections are a push-fit over the radiator unions.

8 Refill the cooling system as described in Chapter 1, Section 31.

9 Check thoroughly for leaks as soon as possible after disturbing any part of the cooling system.

3 Radiator – removal, inspection and refitting

Removal

1 Switch off the ignition and all electrical consumers.

2 Apply the handbrake then jack up the front of the car and support it on axle stands (see *Jacking and vehicle support*). Remove the engine undertray.

3 Remove the front bumper and the impact absorber as described in Chapter 11, Section 8.

4 Remove the left-hand headlight unit as described in Chapter 12 Section 8.

5 Remove the intercooler as described in Chapter 4B, Section 6.

6 Disconnect the wiring connector(s) for the electric cooling fan(s).

7 With reference to Section 2, disconnect the coolant hoses at the radiator.

2.3a On some hoses, prise up the retaining clip a little, and pull the hose from the connection...

2.3b...whilst on others, squeeze together the ends of the clip to release them

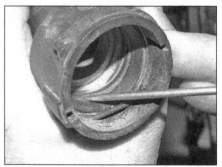
2.7 Renew the radiator hose connection O-rings

3.9 Press in the clip and prise up the radiator retaining pins.

4.1a Location of thermostat

4.3 Slacken the upper and lower clips and disconnect the air hose

8 On models with Multitronic transmission, wipe clean the area around the fluid pipe unions on the radiator. Slacken and remove the retaining bolts then carefully ease both pipes out from the radiator. Plug the pipe ends and cooler ports to minimise fluid loss and prevent the entry of dirt into the hydraulic system. Discard the sealing rings from the pipe end fittings and obtain new sealing rings for refitting.

9 Using a screwdriver, release the upper retaining pin on each side of the radiator and remove the retaining pins by pulling them upward from their locations **(see illustration)**.

10 Enlist the help of an assistant to support the radiator. From under the car, undo the bolt each side securing the radiator brackets to the lock carrier and lower the radiator slightly.

11 Depress the retaining catch on each side and lift the condenser up and out of its mountings on the radiator. Move the condenser forward slightly and suitably support it. DO NOT disconnect the refrigerant pipes.

12 Remove the radiator from the car.

13 If required, depress the locking tab on each side of the cooling fan shroud and lift the shroud and fan(s) off the radiator.

Inspection

14 If the radiator has been removed due to suspected blockage, reverse flush it as described in Chapter 1, Section 31.

15 Clean dirt and debris from the radiator fins, using an airline (in which case, wear eye protection) or a soft brush. Be careful, as the fins are sharp and easily damaged.

16 It necessary, a radiator specialist can perform a 'flow test' on the radiator, to establish whether an internal blockage exists.

17 A leaking radiator must be referred to a specialist for permanent repair. Do not attempt to weld or solder a leaking radiator, as damage may result.

18 Check the radiator mounting rubbers, and renew if necessary.

Refitting

19 Refitting is a reversal of removal, bearing in mind the following points:

a) On models with Multitronic transmission, fit new sealing rings to the fluid pipe end fittings, lubricating them with fresh transmission fluid to ease installation. Ease both pipes fully into position before refitting the retaining bolts and tighten them securely.

b) Make sure all coolant hoses are correctly reconnected and securely retained by their clips.

c) Refil the cooling system as described in Chapter 1, Section 31.

d) On models with Multitronic transmission, have the transmission fluid level checked at the earliest opportunity.

4 Thermostat – removal, testing and refitting

Removal

1 The thermostat is located behind the alternator on the left-hand side of the engine cylinder block **(see illustration)**. There are two types of thermostat fitted:

a) Single hose to the thermostat cover, and the thermostat can be renewed separately.

b) Three hoses to the thermostat housing, the thermostat is part of the housing and can only be renewed as a complete assembly.

2 Drain the cooling system as described in Chapter 1, Section 31. If the coolant is not due for renewal, it may be re-used if it is collected in a clean container.

3 Slacken the hose clips and disconnect the air hose from the throttle valve housing/module and intercooler air duct **(see illustration)**.

4 Release the securing clip(s) and disconnect the coolant hose(s) from the thermostat cover/housing **(see illustration)**.

5 Unscrew the two securing bolts, and remove the thermostat cover/housing complete with the thermostat. Note the locations of any brackets secured by the bolts. Recover the O-ring if it is loose **(see illustrations)**.

6 On models with one hose connection to the thermostat cover, remove the thermostat by turning it through 90° then pull it from the cover.

7 On models with three hose connections to the thermostat housing, the thermostat cannot be removed, renew the complete unit.

Testing

Note: *If there is any question about the operation of the thermostat, it's best to renew it – they are not usually expensive items.*

4.4 Release the retaining clip

4.5a Remove the thermostat housing...

4.5b...and renew the seal

5.3 Undo the bolts and detach the motor from the shroud

Testing involves heating in, or over, an open pan of boiling water, which carries with it the risk of scalding. A thermostat that has seen more than five years' service may well be past its best already.

8 A rough test of the thermostat, may be made by suspending it with a piece of string in a container full of water, but not touching the container. Heat the water to bring it to the boil – the thermostat must open by the time the water boils. If not, renew it.

9 If a thermometer is available, the precise opening temperature of the thermostat may be determined, and compared with the figures given in the Specifications. The opening temperature is also marked on the thermostat.

10 A thermostat which fails to close as the water cools must also be renewed.

Refitting

11 Refitting is a reversal of removal, bearing in mind the following points.
a) *Refit the thermostat using a new O-ring.*
b) *Insert the thermostat into the cover and twist 90° (where applicable). The thermostat should be fitted with the brace almost vertical.*
c) *Ensure that any brackets are in place on the thermostat cover bolts as noted before removal.*

d) *Refill the cooling system with the correct type and quantity of coolant as described in Chapter 1, Section 33.*

5 Electric cooling fans – removal and refitting

Removal

1 Remove the radiator as described in Section 3.

2 Depress the locking tab on each side of the cooling fan shroud and lift the shroud and fan(s) off the radiator.

3 To remove the fan(s) and motor(s) from the shroud, first disconnect and release the wiring plugs, then unscrew the three bolts and remove the units **(see illustration)**.

Refitting

4 Refitting is a reversal of removal.

6 Cooling system electrical sensors – removal and refitting

Radiator outlet temperature sensor
Removal

1 The sensor is located in the coolant pipe at the rear of the engine.

2 The engine should be cold before removing the sensor. Switch off the ignition and all electrical consumers.

3 Either drain the cooling system (as described in Chapter 1, Section 31), or have ready a suitable plug which can be used to plug the sensor aperture whilst it is removed.

4 Disconnect the wiring plug from the sensor.

5 Unscrew the sensor from the coolant pipe and recover the O-ring seals. Check the condition of the O-ring seals and renew if necessary.

Refitting

6 Refitting is a reversal of removal. On completion, refill the cooling system with the correct type and quantity of coolant as described in Chapter 1, Section 31, or top-up as described in *Weekly checks*.

Coolant temperature sensor
Removal

7 The sensor is fitted in the coolant outlet housing at the rear of the engine.

8 The engine should be cold before removing the sensor. Switch off the ignition and all electrical consumers.

9 Either drain the cooling system (as described in Chapter 1, Section 31), or have ready a suitable plug which can be used to plug the sensor aperture whilst it is removed.

10 Remove the braking system vacuum pump as described in Chapter 9, Section 18.

11 Disconnect the wiring from the sensor.

12 Pull out the retaining clip and withdraw the sensor from the housing. Recover the O-ring **(see illustrations)**.

Refitting

13 Refitting is a reversal of removal. Bearing in mind the following points.
a) *Refit the sensor with a new O-ring.*
b) *Refit the braking system vacuum pump as described in Chapter 9, Section 18.*
c) *Refill the cooling system with the correct type and quantity of coolant as described in Chapter 1, Section 31, or top-up as described in Weekly checks.*

7 Coolant pump – removal and refitting

Belt driven coolant pump

1 Drain the cooling system as described in Chapter 1, Section 31.

2 Remove the timing belt as described in Chapter 2A, Section 7.

6.12a Pull out the clip and remove the sensor...

6.12b...recover the O-ring from the housing

7.3a Undo the coolant pump bolts...

7.3b...remove it from the cylinder block...

7.3c...and renew the O-ring seal

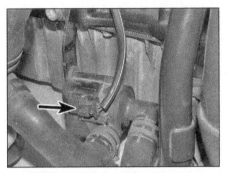

7.7 Disconnect the wiring connector

7.8 Disconnect the coolant hoses

3 Unscrew the coolant pump retaining bolts, and remove the pump from the engine block. Recover the O-ring seal from the groove in the pump. If the pump is faulty, it must be renewed **(see illustrations)**.
4 Refitting is a reversal of removal, bearing in mind the following points.
a) Fit the coolant pump with a new O-ring.
b) Lubricate the O-ring with coolant.
c) Refit the timing belt as described in Chapter 2A, Section 7.
d) Refill the cooling system as described in Chapter 1, Section 31.

Electric circulation pump

5 Raise the front of the vehicle and support is securely on axle stands (see *Jacking and vehicle support*).
6 Undo the fasteners and remove the engine undertray.

7 Disconnect the wiring plug connector to the pump **(see illustration)**.
8 Fit hose clamps to the coolant hoses connected to the pump, and release the clips and disconnect the hoses from the pump **(see illustration)**. Be prepared for some loss of coolant.
9 Undo the retaining bolt and remove the pump **(see illustration)**.
10 Refitting is a reversal of removal. Top up the coolant, as described in *Weekly checks*.

8 Heating and ventilation system – general information

1 The heating/ventilation system consists of a four-speed blower motor (housed in the passenger compartment), face-level vents in

the centre and at each end of the facia, and air ducts to the front and rear footwells.
2 The control unit is located in the facia, and the controls operate flap valves to deflect and mix the air flowing through the various parts of the heating/ventilation system. The flap valves are contained in the air distribution housing, which acts as a central distribution unit, passing air to the various ducts and vents.
3 Cold air enters the system through the grille at the rear of the engine compartment. A pollen filter is fitted to filter out dust, soot, pollen and spores from the air entering the vehicle.
4 The airflow, which can be boosted by the blower, flows through the various ducts, according to the settings of the controls. Stale air is expelled through ducts beneath the rear bumper. If warm air is required, the cold air is passed through the heater matrix, which is heated by the engine coolant.
5 If necessary, the outside air supply can be closed off, allowing the air inside the vehicle to be recirculated. This can be useful to prevent unpleasant odours entering from outside the vehicle, but should only be used briefly, as the recirculated air quality inside the vehicle will soon deteriorate.

9 Heating and ventilation system components – removal and refitting

Note: *The information in this Section is applicable to the heating and ventilation elements of the vehicle. The air conditioning elements are described in Section 10.*

Heater/ventilation/air conditioning control panel

1 Switch off the ignition and all electrical consumers.
2 Audi special tool 3438 is available for removal of the control panel. Essentially this tool is just a thin wire hook and a suitable alternative can be fabricated out of a length of welding rod or similar material **(see illustration)**.
3 Insert the hooked end of the tool into one of the two openings at the base of the control panel facia plate. Pull on the tool to

7.9 Undo the pump bracket retaining bolt

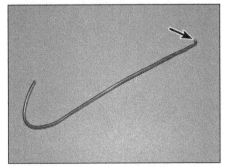

9.2 Removal tool with hooked end fabricated from a length of welding rod

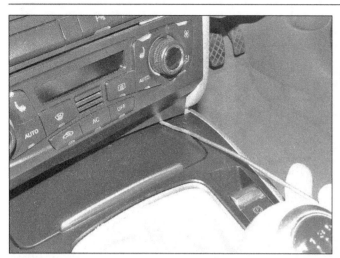

9.3a Insert the removal tool into one of the two openings in the control panel facia plate, then pull on the tool to release the control panel from the retaining clips

9.3b Once the panel is free, pull it further out by engaging the tool with the upper edge

release the control panel from the retaining clips in the centre console support bracket. Once the base of the control panel has been released, pull the upper edge of the panel until the unit can be pulled from its location **(see illustrations)**. If necessary, release the other side of the control panel in the same way.

4 Withdraw the control panel from its location, disconnect the wiring connectors and remove the panel **(see illustration)**.

5 Refitting is a reversal of removal. Note

that if a new control panel has been fitted it will be necessary to carry out a basic setting procedure which necessitates the use of Audi diagnostic equipment. Consequently, this task should be entrusted to an Audi dealer, or suitably-equipped specialist.

Blower motor/control unit

6 Switch off the ignition and all electrical consumers.

7 Remove the glovebox as described in Chapter 11, Section 23.

8 Disconnect the wiring connectors at the blower motor control unit **(see illustration)**.

9 Undo the two bolts securing the control unit to the blower motor and remove the unit from the motor **(see illustrations)**.

10 Release the locking tab at the top of the blower motor, turn the motor anti-clockwise and withdraw it from the air distribution housing **(see illustration)**.

Note: *On some models there may be a screw fitted, if so, undo the screw before removal.*

11 Refitting is a reversal of removal.

Heater matrix

12 Removal and refitting of the heater matrix is an extremely complicated operation with extensive dismantling of the vehicle interior required. In addition, there are numerous variations of heater housing and heater matrix depending on year of manufacture, vehicle specification and whether the original unit is still fitted or has been renewed previously. It is therefore recommended that any work on the heater matrix or its associated components should be entrusted to an Audi dealer or a suitably equipped independent garage

9.4 Disconnect the wiring connectors and remove the control panel

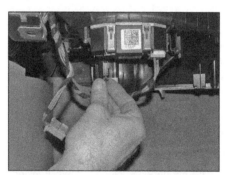

9.8 Disconnect the wiring connectors at the blower motor control unit

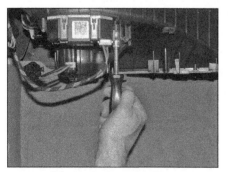

9.9a Undo the two bolts...

9.9b...then remove the control unit from the blower motor

9.10 Release the locking tab, turn the motor anti-clockwise and withdraw it from the air distribution housing

9.14a Insert the removal tool into the vent, engage the tool with the removal hole and pull on the tool to release the vent retaining clips

9.14b Withdraw the vent from the facia...

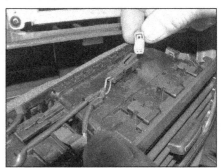

9.14c...then disconnect the wiring connectors and remove the vent

9.16a Insert the removal tool into the vent, engage the tool with the removal hole and pull on the tool to release the vent retaining clips

9.16b Withdraw the vent from the centre console...

9.16c...and disconnect the wiring connector

Facia air vents

13 Audi special tool 3438 is available for removal of the control panel. Essentially this tool is just a thin wire hook and a suitable alternative can be fabricated out of a length of welding rod or similar material **(see illustration 9.3)**.

14 Insert the hooked end of the tool into the vent and engage the tool with the removal hole in the vent. Pull on the tool to release the vent retaining clips, then withdraw the vent from the facia. Where applicable, disconnect the wiring connectors and remove the vent **(see illustrations)**.

15 To refit the vent, reconnect the wiring connectors, where applicable, then push the vent into its location until the retaining clips engage.

Centre console air vents

16 Proceed as described in paragraphs 13 to 15 for the facia air vents **(see illustrations)**.

10 Air conditioning system
– general information and precautions

1 Air conditioning is fitted as standard equipment to all models. It combines a conventional air heating system with an air cooling and dehumidifying system. This allows greater control over the temperature and humidity of the air inside the car, giving increased comfort and rapid window demisting.

2 The cooling side of the system works in the same way as a domestic refrigerator. Refrigerant gas is drawn into a belt-driven compressor and passes into a condenser mounted in front of the radiator, where it loses heat and becomes liquid. The liquid passes through an expansion valve to an evaporator, where it changes from liquid under high pressure to gas under low pressure. This change is accompanied by a drop in temperature, which cools the evaporator. The refrigerant returns to the compressor and the cycle begins again.

3 Air blown through the evaporator passes to the air distribution unit, where it is mixed with hot air blown through the heater matrix to achieve the desired temperature in the passenger compartment.

4 The heating side of the system operates as described in Section 8.

5 The operation of the system is controlled electronically by coolant temperature switches, and pressure switches which are screwed into the compressor high-pressure line. Any problems with the system should be referred to an Audi dealer or an air conditioning specialist.

6 The only operation, which can be carried out easily without discharging the refrigerant, is the renewal of the compressor drivebelt, which is covered in Chapter 1, Section 8. Removal of the evaporator and condenser requires the evacuation of the refrigerant. If necessary the compressor can be unbolted and moved aside, without disconnecting its flexible hoses, after removing the drivebelt **(see illustration)**.

10.6 Air conditioning compressor bolted to the left-hand side of the cylinder block

Precautions

7 It is necessary to observe special precautions whenever dealing with any part of the air conditioning system, its associated components and any items which require disconnection of the system. If for any reason the system must be disconnected, entrust this task to your Audi dealer or an air conditioning specialist.

8 Do not operate the air conditioning system if it is known to be short of refrigerant, as this may damage the compressor.

Caution: The air conditioning compressor is driven permanently by the auxiliary drivebelt, and is not fitted with a magnetic clutch. The engine should not be started without refrigerant being present in the system, as the compressor may overheat causing internal damage.

 Warning: The refrigeration circuit contains a refrigerant and it is therefore dangerous to disconnect any part of the system without specialised knowledge and equipment. The refrigerant is potentially dangerous and should only be handled by qualified persons. If it is splashed onto the skin it can cause frostbite. It is not itself poisonous, but in the presence of a naked flame (including a cigarette) it forms a poisonous gas. Uncontrolled discharging of the refrigerant is dangerous and potentially damaging to the environment.

Chapter 4 Part A
Fuel systems

Contents

Degrees of difficulty

Easy, suitable for novice with little experience		**Fairly easy,** suitable for beginner with some experience	⚑	**Fairly difficult,** suitable for competent DIY mechanic	⚑	**Difficult,** suitable for experienced DIY mechanic	⚑	**Very difficult,** suitable for expert DIY or professional	

Specifications

General

Fuel injection system	Electronic, direct, common rail injection
Firing order.	1-3-4-2
Maximum engine speed.	N/A (ECU controlled)
Engine fast idle speed	N/A (ECU controlled)
Turbocharger type	Garrett or KKK

Torque wrench settings

	Nm	lbf ft
Camshaft position sensor (Hall sender)	10	7
EGR pipe flange-to-inlet manifold bolts.	8	6
Engine speed/TDC sender	5	4
Flap motor housing	10	7
Fuel pressure regulating valve	80	59
Fuel pressure sender	100	74
Fuel pump bolts*:		
Two lower bolts (long):		
Stage 1	20	15
Stage 2	Angle-tighten a further 180°	
One upper bolt (short):		
Stage 1	20	15
Stage 2	Angle-tighten a further 45°	
Fuel rail 22	16	
Fuel pump hub nut.	95	70
Fuel pump sprocket bolts*	20	15
High-pressure fuel pipe unions	28	20
Injector clamp/cover mounting:		
Engine codes CGLC, CGLD, CJCA, CJCB, CJCC, CJCD, CMBG,		
CMFA, CMFB and CMGB:		
Clamp bolt*:		
Stage 1	8	6
Stage 2	Angle-tighten a further 270°	
Engine codes CAGA, CAGB, CAGC, CAHA, CAHB, and CMEA:		
Clamp nut	10	7
Cover bolt.	5	4
Inlet manifold to cylinder head	8	6
Oxygen (Lambda probe) sensor.	55	41

*Use new fasteners

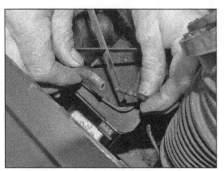

2.2 Disconnect the air cleaner vacuum hose

1 General information and precautions

General information

1 The engines covered in this Chapter are fitted with a direct-injection fuelling system, incorporating a fuel tank, an under-body mounted fuel filter, fuel supply and return lines and four fuel injectors.
2 The fuel system is the familiar Common Rail system, where fuel is supplied from a timing belt-driven high-pressure pump to a common fuel rail (or reservoir). The four injectors are fitted into the cylinder head and are connected to the fuel rail by rigid metal pipes. The precise timing of the pre-, main, and post-injections are controlled by the engine management ECU and an electrically operated Piezo crystal incorporated into the injector design. All engines are fitted with a turbocharger.
3 The direct-injection fuelling system is controlled electronically by a diesel engine management system, comprising an Electronic Control Unit (ECU) and its associated sensors, actuators and wiring. In addition, the ECU manages the operation of the Exhaust Gas Recirculation (EGR) emission control system, the turbocharger boost pressure control system and the glow plug control system.
4 A flap valve/throttle valve module fitted to the inlet manifold is closed by the ECU for 3 seconds as the engine is switched off, to minimise the air intake as the engine shuts down. This minimises the vibration felt as the pistons come up against the volume of highly compressed air present in the combustion chambers.
5 It should be noted that fault diagnosis of the diesel engine management system is only possible with dedicated electronic test equipment. Problems with the system's operation should therefore be referred to an Audi dealer or suitably equipped specialist for assessment. Once the fault has been identified, the removal/refitting sequences detailed in the following Sections will then allow the appropriate component(s) to be renewed as required.

2.4 Lift the air cleaner body upwards and remove it from the engine compartment

6 The Electronic On-Board Diagnostic (EOBD) connector is located under the driver's side of the facia.

Precautions

7 Many of the operations described in this Chapter involve the disconnection of fuel lines, which may cause an amount of fuel spillage. Before commencing work, refer to the warnings below and the information in *Safety first!*.

 Warning: When working on any part of the fuel system, avoid direct contact skin contact with diesel fuel – wear protective clothing and gloves when handling fuel system components. Ensure that the work area is well ventilated to prevent the build-up of diesel fuel vapour.

Warning: Fuel injectors operate at extremely high pressures and the jet of fuel produced at the nozzle is capable of piercing skin, with potentially fatal results. When working with pressurised injectors, take care to avoid exposing any part of the body to the fuel spray. It is recommended that a diesel fuel systems specialist should carry out any pressure testing of the fuel system components.

Warning: Under no circumstances should diesel fuel be allowed to come into contact with coolant hoses – wipe off accidental spillage immediately. Hoses that have been contaminated with fuel for an extended period should be renewed.

3.2 Slacken the retaining clip and disconnect the intake hose

 Warning: Diesel fuel systems are particularly sensitive to contamination from dirt, air and water. Pay particular attention to cleanliness when working on any part of the fuel system, to prevent the ingress of dirt. Thoroughly clean the area around fuel unions before disconnecting them. Only use lint-free cloths and clean fuel for component cleansing.

Warning: Store dismantled components in sealed containers to prevent contamination and the formation of condensation.

2 Air cleaner assembly – removal and refitting

Removal

1 Remove the air filter element as described in Chapter 1, Section 27.
2 Where fitted, disconnect the bypass flap valve vacuum hose from the air cleaner body **(see illustration)**.
3 Disconnect the water drain hose and the wiring connector from the base of the air cleaner body.
4 Lift the air cleaner body upwards to release it from the retainer and the two rubber grommets and remove it from the engine compartment **(see illustration)**.

Refitting

5 Refitting is the reversal of removal.

3 Diesel engine management system – component removal and refitting

Throttle valve housing/module

1 Carefully pull the engine top cover off the four retaining pins, one after the other. Do not jerk the cover away and do not try to pull on one side only.
2 Slacken the hose clip and disconnect the air intake hose from the throttle valve housing/ module **(see illustration)**.
3 Disconnect the wiring plug connector, from the throttle housing/module **(see illustration)**.

3.3 Disconnect the wiring connector

3.4 Undo the dipstick tube retaining bolt

3.5a Undo the three retaining bolts ...

3.5b ... and remove the throttle housing module

3.6 Fit a new seal to the housing on refitting

3.8 Disconnect the wiring connector

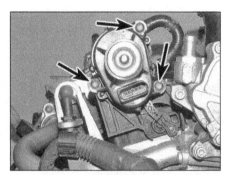

3.9 Undo the three retaining bolts

4 Undo the retaining bolt and disconnect the dipstick guide tube from the throttle housing **(see illustration)**.

5 Unscrew and remove the retaining bolts, then lift the throttle housing/module away from the inlet manifold **(see illustrations)**. Recover the O-ring seal; a new one will be required for refitting.

6 Refitting is a reversal of removal, noting the following:

a) Use a new throttle housing-to-inlet manifold seal **(see illustration)**.

b) Tighten the throttle housing bolts evenly to the specified torque.

c) Ensure that all hoses and electrical connectors are refitted securely.

Inlet manifold flap motor

Note: On some engines there is an electrically operated flap motor located on the inlet manifold, this is not fitted to all models.

7 Carefully pull the engine top cover off the four retaining pins, one after the other. Do not jerk the cover away and do not try to pull on one side only.

8 Disconnect the flap control motor wiring plug from the lower part of the housing **(see illustration)**.

9 Unscrew the bolts securing the flap motor housing to the manifold **(see illustration)**, remove the flap housing and recover the O-ring seal.

10 Refitting is a reversal of removal. Renew the O-ring seal if it appears damaged.

Air mass meter

11 The air mass meter is located in the air cleaner assembly cover on the right-hand side of the engine compartment.

12 Disconnect the wiring plug connector from the air mass meter **(see illustration)**.

13 Slacken the retaining clamp and detach the air outlet duct from the air mass meter **(see illustration)**.

14 Undo the retaining screws securing the meter to the air cleaner. Withdraw the meter and recover the O-ring seal.

Caution: Handle the air mass meter carefully – its internal components are easily damaged.

15 Refitting is a reversal of removal. Renew the O-ring seal if it appears damaged.

Charge air pressure/ temperature sensor

16 The charge air pressure/temperature sensor is fitted in the air ducting from the intercooler to the throttle housing/inlet manifold, on the left-hand side of the engine compartment. **(see illustration)**.

3.12 Disconnect the air mass meter wiring plug

3.13 Slacken the clamp and detach the air outlet duct

3.16 Charge air pressure sensor location

3.19 Fuel pressure regulating valve location

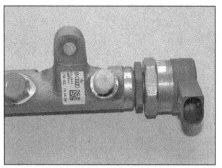

3.23 Pressure regulating valve fitted to the rear of the fuel rail

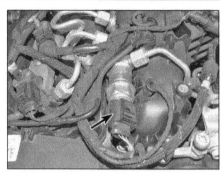

3.26 Disconnect the wiring connector from the fuel pressure sender

17 Disconnect the wiring then undo the two retaining screws and remove the sensor from the intake ducting.

18 Refit the sensor by reversing the removal procedure, using a new O-ring seal.

Fuel pressure regulating valve

19 The fuel pressure regulating valve is fitted to the rear of the fuel rail (see illustration).If the valve is removed from the fuel rail, then it will need to be renewed, as it has a deformable sealing lip as part of the valve. To gain access to the valve, carefully pull the engine top cover off the four retaining pins, one after the other. Do not jerk the cover away and do not try to pull on one side only.

20 To check the operation of the regulating valve, first disconnect the fuel return hose from the fuel rail and plug the end (see illustration 11.04). Then fit a piece of hose to

the fuel rail and the other end into a container. There are three checks that can be made, the first two with the engine running and the third if the vehicle will not start:

a) Start the engine and run at idle for 30 seconds, there should be approximately 75 ml of fuel in the container.

b) Start engine and increase engine speed to 2000rpm, there should be no fuel in the container (allow for a few droplets of fuel).

c) On vehicles that will not run, turn the ignition key and crank the engine, there should be no fuel in the container (allow for a few droplets of fuel).

21 If any of these readings are not attained, renew the regulating valve.

22 To renew the valve, remove the fuel rail as described in Section 11.

23 Clean around the valve, then slacken the valve from the end of the fuel rail (see

illustration) ; counterhold the fuel rail using the flats on the housing. Plug the end of the rail to prevent dirt from entering.

24 Fit the new valve by reversing the removal procedure, making sure that the threads are all clean before fitting. Check the deformable seal on the new valve, before fitting, to check it is not damaged. Apply a small amount of Molybdenum grease to seal and threads.

Fuel pressure sender

25 The fuel pressure sender is fitted to the front of the fuel rail. To gain access to the valve, carefully pull the engine top cover off the four retaining pins, one after the other. Do not jerk the cover away and do not try to pull on one side only. If the engine will not start, disconnect the fuel pressure sender wiring connector and see if the engine will start. If the engine starts, the fuel pressure sender is faulty. With the connector removed a value is taken from the control unit, so that the engine will start, in this mode the maximum engine speed is limited to 3000 rpm.

26 To renew the sender, first disconnect the wiring plug connector (see illustration).

27 Clean around the sender, then slacken it from the end of the fuel rail (see illustration); plug the end of the rail to prevent dirt from entering.

28 Refit the pressure sender by reversing the removal procedure, making sure that the threads are all clean before refitting. Keep the threads free of oil and grease.

Coolant temperature sensors

29 Refer to Chapter 3, Section 6.

Camshaft position sensor

30 The camshaft position sensor (Hall sender) is located behind the timing belt cover, below the camshaft sprocket (see illustration).

31 Remove the timing belt, as described in Chapter 2A, Section 7.

32 Disconnect the sensor wiring plug connector, located at the rear of the oil filter housing against the cylinder block (see illustration).

33 To make access easier undo the retaining bolt and remove the timing belt idler pulley (see illustration).

3.27 The fuel pressure sender is fitted to the front of the fuel rail

3.30 Camshaft position sensor

3.32 Disconnect the sensor wiring connector

3.33 Unbolt the Idler pulley

3.34 Prise up the aperture cover

3.37 Crankshaft position speed sensor

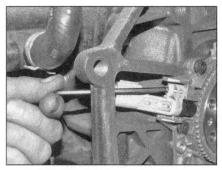

3.39a Undo the retaining bolt...

34 Using a screwdriver prise out the aperture cover in the rear plastic cover, then withdraw the wiring plug through the cover, unhooking it from the rear cover **(see illustration)**.

35 Undo the retaining bolt and remove the camshaft sensor from the cylinder head.

36 Refitting is a reversal of removal, but tighten the bolt to the specified torque setting and fit rubber plugs to the aperture for the wiring in the rear plastic cover.

Engine speed/TDC sensor

37 The engine speed/TDC sensor is mounted on the left-hand side of the cylinder block, adjacent to the mating surface of the block and transmission bellhousing **(see illustration)**.

38 Access is from beneath the engine compartment. Apply the handbrake, and then jack up the front of the vehicle and support it on axle stands (see *Jacking and vehicle support*). Remove the engine undertray.

39 Remove the retaining bolt and withdraw the sensor from the cylinder block **(see illustrations)**.

40 Refit the sensor by reversing the removal procedure.

Oxygen (lambda probe) sensor

⚠️ *Warning: Working on the sensors is only advisable with the engine (and therefore the exhaust system) completely cold. The particulate filter in particular will be very hot for some time after the engine has been switched off.*

41 All models have a sensor threaded into the top of the diesel particulate filter **(see illustration)**. To gain access, carefully pull the engine top cover off the four retaining pins, one after the other. Do not jerk the cover away and do not try to pull on one side only.

42 Working from the sensor, trace the wiring harness from the oxygen sensor back to the connector, and disconnect it. Unclip the sensor wiring from any retaining clips, noting how it is routed.

43 Unscrew and remove the sensor, taking care to avoid damaging the sensor probe as it is removed.

Note: *As a flying lead remains connected to the sensor after it has been disconnected, if the correct-size spanner is not available, a slotted socket will be required to remove the sensor.*

44 Apply a little high-temperature anti-seize grease to the sensor threads – avoid contaminating the probe tip.

45 Refit the sensor, tightening it to the specified torque. Reconnect the wiring; making sure that the wiring loom is secured in its retaining clips.

Throttle pedal/position sensor

46 Refer to Chapter 11, Section 23 and remove the trim panel from below the steering column.

47 Push the release tab upwards and disconnect the wiring connector from the top of the accelerator pedal **(see illustration)**.

48 Undo the bolt securing the accelerator pedal to the brake pedal bracket.

49 Move the pedal downward to disengage the lower retainer and remove the pedal assembly from the footwell.

50 Refitting is a reversal of removal.

Clutch pedal switch

51 The clutch pedal switch is clipped to the clutch master cylinder on the pedal bracket. Remove the master cylinder as described in Chapter 6, Section 4.

52 Unclip the pedal switch from the bottom of the master cylinder.

53 Refitting is a reversal of removal.

Electronic control unit (ECU)

Caution: Always wait at least 30 seconds after switching off the ignition before disconnecting the wiring from the ECU. When the wiring is disconnected, all the learned values are erased, although any Specifications of the fault memory are retained. After reconnecting the wiring, the basic settings must be reinstated by an Audi dealer using a special test instrument. Note also that if the ECU is renewed, the identification of the new ECU must be transferred to the immobiliser control unit by an Audi dealer.

54 The ECU is located in the engine compartment electronics box at the rear right-hand side of the engine compartment, under the plenum chamber cover. To gain access, remove the plenum chamber cover as described in Chapter 11, Section 21.

3.39b ...and withdraw the sensor

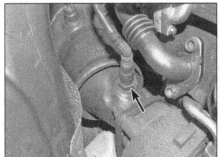

3.41 Oxygen sensor location in the particulate filter

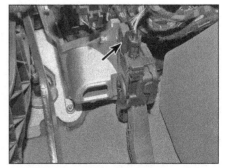

3.47 Disconnect the wiring connector from the accelerator pedal

3.55 Remove the cover from the engine compartment electronics box

3.56a Release the catch on each side of the ECU...

3.56b...and lift the ECU out of the electronics box

55 Undo the three bolts and lift off the cover from the engine compartment electronics box **(see illustration)**.

56 Release the catch on each side of the engine management ECU and lift the ECU out of the electronics box**(see illustrations)**.

57 Place a piece of cardboard under the ECU and either drill out the shear bolts that are holding the wiring connector security cover together, or cut a slot in them and unscrew them with a screwdriver. New shear bolts will be required for refitting. Note that the two lower bolts that are not screwed into the ECU are secured with locking fluid and it will be necessary to heat them with a hot air gun to assist removal. The two upper bolts which are screwed into the ECU are not secured with locking fluid and must not be heated.

58 With the shear bolts removed, separate the two halves of the security cover.

59 Disconnect the wiring plugs from the

ECU by sliding the locking levers outwards, to release them from the top of the ECU. Remove the ECU from the vehicle.

60 Refitting is a reversal of removal, using new shear bolts to secure the wiring cover. Bear in mind the comments made in the Caution above – the ECU will not work correctly until it has been electronically coded.

---

4 Injectors – general information, removal and refitting

⚠️ *Warning: Exercise extreme caution when working on the fuel injectors. Never expose the hands or any part of the body to injector spray, as the high pressure can cause the fuel to penetrate the skin, with possibly fatal results. You are strongly advised to*

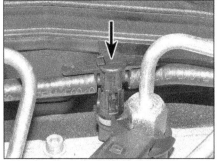

4.5a Hold down the outer tabs, and prise up the centre piece...

4.5b...then pull the return hose connector upwards from the injector

4.6a Use two spanners to counterhold the fuel pipe to the injector...

4.6b...and remove the high pressure fuel pipes

have any work which involves testing the injectors under pressure carried out by a dealer or fuel injection specialist. Refer to the precautions given in Section 1 of this Chapter before proceeding.

General information

1 Injectors do deteriorate with prolonged use, and it is reasonable to expect them to need reconditioning or renewal after 60,000 miles (100,000 km) or so. Accurate testing, overhaul and calibration of the injectors must be left to a specialist.

Removal

Note: *Take care not to allow dirt into the injectors or fuel pipes during this procedure. Do not drop the injectors or allow the needles at their tips to become damaged. The injectors are precision-made to fine limits, and must not be handled roughly. Keep the injectors identified for position to ensure correct refitting.*

2 Carefully pull the engine top cover off the four retaining pins, one after the other. Do not jerk the cover away and do not try to pull on one side only. Where fitted, remove the foam insulation over the injectors.

3 Ensure the area around the injectors and the pipes/return hoses is clean and free from debris. The use of a vacuum cleaner is recommended. Plug all fuel lines when they have been disconnected to prevent any dirt ingress.

Engine codes CGLC, CGLD, CJCA, CJCB, CJCC, CJCD, CMBG, CMFA, CMFB and CMGB

4 Disconnect the injector wiring plug connectors.

5 Push the return hose connector downwards at its outer tabs, then pull up the centre piece and disconnect them from the top of the injectors **(see illustrations)**. Plug the openings to prevent contamination.

6 Undo the unions and remove the high-pressure pipes from between the fuel rail and the injectors. Counterhold the injector with an open-ended spanner when releasing the pipe union **(see illustrations)**.

7 Undo the bolt securing the injector clamp between the two injectors, note that one clamp secures two injectors in place.

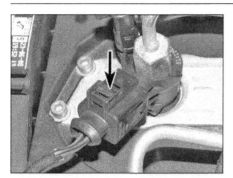

4.10 Lever up the clip and disconnect the injector wiring plugs

4.12 Undo the unions and remove the high-pressure pipes between the common rail and the injectors

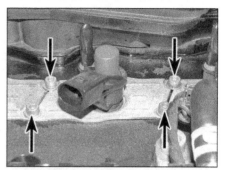

4.13a Undo the injector clamp cover bolts...

4.13b ...then lift and rotate it 90°

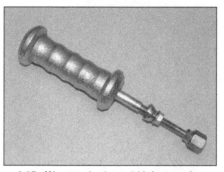

4.15a We attached an old injector pipe union onto the end of the slide hammer...

4.15b ...screwed it onto the top of the injector...

8 Audi technicians use a slide hammer (tool T10055) and adapter (T10415) to pull the injector from the cylinder head. If this tool is not available, it may be possible to fabricate an equivalent tool to pull the injector out of the cylinder head.

9 Two injectors will need to be removed together, as the clamping piece is slotted into both injectors. Recover the copper seal and O-rings and discard. New ones must be used for refitting.

Note: *The injectors can only be refitted to their original positions. Mark the injectors to avoid confusion if refitting the original injectors.*

Engine codes CAGA, CAGB, CAGC, CAHA, CAHB, and CMEA

10 Disconnect the injector wiring plugs **(see illustration)**.

11 Ensure the area around the injectors

and the pipes/return hoses is clean and free from debris. The use of a vacuum cleaner is recommended. Push the return hose connector downwards at its tabs, then pull up the centre piece and disconnect them from the injectors **(see illustrations 4.5a and 4.5b)**.

12 Undo the unions remove the high-pressure pipes between the common fuel rail and the injectors **(see illustration)**. Plug the openings to prevent contamination.

13 Undo the bolts securing the injector clamp cover, the slightly lift the cover and rotate it 90° for access to the injector retaining nuts **(see illustrations)**.

14 Unscrew the injector retaining nuts.

15 Audi technicians use a slide hammer (tool T10055) and adapter (T10055/1) to pull the injector from the cylinder head. This is a slide hammer with an adapter that screws onto the

top of the injector. If this tool is not available, it is possible to fabricate an equivalent using a slide hammer with the union from an old injector pipe brazed/welded onto the end. Screw the tool onto the top of the injector, and pull the injector out using a few gently taps. Recover the clamping piece, copper seal and O-rings and discard. New ones must be used for refitting **(see illustrations)**.

Note: *The injectors can only be refitted to their original positions. Mark the injectors to avoid confusion if refitting the original injectors.*

Refitting

16 If required, renew the injector seals in the top of the camshaft cover. Using a screwdriver, prise the seal out from the cover; the new seal can then be pressed firmly into the cover **(see illustrations)**. There are different size seals depending on engine code, make sure the

4.15c ...and pulled it from the cylinder head

4.16a Carefully prise out the seal...

4.16b ...making sure the spring does not fall into the cover

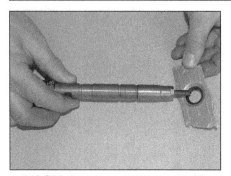

4.18 Slide the new cover plate onto the injector

4.19a Clean off the carbon around the end of the injector...

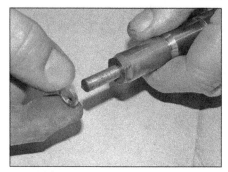

4.19b...and fit a new sealing washer

4.20 Fit the new return pipe O-ring to the top of the injector

4.21 Fit a new main O-ring seal without twisting it

4.22 Slide the new clamping piece onto the injector

correct seals are supplied. Also make sure the spring on the inside lip of the seal does not drop into the camshaft cover.

17 Ensure the area around the injector locations in the cylinder head are clean and free from debris. Use a vacuum cleaner if available. Clean any carbon deposits from the injector and sealing surfaces with a cloth soaked in clean engine oil or rust-releasing spray.

18 Depending on engine code, if new cover plates are to be fitted, slide them on now **(see illustration)**.

19 To remove the copper sealing washer, spray rust-releasing spray around the injector nozzle, then clamp the seal in a vice, and use a twisting motion to pull the injector from the seal. Push the new copper seal into place **(see illustrations)**. Do not touch the very end of the injector, or you could block up the nozzle.

20 Apply a little clean engine oil to the return

pipe connection on the injector, and fit the new O-ring **(see illustration)**.

21 To renew the main injector O-ring seal, Audi specify the use of tool no. T10377. This tool allows the O-ring to slide over the end of the injector without twisting. With care, the seals can be fitted without the tool **(see illustrations)**.

22 Depending on engine code, slide the new clamping piece onto injector as shown **(see illustration)**.

23 Apply a smear of clean engine oil to the main O-ring seal, and insert the injector into place in the cylinder head **(see illustrations)**. Note that if the original injectors are being refitted, they must go into their original positions. Tighten the injector clamping bolt/nut to the specified torque.

24 Depending on engine code, rotate the cover back to position and tighten the retaining bolt to the specified torque.

25 Refit the high-pressure fuel pipes and tighten the unions to the specified torque. Note that the pipes may be re-used providing the tapered seats are undamaged and the pipes are not deformed, constricted or corroded. Where applicable, counterhold the injector with an open-ended spanner when tightening the pipe union.

26 The remainder of refitting is a reversal of removal, noting the following:

a) If one or more injectors have been renewed, the 'injector delivery calibration values' and 'injector voltage calibration values' must be entered into the ECU using Audi diagnostic equipment. Entrust this task to an Audi dealer or suitably equipped specialist.

b) After completion of the work, the fuel system must be bled as described in Section 10.

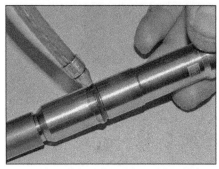

4.23a Lubricate the seal with some clean oil...

4.23b ...then slide the injectors down into the cylinder head

5 Inlet manifold – removal and refitting

Removal

Plastic manifold

1 Remove the throttle valve housing/module, as described in Section 3 of this Chapter.

2 Remove the fuel rail from the top of the inlet manifold, as described in Section 11 of this Chapter.

3 Undo the two retaining screws and move

5.3 Undo the coolant pipe retaining screws

5.4 Undo the fuel line retaining screws

5.5 Disconnect the wiring connector

the coolant return pipe to one side **(see illustration)**.

4 Undo the two retaining screws and move the fuel return pipe to one side **(see illustration)**.

5 Where fitted, disconnect the wiring plug connector from the manifold flap motor **(see illustration)**.

6 Undo the retaining screw and remove the EGR cooler changeover valve from the manifold **(see illustration)**.

7 Slacken the retaining clamp and disconnect the EGR pipe **(see illustration)**.

8 Undo the manifold retaining bolts, starting from the outside and working inwards in a diagonal sequence **(see illustrations)**. Lift the manifold from the cylinder head and retrieve the gasket seals; discard, as new ones will be required for refitting.

Aluminium manifold

9 Remove the throttle valve housing/module and manifold flap motor (where fitted), as described in Section 3 of this Chapter.

10 Using thin, long-nosed pliers, carefully pull the wiring plugs from the top of the glow plugs **(see illustration)**.

11 With reference to Section 4, disconnect the fuel return pipes from the injectors, fuel rail, and high-pressure pump.

12 Undo the retaining nut and remove the fuel return pipe **(see illustration)**.

13 Undo the unions and disconnect the

5.6 Undo the solenoid valve mounting bracket securing bolt

5.7 Slacken the EGR pipe retaining clamp

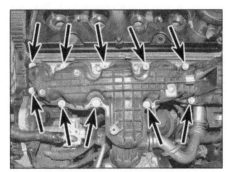

5.8a Undo the retaining bolts...

5.8b ...and remove the inlet manifold

5.8c Cover the inlet manifold recess with tape

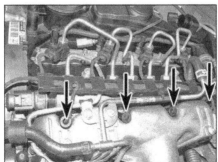

5.10 Pull the wiring plugs from the glow plugs

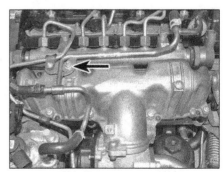

5.12 Fuel return pipe nut

5.17 Renew the inlet manifold seals

7.6 Fuel supply and return hoses

7.7 Use a suitable tool to unscrew the securing ring

high-pressure fuel pipe between the pump and fuel rail.

14 Disconnect the wiring plug from the manifold change-over motor.

15 Where applicable, undo the 2 retaining bolts and pull the engine oil level dipstick guide tube upwards from place.

16 Undo the retaining bolts, starting from the outside and working inwards in a diagonal sequence, then manoeuvre the manifold from position.

Refitting

17 Refitting is a reversal of removal, using new seals and gaskets **(see illustration)**. Remember to renew any self-locking nuts. Tighten the manifold retaining bolts to the specified torque setting, starting from the inside and working outwards in a diagonal sequence.

6 Fuel filter – renewal

Note: *Observe the precautions in Section 1 before working on any component in the fuel system.*

1 Refer to Chapter 1, Section 24.

7 Fuel lift pump and gauge sender unit – removal and refitting

Note: *Observe the precautions in Section 1 before working on any component in the fuel system.*

⚠ **Warning: Avoid direct skin contact with fuel – wear protective clothing and gloves when handling fuel system components. Ensure that the work area is well-ventilated to prevent the build-up of fuel vapour.**

General information

1 The fuel lift pump and gauge sender unit are combined in one assembly, which is mounted in the top of the fuel tank. Access is beneath the rear seat cushion in the floor panel. The unit protrudes into the fuel tank, and its removal involves exposing the contents of the tank to the atmosphere.

Removal

Note: *A new securing ring and rubber seal will be required for refitting.*

2 Ensure that the vehicle is parked on a level surface, then disconnect the battery negative lead and position it away from the terminal. Refer to Disconnecting the battery in Chapter 5, Section 3.

3 Remove the rear seat cushion, and lift the carpet section from the floor panel.

4 Undo the three bolts and lift off the access cover from the floor.

5 Disconnect the wiring connector from the top of the lift pump/gauge sender unit.

6 Pad the area around the supply and return fuel hoses with rags to absorb any spilt fuel from the fuel lines, and then squeeze the catches to release the hose clips and disconnect them **(see illustration)**. Observe the supply and return arrow markings on the ports – label the fuel hoses accordingly to ensure correct refitting later. The supply pipe is black, and may have white markings, while the return pipe is blue, or has blue markings.

7 Unscrew and remove the pump/sender unit securing ring. Use a pair of water pump pliers (or home-made tool) to grip and rotate the securing ring **(see illustration)**. The plastic detent on the threaded ring will break off when the securing ring is unscrewed, but this can be disregarded.

8 Lift out the lift pump/gauge sender unit, holding it above the level of the fuel in the tank until the excess fuel has drained out. Recover the rubber seal **(see illustration)**.

9 With the pump/sender unit removed from

7.8 Recover the rubber seal from the tank

the car, place it on an absorbent card or rag. Inspect the float at the end of the sender unit swinging arm for punctures and fuel ingress – renew the unit if it appears damaged.

10 Inspect the sender unit wiper and track; clean off any dirt and debris that may have accumulated, and look for breaks in the track.

11 If required, the sender unit can be separated from the assembly, as follows. Disconnect the wiring connector on the underside of the pump flange, then release the retaining tabs and slide the unit from the pump.

Refitting

12 Place a new rubber seal in position on the top of the fuel tank and engage it with the groove on the tank.

13 Place the pump/sender unit in the tank, taking care not to bend the float arm as the unit is fitted. Position the unit so that the lug on the pump flange is between the two tabs on the threaded ring.

14 Slip the new securing ring over your left arm and use your left hand to keep the pump flange pushed firmly down and in the correct position. Using your right hand, position the securing ring on the tank with the double ridge on the ribs aligned with the lug on the flange (approximately the 10 o'clock position). This will allow the threads on the securing ring to engage immediately when tightening.

15 Keep the pump flange pushed firmly down with your left hand and turn the securing ring with your right hand through approximately 480°. The double ridge on the ribs of the securing ring should now be in the 2 o'clock position.

16 Using the tool used for removal, tighten the securing ring further until the double ridge on the ribs of the securing ring are between the 7 o'clock and 8 o'clock position.

17 The remainder of refitting is a reversal of removal.

8 Fuel tank – removal and refitting

Note: *Observe the precautions in Section 1 before working on any component in the fuel system.*

9.2 Disconnect the pump wiring connector

9.3a Undo the high-pressure fuel pipe union at the fuel pump...

Removal

1 Before the tank can be removed, it must be drained of as much fuel as possible. As no drain plug is provided, it is preferable to carry out this operation with the tank almost empty.

2 Open the fuel filler flap, and unscrew the fuel filler cap – leave the cap loosely in place.

3 Disconnect the battery negative lead and position it away from the terminal. Refer to Disconnecting the battery in Chapter 5, Section 3. Using a hand pump or siphon, remove any remaining fuel from the bottom of the tank.

4 Loosen the right-hand rear wheel bolts, then jack up and securely support the rear of the car. See *Jacking and vehicle support*. Remove the right-hand rear wheel.

5 Remove the right-hand rear wheel arch liner as described in Chapter 11 Section 21.

6 From under the wheel arch undo the two bolts securing the fuel filler neck to the underbody.

7 Gain access to the top of the fuel lift pump/sender unit as described in Section 7, and disconnect the wiring harness from the top of the pump/sender unit at the multiway connector.

8 Remove the exhaust system rear section as described in Chapter 4B, Section 8.

9 Remove the rear subframe as described in Chapter 10, Section 11.

10 Release the quick-release connectors and disconnect the fuel tank supply and return lines at the fuel cooler. Be prepared to collect escaping fuel.

11 Position a trolley jack under the centre of the tank. Insert a block of wood between the jack head and the tank to prevent damage to the tank surface. Raise the jack until it just takes the weight of the tank.

12 Unscrew the mounting bolts and detach the tank retaining straps.

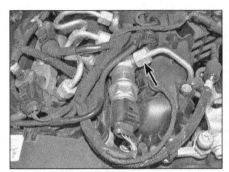

9.3b...and at the fuel rail

13 Lower the jack and tank away from the underside of the vehicle.

14 If the tank is contaminated with sediment or water, remove the fuel lift pump/sender unit (see Section 7) and swill the tank out with clean fuel. The tank is injection-moulded from a synthetic material, and if damaged, it should be renewed. However, in certain cases it may be possible to have small leaks or minor damage repaired. Seek the advice of a suitable specialist before attempting to repair the fuel tank.

Refitting

15 Refitting is the reverse of the removal procedure, noting the following points:

a) *When lifting the tank back into position, make sure the mounting rubbers are correctly positioned, and take care to ensure none of the hoses get trapped between the tank and vehicle body.*

b) *Ensure that all pipes and hoses are correctly routed, are not kinked, and are securely held in position with their retaining clips.*

c) *On completion, refill the tank with fuel, and exhaustively check for signs of leakage prior to taking the vehicle out on the road.*

9.4 Disconnect the fuel hoses from the pump

9 Fuel pump – removal and refitting

Removal

1 Remove the timing belt as described in Chapter 2A, Section 7.

2 Disconnect the wiring connector from the fuel metering valve on top of the fuel pump **(see illustration)**.

3 Undo the high-pressure fuel pipe unions at the pump and at the fuel rail **(see illustrations)**. Undo the high-pressure fuel pipe retaining clip bolt and remove the high-pressure fuel pipe. Suitably cover or plug all disconnected unions.

4 Release the retaining clips and disconnect the two fuel hoses from the top of the fuel pump **(see illustration)**.Suitably cover or plug all disconnected unions.

5 Undo the fuel pipe retaining clip bolts and move the two fuel pipes to one side.

6 Undo the three bolts and remove the fuel pump sprocket from the pump hub.

7 Counterhold the pump hub using VAG tool No. T10051, and undo the pump hub nut. In the absence of this special tool, counterhold

9.7 Counterhold the pump hub with a C-spanner, and undo the nut

9.8a Use a two-legged puller and 8 mm bolts to pull the hub from the pump shaft

9.8b Note the locating peg in the pump shaft

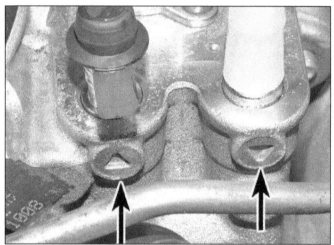

9.10 The triangles adjacent to the pump apertures indicate fuel flow

the hub using a suitable C-spanner **(see illustration)**.

8 Using a suitable two-legged puller and two 8 mm bolts, remove the hub from the pump shaft **(see illustrations)**.

9 Undo the 3 retaining bolts and remove the pump.

Refitting

10 Refitting is a reversal of removal, noting the following points:

a) *Ensure all fuel pipes/hose connections are clean and free from debris.*

b) *The high-pressure fuel pipe from the pump to the common rail maybe re-used providing it's not been damaged.*

c) *Tighten all fasteners to their specified torque where given.*

d) *Fill the pump with clean fuel through the fuel supply pipe aperture prior to starting* **(see illustration)**.

e) *Bleed the fuel system as described in Section 10.*

10 Fuel system bleeding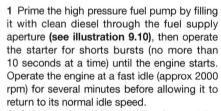

1 Prime the high pressure fuel pump by filling it with clean diesel through the fuel supply aperture **(see illustration 9.10)**, then operate the starter for shorts bursts (no more than 10 seconds at a time) until the engine starts. Operate the engine at a fast idle (approx 2000 rpm) for several minutes before allowing it to return to its normal idle speed.

2 If the engine fails to start, it must be filled/bled using Audi diagnostic equipment (VAS5051 etc.). Using this equipment operates the electric fuel pumps for 3 minutes.

3 Once the engine has been started, test drive the vehicle over a distance of at least 15 miles with at least one period of full acceleration. If there is any air left in the fuel system, the engine management ECU may switch to 'limp home'

mode, and store a fault code. Have the fault code cleared and road test the vehicle again.

11 Fuel rail – removal and refitting

Note: *Observe the precautions in Section 1 before working on any component in the fuel system.*

Removal

1 Pull the plastic cover on the top of the engine upwards from it's mountings and remove the foam insulation (where fitted). Ensure the area around the fuel rail and pipes is clean and free from debris. If available, use a vacuum cleaner.

2 Disconnect the wiring connector from the fuel metering valve on top of the fuel pump **(see illustration 9.2)**.

3 Undo the high-pressure fuel pipe unions at

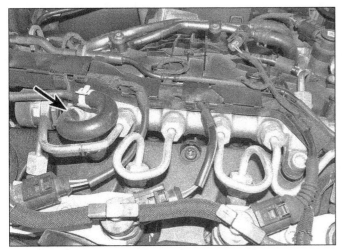

11.4 Disconnect the fuel return hose from the fuel rail

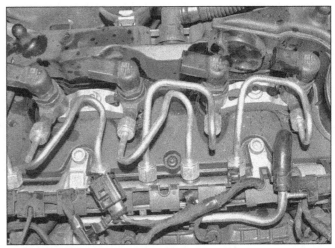

11.7a Remove the high pressure pipes from the rail and injectors...

11.7b...and fit sealing caps to prevent dirt ingress

11.8 Undo the fuel rail retaining bolts

the pump and at the fuel rail **(see illustrations 9.3a and 9.3b)**. Undo the high-pressure fuel pipe retaining clip bolt and remove the high-pressure fuel pipe. Suitably cover or plug all disconnected unions.

4 Release the retaining clip and disconnect the fuel return hose from the fuel rail **(see illustration)**.

5 Disconnect the wiring connectors from the fuel injectors.

6 Disconnect the wiring plugs from the glow plugs, fuel pressure regulating valve, and the fuel pressure sensor at each end of the fuel rail. Unclip the wiring loom retaining bracket from the top of the fuel rail and move it to one side.

7 Where necessary, counterhold the injector with an open-ended spanner when releasing the pipe union. Undo the unions and remove the high-pressure pipes from between the fuel rail and the injectors **(see illustrations)**. Plug the openings to prevent contamination.

8 Undo the multi-spline retaining bolts and remove the fuel rail **(see illustrations)**.

9 If required, note their fitted positions, then unscrew the fuel pressure sensor and pressure regulating valve from the fuel rail, as described in Section 3.

Note: *Audi insist that once removed, the pressure regulating valve cannot be re-used.*

Refitting

10 Where applicable, refit the fuel pressure sensor and the new regulating valve to the fuel rail, and tighten them to the specified torque. Note that the threads of the sensors must be clean and free from oil and grease.

11 The remainder of refitting is a reversal of removal, noting the following points:

a) *Refit the high-pressure fuel pipes and tighten the unions to the specified torque. Note that the high-pressure fuel pipes may be re-used providing the tapered seats are undamaged and the pipes are not deformed, constricted or corroded.*

b) *After completion of the work, the fuel system must be bled as described in Section 10.*

Notes

Chapter 4 Part B
Emission control and exhaust systems

Contents

Degrees of difficulty

Easy, suitable for novice with little experience	**Fairly easy,** suitable for beginner with some experience	**Fairly difficult,** suitable for competent DIY mechanic	**Difficult,** suitable for experienced DIY mechanic	**Very difficult,** suitable for expert DIY or professional

Specifications

Emission control applications

All models . . . . Particulate filter, with catalytic converter and oxygen (lambda probe) sensor, EGR system with exhaust gas temperature sensors and exhaust gas pressure sensor.

Torque wrench settings

	Nm	lbf ft
EGR cooler mounting bolts	9	6
EGR valve retaining bolts	8	6
Exhaust clamp nuts	25	18
Exhaust gas pressure sensors-to-particulate filter	45	33
Exhaust gas temperature sensors:		
To particulate filter	60	44
To turbocharger	45	33
Exhaust manifold to cylinder head	25	18
Exhaust manifold heat shield nuts	25	18
Particulate filter-to-front pipe nuts*	23	17
Particulate filter-to-turbocharger nuts*	23	17
Turbocharger oil return pipe flange bolts*	15	11
Turbocharger oil return banjo bolt*	40	30
Turbocharger oil supply union nuts	22	16
Turbocharger-to-exhaust manifold*	25	18

*Use new fasteners

1 General Information

Emission control systems

1 All engines have a crankcase emission control system, and in addition, are fitted with a diesel particulate filter. All engines are also equipped with an Exhaust Gas Recirculation (EGR) system to reduce exhaust emissions.

Crankcase emission control

2 To reduce the emission of unburned hydrocarbons from the crankcase into the atmosphere, the engine is sealed and the blow-by gases and oil vapour are drawn from inside the crankcase, through a wire mesh oil separator, into the inlet tract to be burned by the engine during normal combustion.

3 Under conditions of high manifold depression, the gases will be sucked positively out of the crankcase. Under conditions of low manifold depression, the gases are forced out of the crankcase by the (relatively) higher crankcase pressure. If the engine is worn, the raised crankcase pressure (due to increased blow-by) will cause some of the flow to return under all manifold conditions.

Exhaust emission control

4 A diesel particulate filter incorporating an oxidation catalyst is fitted in the exhaust system of all models. This has the effect of removing a large proportion of the gaseous hydrocarbons, carbon monoxide, soot and particulates present in the exhaust gas.

5 An Exhaust Gas Recirculation (EGR) system is also fitted. This reduces the level of nitrogen oxides produced during combustion by introducing a proportion of the exhaust gas back into the inlet manifold under certain engine operating conditions. The system is controlled electronically by the engine management ECU.

Exhaust systems

6 The exhaust system consists of the exhaust manifold, the turbocharger, the particulate filter, the front pipe and the centre section which is combined in one unit with the rear silencer as original equipment.

7 The system is supported by various metal brackets screwed to the vehicle floor, with rubber vibration dampers fitted to suppress noise.

2 Crankcase emission system – general information

1 The crankcase emission control system consists of hoses connecting the crankcase to the air cleaner or inlet manifold.

2 The system requires no attention other than to check at regular intervals that the hoses and pressure-regulating valve are free of blockages and in good condition.

3 Exhaust Gas Recirculation (EGR) system – component removal and refitting

1 The EGR system consists of the EGR valve, which directs exhaust gas from the exhaust manifold to the inlet manifold, and a control (changeover) valve that actuates the system according to engine load and speed. There is a vacuum-operated changeover unit, which is fitted on the EGR cooler for recirculating the exhaust gas. All this is connected by a series of vacuum hoses, and metal corrugated cooler pipes. There is also a recirculation potentiometer fitted to the EGR valve, this is controlled directly from the engine management ECU, which then activates the control motor.

2 On engine codes CAGA, CAGB, CAGC, CAHA, CAHB and CMEA, the EGR valve is mounted between the throttle valve housing/module and the inlet manifold. On the side of the EGR valve is a metal connecting pipe that goes to the EGR cooler, which is bolted to the right-hand side of the engine. The EGR cooler uses coolant from the engine cooling system to cool the exhaust gases before passing them to the inlet manifold. The system is activated by a solenoid valve which is controlled by the ECU.

3 On all other engines the EGR valve is integral with the EGR cooler, which is bolted to the right-hand side of the engine. It is joined to the exhaust manifold and cylinder head, by flanged corrugated metal pipes. The system is activated by a solenoid valve which is controlled by the ECU.

EGR valve

Engine codes CAGA, CAGB, CAGC, CAHA, CAHB and CMEA

4 Remove the throttle valve housing/module from the inlet manifold, as described in Chapter 4A, Section 3.

5 Undo the bolts securing the pipe to the rear of the EGR valve **(see illustration)**.

6 Disconnect the wiring plug connector from the front of the EGR valve.

7 Undo the bolts and detach the valve from the inlet manifold. Discard the O-ring seal – a new one must be fitted.

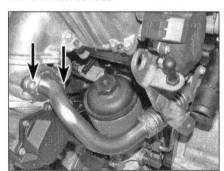

3.5 EGR pipe-to-valve bolts

8 Refitting is a reversal of removal, using a new EGR valve O-ring seal, and tightening the retaining bolts to the specified torque.

All other engine codes

9 The EGR valve is incorporated into the EGR cooler. Remove and refit the cooler as described in paragraphs 17 to 28. At the time of writing, it was not possible to separate the EGR valve from the cooler.

EGR cooler

Engine codes CAGA, CAGB, CAGC, CAHA, CAHB and CMEA

10 Carefully pull the engine top cover off the four retaining pins, one after the other. Do not jerk the cover away and do not try to pull on one side only.

11 Remove the air cleaner assembly as described in Chapter 4A, Section 2.

12 Using suitable hose clamps, clamp off the two coolant hoses at the top of the EGR cooler.

13 Undo the two bolts securing the EGR metal connecting pipe to the rear of the cooler. Similarly, undo the two bolts securing the metal connecting pipe to the exhaust manifold.

14 Disconnect the vacuum hose from the vacuum unit on the front of the EGR cooler.

15 Undo the three bolts securing the EGR cooler to the mounting bracket and remove the cooler from the engine.

16 Refitting is a reversal of removal, using new gaskets, and tightening the retaining bolts to the specified torque.

All other engine codes

17 Carefully pull the engine top cover off the four retaining pins, one after the other. Do not jerk the cover away and do not try to pull on one side only.

18 Drain the cooling system as described in Chapter 1, Section 31.

19 Remove the plenum chamber partition panel as described in, Section.

20 Remove the air cleaner assembly as described in Chapter 4A, Section 2.

21 Disconnect the crankcase ventilation hose from the camshaft cover **(see illustration)**, then slacken the retaining clip and remove the air intake duct from the turbocharger.

3.21 Disconnect the crankcase ventilation hose from the camshaft cover

3.22 Release the retaining clip and disconnect the coolant hose

3.23 Undo the two bolts securing the EGR connecting pipe to the manifold

3.25 Disconnect the vacuum hose and wiring connectors as shown

22 Release the retaining clip and disconnect the coolant hose from the metal coolant pipe at the front of the EGR cooler **(see illustration)**. Undo the nut and bolt securing the metal coolant pipe to the rear of the engine.
23 Undo the two bolts securing the front EGR connecting pipe to the exhaust manifold **(see illustration)**.
24 Undo the two bolts securing the rear EGR connecting pipe to the EGR cooler.
25 Disconnect the vacuum hose and wiring connectors at the EGR valve and EGR cooler **(see illustration)**.
26 Release the retaining clip and disconnect the coolant hose at the rear of the EGR cooler.
27 Undo the two bolts at the front and two bolts at the rear and remove the EGR cooler from the engine.
28 Refitting is a reversal of removal, using new gaskets **(see illustration)**, and tightening the retaining bolts to the specified torque. On completion refill the cooling system as described in Chapter 1, Section 31.

4   Turbocharger – general information and precautions

1 A turbocharger is fitted to all engines, and is bolted to the exhaust manifold.
2 The turbocharger increases engine efficiency by raising the pressure in the inlet manifold above atmospheric pressure. Instead of the air simply being sucked into the cylinders, it is forced in.
3 Energy for the operation of the turbocharger comes from the exhaust gas. The gas flows through a specially-shaped housing (the turbine housing) and in so doing, spins the turbine wheel. The turbine wheel is attached to a shaft, at the end of which is another vaned wheel, known as the compressor wheel. The compressor wheel spins in its own housing, and compresses the inducted air on the way to the inlet manifold.
4 Between the turbocharger and the inlet manifold, the compressed air passes through an intercooler (see Section 6 for details). The purpose of the intercooler is to remove from the inducted air some of the heat gained in being compressed. Because cooler air is

denser, removal of this heat further increases engine efficiency.
5 Boost pressure (the pressure in the inlet manifold) is limited by a wastegate, which diverts the exhaust gas away from the turbine wheel in response to a pressure-sensitive actuator.
6 The turbo shaft is pressure-lubricated by an oil feed pipe from the engine oil filter mounting. The shaft 'floats' on a cushion of oil. Oil is returned to the sump through a return pipe that connects to the sump.

Precautions

7 The turbocharger operates at extremely high speeds and temperatures. Certain precautions must be observed to avoid premature failure of the turbo, or injury to the operator.

● *Do not operate the turbo with any parts exposed – foreign objects falling onto the rotating vanes could cause excessive damage and (if ejected) personal injury.*
● *Cover the turbocharger air inlet ducts to prevent debris entering, and clean using lint-free cloths only.*
● *Do not race the engine immediately after start-up, especially if it is cold. Give the oil a few seconds to circulate.*
● *Observe the recommended intervals for oil and filter changing, and use a reputable oil of the specified quality. Neglect of oil changing, or use of inferior oil, can cause carbon formation on the turbo shaft and subsequent failure.*
● *Thoroughly clean the area around all oil pipe unions before disconnecting them, to prevent the ingress of dirt.*
● *Store dismantled components in a sealed container to prevent contamination.*

5   Turbocharger – removal and refitting

Removal

Engine codes CAGA, CAGB, CAGC, CAHA, CAHB and CMEA

1 Apply the handbrake, then jack up the front of the vehicle and support it on axle stands

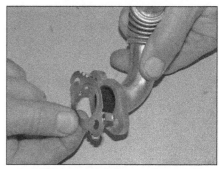

3.28 Fit new gaskets to the EGR pipes

(see *Jacking and vehicle support*). Remove the engine compartment undertrays.
2 Remove the EGR cooler as described in Section 3.
3 Remove the exhaust front pipe as described in Section 8.
4 From under the car, unfasten the spring connection, then undo the retaining bolt and take out the mounting for the particulate filter.
5 Slacken the retaining clip and disconnect the intercooler air duct from the turbocharger.
6 Undo the two bolts and remove the support strut from under the turbocharger.
7 Undo the two upper flange bolts and the lower union nut and remove the turbocharger oil return pipe.
8 Disconnect the wiring plug for the exhaust gas temperature sender and release the wiring from the cylinder block.
9 Undo the three nuts securing the particulate filter to the turbocharger.
10 Disconnect the wiring connector and vacuum pipe from the vacuum unit on top of the turbocharger.
11 Undo the union nut and disconnect the oil supply pipe from the top of the turbocharger.
12 Unclip the wiring from the cylinder block.
13 Undo the two retaining nuts and remove the turbocharger from the exhaust manifold.

All other engine codes

14 Carefully pull the engine top cover off the four retaining pins, one after the other. Do not jerk the cover away and do not try to pull on one side only.
15 Remove the air cleaner assembly as described in Chapter 4A, Section 2.

5.20 Slacken the retaining clip and remove the air intake duct from the turbocharger

16 Apply the handbrake, then jack up the front of the vehicle and support it on axle stands (see *Jacking and vehicle support*). Remove the engine compartment undertrays.
17 Remove the right-hand front roadwheel, then remove the cover for the driveshaft from under the wheel arch.
18 Remove the exhaust front pipe as described in Section 8.
19 Unfasten the spring connection, then undo the retaining bolt and take out the mounting for the particulate filter.
20 Disconnect the crankcase ventilation hose from the camshaft cover **(see illustration 3.21)**, then slacken the retaining clip and remove the air intake duct from the turbocharger **(see illustration)**.
21 Slacken the retaining clip and disconnect the intercooler air duct from the turbocharger.

6.6a Using a screwdriver, release the catches on the right-hand air deflector (shown with air deflector removed)...

22 Undo the two bolts and remove the support strut from under the turbocharger.
23 Undo the two upper flange bolts and the lower union nut and remove the turbocharger oil return pipe.
24 Disconnect the wiring plug for the exhaust gas temperature sender and release the wiring from the cylinder block.
25 Unscrew the exhaust gas temperature sender from the particulate filter.
26 Remove the oxygen (lambda probe) sensor as described in Chapter 4A, Section 3.
27 Undo the pressure differential sender retaining bolt, move the hoses clear at the mounting bracket, and move the pressure differential sender to the rear.
28 Undo the three nuts securing the particulate filter to the turbocharger and move the particulate filter to the rear.
29 Undo the oil supply pipe union nut from the top of the turbocharger.
30 Disconnect the wiring connector and vacuum pipe from the vacuum unit on top of the turbocharger.
31 Undo the retaining nuts and remove the turbocharger from the exhaust manifold.

Refitting

32 Refit the turbocharger by following the removal procedure in reverse, noting the following points:
a) *Renew all disturbed gaskets, sealing washers and O-rings.*
b) *Before reconnecting the oil supply pipe,*

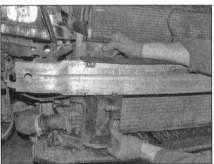

6.6b...and swivel the air deflector toward the centre to remove

fill the turbocharger with fresh oil using an oil can.
c) *Tighten all nuts and bolts to the specified torque, where given.*
d) *When the engine is started after refitting, allow it to idle for approximately one minute to give the oil time to circulate around the turbine shaft bearings. Check for signs of oil or coolant leakage from the relevant unions.*

6   Intercooler – general information, removal and refitting

General information

1 The intercooler is effectively an 'air radiator', used to cool the pressurised inlet air before it enters the engine.
2 When the turbocharger compresses the inlet air, one side effect is that the air is heated, causing the air to expand. If the inlet air can be cooled, a greater effective volume of air will be inducted, and the engine will produce more power.
3 The compressed air from the turbocharger, which would normally be fed straight into the inlet manifold, is instead ducted around the engine to the base of the intercooler. The intercooler is mounted at the front of the car, in the airflow. The heated air entering the base of the unit rises upwards, and is cooled by the airflow over the intercooler fins, much as with the radiator. When it reaches the top of the intercooler, the cooled air is then ducted into the throttle housing.

Removal

4 The intercooler is located in front of the air conditioning condenser and the radiator, on the lock carrier.
5 Remove the front bumper as described in Chapter 11, Section 8.
6 Release the catches on the left-hand and right-hand air deflectors, swivel the air deflectors towards the centre of the vehicle and remove them from each side of the intercooler **(see illustrations)**.
7 Slacken the retaining clips and disconnect the air ducts from the elbows on each side of the intercooler **(see illustrations)**.

6.6c Similarly, release the catches on the left-hand air deflector...

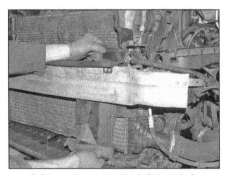

6.6d...and remove the left-hand air deflector in the same way

6.7a Slacken the retaining clips and disconnect the right-hand air duct...

6.7b...and left-hand air duct from the intercooler

6.8 Undo the intercooler retaining screw

8 Undo the screw securing the left-hand side of the intercooler to the lock carrier **(see illustration)**.

9 Push down on the retaining clip at the right-hand side of the intercooler, then tip it forward and remove it from the car **(see illustrations)**.

10 Examine the intercooler for any damage, and check the air hoses for splits.

Refitting

11 Refitting is a reversal of removal.

7 Exhaust manifold – removal and refitting

Removal

1 Remove the turbocharger as described in Section 5.
2 Undo the bolt securing the turbocharger oil supply pipe retaining clip.
3 Undo the four bolts and detach the EGR pipe.
4 Undo the two nuts and remove the exhaust manifold heat shield.
5 Undo the eight retaining nuts and remove the exhaust manifold from the cylinder head studs. Obtain a new gasket and new manifold retaining nuts for refitting.

Refitting

6 Refitting is a reversal of removal tightening all nuts and bolts to the specified torque (where given).

8 Exhaust system – component renewal

 Warning: Allow ample time for the exhaust system to cool before starting work. In particular,

note that the particulate filter/catalytic converter runs at very high temperatures. If there is any chance that the system may still be hot, wear suitable gloves.

Removal

Note: *The following procedures describe the general work required for component renewal. Some differences will be experienced according to model, but the procedures are essentially the same*
1 The original Audi system fitted in the factory is in multiple sections. The particulate filter is attached to the exhaust manifold at the front and has the exhaust system front pipe attached to it at the rear. Attached to the front pipe is the centre section which contains the centre silencer and is combined in one unit with the rear silencer. The centre section and rear silencer are available separately for repair purposes.
2 To remove part of the system, first jack up the front or rear of the car and support it on axle stands (see *Jacking and vehicle support*). Alternatively, position the car over an inspection pit or on car ramps. Remove the engine undertrays as necessary for access.

Particulate filter

3 Carefully pull the engine top cover off the four retaining pins, one after the other. Do not

6.9a Push down on the retaining clip...

jerk the cover away and do not try to pull on one side only.
4 Drain the cooling system as described in Chapter 1, Section 31.
5 Remove the plenum chamber partition panel as described in Chapter 11 Section 21.
6 Remove the air cleaner assembly as described in Chapter 4A, Section 2.
7 Remove the exhaust system front pipe as described later in this Section.
8 Unscrew the exhaust gas temperature sender from the particulate filter.
9 Unfasten the spring connection, then undo the retaining bolt and take out the mounting for the particulate filter.
10 Remove the right-hand front roadwheel, then remove the cover for the driveshaft from under the wheel arch.
11 Remove the oxygen (lambda probe) sensor as described in Chapter 4A, Section 3.
12 Undo the pressure differential sender retaining bolt, move the hoses clear at the mounting bracket, and move the pressure differential sender to the rear.
13 Undo the three nuts securing the particulate filter to the turbocharger and move the particulate filter to the rear.
14 Undo the nut and bolt securing the coolant pipe to the rear and right-hand side of the engine. Slacken the retaining clips,

6.9b...and remove the intercooler from the car

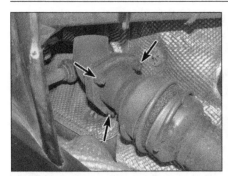

8.20 Undo the nuts securing the front pipe to the particulate filter

8.21 Undo the two nuts at the clamp connecting the front pipe to the centre section

disconnect the three coolant hoses and remove the coolant pipe from the engine.

15 Remove the EGR cooler as described in Section 3.

16 Remove the turbocharger as described in Section 5.

17 Disconnect the wiring connector, then unscrew the oil pressure warning light switch from the rear of the cylinder head.

18 Undo the two bolts and detach the EGR pipe.

19 Undo the retaining bolt and retaining nut and push the rear coolant pipe to one side, then move the particulate filter forwards and remove it from the engine compartment.

Front pipe

Caution: Handle the flexible, braided section of the front pipe carefully, and do not bend it excessively.

20 Undo the three nuts securing the front pipe to the particulate filter **(see illustration)**.

21 Undo the two nuts at the clamp connecting the front pipe to the centre section **(see illustration)**. Move the clamp to the rear and remove the front pipe from under the car.

Centre section

22 Undo the two nuts at the clamp connecting the front pipe to the centre section. Move the clamp forward to release the front pipe from the centre section.

23 Suitably support the centre section then release the front and rear mounting rubbers. Alternatively unbolt the mounting rubber brackets from the underbody.

24 Withdraw the centre section from under the car.

Rear pipe and silencers

25 If the factory-fitted Audi centre/rear section is being worked on, examine the pipe just forward of the rear silencer for three pairs of punch marks, or three line markings. The centre marking indicates the point at which to cut the pipe, while the outer marks indicate the position for the ends of the new clamp required when refitting. Cut through the pipe using the centre mark as a guide, making the cut as square to the pipe as possible if either resulting section is to be re-used.

26 If the factory-fitted rear section has already been renewed, unscrew the clamp bolts between the two sections.

Refitting

27 Each section is refitted by a reversal of the removal sequence, noting the following points:

a) Ensure that all traces of corrosion have been removed from the flanges or pipe ends, and renew all necessary gaskets.

b) The design of the clamps used between the exhaust sections means that they play a greater role in ensuring a gas-tight seal – fit new clamps if they are in less than perfect condition.

c) When fitting the clamps, use the markings on the pipes as a guide to the clamp's correct fitted position.

d) Inspect the mountings for signs of damage or deterioration, and renew as necessary.

e) If using exhaust assembly paste, make sure this is only applied to joints downstream of the particulate filter.

f) Prior to tightening the exhaust system mountings and clamps, ensure that all rubber mountings are correctly located and that there is adequate clearance between the exhaust system and vehicle underbody

9 Particulate filter/catalytic converter – general information and precautions

1 The particulate filter which incorporates the catalytic converter needs to be treated with respect to avoid problems. The unit is a reliable and simple device which needs no maintenance in itself, but there are some facts of which an owner should be aware if the converter/particulate filter is to function properly for its full service life:

a) DO NOT use fuel or engine oil additives – these may contain substances harmful to the particulate filter.

b) DO NOT continue to use the car if the engine burns (engine) oil to the extent of leaving a visible trail of blue smoke.

c) Remember that the particulate filter is FRAGILE – do not strike it with tools during servicing work, and take care handling it when removing it from the car for any reason.

d) The particulate filter, used on a well-maintained and well-driven car, should last for between 50,000 and 100,000 miles – if the unit is no longer effective, it must be renewed.

Chapter 5
Starting and charging systems

Contents

Degrees of difficulty

Easy, suitable for novice with little experience | **Fairly easy,** suitable for beginner with some experience | **Fairly difficult,** suitable for competent DIY mechanic | **Difficult,** suitable for experienced DIY mechanic | **Very difficult,** suitable for expert DIY or professional

Specifications

General
System type . . . . 12 volt, negative earth

Starter motor
Type . . . . Pre-engaged

Battery
Rating . . . . 44 to 80 Ah (depending on model and market)

Alternator
Type . . . . Bosch or Valeo
Rating . . . . 70, 90 or 120 amp
Minimum brush length . . . . 5.0 mm

Torque wrench settings	Nm	lbf ft
Alternator mounting bolts	23	17
Glow plugs	17	13
Starter motor	65	48

1 General information and precautions

1 The engine electrical system consists mainly of the charging, starting, and diesel preheating systems. Because of their engine-related functions, these are covered separately from the body electrical devices such as the lights, instruments, etc, which are covered in Chapter 12.

2 The electrical system is of the 12 volt negative earth type.

3 The battery, which is of the maintenance-free (sealed for life) type, is charged by the alternator, which is belt-driven from the crankshaft pulley. The battery is located under the floor panel in the luggage compartment. To enable jump starting or battery charging to be carried out, separate positive (+) and negative (-) terminal connectors are located in the engine compartment.

4 The starter motor is of the pre-engaged type, with an integral solenoid. On starting, the solenoid moves the drive pinion into engagement with the driveplate ring gear before the starter motor is energised. Once the engine has started, a one-way clutch prevents the motor armature being driven by the engine until the pinion disengages from the ring gear.

5 To assist cold starting, the engines are fitted with a preheating system, which comprises four glow plugs, a glow plug control unit (incorporated in the ECU), a facia-mounted warning lamp and the associated electrical wiring.

6 The glow plugs are miniature electric heating elements, encapsulated in a metal or ceramic case with a probe at one end and electrical connection at the other. Each combustion chamber has a glow plug threaded into it, which is positioned directly in line with the incoming spray of fuel. When the glow plug is energised, the air in the combustion chamber is heated, allowing optimum combustion temperature to be achieved more quickly.

7 The duration of the preheating period is governed by the ECU which monitors the temperature of the engine via the coolant temperature sensor and alters the preheating time to suit the conditions. Preheating only takes place at coolant temperatures below 9ºC.

8 A facia-mounted warning light informs the driver that preheating is taking place. The light extinguishes when sufficient preheating has taken place to allow the engine to be started, but power will still be supplied to the glow plugs for a further period until the engine is started. If no attempt is made to start the engine, the power supply to the glow plugs is switched off to prevent battery drain and glow plug burn-out. After the engine is started, there is a period of post-heating which takes place irrespective of whether it is preceded by preheating or not. This period lasts for a maximum of 4 minutes after the engine has been started, at engine speeds of under 2500 rpm. The heating is switched off after this period, or if the engine speed exceeds 2500 rpm. Post-heating reduces combustion noise and improves idling quality, and additionally reduces hydrocarbon emissions.

9 The warning light comes on when the ignition is initially switched on with a cold engine, and indicates that the glow plugs are being energised. If the light does not come on in these conditions, there is a defect in the glow plug system which should be investigated. When the engine is warm, the light may not come on, and the engine can be started straight away, and any post-heating will take place automatically.

10 Further details of the various systems are given in the relevant Sections of this Chapter. While some repair procedures are given, the usual course of action is to renew the component concerned.

Precautions

⚠ *Warning: It is necessary to take extra care when working on the electrical system to avoid damage to semi-conductor devices (diodes and transistors), and to avoid the risk of personal injury. In addition to the precautions given in 'Safety first!', observe the following when working on the system:*

● *Always remove rings, watches, etc, before working on the electrical system. Even with the battery disconnected, capacitive discharge could occur if a component's live terminal is earthed through a metal object. This could cause a shock or nasty burn.*

● *Do not reverse the battery connections. Components such as the alternator, electronic control units, or any other components having semi-conductor circuitry could be irreparably damaged.*

● *Never disconnect the battery terminals, the alternator, any electrical wiring or any test instruments when the engine is running.*

● *Do not allow the engine to turn the alternator when the alternator is not connected.*

● *Never test for alternator output by 'flashing' the output lead to earth.*

● *Always ensure that the battery negative lead is disconnected when working on the electrical system.*

● *If the engine is being started using jump leads and a slave battery, connect the batteries negative-to-negative and positive-to-positive. This also applies when connecting a battery charger.*

● *Before using electric-arc welding equipment on the car, disconnect the battery, alternator and components such as electronic control modules to protect them from the risk of damage.*

Caution: The radio fitted as standard equipment has a built-in security code to deter thieves. If the power source to the unit is cut, the anti-theft system will activate. Even if the power source is immediately reconnected, the radio will not function until the correct security code has been entered. Therefore, if you do not know the correct security code for the radio, do not disconnect the battery negative terminal or remove the radio from the vehicle.

2 Battery – testing and charging

Testing

Standard and low-maintenance battery

1 If the vehicle covers a small annual mileage, it is worthwhile checking the specific gravity of the electrolyte every three months to determine the state of charge of the battery. Use a hydrometer to make the check, and compare the results with the following table. Note that the specific gravity readings assume an electrolyte temperature of 15°C; for every 10°C below 15°C subtract 0.007. For every 10°C above 15°C add 0.007.

	Above 25°C	Below 25°C
Fully-charged	1.210 to 1.230	1.270 to 1.290
70% charged	1.170 to 1.190	1.230 to 1.250
Discharged	1.050 to 1.070	1.110 to 1.130

2 If the battery condition is suspect, first check the specific gravity of electrolyte in each cell. A variation of 0.040 or more between any cells indicates loss of electrolyte or deterioration of the internal plates.

3 If the specific gravity variation is 0.040 or more, the battery should be renewed. If the cell variation is satisfactory but the battery is discharged, it should be charged as described later in this Section.

Maintenance-free battery

4 In cases where a sealed for life maintenance-free battery is fitted, topping-up and testing of the electrolyte in each cell is not possible. The condition of the battery can therefore only be tested using a battery condition indicator or a voltmeter.

5 Certain models may be fitted with a maintenance-free battery with a built-in charge condition indicator. The indicator is located in the top of the battery casing and indicates the condition of the battery from its colour. If the indicator shows green, then the battery is in a good state of charge. If the indicator turns darker, eventually to black, then the battery requires charging, as described later in this Section. If the indicator shows clear/yellow, then the electrolyte level in the battery is too low to allow further use, and the battery should be renewed. Do not

attempt to charge, load or jump start a battery when the indicator shows clear/yellow.

All battery types

6 If testing the battery using a voltmeter, connect the voltmeter across the battery and note the voltage. The test is only accurate if the battery has not been subjected to any kind of charge for the previous six hours. If this is not the case, switch on the headlights for 30 seconds, then wait four to five minutes before testing the battery after switching off the headlights. All other electrical circuits must be switched off, so check that the doors and tailgate are fully shut when making the test.

7 If the voltage reading is less than 12.2 volts, then the battery is discharged, whilst a reading of 12.2 to 12.4 volts indicates a partially-discharged condition.

Charging

Note: *The following is intended as a guide only. Always refer to the manufacturer's recommendations (often printed on a label attached to the battery) before charging a battery.*

Standard and low-maintenance battery

8 Charge the battery at a rate equivalent to 10% of the battery capacity (eg, for a 45 Ah battery charge at 4.5 A) and continue to charge the battery at this rate until no further rise in specific gravity is noted over a four-hour period.

9 Alternatively, a trickle charger charging at the rate of 1.5 amps can safely be used overnight.

10 Specially rapid boost charges which are claimed to restore the power of the battery in 1 to 2 hours are not recommended, as they can cause serious damage to the battery plates through overheating.

11 While charging the battery, note that the temperature of the electrolyte should never exceed 38°C.

Maintenance-free battery

12 This battery type takes considerably longer to fully recharge than the standard type, the time taken being dependent on the extent of discharge, but it can take anything up to three days.

13 A constant voltage type charger is required, to be set, when connected, to 13.9 to 14.9 volts with a charger current below 25 amps. Using this method, the battery should be useable within three hours, giving a voltage reading of 12.5 volts, but this is for a partially-discharged battery and, as mentioned, full charging can take far longer.

14 If the battery is to be charged from a fully-discharged state (condition reading less than 12.2 volts), have it recharged by your local automotive electrician, as the charge rate is higher and constant supervision during charging is necessary.

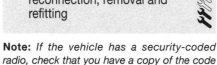

3 Battery – disconnection, reconnection, removal and refitting

Note: *If the vehicle has a security-coded radio, check that you have a copy of the code number before disconnecting the battery cable; refer to the caution in Section 1.*

Disconnection and reconnection

1 On Saloon models, open the boot lid, then lift the luggage compartment floor and hook it onto the body. On Avant models, open the tailgate and take out the luggage compartment floor.

2 Where fitted, remove the subwoofer located at the rear of the battery.

3.3 Undo the centre retainer and lift out the spare wheel, or lift off the tool kit cover (as applicable)

3.5 Remove the mounting frame for the tool kit cover or spare wheel

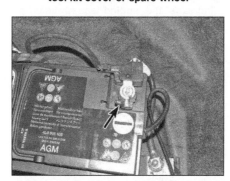

3.7 Loosen the clamp nut and disconnect the battery negative (-) lead

3 Undo the centre retainer and either lift out the spare wheel (if fitted) or lift off the cover over the tool kit **(see illustration)**.

4 Remove the tool kit or the jack (as applicable) **(see illustration)**.

5 Undo the four bolts and lift out the mounting frame for the tool kit cover or spare wheel **(see illustration)**.

6 Using a screwdriver, release the two catches and remove the cover over the battery negative terminal **(see illustration)**.

7 Loosen the clamp nut and disconnect the battery negative (-) lead from the terminal **(see illustration)**.

8 Lift the plastic flap where fitted, then loosen the clamp nut and disconnect the battery positive (+) lead from the terminal **(see illustration)**.

3.4 Lift out the tool kit or the jack from the battery location

3.6 Remove the cover over the battery negative terminal

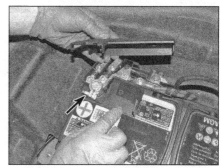

3.8 Lift the plastic flap, loosen the clamp nut and disconnect the battery positive (+) lead

3.13 Unscrew the battery retainer plate retaining bolt

5.2 Remove the air intake hose

voltmeter reading remains steady; the reading should be approximately 12 to 13 volts, and no more than 14 volts.

7 Switch on as many electrical accessories as possible (eg, the headlights, heated rear window and heater blower), and check that the alternator maintains the regulated voltage at around 13 to 14 volts.

8 If the regulated voltage is not as stated, this may be due to worn brushes, weak brush springs, a faulty voltage regulator, a faulty diode, a severed phase winding or worn or damaged slip-rings. Have the alternator checked and tested by an auto-electrician.

9 Reconnection is a reversal of disconnection, ensuring the battery positive (+) lead is reconnected first.

10 After both leads have been reconnected, note the following:
a) Re-activate the radio by inserting the security code.
b) Open the electric windows, then pull and hold each window switch until the window is fully closed. Release the switch, then pull it again for at least one second. This will restore the one-touch open and close function of the window.
c) The ESP warning light on the instrument panel may illuminate until the vehicle has be driven several metres.

Removal

11 Disconnect the battery terminals as described previously in this Section.

12 Disconnect the vent pipe from the side of battery. Note on some models the vent incorporates a flashback arrester.

13 Unscrew the bolt from the battery retainer plate and lift out the plate and bolt **(see illustration)**.

14 Lift up the battery and remove it from the luggage compartment.

Refitting

15 Clean the battery mounting, then refit the battery in position and refit the retainer plate. Tighten the retainer plate bolt securely.

16 Refit the vent pipe to the battery.

17 Reconnect the battery terminals as described previously in this Section.

4 Alternator/charging system – testing in vehicle

Note: *Refer to Section 1 of this Chapter before starting work.*

1 If the charge warning light fails to illuminate when the ignition is switched on, first check the alternator wiring connections for security. Check the condition of the auxiliary drivebelt. If all is satisfactory, the alternator maybe at fault and should be renewed or taken to an auto-electrician for testing and repair.

2 Similarly, if the charge warning light comes on with the ignition, but is then slow to go out when the engine is started, this may indicate an impending alternator problem. Check all the items listed in the preceding paragraph, and refer to an auto-electrical specialist if no obvious faults are found.

3 If the charge warning light illuminates when the engine is running, stop the engine and check that the drivebelt is correctly tensioned (see Chapter 1, Section 8) and that the alternator connections are secure. If the fault persists, the alternator should be renewed, or taken to an auto-electrician for testing and repair.

4 If the alternator output is suspect even though the warning light functions correctly, the regulated voltage may be checked as follows.

5 Connect a voltmeter across the battery terminals, and start the engine.

6 Increase the engine speed until the

5 Alternator – removal and refitting

Removal

1 Disconnect the battery negative lead and position it away from the terminal, as described in Section 3.

2 Slacken the retaining clips and remove the air intake hose from the throttle housing **(see illustration)**. To give more access to the alternator, also undo the retaining bolts and lower the plastic air ducting away from the rear of the alternator.

3 Disconnect the wiring connector from the electric coolant circulation pump.

4 Undo the electric coolant circulation pump bracket retaining bolt and move the pump to one side. Do not disconnect the coolant hoses.

5 Remove the auxiliary drivebelt as described in Chapter 1, Section 8. Mark the drivebelt for direction to ensure it is refitted in the same position.

6 Release the retaining clip and disconnect the wiring connector from the alternator **(see illustration)**.

7 Remove the protective plastic cap, unscrew and remove the nut (washer), then disconnect the battery positive cable from the alternator terminal. Where applicable, unscrew the nut and remove the cable guide **(see illustration)**.

8 Unscrew and remove the lower, then upper bolts, then lift the alternator away from its bracket **(see illustrations)**.

5.6 Disconnecting the alternator wiring plug connector

5.7 Pull the plastic cover off and undo the retaining nut

5.8 Alternator mounting bolts

5.9 Tap the spacer down slightly to aid refitting

6.3 On the Bosch type, remove the outer cover...

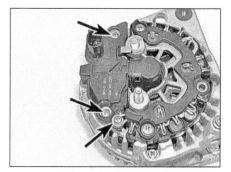

6.4a...undo the screws...

Refitting

9 Refitting is a reversal of removal. Refer to Chapter 1, Section 8, for details of refitting the auxiliary drivebelt. Tighten the alternator mounting bolts to the specified torque. Before fitting the alternator, it may be necessary to tap the sliding sleeve in the alternator housing back a couple of millimeters **(see illustration)**, so that it can be refitted to the mounting bracket easier.

6 Alternator – brush holder/ regulator module renewal

Removal

1 Remove the alternator, as described in Section 5.

2 Place the alternator on a clean work surface, with the pulley facing down.

Bosch

3 Undo the screw and the two retaining nuts, and lift away the outer plastic cover **(see illustration)**.
4 Unscrew the three securing screws, and remove the voltage regulator **(see illustrations)**.

Valeo

5 Prise off the spring clips, and remove the outer plastic cover **(see illustration)**.
6 Undo the two screws and single nut, and remove the voltage regulator **(see illustrations)**.
7 Slide off the brush cover by depressing the lugs on each side.

Inspection

8 Measure the free length of the brush contacts **(see illustration)**. Check the measurement with the Specifications; renew the module if the brushes are worn below the minimum limit.
9 Clean and inspect the surfaces of the slip-rings **(see illustration)**, at the end of the alternator shaft. If they are excessively worn, or damaged, the alternator must be renewed.

Refitting

Bosch

10 Refit the voltage regulator using a reversal of the removal procedure, tightening the screws securely. On completion, refer to Section 5 and refit the alternator.

6.4b...and remove the brush holder/ regulator

6.5 On the Valeo type, remove the outer plastic cover...

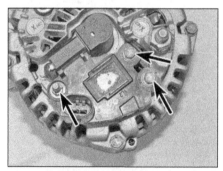

6.6a...undo the two bolts and single nut...

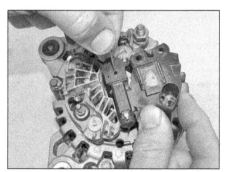

6.6b...and remove the voltage regulator

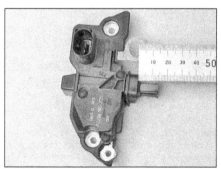

6.8 Measure the brush length

6.9 Clean and inspect the surfaces of the slip-rings

8.7 Disconnecting the starter wiring plug connector

8.8a Remove the plastic cap, undo the nut...

8.8b ...and disconnect the wiring from the starter motor

Valeo

11 Depress the carbon brushes into the housing, then refit the voltage regulator and tighten the screws and nut securely. Slide on the brush cover until it is heard to engage. On completion, refer to Section 5 and refit the alternator.

7 Starting system – testing

Note: *Refer to Section 1 of this Chapter before starting work.*
1 If the starter motor fails to operate when the ignition key is turned to the appropriate position, the following possible causes may be to blame:
a) *The battery is faulty.*
b) *The electrical connections between the switch, solenoid, battery and starter motor are somewhere failing to pass the necessary current from the battery through the starter to earth.*
c) *The solenoid is faulty.*
d) *The starter motor is mechanically or electrically defective.*
2 To check the battery, switch on the headlights. If they dim after a few seconds, this indicates that the battery is discharged – recharge (see Section 2) or renew the battery. If the headlights glow brightly, operate the ignition switch and observe the lights. If they dim, then this indicates that current is reaching the starter motor, therefore the fault must lie in the starter motor. If the lights continue to glow brightly (and no clicking sound can be heard from the starter motor solenoid), this indicates that there is a fault in the circuit or solenoid – see following paragraphs. If the starter motor turns slowly when operated, but the battery is in good condition, then this indicates that either the starter motor is faulty, or there is considerable resistance somewhere in the circuit.
3 If a fault in the circuit is suspected, disconnect the battery leads (including the earth connection to the body), the starter/solenoid wiring and the engine/transmission earth strap. Thoroughly clean the connections, and reconnect the leads and wiring, then use a

voltmeter or test light to check that full battery voltage is available at the battery positive lead connection to the solenoid, and that the earth is sound.
4 If the battery and all connections are in good condition, check the circuit by disconnecting the wire from the solenoid blade terminal. Connect a voltmeter or test light between the wire end and a good earth (such as the battery negative terminal), and check that the wire is live when the ignition switch is turned to the start position. If it is, then the circuit is sound – if not the circuit wiring can be checked as described in Chapter 12 Section 2.
5 The solenoid contacts can be checked by connecting a voltmeter or test light between the battery positive feed connection on the starter side of the solenoid, and earth. When the ignition switch is turned to the start position, there should be a reading or lighted bulb, as applicable. If there is no reading or lighted bulb, the solenoid is faulty and should be renewed.
6 If the circuit and solenoid are proved sound, the fault must lie in the starter motor. Remove the starter motor, and have it inspected by an auto-electrician.

8 Starter motor – removal and refitting

Removal

1 Disconnect the battery negative lead as described in Section 3
2 Apply the handbrake, then jack up the front of the vehicle and support it on axle stands (see *Jacking and vehicle support*). Remove the engine undertray.
3 Release the diesel particulate filter sufficiently to allow access to the starter motor.
4 Remove the right-hand engine mounting and the mounting bracket on the cylinder block as described in Chapter 2A, Section 14.
5 Undo the two bolts and remove the turbocharger support bracket.
6 Undo the bolt securing the engine wiring harness retainer and move to one side.
7 Slide the locking element to the rear, press

down the release catch and disconnect the wiring connector from the solenoid **(see illustration)**.
8 Unclip the plastic cover from the wiring connector and unscrew the nut to disconnect the battery positive lead from the starter motor **(see illustrations)**.
9 Unscrew the mounting bolts noting the fitted position of the spacer sleeve on the upper bolt, then guide the starter motor out of the bellhousing aperture and out of the engine compartment.

Refitting

10 Refit the starter motor by following the removal procedure in reverse. Tighten the mounting bolts to the specified torque.

9 Starter motor – testing and overhaul

1 If the starter motor is thought to be defective, it should be removed from the vehicle and taken to an auto-electrician for assessment. In the majority of cases, new starter motor brushes can be fitted at a reasonable cost. However, check the cost of repairs first as it may prove more economical to purchase a new or exchange motor.

10 Glow plugs – testing, removal and refitting

Testing

1 If the system malfunctions, testing is ultimately by substitution of known good units, but some preliminary checks may be made as described in the following paragraphs.
2 Before testing the system, check that the battery voltage is at least 11.5 volts using a voltmeter. Switch off the ignition.
3 Carefully pull the engine top cover off the four retaining pins, one after the other. Do not jerk the cover away and do not try to pull on one side only.
4 Disconnect the wiring plug from the coolant temperature sender at the rear of the engine. Disconnecting the sender in this way simulates

a cold engine, which is a requirement for the glow plug system to activate.

5 Disconnect the wiring connector from the most convenient glow plug, and connect a suitable voltmeter between the wiring connector and a good earth.

6 Have an assistant switch on the ignition. Battery voltage should be displayed for approximately 20 seconds – note that the voltage will drop to zero when the pre- and post-heating periods end.

7 If no supply voltage can be detected at the glow plug, then either the glow plug relay (where applicable) or the supply wiring must be faulty. Also check that the glow plug fuse or fusible link (usually located on top of the battery) has not blown – if it has, this may indicate a serious wiring fault; consult an Audi dealer or specialist for advice.

8 To locate a faulty glow plug, first disconnect the battery negative lead as described in Section 3.

9 Disconnect the wiring plug from the glow plug terminal. Measure the electrical resistance between the glow plug terminal and the engine earth. Ceramic glow plugs should have a resistance of no more than 1 ohm, and as a guide on metal glow plugs, more than a few ohms indicates that the plug is defective. Ceramic glow plugs are identified by a white or silver seal around the top of plug. Metal plugs have a red seal around the top of the plug.

10 If a suitable ammeter is available, connect it between the glow plug and its wiring connector, and measure the steady-state current consumption (ignore the initial current surge, which will be about 50% higher). As a guide, high current consumption (or no current draw at all) indicates a faulty glow plug.

11 As a final check, remove the glow plugs and inspect their stems for signs of damage.

10.14a Using long nose pliers...

A badly burned or charred stem may be an indication of a faulty fuel injector.

Removal

12 Ceramic or metal glow plugs may be fitted, depending on engine code. Ceramic glow plugs are identified by a white or silver seal at the top of the plug. Due to the materials used in their construction, special rules must be followed regarding their handling:

a) *Do not remove the plugs from the packaging until you are ready to fit them.*

b) *Ceramic plugs are very delicate. Protect them from knocks. Audi claim that plugs which have been dropped (even from 2 cm) must not be fitted*

c) *Damaged glow plugs may cause engine damage. Remove any fragments of damaged ceramic heater tips from the combustion chamber.*

d) *The software within the ECU is specific to ceramic plugs. Therefore, these type of plugs are not interchangeable with metal plugs.*

13 Carefully pull the engine top cover off the four retaining pins, one after the other. Do not

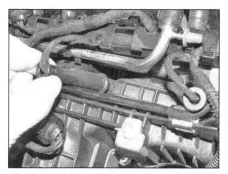

10.14b...pull the connectors from the top of the glow plugs

jerk the cover away and do not try to pull on one side only.

14 Pull the connectors from the top of the glow plugs and move the wiring loom to one side. Be sure to only pull on the underside of the ridge at the top of the connectors **(see illustrations)**.

15 Clean the area around the glow plugs; use a vacuum cleaner if possible. Spray brake cleaner (or similar) around the glow plug opening, letting it penetrate briefly, and then blow out with compressed air.

16 Using a universal joint, extension and a deep 10 mm socket, unscrew and remove the glow plug(s) from the cylinder head. Note that the plug must be kept 'straight' when being removed – if the ceramic heater tip touches the cylinder head, etc, it may easily be damaged.

Refitting

17 Ensure the threads in the cylinder head and glow plugs are clean, then refit the plugs to the cylinder head.

18 Tighten the plugs to the specified torque.

19 Reconnect the glow plug wiring plugs.

20 The remainder of refitting is a reversal of removal.

Chapter 6
Clutch

Contents

Degrees of difficulty

| **Easy,** suitable for novice with little experience | | **Fairly easy,** suitable for beginner with some experience | | **Fairly difficult,** suitable for competent DIY mechanic | | **Difficult,** suitable for experienced DIY mechanic | | **Very difficult,** suitable for expert DIY or professional | |

Specifications

General
Type . . . . Single dry friction disc, diaphragm spring with spring-loaded hub, self-adjusting pressure plate
Operation . . . . Hydraulic with slave and master cylinders

Torque wrench settings

	Nm	lbf ft
Clutch slave cylinder mounting bolt*	20	15
Pressure plate-to-flywheel bolts: *		
Stage 1	22	16
Stage 2	Angle-tighten a further 90°	

Use new fasteners

1 General Information

1 The clutch assembly consists of the clutch friction disc, diaphragm spring pressure plate and a dual-mass flywheel. These components form what Audi refer to as a 'clutch module' **(see illustration)**. This clutch module is in turn bolted to a driveplate attached to the engine crankshaft. The arrangement is unusual in that the clutch module remains in place on the transmission input shaft when the transmission is removed from the car and is then removed from the input shaft with the transmission on the bench.
2 The clutch pressure plate is bolted to the rear face of the flywheel, and the friction disc is located between the pressure plate and the flywheel friction surface. The disc hub is splined to the transmission input shaft and is

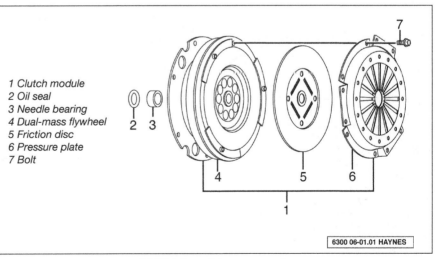

1 Clutch module
2 Oil seal
3 Needle bearing
4 Dual-mass flywheel
5 Friction disc
6 Pressure plate
7 Bolt

1.1 Clutch module components

free to slide along the splines. Friction lining material is riveted to each side of the disc and the disc hub incorporates cushioning springs to absorb transmission shocks and ensure a smooth take-up of drive. The flywheel is manufactured in two parts instead of the conventional single unit; the friction surface has a limited buffered movement in relation to the main flywheel mass bolted to the rear of the crankshaft. This has the effect of absorbing the initial clutch engagement shock and makes for a smoother gearchange.

3 When the clutch pedal is depressed, the slave cylinder pushrod moves the release lever forwards, and the release bearing is forced onto the diaphragm spring fingers. As the centre of the spring is pushed in, the outer part of the spring moves out and releases the pressure plate from the friction disc. Drive then ceases to be transmitted to the transmission.

4 When the clutch pedal is released, the diaphragm spring forces the pressure plate into contact with the linings on the friction disc, and at the same time pushes the disc slightly forward along the input shaft splines into engagement with the flywheel. The friction disc is now firmly sandwiched between pressure plate and flywheel. This causes drive to be taken up.

5 An over-centre spring is fitted to the clutch pedal to equalise the operating effort over the full pedal stroke.

6 As the linings wear on the friction disc, the pressure plate rest position moves closer to the flywheel resulting in the 'rest' position of the diaphragm spring fingers being raised. This is compensated for by means of a self-adjusting clutch. On these units, as the friction plate wears, an adjustment ring of varied thickness within the pressure plate assembly rotates slightly to compensate. This should ensure a more consistent feel to the clutch pedal.

7 The hydraulic system requires no adjustment since the quantity of hydraulic fluid in the circuit automatically compensates for wear every time the clutch pedal is operated.

2 Hydraulic system – bleeding

⚠ **Warning: Hydraulic fluid is poisonous, thoroughly wash off spills from bare skin without delay. Seek immediate medical advice if any fluid is swallowed or gets into the eyes. Certain types of hydraulic fluid are inflammable and may ignite when brought into contact with hot components. Hydraulic fluid is also an effective paint stripper. If spillage occurs onto painted bodywork or fittings, it should be washed off immediately, using copious quantities of cold water. It is also hygroscopic (i.e. it can absorb moisture from the air) which then renders it useless. Old fluid may have**

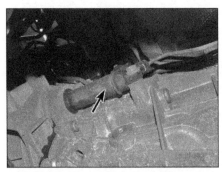

2.3 Clutch slave cylinder location on the left-hand side of the transmission

suffered contamination, and should never be re-used.

Note: *Suitable pressure-bleeding equipment will be required for this operation.*

1 If any part of the hydraulic system is dismantled, or if air has accidentally entered the system, the system will need to be bled. The presence of air is characterised by the pedal having a spongy feel and it results in difficulty in changing gear.

2 The design of the clutch hydraulic system does not allow bleeding to be carried out using the conventional method of pumping the clutch pedal. In order to remove all air present in the system, it is necessary to use pressure bleeding equipment. This is available from auto accessory shops at relatively low cost.

3 The pressure bleeding equipment should be connected to the brake/clutch hydraulic fluid reservoir in accordance with the manufacturer's instructions. The system is bled through the bleed screw of the clutch slave cylinder, which is located on the left-hand upper side of the transmission **(see illustration)**.

4 Bleed the system until the fluid being ejected is free from air bubbles. Close the bleed screw, then disconnect and remove the bleeding equipment.

5 Check the operation of the clutch to see that it is satisfactory. If air still remains in the system, repeat the bleeding operation.

6 Discard any fluid that is bled from the system, even if it looks clean. Hydraulic fluid absorbs water and its re-use can cause internal corrosion of the master and slave cylinders, leading to excessive wear and failure of the seals.

3 Clutch pedal – removal and refitting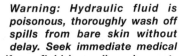

Removal

Note: *Audi special tool T40025 will be required for this operation.*

1 Remove the brake pedal mounting bracket, complete with clutch and brake pedals as described in Chapter 9, Section 12.

2 Extract the retaining pin securing the master cylinder push rod to the clutch pedal.

3 Depress the clutch pedal and use Audi special tool T40025 to retain the over-centre spring in the tension position. Release the pedal and remove the over-centre spring, noting its fitted position.

4 Extract the retaining clip from the clutch pedal pivot pin, then withdraw the pivot pin from the pedal mounting bracket.

5 Withdraw the clutch pedal from the mounting bracket.

Refitting

6 Refitting is a reversal of removal, bearing in mind the following points:

a) Apply VAG special grease G 000 450 02 to all bearings and contact surfaces.

b) Ensure that the over-centre spring is fitted with the black side towards the clutch pedal.

c) Refit the brake pedal mounting bracket as described in Chapter 9, Section 12.

4 Master cylinder – removal, overhaul and refitting

Note: *Refer to the warning at the beginning of Section 2 regarding the hazards of working with hydraulic fluid.*

Removal

Note: *Audi special tool 3355 (32 mm open ring spanner) and T40025 or suitable alternatives will be required for this operation.*

1 Disconnect the battery negative lead and position it away from the terminal, as described in Chapter 5, Section 3.

2 Remove the engine compartment electronics box as described in Chapter 12 Section 16.

3 Place cloth rags beneath the clutch master cylinder fluid supply hose, then fit a hose clamp to the hose and disconnect it from the master cylinder. Plug the open end of the hose to prevent dirt ingress. The hose supplies the master cylinder with fluid from the brake master cylinder reservoir. Be prepared for fluid spillage.

4 Using a small screwdriver, release the retaining clip and pull it out to its limit stop, then remove the fluid pressure pipe from the clutch master cylinder.

5 From inside the car, refer to, Section and remove the trim panel from below the steering column.

6 Undo the retaining bolt and remove the footwell vent over the pedal assembly.

7 Extract the retaining pin securing the master cylinder push rod to the clutch pedal.

8 Depress the clutch pedal and use Audi special tool T40025 to retain the over-centre spring in the tension position. Release the pedal and remove the over-centre spring, noting its fitted position.

9 Engage Audi special tool 3355 over the

master cylinder and turn the tool clockwise to release the master cylinder from its location.

10 From within the engine compartment, withdraw the master cylinder, release and disconnect the wiring connector, then remove the cylinder from the car.

Overhaul

11 At the time of writing, it would appear repair kits are not available. Check with your local Audi dealer or parts specialist.

Refitting

12 Refitting is a reversal of removal, bearing in mind the following points:
a) Locate the master cylinder in position and turn it anti-clockwise using Audi tool 3355 to retain it in position.
b) Apply VAG special grease G 000 450 02 to all bearings and contact surfaces.
c) Refit the engine compartment electronics box as described in Chapter 12 Section 16.
d) Bleed the clutch hydraulic system as described in Section 2 on completion.

5 Slave cylinder – removal, overhaul and refitting

Note: *Refer to the warning at the beginning of Section 2 regarding the hazards of working with hydraulic fluid.*

Removal

1 The slave cylinder is located on top of the transmission on the left-hand side.

2 Apply the handbrake, then jack up the front of the vehicle and support it on axle stands (see *Jacking and vehicle support*). Remove the engine undertray.

3 Clamp the rubber section of the hydraulic hose leading from the master cylinder to the slave cylinder using a brake hose clamp, to prevent loss of hydraulic fluid.

4 Using a small screwdriver, release the retaining clip and pull it out to its limit stop, then remove the fluid pressure pipe from the slave cylinder. Tape or plug the end of the pipe and the slave cylinder aperture.

5 Unscrew the mounting bolt and remove the slave cylinder.

Caution: Do not depress the clutch pedal with the slave cylinder removed.

Overhaul

6 At the time of writing, it would appear that slave cylinder overhaul kits are not available. Check with your local Audi dealer or spare parts specialist.

Refitting

7 Refitting is a reversal of removal, but smear a little lithium-based grease to the outer surface of the rubber boot before locating the slave cylinder in the transmission aperture **(see illustration)**. Tighten the mounting

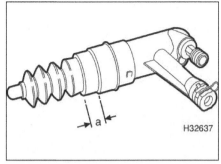

5.7 Apply a thin layer of lithium grease to the area (a) of the slave cylinder before inserting it into the transmission housing

bolt to the specified torque and finally bleed the hydraulic system as described in Section 2.

8 The end of the pushrod which contacts the release lever should be lightly lubricated with a molybdenum disulphide grease and care must be taken to ensure that the pushrod actually engages with the depression in the lever. The slave cylinder must be pressed into the transmission casing before the mounting bolt can be inserted. Due to the limited access and the fact that the slave cylinder must be pushed against the considerable force of the internal return spring, refitting should be made in stages.

9 First fully insert the cylinder, ensuring that the bolt hole is correctly aligned. With the cylinder held in this position, insert the mounting bolt and tighten to the specified torque.

10 Upon completion, check the action of the clutch pedal. If unusually strong resistance is felt, it is possible that the slave cylinder operating rod has been guided past the release lever. Do not apply excessive pressure on the clutch pedal – Audi state that the slave cylinder will be damaged if the applied force exceeds 300 N – normal pedal force is approximately 115 N.

6 Clutch module – removal and refitting

Removal

1 Remove the manual transmission as described in Chapter 7A, Section 3. With the transmission removed, position it in such a way that it is inclined slightly to the rear.

2 Undo the three bolts securing the left-hand drive flange mounting bracket to the transmission casing.

3 Pull the drive flange out of the transmission, taking care not to damage the differential inner oil seal as the splines on the inner end of the drive flange pass through it **(see illustration)**. If the drive flange cannot be removed by hand, attach a suitable slide hammer to the

flange end and use the slide hammer to draw the flange out.

4 If available, attach Audi special tool T40176 to the dual-mass flywheel and secure it in place with the retaining nut. This special tool is essentially just a handle for you to hold when lifting the clutch module off the transmission input shaft. In the absence of the Audi tool, a long bolt secured to the flywheel with two nuts could be used instead.

5 Turn the clutch module so that the holding tool is at the top. Take hold of the tool with one hand, and using your other hand to keep the clutch module upright, carefully pull the module off the transmission input shaft. As the module is being removed, take care not to damage the oil seals and needle bearing in the dual mass flywheel.

Caution: The clutch module weighs approximately 20 kg. Ensure that the module is adequately supported as it slides off the input shaft.

6 With the clutch module removed, lay it down with the dual-mass flywheel driveplate flange facing upward. The driveplate flange could become distorted if the weight of the clutch module is allowed to rest on it.

Refitting

7 Refitting is the reverse sequence to removal, bearing in mind the following points:
a) Apply a thin coating of VAG special grease G 000 100 to the transmission input shaft splines.
b) Slide the guide flange into the transmission keeping it level as it enters the differential inner oil seal.
c) Tighten all nuts and bolts to the specified torque (where given).
d) Refit the manual transmission as described in Chapter 7A, Section 3.

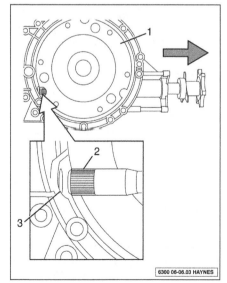

6.3 Drive flange removal

1 Dual-mass flywheel
2 Drive flange splines
3 Differential inner oil seal

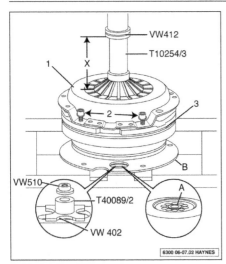

7.2 Arrangement of Audi special tools for clutch friction disc and pressure plate removal

1 Pressure plate	A Bearing washer
2 Retaining bolts	B Drive plate flange
3 Dual-mass flywheel	X = 8.0 to 9.0 mm

7 Clutch friction disc, pressure plate and flywheel – removal, inspection and refitting

⚠ *Warning: Dust created by clutch wear and deposited on the clutch components may contain asbestos, which is a health hazard. DO NOT blow it out with compressed air or inhale any of it. DO NOT use petrol or petroleum-based solvents to clean off the dust. Brake system cleaner or methylated spirit should be used to flush the dust into a suitable receptacle. After the clutch components are wiped clean with clean rags, dispose of the contaminated rags and cleaner in a sealed container.*

Removal

Note: *Access to an hydraulic press and numerous Audi special tools will required for this operation.*

1 Remove the clutch module as described in Section 6.

2 Place the Audi special tools on the press bed, then position the clutch module so that the thrust pad (Audi tool VW 510) makes contact with the bearing washer in the centre of the dual-mass flywheel **(see illustration)**.

Caution: If the dual-mass flywheel is supported on the drive plate flange, rather than on the bearing washer, the drive plate flange will become distorted and renewal of the dual-mass flywheel will be necessary.

3 With the Audi tools in position on the diaphragm spring fingers, operate the press through a distance of travel of approximately 8.0 to 9.0 mm.

4 Mark the clutch pressure plate and

7.7 Examine the fingers of the diaphragm spring for wear or scoring

dual-mass flywheel in relation to each other. Note that on some models, Audi used a white spot on the flywheel and pressure plate cover to indicate the correct assembly position.

5 Undo the six bolts, ¼ of a turn at a time, securing the pressure plate to the dual-mass flywheel, then release the press. Remove all the bolts, noting that new bolts will be required for refitting, then lift the clutch pressure plate and friction disc from the flywheel.

Inspection

Friction disc and pressure plate

Note: *Due to the amount of work necessary to remove and refit clutch components, it is usually considered good practice to renew the clutch friction disc, pressure plate assembly and release bearing as a matched set, even if only one of these is actually worn enough to require renewal. It is also worth considering the renewal of the clutch components on a preventative basis if the engine and/or transmission have been removed for some other reason.*

6 Clean the pressure plate friction surface, clutch friction disc and flywheel. Do not inhale the dust, as it may contain asbestos which is dangerous to health.

7 Examine the fingers of the diaphragm spring for wear or scoring **(see illustration)**. If the depth of wear exceeds half the thickness of the fingers, a new pressure plate assembly must be fitted.

8 Examine the pressure plate for scoring, cracking, distortion and discoloration. Light scoring is acceptable, but if excessive, a new pressure plate assembly must be fitted. If

7.12 Flywheel warpage – see text

7.9 Examine the friction disc linings for wear and cracking

the distortion of the friction surface exceeds 1.0 mm, renew it.

9 Examine the friction disc linings for wear and cracking, and for contamination with oil or grease **(see illustration)**. The linings are worn excessively if they are worn down to, or near, the rivets. Check the disc hub and splines for wear by temporarily fitting it on the transmission input shaft. Renew the friction disc as necessary.

Dual-mass flywheel

10 The following are guidelines only, but should indicate whether professional inspection is necessary. The dual-mass flywheel should be checked as follows:

Warpage

11 There should be no cracks in the drive surface of the flywheel. If cracks are evident, the flywheel may need renewing.

12 Place a straightedge across the face of the drive surface, and check by trying to insert a feeler gauge between the straightedge and the drive surface **(see illustration)**. The flywheel will normally warp like a bowl – i.e. higher on the outer edge. If the warpage is more than 0.40 mm, the flywheel may need renewing.

Free rotational movement

13 This is the distance the drive surface of the flywheel can be turned independently of the flywheel primary element, using finger effort alone. Move the drive surface in one direction and make a mark where the locating pin aligns with the flywheel edge. Move the drive surface in the other direction (finger pressure only) and make another mark **(see illustration)**. The total of

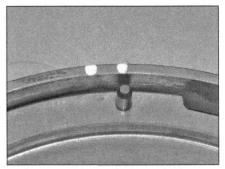

7.13 Flywheel free rotational movement check alignment marks – see text

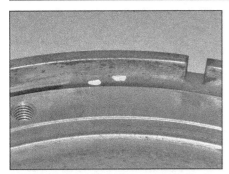

7.15 Flywheel lateral movement check marks – see text

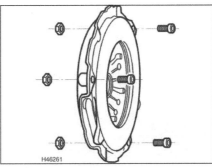

7.18 Insert three 8 mm bolts from the flywheel side, and secure with nuts

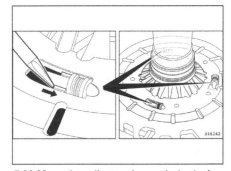

7.20 Move the adjuster ring anti-clockwise to the stop

free movement should not exceed 20.0 mm. If it's more, the flywheel may need renewing.

Total rotational movement

14 This is the total distance the drive surface can be turned independently of the flywheel primary element. Insert two bolts into the clutch pressure plate/damper unit mounting holes, and with the crankshaft/flywheel held stationary, use a lever/pry bar between the bolts and use some effort to move the drive surface fully in one direction – make a mark where the locating pin aligns with the flywheel edge. Now force the drive surface fully in the opposite direction, and make another mark. The total rotational movement should not exceed 44.0 mm. If it does, have the flywheel professionally inspected.

Lateral movement

15 The lateral movement (up and down) of the drive surface in relation to the primary element of the flywheel should not exceed 2.0 mm. If it does, the flywheel may need renewing. This can be checked by pressing the drive surface down on one side into the flywheel (flywheel horizontal) and making an alignment mark between the drive surface and the inner edge of the primary element. Now press down on the opposite side of the drive surface, and make another mark above the original one. The difference between the two marks is the lateral movement **(see illustration)**.

Refitting

16 Ensure that all parts are clean, and free of oil or grease, before reassembling. Note that new pressure plates and clutch covers may be coated with protective grease. It is only permissible to clean the grease away from the friction disc lining contact area. Removal of the grease from other areas will shorten the service life of the clutch.

17 Where a new friction disc is fitted, but the pressure plate is to be re-used, it is necessary to reset the pressure plate adjusting ring prior to assembly as follows.

18 Insert three 8 mm bolts into the pressure plate mounting holes at intervals of 120°. The bolts should be inserted from the flywheel side, and retained by nuts **(see illustration)**.

19 Place the pressure plate face down on the hydraulic press so that only the heads of the

bolts make contact with the press bed, then place a circular spacer over the ends of the diaphragm springs fingers.

20 Use 2 screwdrivers to attempt to rotate the adjuster ring anti-clockwise. Apply just enough pressure with the hydraulic press until it's just possible to move the adjuster ring **(see illustration)**.

21 Once the adjuster ring is against its stop, relieve the pressure on the press and remove the three nuts and bolts from the pressure plate.

Note: *New pressure plates are supplied in this reset position.*

22 Commence reassembly by placing the Audi special tools on the press bed, then position the dual-mass flywheel so that the thrust pad (Audi tool VW 510) makes contact with the bearing washer in the centre of the dual-mass flywheel.

23 Locate the friction disc on the flywheel, with the raised side of the hub facing towards the pressure plate (normally marked 'Getriebeseite' or 'Gearbox side').

24 Place the pressure plate over the friction disc and engage it with the dowels on the flywheel. If refitting the original pressure plate, make sure that the previously made marks are aligned. Centralise the friction disc by inserting the centring mandrel (Audi tool T40171) through the diaphragm spring fingers and into the friction disc hub.

25 Place the Audi tool T10254/3 over the centring mandrell, then apply pressure with the hydraulic press until the pressure plate just

makes contact with the dual-mass flywheel.

26 Insert the new pressure plate retaining bolts and tighten them progressively and in a diagonal sequence to the specified Stage 1 torque setting. When all the bolts have been tightened to the Stage 1 torque setting, tighten them progressively and in a diagonal sequence through the specified Stage 2 angle.

27 Release the hydraulic press and remove all of the special tools.

28 Check the release bearing in the transmission bellhousing for smooth operation, and if necessary renew it with reference to Section 8.

29 Refit the clutch module as described in Section 6.

---

8 Release bearing and lever – removal, inspection and refitting

Removal

1 Remove the transmission as described in Chapter 7A, Section 3.

2 Use a screwdriver to prise the release lever from the ball-stud inside the transmission bellhousing. If this proves difficult, push the spring clip from the pivot end of the release lever by pushing it through the hole. This will release the pivot end of the lever from the ball-stud. Now withdraw the lever together with the release bearing from the guide sleeve **(see illustrations)**.

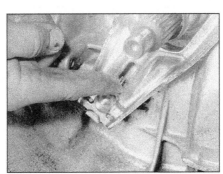

8.2a Push the spring clip to release the arm from the pivot stud

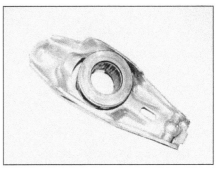

8.2b Release lever and bearing removed from the transmission

3 Use a screwdriver to depress the plastic tabs and separate the bearing from the lever **(see illustrations)**.

Inspection

4 Spin the release bearing by hand, and check it for smooth running. Any tendency to seize or run rough will necessitate renewal of the bearing. If it is to be re-used, wipe it clean with a dry cloth; on no account should the bearing be washed in a liquid solvent, otherwise the internal grease will be removed.

Refitting

5 Apply VAG special grease G 000 150 to all bearings and contact surfaces.
6 Commence refitting by lubricating the ball-stud and pivot with VAG special grease. Also smear a little grease on the release

8.3a Depress the plastic tabs...

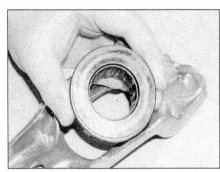

8.3b...and remove the bearing from the lever

bearing surface which contacts the diaphragm spring fingers and the release lever, and also on the guide sleeve. Wipe off any excess grease.

7 Fit the spring onto the release lever. Refit the lever together with the bearing and press the release lever onto the ball-stud until the spring holds it in position **(see illustrations)**.

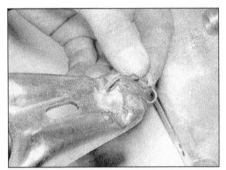

8.7a Locate the spring over the end of the release lever...

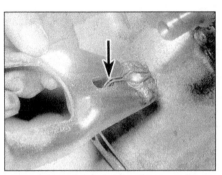

8.7b...and press the spring into the hole...

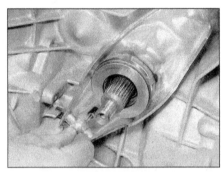

8.7c...then press the release lever onto the ball-stud until the spring clip holds it in position

Chapter 7 Part A
Manual transmission

Contents

Degrees of difficulty

Easy, suitable for novice with little experience	Fairly easy, suitable for beginner with some experience	Fairly difficult, suitable for competent DIY mechanic	Difficult, suitable for experienced DIY mechanic	Very difficult, suitable for expert DIY or professional

Specifications

General

Type	Transmission mounted on rear of engine, with drive flanges to front wheels. Six forward speeds and reverse, synchromesh on all gears, integral final drive
Transmission code	0B1
Lubricant capacities	See Chapter 1, Section 0

Torque wrench settings

	Nm	lbf ft
Clutch module-to-driveplate bolts*	60	44
Clutch slave cylinder mounting bolt*	20	15
Driveshaft left-hand drive flange mounting bracket bolts: *	24	18
Driveshaft-to-transmission flange socket-head bolts*	70	52
Engine-to-transmission bolts:		
M10 steel bolt	65	48
M10 aluminium bolt: *		
Stage 1	15	11
Stage 2	Angle-tighten a further 90°	
M12 aluminium bolts: *		
Stage 1	30	22
Stage 2	Angle-tighten a further 90°	
Exhaust system clamp nuts	23	17
Gearchange linkage push rod and connecting rod bolts	20	15
Gear detection sensor retaining bolt: *		
Stage 1	10	7
Stage 2	Angle-tighten a further 45°	
Gear detector switch	20	15
Neutral position sender retaining bolt: *		
Stage 1	10	7
Stage 2	Angle-tighten a further 45°	
Oil drain plug	45	33
Oil filler plug	45	33
Right-hand driveshaft heat shield bolts	23	17
Selector lever-to-selector shaft retaining nut	20	15
Starter motor mounting bolts	65	48
Steering column universal joint pinch-bolt: *		
Stage 1	30	22
Stage 2	Angle-tighten a further 90°	
Subframe cross-brace guard plate bolts	20	15

Torque wrench settings (continued)

	Nm	lbf ft
Subframe cross-brace retaining bolts: *		
Vehicles with hydraulic power steering:		
Stage 1	90	66
Stage 2	Angle-tighten a further 135°	
Vehicles with electro-mechanical power steering:		
Front bolts (2):		
Stage 1	90	66
Stage 2	Angle-tighten a further 90°	
Rear bolts (4):		
Stage 1	90	66
Stage 2	Angle-tighten a further 135°	
Torque reaction support-to-engine bolts	40	30
Transmission crossmember retaining bolts	70	52

*Use new fasteners

1 General Information

1 The transmission is bolted to the rear of the in-line engine. The front-wheel-drive configuration transmits the power to a differential unit located at the side of the transmission, through driveshafts, to the front wheels. All gears, including reverse, incorporate a synchromesh engagement.
2 Gearchange is by a floor-mounted lever. A selector rod connects the bottom of the gear lever to a selector lever which protrudes from the side of the transmission.

2 Gearchange linkage – adjustment

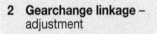

1 Remove the heater/ventilation/air conditioning control panel as described in Chapter 3, Section 9.
2 Ensure the transmission is in the neutral position, then prise up the gear lever gaiter from the centre console using a plastic spatula or similar tool (see illustration). Pull the gaiter up around the gear lever knob.
3 Reach through the gear lever gaiter aperture in the MMI control panel and pull the panel up at the rear to disengage the retaining clips. Lift the panel up and feed the gear lever gaiter through the panel aperture. Disconnect

2.2 Carefully prise up the gear lever gaiter from the centre console

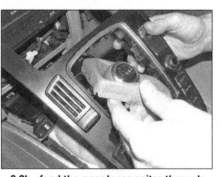

2.3b...feed the gear lever gaiter through the panel aperture...

the wiring connectors and remove the MMI control panel (see illustrations).
4 Undo the two bolts securing the front ashtray to the centre console. Move the ashtray

2.3a Pull the MMI control panel up at the rear to disengage the retaining clips...

2.3c...then turn the panel over and disconnect the wiring connector

rearwards to disengage the front mounting lugs, then disconnect the wiring connector and remove the ashtray (see illustrations).
5 At the base of the gear lever knob, open the

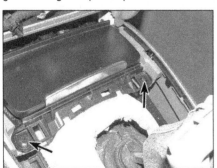

2.4a Undo the two bolts...

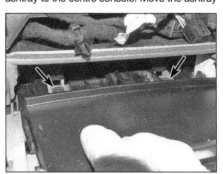

2.4b...disengage the front mounting lugs...

2.4c...then disconnect the wiring connector and remove the ashtray retaining clip and lift the knob, together with the gaiter, off the gear lever.

6 Lift out the foam insulation from around the gear lever.

7 Release the retaining tab on each side of the gear lever boot, and lift the boot at the rear. Disengage the locating tabs at the front and slide the boot up and off the gear lever.

8 Measure the distance between the rear internal edge of the gear lever housing mounting bracket and the protrusion on the side of the housing **(see illustration)**. If the dimension is not as specified, slacken the adjustment bolt in the front of the housing. Move the housing forward or backward as necessary until the specified dimension is obtained, then tighten the adjustment bolt.

9 Slacken the selector rod bolt, located below and to the left of the gear lever housing adjustment bolt and position the gear lever in the dead centre of the ball socket. Now move the lever slightly to the right, so that it is approximately 3° from the vertical **(see illustration)**. Hold the lever in this position and tighten the selector rod bolt securely.

10 Check the correct operation of the selector mechanism, then refit all the components removed for access, using the reverse of the removal procedure..

---

3 Manual transmission – removal and refitting

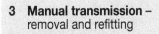

Removal

1 Select a solid, level surface to park the vehicle upon. Give yourself enough space to move around it easily.

2 Apply the handbrake, then jack up the front of the vehicle and support it on axle stands (see *Jacking and vehicle support*). Remove the engine and transmission undertrays.

3 Set the front roadwheels in the straight-ahead position and select 6th gear with the gear lever.

4 Disconnect the battery negative lead as described in Chapter 5, Section 3.

5 Carefully pull the engine top cover off the four retaining pins, one after the other. Do not jerk the cover away and do not try to pull on one side only.

6 Attach an engine compartment crossbrace or hoist to the cylinder head to steady the engine when the transmission is removed.

Models with hydraulic power steering

7 From under the front of the car, undo the retaining bolt and release the power steering fluid line from the left-hand side of the front subframe cross-brace.

Models with electro-mechanical power steering

8 From under the front of the car, detach the wiring harness from the left-hand side of the front subframe cross-brace.

9 If fitted, undo the five bolts and remove the

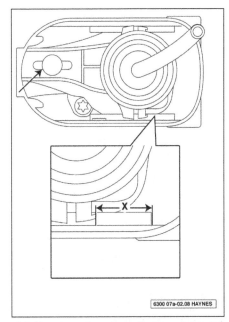

2.8 Gear lever housing adjustment details
X = 25.0 mm

guard plate from the front of the subframe cross-brace.

All models

10 Undo the six retaining bolts and remove the cross-brace from the front subframe **(see illustration)**.

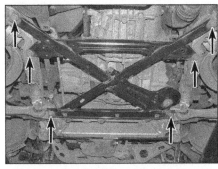

3.10 Undo the retaining bolts and remove the front subframe cross-brace

3.12a Pull off the rubber cover from the bellhousing...

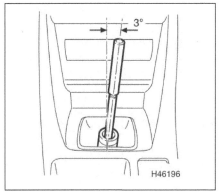

2.9 Position the lever 3° from vertical

11 Undo the steering column intermediate shaft universal joint pinch-bolt, then disengage the universal joint from the steering gear pinion **(see illustration)**. Do not alter the position of the roadwheels or the steering wheel whilst the universal joint is disconnected.

12 Pull off the rubber cover from the lower left-hand side of the transmission bellhousing. Using a spanner or socket on the crankshaft sprocket bolt, turn the crankshaft in the normal direction of rotation (clockwise) until one of the three bolts securing the clutch module to the driveplate on the crankshaft becomes accessible through the bellhousing aperture **(see illustrations)**.

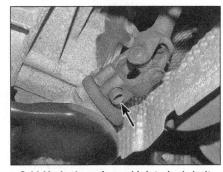

3.11 Undo the universal joint pinch-bolt and disengage the joint from the steering gear pinion

3.12b...then turn the crankshaft until one of the clutch module retaining bolts becomes accessible

13 Undo the first accessible bolt, then turn the crankshaft 120° each time and remove the remaining bolts. Note that new bolts will be required for refitting.

14 Refer to Chapter 4B and remove the exhaust front pipe and catalytic converter/ particulate filter. Take care not to excessively bend the flexible section of the front pipe.

15 If fitted, undo the retaining bolts and remove the left-hand and right-hand subframe shields.

16 Using an Allen key, undo the three retaining bolts and remove the heat shield from over the inner end of the right-hand driveshaft.

17 Remove the left- and right-hand drive-shafts with reference to Chapter 8, Section 2. Note that it is permissible to disconnect the shafts from the transmission drive flanges and tie them to one side.

18 Undo the bolt securing the clutch slave cylinder to the left-hand side of the transmission **(see illustration)**. Withdraw the slave cylinder from its location and tie it up to a convenient place on the underbody.

19 Undo the nut securing the gearchange selector lever to the transmission selector shaft. Using a small puller, pull the selector lever off the shaft.
Caution: Do not attempt to remove the selector lever by prising or knocking it off as damage to the selector shaft may occur. Always use a puller when removing the selector lever.

20 Undo the accessible lower bolts securing the transmission to the engine.

21 Position a trolley jack under the transmission and take the weight. With the transmission securely supported, undo the four bolts securing the transmission crossmember to the vehicle underbody.

22 Lower the jack slightly so that the transmission drops by approximately 80 mm.

23 Note their fitted positions and disconnect all wiring plugs and wiring harnesses from the transmission.

24 Undo the bolt securing the gearchange linkage push rod and the connecting rod to the transmission.

25 Unbolt the starter motor from the engine and move it to one side. There is no need to disconnect the starter wiring.

26 Ensure the transmission is adequately supported, then remove the remaining bolts securing the transmission to the engine.

27 Enlist the help of an assistant, then slowly and carefully lower the transmission and manoeuvre it from the underside of the vehicle. Note that the transmission is heavy.

Refitting

28 Before refitting the transmission, make sure that the location dowels are correctly positioned in the engine cylinder block rear face. It is recommended that the clutch friction disc, pressure plate and release bearing are checked as described in Chapter 6, and renewed if necessary.

29 Refitting the transmission is a reversal of the removal procedure, but note the following points:
a) If the crankshaft driveplate is of the type containing locating pins for the clutch module, ensure that the locating pins engage in the large holes in the clutch module.
b) Hand-tighten the three clutch module-to-driveplate retaining bolts first, then tighten them to the specified torque.
c) Tighten all nuts and bolts to the specified torque where given.
d) On completion, refer to Section 2 and check the gearchange linkage adjustment.

4 Manual transmission overhaul – general information

1 Overhauling a manual transmission unit is a difficult and involved job for the DIY home mechanic. In addition to dismantling and reassembling many small parts, clearances must be precisely measured and, if necessary, changed by selecting shims and spacers. Internal transmission components are also often difficult to obtain and in many instances, extremely expensive. Because of this, if the transmission develops a fault or becomes noisy, the best course of action is to have the unit overhauled by a specialist repairer or to obtain an exchange reconditioned unit.

2 Nevertheless, it is not impossible for the more experienced mechanic to overhaul the transmission if the special tools are available and the job is carried out in a deliberate step-by-step manner, to ensure that nothing is overlooked.

3 The tools necessary for an overhaul include internal and external circlip pliers, bearing pullers, a slide hammer, a set of pin punches, a dial test indicator and possibly a hydraulic press. In addition, a large, sturdy workbench and a vice will be required.

4 During dismantling of the transmission, make careful notes of how each component is fitted to make reassembly easier and accurate.

5 Before dismantling the transmission, it will help if you have some idea of where the problem lies. Certain problems can be closely related to specific areas in the transmission which can make component examination and renewal easier. Refer to the Fault finding Section in this manual for more information.

5 Transmission switches – renewal

Gear detector switch

Note: A gear detector switch is only fitted to vehicles up to model year 2012.

1 The gear detector switch is located on the upper right-hand side of the transmission.

2 Apply the handbrake, then jack up the front of the vehicle and support it on axle stands (see *Jacking and vehicle support*). Remove the engine and transmission undertrays.

3 Undo the three bolts and detach the torque reaction support from the engine **(see illustration)**.

4 Undo the nuts, remove the two bolts and slide the exhaust system clamp rearwards to release the exhaust front pipe from the intermediate pipe **(see illustration)**. Suitably tie up the front pipe to one side of the intermediate pipe.

5 Position a trolley jack under the transmission and take the weight. With the transmission securely supported, undo the four bolts securing the transmission crossmember to the vehicle underbody.

3.18 Undo the retaining bolt and withdraw the slave cylinder from the transmission

5.3 Torque reaction support retaining bolts

5.4 Undo the nuts, remove the bolts and slide the exhaust system clamp rearwards

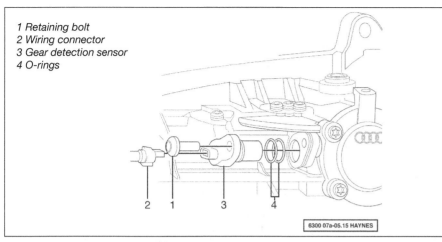

1 Retaining bolt
2 Wiring connector
3 Gear detection sensor
4 O-rings

5.15 Gear detection sensor details

6 Lower the jack slightly so that the transmission drops by approximately 80 mm.
7 Disconnect the wiring connector, then unscrew the gear detector switch using a 24 mm socket.
8 Refit the switch using the reverse of the removal procedure, tightening all nuts and bolts to the specified torque (where given).

Gear detection sensor

Note: A gear detection sensor is fitted to vehicles from model year 2013 onward
9 The gear detection sensor is located on the upper right-hand side of the transmission.
10 Apply the handbrake, then jack up the front of the vehicle and support it on axle stands (see Jacking and vehicle support. Remove the engine and transmission undertrays.
11 Undo the nuts, remove the two bolts and slide the exhaust system clamp rearwards to release the exhaust front pipe from the intermediate pipe **(see illustration 5.4)**. Suitably tie up the front pipe to one side of the intermediate pipe.
12 Position a trolley jack under the transmission and take the weight. With the transmission securely supported, undo

the four bolts securing the transmission crossmember to the vehicle underbody.
13 Lower the jack slightly so that the transmission drops by approximately 80 mm.
14 Disconnect the gear detection sensor wiring connector.
15 Undo the retaining bolt and pull the sensor out of its location in the transmission **(see illustration)**. Recover the two O-rings from the sensor.
16 Refit the sensor using the reverse of the removal procedure, bearing in mind the following points:
a) Renew the two O-rings and lubricate them with gear oil.
b) If the sensor is a tight fit in the transmission casing, carefully push it in using a suitable tool such as a hammer handle. Do not knock the sensor in or attempt to draw it in by tightening the retaining bolt.
c) Renew the sensor retaining bolt.
d) Tighten all nuts and bolts to the specified torque (where given).

Neutral position sender

Note: A neutral position sender is only fitted to vehicles with a start/stop system

17 The neutral position sender is located on the left-hand side of the transmission, above the clutch slave cylinder.
18 Apply the handbrake, then jack up the front of the vehicle and support it on axle stands (see Jacking and vehicle support). Remove the engine and transmission undertrays.
19 Place the transmission in 4th gear.
20 Disconnect the neutral position sender wiring connector.
21 Undo the retaining bolt and pull the sender out of its location in the transmission. Recover the O-ring from the sender.
22 Refit the sender using the reverse of the removal procedure, bearing in mind the following points:
a) Renew the sender O-ring.
b) Renew the sender retaining bolt.
c) Tighten all nuts and bolts to the specified torque (where given).

6 Oil seals – renewal

Driveshaft flange oil seal – right-hand side

1 Apply the handbrake, then jack up the front of the vehicle and support it on axle stands (see Jacking and vehicle support). Remove the right-hand roadwheel, then remove the engine and transmission undertrays.
2 Using an Allen key, undo the three retaining bolts and remove the heat shield from over the inner end of the right-hand driveshaft.
3 Remove the right-hand drive- shafts with reference to Chapter 8, Section 2. Note that it is permissible to disconnect the shaft from the transmission drive flange and tie it to one side.
4 Position a suitable container beneath the transmission to catch spilled oil.
5 The drive flange is held in the differential sun gear by an internal circlip, and the flange must be pulled outwards to release the circlip. To do this, locate a suitable distance piece (such as a chisel) between the flange and the transmission casing, then screw a bolt through the flange onto the distance piece. As the bolt is tightened, the flange will be forced outwards and the circlip released from its groove **(see illustration)**. If the flange is tight, turn it 180° and repeat the removal procedure.
6 With the flange out, note the fitted depth of the oil seal in the housing, then prise it out using a large flat-bladed screwdriver **(see illustration)**.
7 Clean all traces of dirt from the area around the oil seal aperture, then apply a smear of grease to the lips of the new oil seal.
8 Ensure the seal is correctly positioned, with its sealing lip facing inwards, and tap it squarely into position, using a suitable tubular drift (such as a socket) which bears

6.5 Screw a bolt through the driveshaft flange and onto a distance piece placed against the transmission casing

6.6 Note the depth of the fitted seal, then prise it out using a flat-bladed screwdriver

only on the hard outer edge of the seal **(see illustration)**.

9 It is recommended that the circlip on the inner end of the drive flange is renewed whenever the flange is removed. To do this, mount the flange in a soft-jawed vice, then prise off the old circlip and fit the new one **(see illustration)**. Lightly grease the circlip.

10 Insert the drive flange through the oil seal and engage it with the differential gear. Using a suitable drift, drive the flange fully into the gear until the circlip is felt to engage.

11 The remainder of reassembly is the reverse of the removal procedure. Refit the driveshaft as described in Chapter 8, Section 2, and check the transmission oil level as described in Chapter 1, Section 13.

Driveshaft flange oil seal – left-hand side

12 To gain access to the driveshaft flange oil seal on the left-hand side, the transmission must be removed from the engine and the differential must be removed from the transmission. This is an involved and complicated operation requiring numerous Audi special tools and is considered beyond the scope of this manual. For this reason oil seal renewal should be entrusted to an Audi dealer or suitably equipped independent garage.

Input shaft oil seal

13 The transmission must be removed for access to the input shaft oil seal. Refer to Section 3 of this Chapter.

14 Remove the clutch module as described in Chapter 6, Section 6.

15 Remove the clutch release bearing and lever as described in Chapter 6, Section 8.

6.8 Using a suitable tubular drift (such as a socket), tap the seal squarely into position

16 Using a suitable hooked tool, carefully prise the oil seal out of the transmission casing.

17 Wipe clean the oil seal location in the transmission.

18 Smear a little multipurpose grease on the lips of the new oil seal, and locate the seal in the transmission with the open side facing inward. Tap the seal squarely into position, using a suitable drift which bears only on the hard outer edge of the seal, until it is against the stop.

19 Refit the clutch release bearing and lever as described in Chapter 6, Section 8.

20 Refit the clutch module as described in Chapter 6, Section 6.

Selector shaft oil seal

21 Apply the handbrake, then jack up the front of the vehicle and support it on axle stands (see *Jacking and vehicle support*). Remove the engine and transmission undertrays.

22 Undo the nut securing the gearchange selector lever to the transmission selector

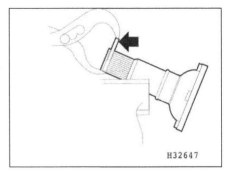

6.9 Fit a new circlip (arrowed) to the groove in the transmission's drive flange

shaft. Using a small puller, pull the selector lever off the shaft.

Note: *Do not attempt to remove the selector lever by prising or knocking it off as damage to the selector shaft may occur. Always use a puller when removing the selector lever.*

23 Using a small screwdriver, carefully prise the oil seal from the housing, taking care not to damage the surface of the selector shaft or housing.

24 Wipe clean the oil seal seating and selector shaft, then smear a little multipurpose grease on the new oil seal lips and locate the seal over the end of the shaft. Make sure the closed side of the seal faces outwards.

25 Tap the seal squarely into position, using a suitable drift which bears only on the outer edge of the seal. The seal should be inserted until it is 2.0 mm below the surface of the transmission.

26 Refit the selector lever to the shaft and tighten the nut to the specified torque.

27 Refit the engine and transmission undertrays, then lower the vehicle to the ground.

Chapter 7 Part B
Multitronic transmission

Contents

Degrees of difficulty

Easy, suitable for novice with little experience	**Fairly easy,** suitable for beginner with some experience	**Fairly difficult,** suitable for competent DIY mechanic	**Difficult,** suitable for experienced DIY mechanic	**Very difficult,** suitable for expert DIY or professional

Specifications

General

Type	Constantly variable transmission with multilink steel belt and multiplate clutch, in a magnesium casing
Designation	0AW
Lubricant capacities	*Lubricants and fluids* in *Weekly checks*

Torque wrench settings

	Nm	lbf ft
Driveshaft left-hand drive flange mounting bracket bolts: *		
Stage 1	10	7
Stage 2	Angle-tighten a further 90°	
Driveshaft-to-transmission flange socket-head bolts*	70	52
Dual-mass flywheel-to-driveplate bolts*	60	44
Engine-to-transmission bolts:		
M10 steel bolt	65	48
M10 aluminium bolt: *		
Stage 1	15	11
Stage 2	Angle-tighten a further 90°	
M12 aluminium bolts: *		
Stage 1	30	22
Stage 2	Angle-tighten a further 90°	
Exhaust system clamp nuts	23	17
Final drive oil filler/level plug*	30	22
Right-hand driveshaft heat shield bolts	23	17
Starter motor mounting bolts	65	48
Steering column universal joint pinch-bolt: *		
Stage 1	30	22
Stage 2	Angle-tighten a further 90°	
Subframe cross-brace guard plate bolts	20	15
Subframe cross-brace retaining bolts: *		
Vehicles with hydraulic power steering:		
Stage 1	90	66
Stage 2	Angle-tighten a further 135°	
Vehicles with electro-mechanical power steering:		
Front bolts (2):		
Stage 1	90	66
Stage 2	Angle-tighten a further 90°	
Rear bolts (4):		
Stage 1	90	66
Stage 2	Angle-tighten a further 135°	
Torque reaction support-to-engine bolts	40	30
Transmission crossmember retaining bolts	70	52
Transmission fluid filler/level plug*	30	22
Transmission mounting to crossmember nuts	20	15

*Use new fasteners

1 General Information

1 The Multitronic transmission is a continuously variable transmission, with a steel link-plate chain running under tension between two pairs of hydraulically adjustable pulley halves. As the pulley halves move towards or away from each other, the ratio between them changes. This provides a wide range of effective ratios that transfers the engine power in a seamless manner, and allows the engine to always operate in its most economical speed range. Drive between the engine and transmission input shaft is controlled by a multiplate clutch, and the differential is enclosed in the same transmission casing. The operation of the whole system is controlled electronically by a dedicated electronic control unit (ECU) located within the transmission end cover.
2 Due to the complexity of the transmission and its control system, major repairs and overhaul operations should be left to an Audi dealer or transmission specialist, who will be equipped to carry out fault diagnosis and repair. The information in this Chapter is therefore limited.
Caution: The Multitronic transmission is fitted into a casing made from a magnesium alloy. In order to eliminate the possibility of contact corrosion, only renew fasteners with those approved by Audi – consult you dealer or spares specialist.

2 Multitronic transmission – removal and refitting

Removal
Note: *The removal and refitting of the Multitronic transmission entails the disconnection of the transmission fluid supply and return lines which will result in the loss of a quantity of transmission fluid. As it is not possible to fill or top-up the transmission without the use of a dedicated Audi transmission fluid filling aparatus and diagnostic test equipment, the contents of this Section is intended to be for information only, or for use if the Audi equipment is available.*
1 Select a solid, level surface to park the vehicle upon. Give yourself enough space to move around it easily.
2 Apply the handbrake, then jack up the front of the vehicle and support it on axle stands (see *Jacking and vehicle support*). Set the front wheels in the straight-ahead position then remove the engine and transmission undertrays.
3 Disconnect the battery negative lead as described in Chapter 5, Section 3.
4 Carefully pull the engine top cover off the four retaining pins, one after the other. Do not

2.12 Undo the retaining bolts and remove the front subframe cross-brace

jerk the cover away and do not try to pull on one side only.
5 Remove the plenum chamber partition panel as described in Chapter 11, Section 21.
6 Undo the retaining bolt and move the bracket containing the exhaust gas pressure sensor and pressure differential sender to one side.
7 Undo the four upper bolts securing the transmission to the engine. Note that one of the bolts also secures the starter motor and contains an additional spacer sleeve.
8 Attach an engine compartment crossbrace or hoist to the cylinder head to steady the engine when the transmission is removed.

Models with hydraulic power steering
9 From under the front of the car, undo the retaining bolt and release the power steering fluid line from the left-hand side of the front subframe cross-brace.

Models with electro-mechanical power steering
10 From under the front of the car, detach the wiring harness from the left-hand side of the front subframe cross-brace.
11 If fitted, undo the five bolts and remove the guard plate from the front of the subframe cross-brace.

All models
12 Undo the six retaining bolts and remove

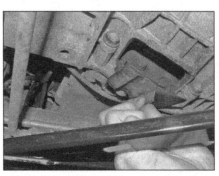
2.16a Pull off the rubber cover from the bellhousing...

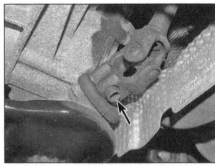
2.13 Undo the universal joint pinch-bolt and disengage the joint from the steering gear pinion

the cross-brace from the front subframe **(see illustration)**.
13 Undo the steering column intermediate shaft universal joint pinch-bolt, then disengage the universal joint from the steering gear pinion **(see illustration)**. Do not alter the position of the roadwheels or the steering wheel whilst the universal joint is disconnected.
14 Undo the bolt securing the automatic transmission fluid pipes to the side of the transmission.
15 Be prepared for fluid spillage, then undo the remaining bolts and disconnect the transmission fluid pipes from the transmission. Suitably plug all disconnected pipes and unions to prevent further fluid loss and protect against dirt ingress.
16 Pull off the rubber cover from the lower left-hand side of the transmission bellhousing. Using a spanner or socket on the crankshaft sprocket bolt, turn the crankshaft in the normal direction of rotation (clockwise) until one of the three bolts securing the dual-mass flywheel to the driveplate on the crankshaft becomes accessible through the bellhousing aperture **(see illustrations)**.
17 Undo the first accessible bolt, then turn the crankshaft 120° each time and remove the remaining bolts. Note that new bolts will be required for refitting.
18 Refer to Chapter 4B, Section 8 and

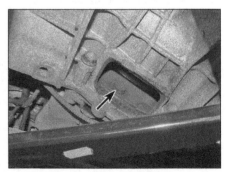
2.16b...then turn the crankshaft until one of the dual-mass flywheel retaining bolts becomes accessible

remove the exhaust system front pipe. Take care not to excessively bend the flexible section of the front pipe.

19 If fitted, undo the retaining bolts and remove the left-hand and right-hand subframe shields.

20 Using an Allen key, undo the three retaining bolts and remove the heat shield from over the inner end of the right-hand driveshaft.

21 Remove the left- and right-hand drive-shafts with reference to Chapter 8, Section 2. Note that it is permissible to disconnect the shafts from the transmission drive flanges and tie them to one side.

22 Using a suitable forked tool carefully prise the ball socket on the end of the selector cable off the transmission selector lever. Undo the two bolts securing the selector cable support bracket to the transmission and move the selector cable to one side.

23 Disconnect the wiring harness at the end of transmission by rotating the locking element anti-clockwise.

24 Position a trolley jack under the transmission and take the weight. With the transmission securely supported, undo the four bolts securing the transmission crossmember to the vehicle underbody. Undo the three nuts securing the transmission crossmember to the transmission mounting and remove the crossmember.

25 Note their fitted positions and disconnect or remove any remaining wiring, hoses brackets or components likely to impede transmission removal.

26 Unbolt the starter motor from the engine and move it to one side. There is no need to disconnect the starter wiring.

27 Ensure the transmission is adequately supported, then remove the remaining bolts securing the transmission to the engine.

28 Enlist the help of an assistant, then slowly and carefully lower the transmission and manoeuvre it from the underside of the vehicle. Note that the transmission is heavy.

Refitting

29 Before refitting the transmission, make sure that the location dowels are correctly positioned in the engine cylinder block rear face. It is recommended that the clutch friction disc, pressure plate and release bearing are checked as described in Chapter 6, and renewed if necessary.

30 Refitting the transmission is a reversal of the removal procedure, but note the following points:
a) *Renew all self-locking nuts and bolts, seals, O-rings and gaskets.*
b) *Hand-tighten the three dual-mass flywheel-to-driveplate retaining bolts first, then tighten them to the specified torque.*
c) *Tighten all nuts and bolts to the specified torque where given.*
d) *Bearing in mind the information contained in the note at the start of this Section, check the final drive oil level and*

transmission fluid level as described in Chapter 1 Section 26.
e) *On completion, refer to Section 5 and check the selector cable adjustment.*

3 Multitronic transmission overhaul – general information

1 In the event of a fault occurring, it will be necessary to establish whether the fault is electrical, mechanical or hydraulic in nature, before repair work can be contemplated. Diagnosis requires detailed knowledge of the transmission's operation and construction, as well as access to specialised test equipment, and so is deemed to be beyond the scope of this manual. It is therefore essential that problems with the automatic transmission are referred to an Audi dealer or specialist for assessment.

2 Note that a faulty transmission should not be removed before the vehicle has been assessed by a dealer, as fault diagnosis is carried out with the transmission in situ.

4 Dual-mass flywheel – removal, inspection and refitting

Removal

1 Remove the multitronic transmission as described in Section 2. With the transmission removed, position it in such a way that it is inclined slightly to the rear.

2 Undo the three bolts securing the left-hand drive flange mounting bracket to the transmission casing.

3 Pull the drive flange out of the transmission, taking care not to damage the differential inner oil seal as the splines on the inner end of the drive flange pass through it **(see illustration)**. If the drive flange cannot be removed by hand, attach a suitable slide hammer to the flange end and use the slide hammer to draw the flange out.

4 If available, attach Audi special tool T40170 to the dual-mass flywheel and secure it in place with the retaining nut. This special tool is essentially just a handle for you to hold when lifting the flywheel off the transmission input shaft. In the absence of the Audi tool, a long bolt secured to the flywheel with two nuts could be used instead.

5 Turn the dual-mass flywheel so that the holding tool is at the top. Take hold of the tool with one hand, and using your other hand to keep the flywheel upright, carefully pull the flywheel off the transmission input shaft. As the flywheel is being removed, take care not to damage the oil seals and needle bearing in the flywheel.

6 With the flywheel removed, lay it down

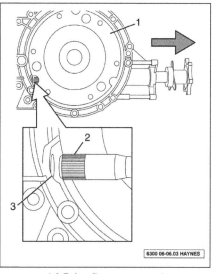

4.3 Drive flange removal

1 *Dual-mass flywheel*
2 *Drive flange splines*
3 *Differential inner oil seal*

with the driveplate flange facing upward. The driveplate flange could become distorted if the weight of the flywheel is allowed to rest on it.

Inspection

7 Carry out a thorough inspection of the dual-mass flywheel as described in Chapter 6, Section 7.

Refitting

8 Refitting is the reverse sequence to removal, bearing in mind the following points:
a) *Apply a thin coating of VAG special grease G 000 100 to the transmission input shaft splines.*
b) *Slide the guide flange into the transmission keeping it level as it enters the differential inner oil seal.*
c) *Tighten all nuts and bolts to the specified torque (where given).*
d) *Refit the transmission as described in Section 2.*

5 Selector cable – removal, refitting and adjustment

Removal

1 Ensure the handbrake is fully applied, then move the selector lever to position D.

2 Prise up the selector lever gaiter retaining frame from the centre console using a plastic spatula or similar tool **(see illustration 2.2 in Chapter 7A)**. Pull the gaiter up around the selector lever knob.

3 Using Audi special tool T40031 or alternatively a suitable long-reach bit,

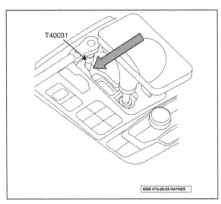

5.3 Using the Audi tool or a long-reach bit, slacken the selector cable clamping bolt approximately 1 turn

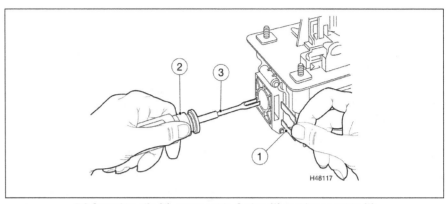

5.6 Securing clip (1), outer cable O-ring (2) and inner cable (3)

slacken the clamping bolt at the rear end of the selector cable approximately 1 turn **(see illustration)**.

4 Apply the handbrake, then jack up the front of the vehicle and support it on axle stands (see *Jacking and vehicle support*). Remove the engine and transmission undertrays.

5 On some models, a noise insulation panel is fitted below the selector lever housing. Prise free the 4 washers securing the panel and slide it forwards. Note that the washers must be renewed.

6 Slide out the clip securing the cable to the housing, and pull the cable forwards from the housing **(see illustration)**.

7 Using a suitable forked tool carefully prise the ball socket on the end of the selector cable off the transmission selector lever. Undo the two bolts securing the selector cable support bracket to the transmission and remove the cable from under the car.

Refitting and adjustment

8 Slide the selector cable through the hole in the noise insulation panel (where fitted). Fit a new O-ring to the outer cable then engage the cable with the selector lever housing.

9 Secure the selector cable with the retaining clip. Note that the angled end of the retaining clip must be towards the selector lever housing.

10 Where applicable, attach the noise insulation panel to the lever housing using new washers.

11 Move the selector lever on the transmission as far rearwards as possible. This should place the transmission in park P. Make sure that both front wheels are locked by attempting to turn them in the same direction at the same time.

Note: *Even though the transmission is locked, it will still be possible to turn the front wheels in opposite directions, since the differential gears are able move in relation to each other.*

12 Now move the selector lever on the transmission forward by three notches to place the transmission in position D.

13 Check that the selector lever inside the car is also still in position D.

14 Carefully press the ball socket on the selector cable back onto the transmission selector lever.

15 Attach the selector cable support bracket to the transmission and secure with the two bolts tightened securely.

16 Tighten the lock nuts to secure the cable to the support bracket.

17 Using Audi special tool T40031 or alternatively a suitable long-reach bit, tighten the clamping bolt at the rear end of the selector cable **(see illustration 5.3)**.

18 Refit the undertrays and lower the car to the ground.

19 Refit the selector lever gaiter to the centre console.

Chapter 8
Driveshafts

Contents

Degrees of difficulty

Easy, suitable for novice with little experience		**Fairly easy,** suitable for beginner with some experience		**Fairly difficult,** suitable for competent DIY mechanic		**Difficult,** suitable for experienced DIY mechanic		**Very difficult,** suitable for expert DIY or professional	

Specifications

Lubrication
Type:
  Outer constant velocity joints. . . . . G 000 603 grease
  Inner constant velocity joints . . . . G 000 605 grease
Amount per joint:
  Outer joint:
    85 mm diameter joint:
      Amount in the joint . . . . 64 g
      Amount in the gaiter . . . . 60 g
    88 mm diameter joint:
      Amount in the joint . . . . 50 g
      Amount in the gaiter . . . . 40 g
    94 mm diameter joint:
      Amount in the joint . . . . 100 g
      Amount in the gaiter . . . . 94 g
    99 mm diameter joint:
      Amount in the joint . . . . 100 g
      Amount in the gaiter . . . . 180 g
    100 mm diameter joint:
      Amount in the joint . . . . 80 g
      Amount in the gaiter . . . . 60 g
    106 mm diameter joint:
      Amount in the joint . . . . 100 g
      Amount in the gaiter . . . . 180 g
  Inner joint:
    Amount in the joint . . . . 80 g
    Amount in the gaiter . . . . 80 g

Torque wrench settings

	Nm	lbf ft
Driveshaft-to-transmission flange socket-head bolts*.	70	52
Hub bolt: *		
Stage 1.	200	148
Stage 2.	Angle-tighten a further 180°	
Roadwheel bolts.	120	89
Upper suspension link arm pinch-bolt/nut*	40	30

*Use new fasteners

1 General Information

1 Drive is transmitted from the differential to the front wheels by means of two steel driveshafts. Both driveshafts are splined at their outer ends, to accept the wheel hubs, and are secured to the hub by a large bolt. The inner end of each driveshaft is bolted to the transmission drive flanges.

2 Constant velocity (CV) joints are fitted to the driveshafts, to ensure the smooth and efficient transmission of drive at all the angles possible as the roadwheels move up-and-down with the suspension, and as they turn from side-to-side under steering. The outer joint is of the ball-and-cage type, and the inner joint is of the tripod type.

3 Rubber or plastic gaiters are secured over both CV joints with steel clips. These contain the grease that is packed into the joint, and also protect the joint from the ingress of dirt and debris.

2 Driveshafts – removal and refitting

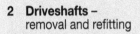

Removal

1 Where fitted, remove the cap from the centre of the wheel, then slacken the hub bolt 90° (one quarter of a turn) with the vehicle resting on its wheels **(see illustration)**. Also slacken the wheel bolts.

2 Chock the rear wheels, firmly apply the handbrake, then jack up the front of the car and support it on axle stands (see *Jacking and vehicle support*). Remove the appropriate front roadwheel. Whilst the wheel is removed, refit at least one of the wheel bolts to ensure the brake disc remains correctly positioned on the hub.

2.1 Prise out the cap in the centre of the wheel

3 Remove the retaining fasteners and remove the transmission undershield to gain access to the driveshafts.

4 Remove the hub bolt. If the bolt was not slackened with the wheels on the ground, refit at least two roadwheel bolts to the front hub, tightening them securely, then have an assistant firmly depress the brake pedal to prevent the front hub from rotating, whilst you slacken and remove the hub bolt.

5 Slacken and remove the bolts securing the inner driveshaft joint to the transmission drive flange. Support the driveshaft by suspending it with wire or string – do not allow it to hang under its weight, or the joint may be damaged.

6 Depending on the model, it may now be possible to pull the inner end of the driveshaft downwards, and slide it from the wheel hub. However, where there is insufficient clearance, remove the upper link arms pinch-bolt, and pull out both upper link arms' balljoints from the hub carrier **(see illustration)**. It should now be possible to pull the upper end of the hub carrier outwards slightly, and slide the driveshaft from place. Discard the pinch-bolt and nut, new ones must be fitted.

Caution: Do not unbolt the steering track rod from the hub carrier.

Caution: Do not allow the vehicle to rest on its wheels with one or both

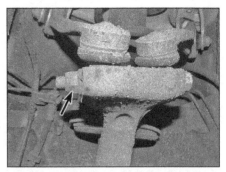

2.6 If necessary, remove the pinch-bolt and pull up the two balljoints

driveshafts removed, as damage to the wheel bearings may result. If moving the vehicle is unavoidable, temporarily insert the outer end of the driveshaft in the hubs and tighten the driveshaft bolts. Support the inner ends of the driveshafts to avoid damage.

Refitting

7 Thoroughly clean the driveshaft outer joint and hub splines and the mating surfaces of the inner joint and transmission flange. Check that all gaiter clips are securely fastened.

8 Manoeuvre the driveshaft into position, engaging the splines with those of the hub, and slide the outer joint into position. Fit the new hub bolt, tightening it by hand only at this stage **(see illustration)**.

9 Align the driveshaft inner joint with the transmission flange then refit the retaining bolts. Tighten all bolts by hand then, working in a diagonal sequence, tighten them to the specified torque **(see illustration)**.

10 Where applicable, refit the front and rear upper suspension links arms to the top of the hub, insert the new pinch-bolt, then fit the new retaining nut and tighten it to the specified torque.

11 Tighten the new hub bolt to the stage one torque setting. Prevent the driveshaft/hub

2.8 Fit a new driveshaft retaining bolt

2.9 Tighten the inner joint-to-transmission flange bolts to the specified torque

from rotating, by having an assistant depress the brake pedal.

12 Refit the roadwheel then lower the vehicle to the ground and tighten the wheel bolts to the specified torque.

13 With the vehicle resting on its wheels, tighten the hub bolt to the specified Stage 2 torque angle, using an angle-measuring gauge to ensure accuracy. If an angle gauge is not available, use white paint to make alignment marks between the bolt head and hub/wheel prior to tightening; the marks can then be used to check that the bolt has been rotated through the correct angle. Where applicable, refit the cap to the centre of the wheel.

3 Driveshafts – overhaul

1 Remove the driveshaft from the vehicle as described in Section 2 and proceed as described under the relevant sub-heading **(see illustration)**.

Outer joint

2 Secure the driveshaft in a vice equipped with soft jaws, and release the gaiter retaining clips. If necessary, the retaining clips can be cut to release them.

3 Fold back the rubber gaiter to expose the outer constant velocity joint. Scoop out the excess grease and dispose of it. If necessary, cut the boot from the shaft.

4 Use a hammer and suitable soft metal drift to sharply strike the inner member of the outer joint to drive it off the end of the shaft, taking great care not to damage the joint **(see illustration)**.

5 Once the joint assembly has been removed, remove the circlip from the groove in the driveshaft splines, and discard it. A new circlip must be fitted on reassembly.

6 If still in place, slide the rubber gaiter off the end of the driveshaft.

7 With the constant velocity joint removed from the driveshaft, thoroughly clean the joint using paraffin, or a suitable solvent, and dry it thoroughly. Carry out a visual inspection of the joint.

8 Move the inner splined driving member from side-to-side, to expose each ball in turn at the top of its track. Examine the balls for cracks, flat spots, or signs of surface pitting.

9 Inspect the ball tracks on the inner and outer members. If the tracks have widened, the balls will no longer be a tight fit. At the same time, check the ball cage windows for wear or cracking between the windows.

10 If the constant velocity joint is found to be worn or damaged, it will be necessary to renew the joint as a complete unit. If the joint is in satisfactory condition, obtain a repair kit; the genuine Audi kit consists of a new gaiter, circlips, retaining clips, and the correct type and quantity of grease.

11 Tape over the splines on the end of the

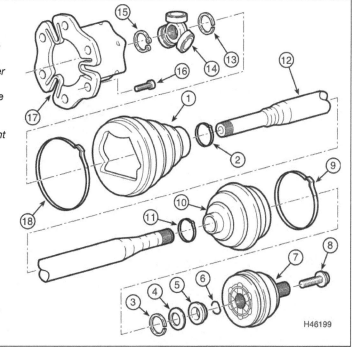

1 Gaiter
2 Clip
3 Circlip (where fitted)
4 Dished washer (where fitted)
5 Spacer (where fitted)
6 Circlip
7 Outer constant velocity joint
8 Hub bolt
9 Clip
10 Gaiter
11 Clip
12 Driveshaft
13 Circlip
14 Triple roller tripod
15 Circlip
16 Multipoint socket head bolts
17 Joint housing
18 Clip

3.1 Driveshaft details

driveshaft, then fit the retaining clip to the small diameter, and slide the new gaiter onto the shaft **(see illustration)**. Remove the tape.

12 Fit the new circlip, making sure it is correctly located in the driveshaft groove **(see illustration)**.

13 Work the specified quantity of the grease supplied well into the ball tracks of the outer joint then fill the gaiter with the remaining grease **(see illustration)**.

14 Locate the outer joint on the driveshaft splines and slide it on until the inner member

3.4 Drive the inner member of the outer joint from the end of the driveshaft

3.11 Slide the new gaiter onto the shaft

3.12 Fit a new circlip to the shaft

3.13 Work the grease well into the ball tracks of the outer joint

3.15 Lift the inner lip of the gaiter to equalise air pressure

3.16a Fit the new clip to the gaiter...

3.16b...and compress its raised section...

3.16c...until it looks like this

3.19 Check the inner joint rollers and bearings for wear

abuts the circlip. Compress the circlip into the outer shaft groove with screwdrivers or pliers, and at the same time tap the joint outer member sharply with hammer and soft-metal drift to force the inner member over the circlip and fully onto the driveshaft. Pull on the joint assembly to make sure the joint is securely retained by the circlip.

15 Locate the outer lip of the gaiter in the groove on the joint outer member and lift the inner lip of the gaiter to equalise the air pressure inside (see illustration).

16 Fit the outer retaining clip to the gaiter and secure both clips in position by compressing its raised section. In the absence of the special tool, carefully compress each clip using a pair of side-cutters taking great care

not to cut through the clip (see illustrations).

17 Check that the constant velocity joint moves freely in all directions, then refit the driveshaft to the vehicle as described in Section 2.

Inner joint

18 Remove the outer constant velocity joint as described above in paragraphs 2 to 6, then release the retaining clips and slide the inner gaiter from the driveshaft. If necessary, cut the gaiter to release it from the shaft. Note that the joint cannot be dismantled without access to an hydraulic press and special pullers.

19 Thoroughly clean the joint using paraffin, or a suitable solvent, and dry it thoroughly. Check the tripod joint bearings and joint outer

member for signs of wear, pitting or scuffing on their bearing surfaces. Check that the bearing rollers rotate smoothly and easily around the tripod joint, with no traces of roughness (see illustration).

20 If on inspection the tripod joint or outer member reveal signs of wear or damage, it will be necessary to renew the complete driveshaft assembly, since the joint is not available separately. If the joint is in satisfactory condition, obtain a repair kit consisting of a new gaiter, retaining clips, and the correct type and quantity of grease. Although not strictly necessary, it is also recommended that the outer constant velocity joint gaiter is renewed, regardless of its apparent condition.

21 On reassembly, pack the inner joint with the grease supplied. Work the grease well into the bearing tracks and rollers, while twisting the joint (see illustration).

22 Clean the shaft, using emery cloth to remove any rust or sharp edges which may damage the gaiter. Tape over the splines on the end of the driveshaft and grease the driveshaft ridges to prevent possible damage to the inner gaiter on installation.

23 Ease the inner gaiter and small clip onto and along the driveshaft and carefully lever it over the driveshaft ridge, taking care not to damage it (see illustrations).

24 Locate the outer lip in the groove on the joint outer member and seat the inner lip correctly on the driveshaft.

3.21 Work the grease well into the bearing tracks and rollers

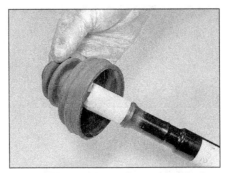

3.23a Tape over the splines and slide the inner gaiter into position...

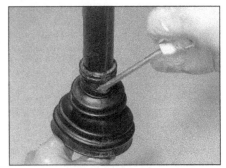

3.23b...levering it carefully over the driveshaft ridge

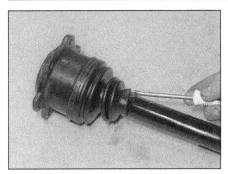

3.25 Lift the inner lip to equalise the pressure

25 Lift the inner lip of the gaiter to equalise the air pressure inside then fit both the inner and outer retaining clips **(see illustration)**.

Secure each clip in position using the method described in paragraph 16.

26 Refit the outer constant velocity joint as described in paragraphs 11 to 17.

27 Check that both constant velocity joints move freely in all directions, then refit the driveshaft to the vehicle as described in Section 2.

4 Driveshaft overhaul – general information

1 If any of the checks described in Chapter 1 reveal wear in any driveshaft joint, first remove the roadwheel centre cap (where fitted) and check that the hub bolt is tight. If the bolt is loose, obtain a new bolt and tighten it to the specified torque (see Section 2). If the bolt is tight, refit the centre cap and repeat the check on the other hub bolt.

2 Road test the vehicle, and listen for a metallic clicking from the front as the vehicle is driven slowly in a circle on full-lock. If a clicking noise is heard, this indicates wear in the outer constant velocity joint; this means that the joint must be renewed.

3 If vibration, consistent with roadspeed, is felt through the car when accelerating, there is a possibility of wear in the inner constant velocity joints.

4 To check the joints for wear, remove the driveshafts, then dismantle them as described in Section 3 ; if any wear or free play is found, the affected joint must be renewed. Refer to your Audi dealer or parts specialist for information on the availability of driveshaft components.

Chapter 9
Braking system

Contents

Degrees of difficulty

Easy, suitable for novice with little experience	**Fairly easy,** suitable for beginner with some experience	**Fairly difficult,** suitable for competent DIY mechanic	**Difficult,** suitable for experienced DIY mechanic	**Very difficult,** suitable for expert DIY or professional

Specifications

Front brakes

Type	Disc, with single-piston FN3 or FBC sliding calipers
Disc diameter:	
FN3 calipers	314.0 mm
FBC calipers	320.0 or 345.0 mm
Disc thickness:	
FN3 calipers:	
New	25.0 mm
Minimum.	23.0 mm
FBC calipers:	
New	30.0 mm
Minimum.	28.0 mm
Maximum disc run-out	0.05 mm
Brake pad wear limit (including backing plate).	10.0 mm

Rear brakes

Type	Disc, with single-piston sliding caliper and integral electronic handbrake
Disc diameter	300.0 or 330.0 mm
Disc thickness:	
New:	
300.0 mm diameter disc.	12.0 mm
330.0 mm diameter disc.	22.0 mm
Minimum:	
300.0 mm diameter disc.	10.0 mm
330.0 mm diameter disc.	20.0 mm
Maximum disc run-out	0.05 mm
Brake pad wear limit (including backing plate).	7.0 mm

ABS systems

Type	Bosch 8.1, with EBD and ESP

Torque wrench settings

	Nm	lbf ft
ABS wheel sensor retaining bolts.	10	7
ESP lateral acceleration sensor, longitudinal acceleration sensor		
and the yaw rate sensor nuts	10	7
Front brake caliper:		
Guide bolts.	30	22
Mounting bracket bolts	196	145
Hydraulic hose unions	20	15
Hydraulic pipe union nuts.	14	10
Master cylinder retaining nuts	49	36
Rear brake caliper:		
Guide pin bolts.	35	26
Mounting bracket bolts: *		
Stage 1	100	74
Stage 2	Angle-tighten a further 100°	
Roadwheel bolts.	120	89
Steering column mounting bolts	20	15
Steering column shaft universal joint clamp bolt: *		
Stage 1	30	22
Stage 2	Angle-tighten a further 90°	
Vacuum pump retaining bolts.	10	7
Vacuum servo unit retaining bolts	25	18

*Use new fasteners

1 General Information

1 All models have disc brakes fitted at the front and rear wheels as standard. ABS (Anti-lock Braking System) is also fitted as standard on all models (refer to Section 16 for further information on ABS operation).

2 The front and rear disc brakes are actuated by single-piston sliding type calipers, which ensure that equal pressure is applied to each disc pad.

3 The electronic handbrake mechanism is built into the rear calipers and provides an independent mechanical (rather than hydraulic) means of rear brake application.

4 Because the diesel engines have no throttle valve, there is insufficient vacuum in the inlet manifold to operate the braking system servo effectively at all times. To overcome this problem, a vacuum pump is fitted to these models, to provide sufficient vacuum to operate the servo unit. The vacuum pump is mounted on the rear of the cylinder head and driven by the camshaft.

5 ESP (Electronic Stability Program) is fitted to all models. The ESP (Electronic Stability Program) incorporates the ABS, EBS (Electronic Brake Assist) system and TCS (Traction Control System). It stabilises the vehicle when oversteering or understeering by applying the brake, or applying increased power to the relevant roadwheel, to increase the driver's control of the vehicle. In order for the ESP system to function, it utilises sensors which provide data concerning the speed of the vehicle around a vertical axis, the lateral movement of the vehicle, the brake pressure and the angle of the front wheels.

Note: *When servicing any part of the system, work carefully and methodically; also observe scrupulous cleanliness when overhauling any part of the hydraulic system. Always renew components (in axle sets, where applicable) if in doubt about their condition, and use only genuine Audi parts, or at least those of known good quality. Note the warnings given in 'Safety first!' and at relevant points in this Chapter concerning the dangers of asbestos dust and hydraulic fluid.*

2 Hydraulic system – bleeding

⚠ **Warning: Hydraulic fluid is poisonous; wash off immediately and thoroughly in the case of skin contact, and seek immediate medical advice if any fluid is swallowed or gets into the eyes. Certain types of hydraulic fluid are inflammable, and may ignite when allowed into contact with hot components; when servicing any hydraulic system, it is safest to assume that the fluid is inflammable, and to take precautions against the risk of fire as though it is petrol that is being handled. Hydraulic fluid is also an effective paint stripper, and will attack plastics; if any is spilt, it should be washed off immediately, using copious quantities of fresh water. Finally, it is hygroscopic (it absorbs moisture from the air) – old fluid may be contaminated and unfit for further use. When topping-up or renewing the fluid, always use the recommended type, and ensure that it comes from a freshly-opened sealed container.**

Note: *If the hydraulic circuit upstream of the ABS modulator has been disturbed, the system may need to be bled using Audi diagnostic equipment. Entrust this task to an Audi dealer or suitably-equipped specialist.*

General

1 The correct operation of any hydraulic system is only possible after removing all air from the components and circuit; this is achieved by bleeding the system.

2 During the bleeding procedure, add only clean, unused hydraulic fluid of the recommended type; never re-use fluid that has already been bled from the system. Ensure that a sufficient quantity of new fluid is available before starting work.

3 If there is any possibility of incorrect fluid being already in the system, the brake components and circuit must be flushed completely with uncontaminated, correct fluid, and new seals should be fitted to the various components.

4 If hydraulic fluid has been lost from the system, or air has entered because of a leak, ensure that the fault is cured before proceeding further.

5 Park the vehicle on level ground, securely chock the wheel then release the handbrake.

6 Check that all pipes and hoses are secure, unions tight and bleed screws closed. Clean any dirt from around the bleed screws.

7 Unscrew the master cylinder reservoir cap, and top the master cylinder reservoir up to the MAX level line; refit the cap loosely, and remember to maintain the fluid level at least above the MIN level line throughout the procedure, or there is a risk of further air entering the system.

8 There is a number of one-man, do-it-yourself brake bleeding kits currently available from motor accessory shops. It is recommended that one of these kits is used whenever possible, as they greatly simplify the bleeding operation, and also reduce the risk of expelled air and fluid being drawn back into the system. If such a kit is not available, the basic (two-man) method must be used, which is described in detail below.

9 If a kit is to be used, prepare the vehicle as described previously, and follow the kit manufacturer's instructions, as the procedure may vary slightly according to the type being used; generally, they are as outlined below in the relevant sub-section.

10 Whichever method is used, the same sequence must be followed (see paragraphs 11 and 12) to ensure the removal of all air from the system.

Bleeding

Sequence

11 If the system has been only partially disconnected, and suitable precautions were taken to minimise fluid loss, it should be necessary only to bleed that part of the system (ie, the primary or secondary circuit).

12 If the complete system is to be bled, then it should be done working in the following sequence:

a) Left-hand front brake.
b) Right-hand front brake.
c) Left-hand rear brake.
d) Right-hand rear brake.

Basic (two-man) method

13 Collect a clean glass jar, a suitable length of plastic or rubber tubing which is a tight fit over the bleed screw, and a ring spanner to fit the screw. The help of an assistant will also be required.

14 Remove the dust cap from the first screw in the sequence. Fit the spanner and tube to the screw, place the other end of the tube in the jar, and pour in sufficient fluid to cover the end of the tube.

15 Ensure that the master cylinder reservoir fluid level is maintained at least above the MIN level line throughout the procedure.

16 Have the assistant fully depress the brake pedal several times to build-up pressure, then maintain it on the final downstroke.

17 While pedal pressure is maintained, unscrew the bleed screw (approximately one turn) and allow the compressed fluid and air to flow into the jar.

18 The assistant should maintain pedal pressure, following it down to the floor if necessary, and should not release it until instructed to do so. When the flow stops, tighten the bleed screw again, have the assistant release the pedal slowly, and recheck the reservoir fluid level.

19 Repeat the steps given in paragraphs 16 to 18 inclusive until the fluid emerging from the bleed screw is free from air bubbles. If the master cylinder has been drained and refilled, and air is being bled from the first screw in the sequence, allow approximately five seconds between cycles for the master cylinder passages to refill.

20 When no more air bubbles appear, tighten the bleed screw securely, remove the tube and spanner, and refit the dust cap. Do not overtighten the bleed screw.

21 Repeat the procedure on the remaining screws in the sequence, until all air is removed from the system and the brake pedal feels firm again. On completion, lower the vehicle to the ground (where necessary).

Using a one-way valve kit

22 As their name implies, these kits consist of a length of tubing with a one-way valve fitted, to prevent expelled air and fluid being drawn back into the system; some kits include a translucent container, which can be positioned so that the air bubbles can be more easily seen flowing from the end of the tube.

23 The kit is connected to the bleed screw, which is then opened **(see illustration)**. The user returns to the driver's seat, depresses the brake pedal with a smooth, steady stroke, and slowly releases it; this is repeated until the expelled fluid is clear of air bubbles.

24 Note that these kits simplify work so much that it is easy to forget to watch the master cylinder reservoir fluid level; ensure that this is maintained at least above the MIN level line at all times, otherwise air will be reintroduced into the system.

Using a pressure-bleeding kit

25 These kits are usually operated by the reservoir of pressurised air contained in the spare tyre. However, note that it will probably be necessary to reduce the pressure to a lower level than normal; refer to the instructions supplied with the kit.

26 By connecting a pressurised, fluid-filled container to the master cylinder reservoir, bleeding can be carried out simply by opening each screw in turn (in the specified sequence), and allowing the fluid to flow out until no more air bubbles can be seen in the expelled fluid.

27 This method has the advantage that the large reservoir of fluid provides an additional safeguard against air being drawn into the system during bleeding.

28 Pressure-bleeding is particularly effective when bleeding difficult systems, or when

bleeding the complete system at the time of routine fluid renewal.

All methods

29 When bleeding is complete, and firm pedal feel is restored, wash off any spilt fluid, tighten the bleed screws securely, and refit their dust caps.

30 Check the hydraulic fluid level in the master cylinder reservoir, and top-up if necessary (see Weekly checks).

31 Discard any hydraulic fluid that has been bled from the system; it will not be fit for re-use.

32 Check the feel of the brake pedal. If it feels at all spongy, air must still be present in the system, and further bleeding is required. Failure to bleed satisfactorily after a reasonable repetition of the bleeding procedure may be due to worn master cylinder seals.

33 Because the clutch hydraulic system shares the same fluid reservoir, we recommend that the clutch is bled at the same time (see Chapter 6, Section 2).

3 Hydraulic pipes and hoses – renewal

Note: Before starting work, refer to the warning at the beginning of Section 2 concerning the dangers of hydraulic fluid.

1 If any pipe or hose is to be renewed, minimise fluid loss by first removing the master cylinder reservoir cap, then tightening it down onto a piece of polythene to obtain an airtight seal. Alternatively, flexible hoses can be sealed, if required, using a proprietary brake hose clamp; metal brake pipe unions can be plugged (if care is taken not to allow dirt into the system) or capped immediately they are disconnected. Place a wad of rag under any union that is to be disconnected, to catch any spilt fluid.

2 If a flexible hose is to be disconnected, unscrew the brake pipe union nut and remove the spring clip which secures the hose to its mounting bracket **(see illustration)**.

3 To unscrew the union nuts, it is preferable

2.23 Connect the brake bleeding kit hose to the caliper bleed screw, then use a spanner to open the screw

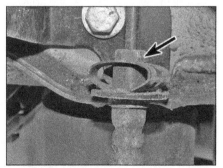

3.2 Undo the union nut and remove the spring clip

to obtain a brake pipe spanner of the correct size; these are available from most large motor accessory shops. Failing this, a close-fitting open-ended spanner will be required, though if the nuts are tight or corroded, their flats may be rounded-off if the spanner slips. In such a case, a self-locking wrench is often the only way to unscrew a stubborn union, but it follows that the pipe and the damaged nuts must be renewed on reassembly. Always clean a union and surrounding area before disconnecting it. If disconnecting a component with more than one union, make a careful note of the connections before disturbing any of them.

4 If a brake pipe is to be renewed, it can be obtained, cut to length with the union nuts and end flares in place, from Audi dealers. All that is then necessary is to bend it to shape, following the line of the original, before fitting it to the car. Alternatively, most motor accessory shops can make up brake pipes from kits, but this requires very careful measurement of the original, to ensure that the new one is of the correct length. The safest answer is usually to take the original to the shop as a pattern.

5 On refitting, do not overtighten the union nuts. It is not necessary to exercise brute force to obtain a sound joint.

6 Ensure that the pipes and hoses are correctly routed, with no kinks, and that they are secured in the clips or brackets provided. After fitting, remove the polythene from the reservoir, and bleed the hydraulic system as described in Section 2. Wash off any spilt fluid, and check carefully for fluid leaks.

4 Front brake pads – renewal

> **Warning: Renew both sets of front brake pads at the same time – never renew the pads on only one wheel, as uneven braking may result. Note that the dust created by wear of the pads may contain asbestos, which is a health hazard. Never blow it out with compressed air, and don't inhale any of it. An approved filtering mask should be worn when working on the brakes. DO NOT use petrol or petroleum-based solvents to clean brake parts; use brake cleaner or methylated spirit only.**

1 Chock the rear wheels, firmly apply the handbrake, then jack up the front of the car and support it on axle stands (see *Jacking and vehicle support*). Remove both front roadwheels.

FN3 calipers

2 Follow the accompanying photos (illustrations 4.2a to 4.2t) for the actual pad renewal procedure. Be sure to stay in order and read the caption under each illustration, and note the following points:

a) The inner pad (with a spring) is marked with an arrow. The arrow must point in the direction of brake disc rotation.

b) New pads may have an adhesive foil on the backplates. Remove this foil prior to installation.

c) Thoroughly clean the caliper guide surfaces, and apply a little brake assembly (polycarbamide) grease.

d) When pushing the caliper piston back to accommodate new pads, keep a close eye on the fluid level in the reservoir.

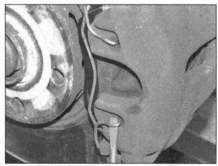

4.2a Use a screwdriver to prise out the ends of the retaining spring...

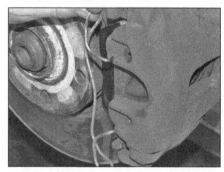

4.2b...and remove it from the caliper

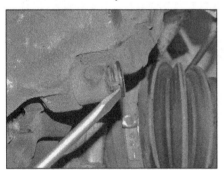

4.2c Prise out the rubber caps over the guide bolts at the top and bottom of the caliper

4.2d Use a 7 mm Allen bit to undo both guide bolts

4.2e Using a small screwdriver to release the clip...

4.2f...disconnect the pad wear sensor wiring plug

4.2g Turn the connector 90° and slide it up from the mounting bracket

4.2h Slide the caliper from the brake disc

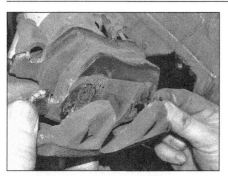

4.2i Remove the outer pad from the caliper...

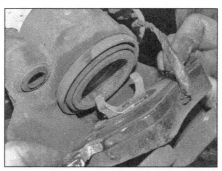

4.2j...then pull the inner pad from the piston

4.2k Use wire to suspend the caliper from the hub carrier, so as not to strain the brake hose

4.2l Measure the thickness of the pad's friction material

4.2m If new pads are to be fitted, use a retraction tool to push the piston back into the caliper. Check the fluid level in the master cylinder reservoir doesn't overflow

4.2n Fit the outer pad to the caliper mounting bracket, ensuring the friction material is against the disc face...

4.2o...then clip the inner pad into the piston

4.2p Slide the pad wear sensor wiring connector into the bracket, and rotate it 90° to lock it in place

4.2q Fit the caliper into position...

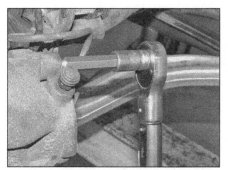

4.2r...then refit the guide bolts, tighten them to the specified torque, and refit the rubber caps

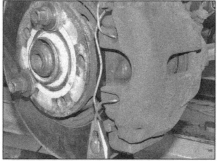

4.2s Insert the ends of the retaining spring into the holes in the caliper body, then use pliers to ease the 'ears' of the spring in front of the lugs on the mounting bracket

4.2t Don't forget to reconnect the pad wear sensor wiring plug

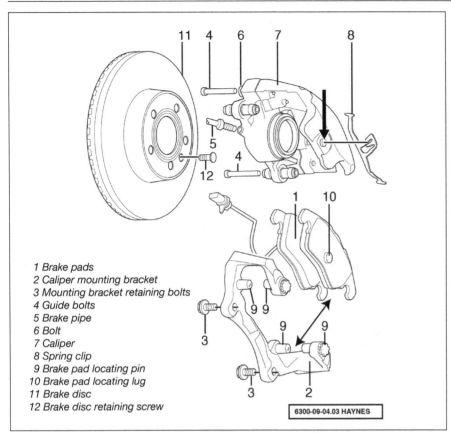

1 Brake pads
2 Caliper mounting bracket
3 Mounting bracket retaining bolts
4 Guide bolts
5 Brake pipe
6 Bolt
7 Caliper
8 Spring clip
9 Brake pad locating pin
10 Brake pad locating lug
11 Brake disc
12 Brake disc retaining screw

6300-09-04.03 HAYNES

4.3 FBC front brake caliper components

FBC calipers

3 The brake pad renewal procedure for the FBC calipers is very similar to the procedure for the FN3 calipers. Use the procedures shown in illustrations 4.2a to 4.2t as a guide but refer to the accompanying illustration of the FBC caliper for details of differences between the two caliper types **(see illustration)**. Also note the following points:

a) New pads may have an adhesive foil on the backplates. Remove this foil prior to installation.

b) Thoroughly clean the caliper guide surfaces, and apply a little brake assembly (polycarbamide) grease.

c) When pushing the caliper piston back to accommodate new pads, keep a close eye on the fluid level in the reservoir.

All calipers

4 Depress the brake pedal repeatedly, until the pads are pressed into firm contact with the brake disc, and normal (non-assisted) pedal pressure is restored.

5 Repeat the above procedure on the remaining front brake caliper.

6 Refit the roadwheels, then lower the vehicle to the ground and tighten the roadwheel bolts to the specified torque.

7 Check the hydraulic fluid level as described in *Weekly checks*.

5.5 Connect the diagnostic tool to the diagnostic socket under the facia

5.6 Set the tool to the correct mode using the buttons on the screen

Caution: New pads will not give full braking efficiency until they have bedded-in. Be prepared for this, and avoid hard braking as far as possible for the first hundred miles or so after pad renewal.

5 Rear brake caliper piston – retracting

1 The design of the electronic handbrake is such that the rear brake caliper piston is applied and retracted by an actuator motor on the caliper, every time the handbrake is applied and released.

2 Before any repair work can be carried out on the caliper (including brake pad renewal) the caliper piston must be retracted further, into the service position. On completion of the work the piston is then returned to its original position.

3 To enable the piston to be retracted and returned to its original position, Audi diagnostic equipment or a suitable alternative will be required. A relatively inexpensive alternative to the Audi equipment is a unit available from SP Diagnostics (www.spdiagnostics.com). This was the tool used in the Haynes workshop during the compilation of this manual and the following is a brief description of the operation of the tool.

4 Chock the front wheels, then jack up the rear of the vehicle and support it on axle stands (see *Jacking and vehicle support*). Ensure that the electronic handbrake is fully released.

5 With the ignition switched off, connect the tool to the diagnostic socket located under the facia on the drivers side **(see illustration)**.

6 Switch the ignition on and set the tool to the correct mode for EPB retraction. To do this, follow the instructions supplied with the tool and use the buttons on the tool screen **(see illustration)**. As the caliper piston retracts the sound of an electric motor turning will be heard at the brake caliper.

7 Once the caliper piston has been retracted, the ignition can be turned off and work on the caliper can commence.

8 On completion of the work the caliper piston is returned to its original position by once again following the instructions supplied with the tool.

9 Check the operation of the electronic parking brake, then refit the roadwheels and lower the car to the ground. Tighten the roadwheel bolts to the specified torque, then remove the diagnostic tool.

6 Rear brake pads – renewal

 Warning: Renew both sets of rear brake pads at the same time – never renew the pads on only one wheel, as uneven braking may result. Note that the dust created by wear of the pads may contain asbestos, which

is a health hazard. Never blow it out with compressed air, and don't inhale any of it. An approved filtering mask should be worn when working on the brakes. DO NOT use petrol or petroleum-based solvents to clean brake parts; use brake cleaner or methylated spirit only.

1 Retract the rear brake caliper piston as described in Section 5. Do not attempt to carry out any work on the rear brakes until the piston has been retracted.

2 Follow the accompanying photos **(see illustrations 6.2a to 6.2n)** for the actual pad renewal procedure. Be sure to stay in order, read the caption under each illustration, and note the following points:

a) If re-installing the original pads, ensure they are fitted to their original positions..
b) New guide pins and protective caps are available as a repair kit.
c) Thoroughly clean the caliper guide surfaces, and apply a little brake assembly (polycarbamide) grease.
d) If new pads are to be fitted, use a piston retraction tool to push the piston back into the caliper – keep an eye on the fluid level in the reservoir whilst retracting the piston.
e) Fit new caliper guide pin bolts – included in the Audi repair kit.
f) On completion, return the caliper piston to its original position as described in the previous Section.

6.2a Remove the caliper guide pin bolts at the top and bottom of the caliper – use an open-ended spanner to prevent the guide pin from rotating

6.2b Slide the caliper from position, and use wire to suspend it from the vehicle bodywork – don't strain the brake hose

6.2c Pull the inner pad from the mounting bracket...

6.2d...and the outer pad

6.2e Remove the upper and lower pad retainers from the caliper mounting bracket

6.2f If new pads are to be fitted, push the piston back into the caliper housing using a piston retracting tool

6.2g Thoroughly clean the caliper and mounting bracket

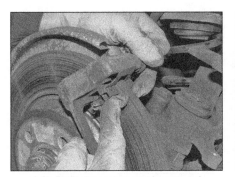

6.2h Refit the upper and lower pad retainers

6.2i Fit the inner pad, ensuring the friction material is against the disc face...

6.2j...followed by the outer pad

6.2k Check the condition of the guide pin gaiters – renew them if they show signs of deterioration or damage

6.2l Refit the caliper to the mounting bracket, ensuring it locates correctly over the ends of the guide pins

6.2m Fit new guide pin bolts...

6.2n...and tighten them to the specified torque. Use an open-ended spanner to prevent the guide pins from rotating

3 Depress the brake pedal repeatedly, until the pads are pressed into firm contact with the brake disc, and normal (non-assisted) pedal pressure is restored.

4 Repeat the above procedure on the remaining brake caliper.

5 Return the caliper pistons to their original position as described in Section 5.

6 Refit the roadwheels, then lower the vehicle to the ground and tighten the roadwheel bolts to the specified torque.

7 Check the hydraulic fluid level as described in *Weekly checks*.

Caution: New pads will not give full braking efficiency until they have bedded-in. Be prepared for this, and avoid hard braking as far as possible for the first hundred miles or so after pad renewal.

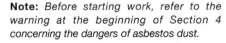

7 Front brake disc – inspection, removal and refitting

Note: *Before starting work, refer to the warning at the beginning of Section 4 concerning the dangers of asbestos dust.*

Inspection

Note: *If either disc requires renewal, BOTH should be renewed at the same time, to ensure even and consistent braking. New brake pads should also be fitted.*

1 Apply the handbrake, then jack up the front of the car and support it on axle stands (see *Jacking and vehicle support*). Remove the appropriate front roadwheel. Whilst the wheel is removed, refit at least one of the wheel bolts to ensure the brake disc remains correctly positioned on the hub; if necessary fit spacers to the wheel bolts to clamp the disc firmly in position **(see illustration)**.

2 Slowly rotate the brake disc so that the full area of both sides can be checked; remove the brake pads if better access is required to the inboard surface. Light scoring is normal in the area swept by the brake pads, but if heavy scoring or cracks are found, the disc must be renewed.

3 It is normal to find a lip of rust and brake dust around the disc's perimeter; this can be scraped off if required. If, however, a lip has formed due to excessive wear of the brake pad swept area, then the disc's thickness must be measured using a micrometer. Take measurements at several places around the disc, at the inside and outside of the pad swept area; if the disc has worn at any point to the specified minimum thickness or less, the disc must be renewed **(see illustration)**.

4 If the disc is thought to be warped, it can be checked for run-out. Secure the disc firmly to the hub by refitting at least two roadwheel bolts – fit plain washers to the roadwheel bolts to ensure that the disc is properly seated on the hub.

5 Either use a dial gauge mounted on any convenient fixed point, while the disc is slowly rotated, or use feeler blades to measure (at several points all around the disc) the clearance between the disc and a fixed point, such as the caliper mounting bracket **(see illustration)**. If the measurements obtained are at the specified maximum or beyond, the disc is excessively warped, and must be renewed, however, it is worth checking first that the hub bearing is in good condition.

6 Check the disc for cracks, especially around the wheel bolt holes, and any other wear or damage, and renew if necessary.

Removal

7 Unscrew and remove the two bolts securing the brake caliper mounting bracket to the hub carrier. Slide the whole caliper assembly off the hub and away from the disc and tie the assembly to the front coil spring, using a piece

7.1 Refit at least one of the wheel bolts to retain the disc

7.3 Use a micrometer to measure the thickness of the disc

7.5 Use a DTI gauge to measure disc run-out

of wire or string, to avoid placing any strain on the hydraulic brake hose **(see illustrations)**.

8 Remove all the wheel bolts and washers used to secure the disc in position, then undo the disc retaining screw. Remove the disc from the wheel hub. If it is tight, lightly tap its rear face with a hide or plastic mallet to free it from the hub.

Refitting

9 Refitting is the reverse of the removal procedure, noting the following points:
a) *Ensure that the mating surfaces of the disc and hub are clean and flat.*
b) *If a new disc has been fitted, use a suitable solvent to wipe any preservative coating from the disc, before refitting the caliper. Note that new brake pads should always be fitted when the disc is renewed.*
c) *Prior to installation, renew the caliper mounting bracket bolts. Slide the caliper into position, making sure the pads pass either side of the disc, and tighten the caliper bracket bolts to the specified torque setting.*
d) *Refit the roadwheel then lower the vehicle to the ground and tighten the wheel bolts to the specified torque. Apply the footbrake several times to force the pads back into contact with the disc before driving the vehicle.*

8 Rear brake disc – inspection, removal and refitting

Note: *Before starting work, refer to the warning at the beginning of Section 6 concerning the dangers of asbestos dust.*

Inspection

Note: *If either disc requires renewal, BOTH should be renewed at the same time, to ensure even and consistent braking. New brake pads should be fitted also.*

1 Retract the rear brake caliper piston on the side concerned as described in Section 5.
2 Inspect the disc as described in Section 7.

Removal

3 If not already done, retract the rear brake caliper piston on the side concerned as described in Section 5.
4 Unclip the brake hydraulic hose and the wiring harness from the bracket on the hub carrier.
5 Unscrew the two bolts securing the brake caliper mounting bracket in position, then slide the whole caliper, bracket and pads off the disc. Using a piece of wire or string, tie the caliper to a suitable place on the underbody, to avoid placing any strain on the hydraulic brake hose.
6 Undo the screw securing the brake disc to the wheel hub, then remove the disc. If it is tight, lightly tap its rear face with a hide or plastic mallet to free it from the hub.

Refitting

7 Refitting is the reverse of the removal procedure, noting the following points:
a) *Ensure that the mating surfaces of the disc and hub are clean and flat.*
b) *If a new disc has been fitted, use a suitable solvent to wipe any preservative coating from the disc, before refitting the caliper. Note that new brake pads should always be fitted when the disc is renewed.*
c) *Prior to installation, renew the caliper bracket mounting bolts. Slide the caliper into position, making sure the pads pass either side of the disc, and tighten the caliper bracket bolts to the specified torque.*
d) *Return the rear brake caliper piston to its original position as described in Section 5.*
e) *Refit the roadwheel then lower the vehicle to the ground and tighten the wheel bolts to the specified torque. Apply the footbrake several times to force the pads back into contact with the disc before driving the vehicle.*

9 Front brake caliper – removal, overhaul and refitting

Note: *Before starting work, refer to the warning at the beginning of Section 2 concerning the dangers of hydraulic fluid, and to the warning at the beginning of Section 4 concerning the dangers of asbestos dust.*

Removal

1 Apply the handbrake, then jack up the front of the vehicle and support it on axle stands (see *Jacking and vehicle support*). Remove the appropriate roadwheel.
2 Minimise fluid loss by first removing the master cylinder reservoir cap, and then tightening it down onto a piece of polythene, to obtain an airtight seal. Alternatively, use a brake hose clamp to clamp the flexible hose.
3 Clean the area around the union, then loosen the brake hose union nut.
4 Remove the brake pads as described in Section 4.
5 Unscrew the caliper from the end of the brake hose, then remove it from the vehicle.

Overhaul

Note: *At the time of writing, it would appear that caliper overhaul kits are available. However, it would be prudent to check with an Audi dealer or parts specialist prior to commencing work.*

6 With the caliper on the bench, wipe away all traces of dust and dirt, but avoid inhaling the dust, as it is injurious to health.
7 Withdraw the partially ejected piston from the caliper body, and remove the dust seal. If the caliper piston is reluctant to move, apply low air pressure (eg, from a foot pump) to the fluid inlet, but note that the piston may be ejected with some force.
8 Using a soft flat-bladed instrument, such as a plastic spatula, extract the piston hydraulic seal, taking great care not to damage the caliper bore **(see illustration)**.
9 Thoroughly clean all components, using only methylated spirit, isopropyl alcohol or clean brake fluid as a cleaning medium. Never use mineral-based solvents such as petrol or paraffin, as they will attack the hydraulic system's rubber components. Dry the components immediately, using compressed air or a clean, lint-free cloth. Use compressed air to blow clear the fluid passages.
10 Check all components, and renew any that are worn or damaged. Check particularly the cylinder bore and piston; these should be renewed if they are scratched, worn or corroded in any way (note that this means the renewal of the complete body assembly).

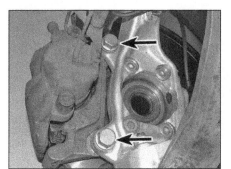

7.7a Undo the caliper mounting bracket bolts

7.7b Slide the caliper and mounting bracket from the hub carrier

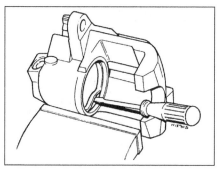

9.8 Use a small screwdriver to extract the caliper piston hydraulic seal

Similarly check the condition of the guide bolts and the bushes in the caliper body; both bolts should be undamaged and (when cleaned) a reasonably tight sliding fit in the bushes. If there is any doubt about the condition of any component, renew it.

11 If the caliper is fit for further use, obtain the appropriate repair kit. All rubber seals should be renewed as a matter of course; these should never be re-used.

12 On commencement of re-assembly, ensure that all components are clean and dry.

13 Soak the seals in the special fluid provided in the overhaul kit for at least 45 minutes – check with the instructions provided in the kit. Smear some of the special fluid on the cylinder bore surface.

14 Fit the new piston (fluid) seal, using only your fingers (no tools) to manipulate it into the cylinder bore groove.

15 Fit the new dust seal to the rear of the piston and seat the outer lip of the seal in the caliper body groove. Carefully ease the piston squarely into the cylinder bore using a twisting motion. Press the piston fully into position and seat the inner lip of the dust seal in the piston groove.

16 If the guide bushes are being renewed, push the old bushes out from the body and press the new ones into position, making sure they are correctly seated.

17 Prior to refitting, fill the caliper with fresh hydraulic fluid by unscrewing the bleed screw and pumping the fluid through the caliper until bubble-free fluid is expelled from the union hole.

Refitting

18 Screw the caliper fully onto the flexible hose union.

19 Refit the brake pads as described in Section 4.

20 Securely tighten the brake pipe union nut.

21 Remove the brake hose clamp or polythene, as applicable, and bleed the hydraulic system as described in Section 2. Note that, providing the precautions described were taken to minimise brake fluid loss, it should only be necessary to bleed the relevant front brake.

22 Refit the roadwheel, then lower the vehicle to the ground and tighten the roadwheel bolts to the specified torque.

10 Rear brake caliper – removal, overhaul and refitting

Note: *Before starting work, refer to the warning at the beginning of Section 2 concerning the dangers of hydraulic fluid, and to the warning at the beginning of Section 6 concerning the dangers of asbestos dust.*

Removal

1 Chock the front wheels, then jack up the rear of the vehicle and support it on axle stands (see *Jacking and vehicle support*). Remove relevant rear wheel.

2 Retract the rear brake caliper piston on the side concerned as described in Section 5.

3 Minimise fluid loss by first removing the master cylinder reservoir cap, and then tightening it down onto a piece of polythene, to obtain an airtight seal. Alternatively, use a brake hose clamp, a G-clamp or a similar tool to clamp the flexible hose.

4 Disconnect the wiring connector from the electronic handbrake actuator motor.

5 Clean the area around the caliper brake hose then slacken the union.

6 Remove the brake pads as described in Section 6.

7 Unscrew the caliper from the end of the brake hose, then remove it from the vehicle.

Overhaul

8 No overhaul procedures or parts were available at the time of writing. Check the availability of spares before dismantling the caliper. Do not attempt to dismantle the handbrake mechanism inside the caliper. If the mechanism is faulty, the complete caliper assembly must be renewed.

Refitting

9 Screw the caliper fully onto the flexible hose union.

10 Refit the brake pads as described in Section 4.

11 Securely tighten the brake pipe union nut.

12 Remove the brake hose clamp or polythene, as applicable, and bleed the hydraulic system as described in Section 2. Note that, providing the precautions

described were taken to minimise brake fluid loss, it should only be necessary to bleed the relevant front brake.

13 Refit the roadwheel, then lower the vehicle to the ground and tighten the roadwheel bolts to the specified torque.

11 Master cylinder – removal, overhaul and refitting

Note: *Before starting work, refer to the warning at the beginning of Section 2 concerning the dangers of hydraulic fluid. A new master cylinder O-ring will be required on refitting.*

Removal

1 Disconnect the battery negative lead as described in Chapter 5, Section 3.

2 Remove the plenum chamber partition panel as described in Chapter 11, Section 21.

3 Remove the master cylinder reservoir cap (disconnect the wiring plug from the brake fluid level warning switch), and siphon the hydraulic fluid from the reservoir **(see illustration)**.

Note: *Do not siphon the fluid by mouth, as it is poisonous; use a syringe or an old poultry baster.*

4 Undo the retaining bolt at the front and lift off the steel cover over the brake fluid reservoir **(see illustration)**.

5 On manual transmission models, disconnect and plug the clutch master cylinder supply hose from the master cylinder reservoir **(see illustration)**.

6 Place absorbent rag beneath the master cylinder to catch any escaping brake fluid, then pull out the retaining pin at the bottom of the fluid reservoir. Lift the reservoir up and off the master cylinder.

7 Wipe clean the area around the brake pipe unions on the side of the master cylinder. Make a note of the correct fitted positions of the unions, then unscrew the union nuts and carefully withdraw the pipes. Plug or tape over the pipe ends and master cylinder orifices, to minimise the loss of brake fluid, and to prevent the entry of dirt into the system. Wash off any spilt fluid immediately with cold water.

11.3 Disconnect the wiring plug from the brake fluid level warning switch

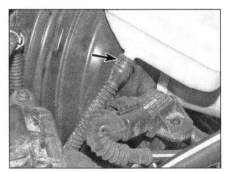

11.4 Remove the cover over the brake fluid reservoir

11.5 Clutch fluid supply hose and union

8 Unscrew and remove the two nuts securing the master cylinder to the vacuum servo unit, then withdraw the unit from the engine compartment. Remove the O-ring from the rear of the master cylinder, and discard it.

Overhaul

9 If the master cylinder is faulty, it must be renewed. Repair kits are not available from an Audi dealer, so the cylinder must be treated as a sealed unit.

10 The only items which can be renewed are the mounting seals for the fluid reservoir; if these show signs of deterioration, prise them out with a screwdriver. Lubricate the new seals with clean brake fluid, and press them into the master cylinder ports.

Refitting

11 Remove all traces of dirt from the master cylinder and servo unit mating surfaces, and fit a new O-ring to the groove on the master cylinder body.

12 Fit the master cylinder to the servo unit, ensuring that the servo unit pushrod enters the master cylinder bore centrally. Refit the master cylinder mounting nuts and tighten them to the specified torque.

13 Wipe clean the brake pipe unions, then refit them to the master cylinder ports and tighten them securely.

14 Place the fluid reservoir in position on the master cylinder and secure with the retaining pin.

15 On manual transmission models, reconnect the clutch master cylinder supply hose to the reservoir.

16 Refit the steel cover to the reservoir and tighten the retaining bolt securely. Reconnect the wiring plug to the brake fluid level warning switch.

17 Reconnect the wiring to the brake level sender unit and brake light switch as applicable.

18 Refit the plenum chamber partition panel as described in Chapter 11, Section 21, then reconnect the battery negative lead.

19 Refill the master cylinder reservoir with new fluid, and bleed the complete hydraulic system as described in Section 2.

12 Brake pedal – removal and refitting

Removal

1 Remove the clutch master cylinder as described in Chapter 6, Section 4.

2 Remove the stop-light switch as described in Section 15.

3 Disconnect the wiring connector from the accelerator pedal module.

4 The brake pedal pivot pin is connected to a remote operating lever to the left of the clutch pedal, which then acts upon the brake servo pushrod. The end of the pushrod is shaped as a ball, and engages with a retaining clip in the

12.4a The end of the servo pushrod is shaped as a ball and engages in the back of the lever

back of the operating lever. To release the clip a special Audi tool is available (T40136), but a suitable alternative can be improvised as shown. Note that the plastic lugs are very stiff, and it will not be possible to release them by hand. Using the tool, release the securing lugs and pull the lever from the servo pushrod (see illustrations).

5 Remove the plenum chamber partition panel as described in Chapter 11, Section 21.

6 Undo the retaining bolt at the front and lift off the steel cover over the brake fluid reservoir (see illustration 11.4).

7 Undo the two long through-bolts securing the master cylinder and vacuum servo unit to the pedal mounting bracket.

8 Undo the two nuts securing the lower corners of the pedal mounting bracket to the bulkhead (see illustration).

9 Turn the steering wheel to set the roadwheels in the straight-ahead position then use the full range of steering column adjustment to move the steering wheel out as far as possible towards the driver's seat.

10 Undo the clamp bolt securing the steering column shaft to the intermediate shaft universal joint (see illustration).

11 Remove the upper and lower steering column shrouds as described in, Chapter 11, Section 23.

12 Undo the hex bolt and the socket headed bolt each side securing the steering column to the facia crossmember.

13 Detach the wiring harness guides from the steering column.

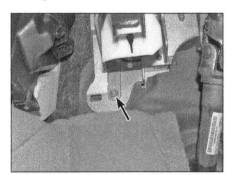

12.8 Left-hand pedal mounting bracket-to-bulkhead retaining nut

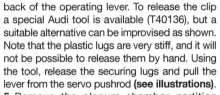

12.4b Improvised special tool constructed from a modified exhaust clamp, used to release the brake lever from the servo pushrod

14 Support the steering column from below and unscrew the four socket headed bolts securing the upper part of the steering column to the facia crossmember.

15 Disengage the steering column shaft from the intermediate shaft universal joint and lay the column down on the floor of the driver's footwell.

16 From inside the car, undo the remaining two retaining bolts and manipulate the pedal mounting bracket out from under the facia.

17 Undo the pedal pivot pin retaining bolt and remove the retaining clip from the left-hand end of the pivot pin. Pull the pivot pin out to the right and remove the brake pedal.

18 Examine all components for signs of wear or damage, renewing them as necessary.

Refitting

19 Refitting is the reverse of the removal procedure, bearing in mind the following points:

a) Tighten all nuts and bolts to the specified torque (where given).

b) Refit the upper and lower steering column shrouds as described in Chapter 11 Section 23.

c) Refit the plenum chamber partition panel as described in Chapter 11, Section 21.

d) Refit the stop-light switch as described in Section 15.

e) Refit the clutch master cylinder as described in Chapter 6, Section 4.

12.10 Steering column shaft clamp bolt

13 Vacuum servo unit – testing, removal and refitting

Testing

1 To test the operation of the servo unit, depress the footbrake several times to exhaust the vacuum, then start the engine whilst keeping the pedal firmly depressed. As the engine starts, there should be a noticeable give in the brake pedal as the vacuum builds-up. Allow the engine to run for at least two minutes, then switch it off. If the brake pedal is now depressed it should feel normal, but further applications should result in the pedal feeling firmer, with the pedal stroke decreasing with each application.

2 If the servo does not operate as described, first inspect the servo unit check valve as described in Section 14. Also check the vacuum pump as described in Section 18.

3 If the servo unit still fails to operate satisfactorily, the fault may lie within the unit itself. Repairs to the unit are not possible – if faulty, the servo unit must be renewed.

Removal

4 Remove the brake master cylinder as described in Section 11.

5 From inside the car, refer to, Chapter 11, Section 23 and remove the trim panel from below the steering column.

6 Undo the retaining bolt and remove the footwell vent over the pedal assembly.

7 Remove the stop-light switch as described in Section 15.

8 Release the servo unit push rod from the brake pedal as described in Section 12, paragraph 4.

9 Carefully ease the vacuum hose connection out from the servo unit, taking care not to damage the grommet.

10 Undo the long through-bolts and manoeuvre the servo unit from its location. Recover the gasket which is fitted between the servo and bulkhead. Examine the gasket for signs of wear or damage and renew if necessary.

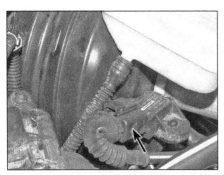

14.3 Vacuum servo pressure sensor wiring connector

Refitting

11 Refitting is the reverse of the removal procedure, bearing in mind the following points:
a) Tighten the servo unit mounting bolts to the specified torque.
b) Refit the stop-light switch as described in Section 15.
c) Refit the trim panel below the steering column.
d) Refit the brake master cylinder as described in, Section 11.

14 Vacuum servo unit check valve – removal, testing and refitting

Note: The valve is an integral part of the servo unit vacuum hose and is not available separately.

Removal

1 Remove the plenum chamber cover as described in Chapter 11, Section 21.

2 Carefully pull the engine top cover off the four retaining pins, one after the other. Do not jerk the cover away and do not try to pull on one side only.

3 Disconnect the wiring connector from the vacuum servo pressure sensor (see illustration).

4 Carefully ease the pressure sensor and vacuum hose connection out from the servo unit, taking care not to damage the grommet.

5 Work back along the hose, freeing it from all the relevant retaining clips whilst noting its correct routing.

6 Slacken the retaining clip then disconnect the vacuum hose from the vacuum pump and remove it from the vehicle.

Testing

7 Examine the vacuum hose for signs of damage, and renew if necessary. The valve may be tested by blowing through it in both directions. Air should flow through the valve in one direction only – when blown through from the servo unit end of the valve. Renew the valve if this is not the case.

8 Examine the servo unit rubber sealing

15.3 The stop-light switch is located on the pedal mounting bracket

grommet and hose(s) linking the main hose to the manifold/pump (as applicable) for signs of damage or deterioration, and renew as necessary.

Refitting

9 Ensure the sealing grommet is in position in the servo unit then carefully ease the vacuum hose end fitting into position, taking care not to displace or damage the grommet.

10 Ensure the hose is correctly routed then connect it to the pump and securely tighten the retaining clip.

11 On completion, start the engine and check the check valve-to-servo unit connection for signs of air leaks.

15 Stop-light switch – removal and refitting

Removal

Note: Audi special tool T40168 will be required to release the switch from its location.

1 From inside the car, refer to, Section and remove the trim panel from below the steering column.

2 Undo the retaining bolt and remove the footwell vent over the pedal assembly.

3 The stop-light switch is located on the pedal mounting bracket under the facia (see illustration).

4 Disconnect the wiring connector from the switch body.

5 Press the switch plunger in with one finger, then with the plunger still pressed in, turn the coloured catch on the sensor body fully anti-clockwise to release the switch.

6 Release the switch plunger.

7 Insert the Audi tool between the brake pedal operating lever and the switch plunger so the tapered part of the tool faces the driver's seat and the slot on the tool corresponds with the recess on the switch. Press the tool against the switch to release the three retaining tabs and withdraw the switch from the mounting bracket.

Refitting and adjustment

8 Insert the switch into its location in the pedal mounting bracket and push it in until the three retaining tabs audibly engage. While doing this, bear in mind the following:
a) The plunger adjusts itself automatically when the switch is inserted.
b) The brake pedal must remain in the normal position as the switch is fitted and must not be depressed.
c) The brake pedal must be connected to the servo unit.

9 With the switch in position, turn the coloured catch fully clockwise to secure the switch.

10 Reconnect the switch wiring connector and check the operation of the stop-lights.

11 Pull the plunger fully out of the switch,

then, with the brake pedal released, guide the plunger through the hole against the pedal, and secure by turning it 45° clockwise.

12 Reconnect the wiring connector, and check the operation of the stop-lights.

13 Refit the footwell vent and the trim panel below the steering column.

16 Anti-lock braking system (ABS) – general information

1 ABS is fitted as standard to all models in the range. The system comprises a hydraulic unit, an electronic control unit (ECU) and four roadwheel sensors. The hydraulic unit contains the eight hydraulic solenoid valves (two for each brake – one inlet and one outlet) and the electrically-driven return pump. The purpose of the system is to prevent the roadwheels locking during heavy braking. This is achieved by automatic release of the brake on the relevant wheel, followed by re-application of the brake. In the case of the rear wheels, both rear brakes are released and applied at the same time.

2 The solenoid valves are controlled by the ECU, which itself receives signals from the four wheel sensors (front sensors are fitted to the hubs and the rear sensors are fitted to the rear axle), which monitor the speed of rotation of each wheel. By comparing these signals, the ECU can determine the speed at which the vehicle is travelling. It can then use this speed to determine when a wheel is decelerating at an abnormal rate, compared to the speed of the vehicle, and therefore predicts when a wheel is about to lock. During normal operation, the system functions in the same way as a non-ABS braking system.

3 If the ECU senses that a wheel is about to lock, it closes the relevant outlet solenoid valves in the hydraulic unit, which then isolates the relevant brake on the wheel which is about to lock from the master cylinder, effectively sealing-in the hydraulic pressure.

4 If the speed of rotation of the wheel continues to decrease at an abnormal rate, the ECU opens the inlet solenoid valves on the relevant brake and operates the electrically-driven return pump which pumps the hydraulic fluid back into the master cylinder, releasing the brake. Once the speed of rotation of the wheel returns to an acceptable rate, the pump stops; the solenoid valves switch again, allowing the hydraulic master cylinder pressure to return to the caliper, which then re-applies the brake. This cycle can be carried out many times a second.

5 The action of the solenoid valves and return pump creates pulses in the hydraulic circuit. When the ABS system is functioning, these pulses can be felt through the brake pedal.

6 The operation of the ABS system is entirely dependent on electrical signals. To prevent the system responding to any inaccurate signals, a built-in safety circuit monitors all signals received by the ECU. If an inaccurate

signal or low battery voltage is detected, the ABS system is automatically shut down, and the warning light on the instrument panel is illuminated to inform the driver that the ABS system is not operational. Normal braking should still be available, however.

7 On all models, the ABS system also includes electronic differential lock and traction control/anti-slip regulation functions. If under acceleration the ECU senses that a wheel is spinning, it uses the hydraulic unit to gradually apply the brake on that wheel until traction is regained. Once the wheel regains traction, the brake is released.

8 The ESP (Electronic Stability Program) function is a further expansion of the ABS system which takes into consideration the angle of the steering wheel, using a steering angle sender and yaw rate sender. Additionally, the system monitors lateral acceleration with a lateral acceleration sender.

9 If a fault does develop in the ABS system, the vehicle must be taken to an Audi dealer or suitably-equipped specialist for fault diagnosis and repair.

17 Anti-lock braking system (ABS) components – removal and refitting

Hydraulic unit

1 Removal and refitting of the hydraulic unit is best entrusted to an audi dealer, as a fault diagnosis check must be performed on completion using specialist equipment.

Electronic control unit (ECU)

2 The ECU is mounted underneath the hydraulic unit and these two components must not be separated.

Wheel sensors

Removal

3 Apply the handbrake, then jack up the front or rear of the vehicle, as appropriate, and support it on axle stands (see *Jacking and vehicle support*). To improve access, remove the roadwheel.

4 Disconnect the sensor wiring connector.

5 Undo the retaining bolt, then carefully pull the sensor out from the relevant hub carrier assembly and remove it from the vehicle.

Refitting

6 Ensure that the mating faces of the sensor and hub carrier are clean and dry then lubricate the wheel sensor surfaces with a small quantity of copper-based grease.

7 Ensure the sensor wiring is correctly positioned then push the sensor firmly into position until it is fully home in the hub carrier, and tighten the retaining bolt to the specified torque.

8 Reconnect the wiring connector.

9 Refit the roadwheel then lower the vehicle and tighten the wheel bolts to the specified torque.

18 Vacuum pump – removal and refitting

Removal

Note: *A new pump O-ring seal will be required for refitting.*

1 Carefully pull the engine top cover off the four retaining pins, one after the other. Do not jerk the cover away and do not try to pull on one side only.

2 The vacuum pump is located at the rear of the cylinder head and is driven by the camshaft.

3 Remove the diesel particulate filter pressure sensor from the bracket on the vacuum pump.

4 Unclip the pressure sensor pipe and carefully move it to one side.

5 Remove the pressure sensor bracket from the vacuum pump.

6 Unclip the adjacent coolant pipe at the bracket and move aside.

7 Detach the vacuum hose from the pump.

8 Undo the retaining bolts and remove the pump from the cylinder head. There are no serviceable parts within the pump. If the pump is faulty, it must be renewed **(see illustration)**.

Refitting

9 Fit the new O-ring seal to the vacuum pump, and apply a smear of oil to aid installation.

10 Manoeuvre the vacuum pump into position, making sure the slot in the pump drive gear engages with the slot on the pump driveshaft.

11 Refit the pump retaining bolts and tighten them to the specified torque.

12 The remainder of refitting is a reversal of removal.

19 ESP system components – removal and refitting

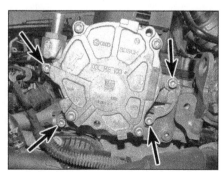

1 The ESP system comprises of the ABS, TCS and EDL system. The ESP, TCS and EDL systems rely on the ABS system components for measuring and reducing wheel speed. In addition to the wheel speed sensors and

18.8 Vacuum pump retaining bolts

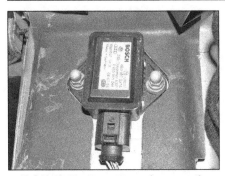

19.3 Undo the two nuts and remove the sensor

brake pressure sensors, the ESP receives information concerning the steering wheel angle, lateral acceleration, longitudinal acceleration and vehicle rotational speed (yaw rate). Testing of the various system components should be entrusted to an Audi dealer or specialist.

Lateral acceleration sensor, longitudinal acceleration sensor and yaw rate sensor

 Warning: Handle the sensor with great care. Severe shakes/jolts can destroy the sensors.

2 The lateral acceleration sensor, longitudinal acceleration sensor and the yaw rate sensor are integrated in one housing, located under the left-hand front seat. Remove the seat as described in Chapter 11, Section 24.

3 Disconnect the wiring plug, unscrew the two retaining nuts and remove the housing **(see illustration)**. No further dismantling is possible.

4 Refitting is a reversal of removal. Ensure the housing is correctly seated tightening the retaining nuts to the specified torque.

Brake pressure sensor

5 The brake pressure sensor is fitted to the ABS hydraulic control unit. These two components must not be separated.

Steering angle sensor

6 The steering angle sensor is incorporated into the airbag contact unit between the steering wheel and column switch. To remove the sensor, refer to Chapter 12, Section 18, and remove the contact unit. Note that if the contact unit has been renewed, specialist equipment is required to perform a 'zero comparison'. This must be entrusted to an Audi dealer or specialist.

Chapter 10
Suspension and steering

Contents

Degrees of difficulty

Easy, suitable for novice with little experience	Fairly easy, suitable for beginner with some experience	Fairly difficult, suitable for competent DIY mechanic	Difficult, suitable for experienced DIY mechanic	Very difficult, suitable for expert DIY or professional

Specifications

Front suspension

Type . . . .   Independent, with four transverse arms and a solid upright (or hub carrier) in an unequal-length, double-wishbone configuration. Coil spring-over-telescopic shock absorber struts and anti-roll bar

Rear suspension

Type . . . .   Independent, with a lower transverse link, upper transverse link and lower track rod. Telescopic shock absorbers coil springs and anti-roll bar

Steering

Type . . . .   Rack-and-pinion with hydraulic or electro-mechanical power assistance, depending on model year

Torque wrench settings	Nm	lbf ft
Front suspension		
Anti-roll bar:		
Drop link:		
Lower joint-to-anti-roll bar bolt: *		
Stage 1	40	30
Stage 2	Angle-tighten a further 90°	
Upper joint-to-suspension strut bolt: *		
Stage 1	40	30
Stage 2	Angle-tighten a further 90°	
Mounting clamp nuts*	25	18
Hub bearing housing-to-hub carrier: *		
Stage 1	80	59
Stage 2	Angle-tighten a further 90°	
Hub bolt: *		
Stage 1	200	148
Stage 2	Angle-tighten a further 180°	
Hub carrier balljoint clamp bolt*	40	30
Lower suspension arms:		
Lower arm-to-hub carrier balljoint nut: *		
M12 hexagon flange nut, 21 mm AF	145	107
M12 hexagon nut with washer, 18 mm AF	110	81
M12 hexagon nut with washer, 21 mm AF	120	89
M14 hexagon nut with washer, 21 mm AF	140	103
Lower arm-to-subframe bolt/nut: *		
Stage 1	70	52
Stage 2	Angle-tighten a further 180°	
Subframe cross-brace bolts: *		
Vehicles with hydraulic power steering:		
Stage 1	90	66
Stage 2	Angle-tighten a further 135°	
Vehicles with electro-mechanical power steering:	Angle-tighten a further 90°	
Front bolts (2):		
Stage 1	90	66
Stage 2	Angle-tighten a further 90°	
Rear bolts (4):		
Stage 1	90	66
Stage 2	Angle-tighten a further 135°	
Suspension strut:		
Lower mounting nut-to-suspension arm: *		
Stage 1	90	66
Stage 2	Angle-tighten a further 90°	
Piston rod nut*	50	37
Strut fork clamp bolt: *		
Stage 1	40	30
Stage 2	Angle-tighten a further 180°	
Upper mounting bolts: *		
Stage 1	40	30
Stage 2	Angle-tighten a further 90°	
Upper suspension arms:		
Hub carrier-to-upper arm clamp bolt/nut*	40	30
Upper arm-to-bracket nut: *		
Stage 1	50	37
Stage 2	Angle-tighten a further 90°	
Rear suspension		
Anti-roll bar:		
Clamp bolts: *		
Stage 1	25	18
Stage 2	Angle-tighten a further 90°	
Drop link bolts: *		
Stage 1	40	30
Stage 2	Angle-tighten a further 90°	
Hub carrier:		
Lower mounting bolts/nuts: *		
Stage 1	120	89
Stage 2	Angle-tighten a further 360°	
Upper mounting nut*	95	70

Torque wrench settings (continued)

	Nm	lbf ft
Rear suspension (continued)		
Lower transverse link inner mounting bolts/nuts: *		
Stage 1	70	52
Stage 2	Angle-tighten a further 180°	
Rear hub flange bolt: *		
Stage 1	200	148
Stage 2	Angle-tighten a further 180°	
Shock absorber:		
Lower mounting bolt: *		
Stage 1	150	111
Stage 2	Angle-tighten a further 180°	
Piston rod nut*	35	26
Upper mounting bolts: *		
Stage 1	50	37
Stage 2	Angle-tighten a further 45°	
Subframe mountings:		
Front mounting bolts: *		
Outer bolts	55	41
Inner bolts:		
Stage 1	115	85
Stage 2	Angle-tighten a further 90°	
Rear mounting bolts: *		
Stage 1	115	85
Stage 2	Angle-tighten a further 90°	
Track rod mounting bolts: *		
Inner mounting bolt/nut	95	70
Outer mounting bolt:		
Stage 1	85	63
Stage 2	Angle-tighten a further 90°	
Upper transverse link inner mounting bolt/nut: *		
Stage 1	70	52
Stage 2	Angle-tighten a further 180°	
Steering		
Power steering pump pressure pipe union nut	38	28
Power steering pump pressure pipe flange retaining bolts	10	7
Power steering pump mounting bolts	25	18
Power steering pump pulley bolts	22	16
Steering column:		
Mounting bolts	20	15
Universal joint clamp bolt: *		
Stage 1	30	22
Stage 2	Angle-tighten a further 90°	
Steering gear:		
Hydraulic pipe union retaining bolts:	20	15
Mounting bolts: *		
Stage 1	80	59
Stage 2	Angle-tighten a further 180°	
Steering wheel retaining bolt: *		
Stage 1	30	22
Stage 2	Angle-tighten a further 90°	
Track rod:		
Balljoint locknut	80	59
Balljoint-to-hub carrier retaining nut: *		
Hexagon flange nut:		
Stage 1	20	15
Stage 2	Angle-tighten a further 90°	
Twelve-point nut with washer	100	74
Hexagon nut with washer	110	81
Track rod to steering gear	100	74
Roadwheels		
Wheel bolts	120	89

*Use new fasteners

1 General Information

1 The front suspension is fully independent, utilising four transverse arms (two upper and two lower) and a solid upright (or hub carrier) in an unequal-length, double-wishbone configuration. Coil spring-over-telescopic shock absorber struts are connected between the front lower transverse arm and upper transverse arm mounting bracket. The hub carriers house the wheel bearings, brake calipers and the hub/disc assemblies, and are connected to the upper and lower transverse arms by means of balljoints. A front anti-roll bar is fitted to all models; the anti-roll bar is rubber-mounted onto the subframe, and is connected to the front lower transverse arms by drop links. The subframe provides mountings for all the lower suspension components as well as the engine and transmission mountings.

2 The rear suspension is fully independent, with a lower transverse link, upper transverse link, and a lower track rod which are connected to the body by rubber bushes. A telescopic shock absorber and separate coil spring is fitted between the hub carrier and rear suspension each side. A rear anti-roll bar is incorporated into the rear axle design to reduce body roll.

3 The suspension type code is stamped on the vehicle identification (VIN) plate and on the identification label in the spare wheel well, or luggage compartment floor.

4 The steering column has a flexible coupling at its lower end and is secured to the steering gear pinion by means of a clamp bolt.

5 The steering gear is mounted onto the subframe and is connected by two track rods, with balljoints at their outer ends, to bosses projecting forward from the suspension hub carriers. The track rod balljoints are threaded, to facilitate adjustment. Power assistance for the steering gear is hydraulic on early models and electro-mechanical on later models. The hydraulic steering system is powered by a belt-driven pump, which is driven off the crankshaft pulley.

2 Front hub bearings and hub carrier – renewal

Front hub bearings

Note: *The bearing is a sealed, pre-adjusted and pre-lubricated, double-row roller type, and is intended to last the car's entire service life without maintenance or attention. Never overtighten the hub bolt in an attempt to adjust the bearing.*

Note: *A hydraulic press will be required to dismantle and rebuild the assembly; if such a tool is not available, a large bench vice and spacers (such as large sockets) may serve as an adequate substitute. The bearing's inner races are an interference fit on the hub; if the inner race remains on the hub when it is pressed out of the hub carrier, a knife-edged bearing puller may be required to remove it.*

1 Where fitted, remove the cap from the centre of the wheel, then slacken the hub bolt 90° (one quarter of a turn) with the vehicle resting on its wheels **(see illustration)**. Also slacken the wheel bolts.

2 Chock the rear wheels, firmly apply the handbrake, then jack up the front of the car and support it on axle stands (see *Jacking and vehicle support*). Remove the appropriate front roadwheel.

3 Remove the hub bolt. If the bolt was not slackened with the wheels on the ground, refit at least two roadwheel bolts to the front hub, tightening them securely, then have an assistant firmly depress the brake pedal to prevent the front hub from rotating, whilst you slacken and remove the hub bolt.

4 On vehicles equipped with gas discharge headlamps, release the clip and disconnect the vehicle level sensor connecting rod from the front lower transverse arm.

5 Remove the brake disc as described in Chapter 9, Section 7.

6 Remove the ABS wheel sensor as described in Chapter 9, Section 17.

7 Undo the bolts and detach the brake disc shield from the hub carrier.

8 Undo the securing nut and extract the clamp bolt from the top of the hub carrier.

Separate the front and rear upper transverse arm balljoints from the top of the hub carrier, but do not force the slots apart with a screwdriver or similar, in an attempt to free the balljoint pins **(see illustration)**. Take care to avoid damaging the balljoint rubber gaiters. Discard the nut and bolt, new ones must be fitted.

9 Pull the hub carrier assembly outwards, and at the same time pull the end of the driveshaft from the wheel hub. Tie the driveshaft to the vehicle body and do not let it hang down or the driveshaft joints may be damaged.

10 Unscrew the 4 multi-splined bolts, and detach the hub bearing housing from the carrier **(see illustration)**.

11 Press the hub from the bearing. If the bearing's inner race remains on the hub, remove it using a bearing puller. Note that new bearings are supplied integral with the bearing housing.

12 Press the new bearing assembly on to the hub, using a tubular spacer which bears only on the inner bearing race.

13 Fit the hub bearing assembly to the hub carrier, then insert the bolts and tighten them to the specified torque.

14 The remainder of refitting is a reversal of removal, noting the following points:
a) Tighten the new driveshaft bolt to the Stage 1 torque setting with the vehicle on axle stands, but only carry out the Stage 2 angle-tightening setting once the vehicle is back on its wheels (see Chapter 8, Section 2).
b) Tighten all fasteners to their specified torque where given.

Hub carrier

15 Proceed as described in paragraphs 1 to 8 of this Section.

16 Loosen the nut securing the steering track rod balljoint to the hub carrier. To do this, fit a ring spanner to the nut, and then hold the balljoint pin stationary using an Allen key. With the nut removed, it may be possible to release the balljoint from the hub carrier by turning the balljoint pin with an Allen key. If not, leave the nut on by a few turns to protect the threads, then use a universal balljoint separator to release the balljoint. Remove

2.1 Prise out the cap in the centre of the wheel

2.8 Undo the nut, remove the clamp bolt and pull up the two balljoints

2.10 Undo the 4 bolts and detach the hub from the carrier

the nut completely once the taper has been released noting that a new nut will be required for refitting.

17 Undo the retaining bolt and detach the brake hose and wiring harness support bracket from the hub carrier.

18 Undo the securing nuts, then separate the front and rear lower transverse arms from the base of the hub carrier, with the aid of a balljoint splitter (see Section 4). Avoid damaging the rubber gaiters.

19 Grasp the hub carrier and gradually draw it off the driveshaft. Use a hub puller if the driveshaft is a tight fit in the hub. Tie the driveshaft to the vehicle body and do not let it hang down or the driveshaft joints may be damaged.

20 If required, undo the 4 countersunk bolts and detach the hub bearing housing from the hub carrier.

21 Refitting is a reversal of removal, noting the following points:

a) *Renew all nuts and bolts securing the driveshaft and suspension components to the hub carrier. Note that their are different versions of the retaining nuts. Refer to an Audi parts stockist for latest recommendations.*

b) *Tighten the new driveshaft bolt to the Stage 1 torque setting with the vehicle on axle stands, but only carry out the Stage 2 angle-tightening setting once the vehicle is back on its wheels (see Chapter 8, Section 2).*

c) *Tighten all fasteners to their specified torque where given.*

d) *Have the front wheel alignment checked at the earliest opportunity.*

3 Front suspension strut – removal, overhaul and refitting

Note: *On vehicles with Dynamic Ride Control the DRC system must be discharged and recharged using specialist Audi equipment. Removal and refitting of the front suspension strut on vehicles with DRC should therefore be entrusted to an Audi dealer.*

Removal

Note: *New retaining nuts and bolts will be required for all suspension component attachments, disturbed in this procedure.*

1 Before commencing work, use a tape measure to measure the distance from the wheel centre to the lower edge of the wheel arch. Record this dimension as it will be used to position the suspension at the normal vehicle ride height when refitting the suspension strut.

2 Chock the rear wheels, firmly apply the handbrake, then jack up the front of the car and support it on axle stands (see *Jacking and vehicle support*). Remove the appropriate front roadwheel, then remove the engine undertrays.

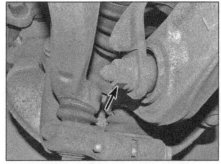

3.7 Undo the nut and remove the suspension strut lower mounting bolt

3 From within the engine compartment, remove the rectangular rubber cover directly above the wheel arch on the side being worked on. Insert a strap, length of rope or something similar down through the opening, wrap it around the top of the hub carrier and feed it up back through the opening. Place a suitable block of wood over the opening and tie the strap or rope around the wood. This will retain the hub carrier when the suspension components are disconnected.

4 On vehicles equipped with gas discharge headlamps, undo the nut and disconnect the vehicle level sensor connecting rod from the front lower transverse arm.

5 Undo the bolts securing the anti-roll bar drop link to the anti-roll bar and suspension strut fork and remove the drop link.

6 Loosen the nut securing the steering track rod balljoint to the hub carrier. To do this, fit a ring spanner to the nut, and then hold the balljoint pin stationary using an Allen key. With the nut removed, it may be possible to release the balljoint from the hub carrier by turning the balljoint pin with an Allen key. If not, leave the nut on by a few turns to protect the threads, then use a universal balljoint separator to release the balljoint. Remove the nut completely once the taper has been released noting that a new nut will be required for refitting.

7 Undo the nut and remove the suspension strut fork lower mounting bolt from the front lower transverse arm **(see illustration)**.

8 Note which way round it is fitted, then unscrew the nut and remove the clamp bolt

3.9 Undo the nut and remove the front lower arm-to-subframe mounting bolt

3.8 Unscrew the nut and remove the suspension strut fork clamp bolt

securing the suspension strut fork to the bottom of the strut **(see illustration)**.

9 Undo the nut then remove the bolt securing the inboard end of the front lower transverse arm to the subframe **(see illustration)**. Pull the arm from its location in the subframe and swivel it forwards.

10 The suspension strut fork must now be released from the bottom of the strut. To do this, Audi technicians insert a special tool into the split in the suspension strut fork, and turn it through 90° to open up the clamp. A similar tool such as an Allen key can be used, or alternatively a suitable cold chisel can be driven into the split as a wedge. Once the split has opened sufficiently, pull the suspension strut fork down and off the base of the strut, then remove it from under the wheel arch.

11 Undo the securing nut and extract the clamp bolt from the top of the hub carrier. Separate the front and rear upper transverse arm balljoints from the top of the hub carrier, but do not force the slots apart with a screwdriver or similar, in an attempt to free the balljoint pins **(see illustration 2.8)**. Take care to avoid damaging the balljoint rubber gaiters.

12 Remove the plenum chamber cover as described in Chapter 11, Section 21.

13 If removing the suspension strut on the right-hand side, undo the three bolts and remove the lid on the engine compartment electronics box **(see illustration)**.

14 If removing the suspension strut on the left-hand side, undo the two retaining nuts, lift the coolant expansion tank from its location and move to one side.

3.13 Undo the bolts and lift off the electronics box lid

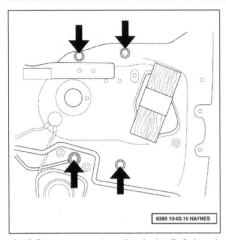

3.15 Strut upper mounting bolts (left-hand side)

15 Undo the four strut upper mounting bolts **(see illustration)**, then withdraw the strut, complete with upper mounting bracket, from under the wheel arch, taking care not to damage the driveshaft or steering rack gaiters.

Overhaul

16 To ensure that the upper mounting bracket is correctly positioned, the suspension strut must be mounted in the Audi suspension strut alignment fixture during reassembly. For this reason, overhaul of the suspension strut must be carried out by an Audi dealer or independent garage with access to the specialist equipment.

Refitting

17 Offer up the suspension strut to the wheel arch and refit the new upper mounting bolts. Tighten the bolts progressively in a diagonal sequence to the specified Stage 1 torque, then through the Stage 2 angle.
18 Reconnect the upper transverse arms to the top of the hub carrier. Refit the new clamp bolt, together with a new retaining nut and tighten it to the specified torque. Press down on both transverse arms as you tighten the nut, to ensure that the balljoints are properly seated in the hub carrier.
19 Open the clamp in the top of the

suspension strut fork using the same method as for removal and engage the base of the strut in the fork. Push the fork fully onto the strut ensuring that the peg on the strut engages with the slot on the fork.
20 Fit the new suspension strut fork clamp bolt, screw on the new nut and tighten the nut to the specified Stage 1 torque, then through the specified Stage 2 angle.
21 Using a new bolt, attach the strut fork lower mounting to the lower transverse arm, fit a new securing nut but hand-tighten it only at this stage. Note the bolt is inserted from the front.
22 Using a new bolt, attach the inboard end of the lower transverse arm to the subframe. Fit a new securing nut but hand-tighten it only at this stage.
23 Position a trolley jack under the hub carrier and raise the suspension to the position recorded in paragraph 1. Take care not to lift the car off the axle stand as the suspension is being raised.
24 With the suspension positioned at the normal vehicle ride height, tighten the lower transverse arm inboard mounting nut and the suspension strut lower mounting nut to the specified Stage 1 torque, then through the specified Stage 2 angle.
25 Using a new nut of the correct type, connect the steering track rod balljoint to the hub carrier as described in Section 19.
26 Using new bolts, attach the anti-roll bar drop link to the anti-roll bar and suspension strut fork. Tighten the bolts to the specified Stage 1 torque, then through the specified Stage 2 angle.
27 The remainder of refitting is a reversal of removal. On completion have the front wheel alignment checked at the earliest opportunity.

4 Front suspension transverse arms – removal, overhaul and refitting

Upper arms

Removal

Note: *New retaining nuts and bolts will be required for all suspension component attachments, disturbed in this procedure.*

1 Before commencing work, use a tape measure to measure the distance from the wheel centre to the lower edge of the wheel arch. Record this dimension as it will be used to position the suspension at the normal vehicle ride height when tightening the transverse link inner mounting bolt.
2 Chock the rear wheels, firmly apply the handbrake, then jack up the front of the car and support it on axle stands (see *Jacking and vehicle support*). Remove the appropriate front roadwheel.
3 Undo the securing nut and extract the clamp bolt from the top of the hub carrier. Separate the front and rear upper transverse arm balljoints from the top of the hub carrier, but do not force the slots apart with a screwdriver or similar, in an attempt to free the balljoint pins **(see illustration 2.8)**. Take care to avoid damaging the balljoint rubber gaiters.
4 Undo the securing nut and remove the bolt securing the appropriate upper transverse arm to the mounting bracket **(see illustrations)**. Withdraw the arm from the bracket and remove it from under the wheel arch.

Overhaul

5 Thoroughly clean the arm and the area around the arm mountings, removing all traces of dirt, thread-locking compound and underseal if necessary, then check carefully for cracks, distortion or any other signs of wear or damage, paying particular attention to the inner pivot bush and outer balljoint. The balljoint is an integral part of the arm and cannot be renewed separately. If the arm or balljoint are damaged then the complete assembly must be renewed.
6 Renewal of the inner pivot bush will require the use of a bush renewal tool or preferably an hydraulic press and several spacers, and is therefore best entrusted to an Audi dealer or garage with access to the necessary equipment. If such equipment is available, press out the old bush and install the new one using a spacer which bears only on the bush outer edge. Ensure the bush is correctly positioned so that the cavities are aligned with the centre axis of the arm **(see illustration)**.

Refitting

7 Offer up the relevant transverse arm to the mounting bracket, insert a new securing bolt

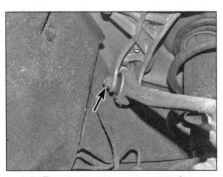

4.4a Front upper transverse arm inner mounting...

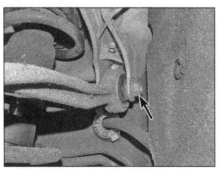

4.4b ...and rear upper arm inner mounting

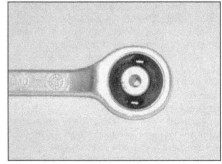

4.6 Align the cavities in the bush with the centre axis of the arm

and screw on a new securing nut. Only tighten the nut hand-tight at this stage.

8 Reconnect the upper transverse arms to the top of the hub carrier. Refit the new clamp bolt, together with a new retaining nut and tighten it to the specified torque. Press down on both transverse arms as you tighten the nut, to ensure that the balljoints are properly seated in the hub carrier.

9 Position a trolley jack under the hub carrier and raise the suspension to the position recorded in paragraph 1. Take care not to lift the car off the axle stand as the suspension is being raised.

10 With the suspension positioned at the normal vehicle ride height, tighten the upper transverse arm inboard mounting nut to the specified Stage 1 torque, then through the specified Stage 2 angle.

11 Refit the roadwheel and lower the car to the ground. Tighten the roadwheel bolts to the specified torque.

Rear lower arm (guide link)

Removal

Note: *New retaining nuts and bolts will be required for all suspension component attachments, disturbed in this procedure.*

12 Before commencing work, use a tape measure to measure the distance from the wheel centre to the lower edge of the wheel arch. Record this dimension as it will be used to position the suspension at the normal vehicle ride height when tightening the nut on the guide link inboard retaining bolt.

13 Chock the rear wheels, firmly apply the handbrake, then jack up the front of the car and support it on axle stands (see *Jacking and vehicle support*). Remove the appropriate front roadwheel and the engine undertrays.

14 Undo the guide link balljoint securing nut until it's flush with the end of the threads (use a 4 mm Allen key to counter-hold the balljoint shank), then separate the link from the base of the hub carrier, with the aid of a universal balljoint separator – avoid damaging the rubber gaiter **(see illustration)**.

15 Undo the nut and remove the retaining bolt at the inboard end of the guide link **(see illustration)**. Withdraw the guide link from the subframe and remove it from under the wheel arch.

Overhaul

Note: *Early models were fitted with a 65 mm conventional bonded rubber bush at the guide link inboard mounting. From model year 2010, 75 mm hydraulic bonded rubber bushes were gradually introduced. If the bush is to be renewed, ensure that the correct type is obtained.*

16 Thoroughly clean the guide link and the area around the mountings, removing all traces of dirt, thread-locking compound and underseal if necessary, then check carefully for cracks, distortion or any other signs of wear or damage, paying particular attention to the inner pivot bush and balljoint. Note

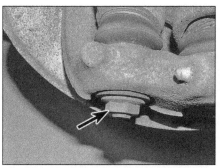

4.14 Undo the guide link balljoint securing nut

that on later models, the inner bush has a hydraulic action; fluid leakage indicates that the bush has been damaged and must be renewed. The balljoint is an integral part of the lower arm and cannot be renewed separately. If the arm or balljoint are damaged then the complete assembly must be renewed.

17 Renewal of the inner pivot bush will require the use of a hydraulic press and several spacers and is therefore best entrusted to an Audi dealer or garage with access to the necessary equipment. If such equipment is available, press out the old bush and install the new one using a spacer which bears only on the bush outer edge. Ensure the bush is correctly positioned in the guide link **(see illustrations)**.

Refitting

18 Offer up the guide link to its location in the subframe, insert a new securing bolt and screw on a new securing nut. Only tighten the nut hand-tight at this stage.

19 Engage the guide link balljoint with the hub carrier, screw on a new nut and tighten the nut to the specified torque.

20 Position a trolley jack under the hub carrier and raise the suspension to the position recorded in paragraph 12. Take care not to lift the car off the axle stand as the suspension is being raised.

21 With the suspension positioned at the normal vehicle ride height, tighten the guide link arm inboard mounting nut to the specified

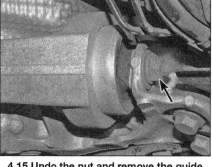

4.15 Undo the nut and remove the guide link inboard bolt.

Stage 1 torque, then through the specified Stage 2 angle.

22 Refit the engine undertrays and roadwheel then lower the car to the ground. Tighten the roadwheel bolts to the specified torque.

Front lower arm (track control link)

Removal

Note: *New retaining nuts and bolts will be required for all suspension component attachments, disturbed in this procedure.*

23 Before commencing work, use a tape measure to measure the distance from the wheel centre to the lower edge of the wheel arch. Record this dimension as it will be used to position the suspension at the normal vehicle ride height when tightening the nut on the track control link inboard retaining bolt.

24 Chock the rear wheels, firmly apply the handbrake, then jack up the front of the car and support it on axle stands (see *Jacking and vehicle support*). Remove the appropriate front roadwheel and the engine undertrays.

25 On vehicles equipped with gas discharge headlamps, undo the nut and disconnect the vehicle level sensor connecting rod from the front lower transverse arm.

26 Undo the nut and remove the suspension strut fork lower mounting bolt from the front lower transverse arm **(see illustration 3.7)**.

27 Loosen the nut securing the steering track rod balljoint to the hub carrier. To do this, fit

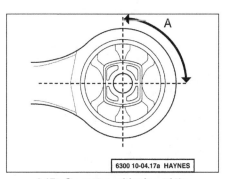

4.17a Correct positioning of the conventional bonded rubber bush in the guide link

A =90°

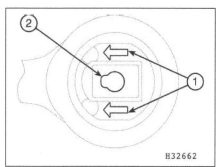

4.17b Correct positioning of the hydraulic bonded rubber bush in the guide link

Ensure the arrows on the bush (1) or the central groove (2) point towards the balljoint

a ring spanner to the nut, and then hold the balljoint pin stationary using an Allen key. With the nut removed, it may be possible to release the balljoint from the hub carrier by turning the balljoint pin with an Allen key. If not, leave the nut on by a few turns to protect the threads, then use a universal balljoint separator to release the balljoint. Remove the nut completely once the taper has been released.

28 Undo the nut then remove the bolt securing the inboard end of the front lower transverse arm to the subframe. Pull the arm from its location in the subframe and swivel it towards the rear.

29 Undo the securing nut until it's flush with the end of the balljoint shank threads, then separate the front lower transverse arm from the base of the hub carrier, with the aid of a universal balljoint separator (avoid damaging the rubber gaiter). If necessary, use a 4 mm Allen key to counter-hold the nut.

30 Position a trolley jack under the hub carrier to prevent the suspension extending to far and damaging the upper link arms. Remove the nut securing the transverse arm balljoint to the hub carrier, then remove the arm from the vehicle.

Overhaul

31 Thoroughly clean the arm and the area around the arm mountings, removing all traces of dirt, thread-locking compound and underseal if necessary, then check carefully for cracks, distortion or any other signs of wear or damage, paying particular attention to the bushes and balljoint. If necessary, the balljoint can be renewed as described in Section 5.

32 Renewal of the two bonded rubber bushes will require the use of a hydraulic press and several spacers and is therefore best entrusted to an Audi dealer or garage with access to the necessary equipment. If such equipment is available, the renewal procedure is the same as described previously for the bonded rubber bush in the guide link.

Refitting

33 Engage the transverse arm balljoint with the hub carrier, screw on a new nut and tighten the nut to the specified torque.

34 Using a new bolt, attach the suspension strut fork lower mounting to the lower transverse arm, fit a new securing nut but hand-tighten it only at this stage. Note the bolt is inserted from the front.

35 Using a new bolt, attach the inboard end of the lower transverse arm to the subframe. Fit a new securing nut but hand-tighten it only at this stage.

36 Position a trolley jack under the hub carrier and raise the suspension to the position recorded in paragraph 23. Take care not to lift the car off the axle stand as the suspension is being raised.

37 With the suspension positioned at the normal vehicle ride height, tighten the lower transverse arm inboard mounting nut and the suspension strut lower mounting nut to the specified Stage 1 torque, then through the specified Stage 2 angle.

38 Using a new nut of the correct type, connect the steering track rod balljoint to the hub carrier as described in Section 19.

39 The remainder of refitting is a reversal of removal. On completion have the front wheel alignment checked at the earliest opportunity.

5 Hub carrier lower arm balljoint – renewal

1 Remove the front lower arm as described in Section 4.

2 Undo and remove the balljoint clamp bolt from the base of the hub carrier.

3 Insert a washer, or similar item into the slot in the hub carrier. Preferably choose a washer of the same thickness as the slot.

4 Screw the previously removed clamp bolt into the hub carrier, this time from the rear, until it makes contact with the washer.

5 Widen the slot in the hub carrier by screwing in the clamp bolt a further half a turn, approximately.

6 Lift the balljoint out of the hub carrier.

7 Fit the new balljoint using the reverse of the removal procedure, bearing in mind the following points:

a) *Ensure that the balljoint is fully inserted into the hub carrier.*

b) *Use a new clamp bolt to secure the balljoint.*

c) *Tighten all nuts and bolts to the specified torque.*

d) *Refit the front lower arm as described in Section 4.*

e) *Have the front wheel alignment checked at the earliest opportunity.*

6 Front anti-roll bar – removal and refitting

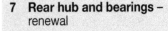

Removal

Note: *New retaining nuts and bolts will be required for all suspension component* attachments, disturbed in this procedure.

1 The anti-roll bar must be removed/refitted with the vehicle resting on its wheels. For this reason the following operation will be much easier if the vehicle can be positioned over an inspection pit. Alternatively drive the vehicle onto ramps to increase the clearance between the front of the vehicle and the ground.

2 Release the fasteners and remove the undertray from beneath the engine to gain access to the anti-roll bar mounting clamps.

3 Undo the nut and remove the bolt securing the anti-roll bar drop link to the anti-roll bar on each side **(see illustration)**.

4 Slacken and remove the nuts securing both the anti-roll bar mounting clamps to the subframe **(see illustration)**. Lower the anti-roll bar, and remove it from under the vehicle.

5 Renew the anti-roll bar if it is damaged or distorted. Renew the mounting bushes if they are perished or worn.

Refitting

6 Manoeuvre the anti-roll bar into position and engage it with the ends of the drop links. Insert the new securing bolts and nuts, tightening them lightly only at this stage.

7 Refit the mounting clamps to the anti-roll bar mounting bushes. Ensure both clamps are correctly located on the bushes then fit the new retaining nuts. Tighten the retaining nuts lightly only at this stage.

8 Rock the vehicle from side-to-side, to settle the anti-roll bar in position. Tighten the drop link nuts to the specified torque settings. Also tighten the anti-roll bar mounting clamp nuts to the specified torque.

9 Refit the undertray and tighten the fixings securely.

7 Rear hub and bearings – renewal

Note: *The rear wheel hub bearings are housed in the rear hub unit. The bearings are an integral assembly with the hub, and are maintenance-free. If defective, the bearings must be renewed with the hub as a complete unit.*

6.3 Undo the nut and remove the anti-roll bar drop link bolt

6.4 Undo the nuts securing the anti-roll bar mounting clamps to the subframe

7.2 Use a chisel to prise off the grease cap

7.4 Use a 17 mm Allen bit to slacken the hub bolt

8.6 Undo the retaining bolt and detach the support bracket from the hub carrier

1 Chock the front wheels, then jack up the rear of the car and support it on axle stands (see *Jacking and vehicle support*). Remove the appropriate rear roadwheel.
2 Prise off the grease cap from the hub **(see illustration)**.
3 Refit the roadwheel and lower the vehicle to the ground.
4 Slacken the hub flange bolt 90° (a quarter of a turn) **(see illustration)**.
5 Raise the vehicle, remove the roadwheel again, then remove the rear brake disc as described in Chapter 9, Section 8.
6 Completely unscrew the flange bolt and pull the hub and bearing from the hub carrier stub axle. If the hub is reluctant to move, undo the four bolts securing the brake backplate to the hub carrier. Use the backplate to pull the hub and bearing slightly off the stub axle. When sufficient clearance exists, reach behind the additional seal on the stub axle and use the seal to pull the hub and brake backplate off the stub axle.
Caution: If the hub unit is to be re-used, when it is removed from the car always lay it down on the brake disc mating face, so that the bearing is pointing upward. Failure to do this may cause damage to the ABS wheel sensor magnetic trigger elements located in the bearing oil seal.
7 Remove the additional seal from the stub axle.
8 Clean the stub axle, additional seal and

brake backplate, then refit the backplate and additional seal. Tighten the backplate retaining bolts securely.
9 Fit the hub bearing unit into position. Fit the new flange bolt, but only tighten it to the specified Stage 1 torque at this stage.
10 Refit the roadwheel, lower the vehicle to the ground, and tighten the flange bolt through the Stage 2 angle-tightening setting.
11 Raise the vehicle and remove the roadwheel again, then drive in the new grease cap.
12 The remainder of refitting is a reversal of removal.

8 Rear hub carrier – removal and refitting

Removal

Note: *New retaining nuts and bolts will be required for all suspension component attachments, disturbed in this procedure.*
1 Before commencing work, use a tape measure to measure the distance from the wheel centre to the lower edge of the rear wheel arch. Record this dimension as it will be used to position the suspension at the normal vehicle ride height when tightening the link arm mounting bolts.

2 If the hub and bearing unit are to be removed from the hub carrier, proceed as described in paragraphs 1 to 7 of Section 7.
3 If the hub and bearing unit are to remain on the hub carrier, begin by jacking up the rear of the vehicle, and supporting it securely on axle stands (see *Jacking and vehicle support*).
4 Disconnect the wiring connector, then undo the retaining bolt, and pull the ABS wheel sensor from the hub carrier.
5 Disconnect the wiring connector from the electronic handbrake actuator on the brake caliper.
6 Undo the retaining bolt and detach the brake hose and wiring loom support bracket from the hub carrier **(see illustration)**.
7 Remove the rear brake disc as described in Chapter 9, Section 8.
8 Remove the coil spring as described in Section 10.
9 Using a felt-tip pen or paint, mark the position of the upper transverse link eccentric bolt in relation to the hub carrier. Undo the nut, remove the eccentric washer, then remove the eccentric bolt **(see illustration)**.
10 Undo and remove the bolt securing the track rod to the hub carrier **(see illustration)**.
11 Unclip the stone deflector surround around the shock absorber lower mounting, then undo the lower mounting bolt **(see illustration)**. Collect the inner washer as the bolt is removed.
12 Undo the nut from the bolt securing the

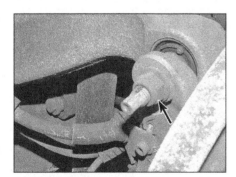
8.9 Undo the nut, remove the eccentric washer, then remove the upper transverse link eccentric bolt

8.10 Undo the bolt securing the track rod to the hub carrier

8.11 Unclip the stone deflector around the shock absorber lower mounting

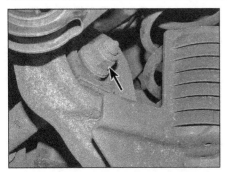

8.12 Undo the nut and remove the lower transverse link-to-hub carrier retaining bolt

lower transverse link to the hub carrier **(see illustration)**. Remove the bolt and collect the spacer tube.

13 Withdraw the hub carrier from under the wheel arch.

Overhaul

14 Renewal of the bonded hub carrier bush requires access to a hydraulic press and a number of specially-shaped extraction/fitment tools. Fabrication of alternative tools is not recommended due to the risk of damage to the bush mountings. For this reason, it's best to entrust bush renewal work to an Audi dealer or suitably-equipped specialist.

Refitting

15 Refitting is a reversal of removal, noting the following points:
a) Obtain new nuts and bolts for all disturbed fastenings.

9.8a Remove the cap...

9.8c...remove the upper mounting bracket...

b) Transfer the alignment mark on the upper transverse link eccentric bolt to the new bolt, then set the bolt to its original position when fitting.
c) Initially tighten the hub carrier attachments hand-tight only. Position a trolley jack under the hub carrier and raise the suspension to the position recorded in paragraph 1. Take care not to lift the car off the axle stand as the suspension is being raised. With the suspension positioned at the normal vehicle ride height, tighten the hub carrier mountings to the specified Stage 1 torque, then through the specified Stage 2 angle.
d) Have the rear wheel alignment checked at the earliest opportunity.

9 Rear shock absorber – removal and refitting

Removal

Note: To maintain the vehicle's handling characteristics, shock absorbers should always be renewed in pairs.
Note: New retaining nuts and bolts will be required for all component attachments, disturbed in this procedure.

1 Before commencing work, use a tape measure to measure the distance from the wheel centre to the lower edge of the rear wheel arch. Record this dimension as it will be used to position the suspension at the normal vehicle ride height when tightening the shock absorber mounting bolt.

9.8b...unscrew the nut while holding the piston rod...

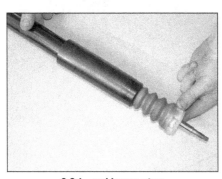

9.8d...and bump stop

2 Chock the rear wheels, firmly apply the handbrake, then jack up the front of the car and support it on axle stands (see Jacking and vehicle support). Remove the appropriate rear roadwheel.

3 Remove the relevant rear wheel arch liner as described in Chapter 11, Section 21.

4 Position a trolley jack underneath the rear hub carrier and raise it until the shock absorber starts to compress.

5 Unclip the stone deflector surround around the shock absorber lower mounting, then undo the lower mounting bolt **(see illustration 8.11)**. Collect the inner washer as the bolt is removed. Note that a new bolt will be required for refitting.

6 Undo and remove the two shock absorber upper mounting bolts from under the wheel arch.

7 Compress the shock absorber and manoeuvre it from the vehicle.

8 With the shock absorber on the bench, remove the cap, then unscrew the nut from the top of the piston rod and remove the upper mounting bracket, followed by the bump stop and protective tube **(see illustrations)**.

9 If necessary, the action of the shock absorber can be checked by mounting it upright in a vice. Fully depress the rod, and then pull it up fully. The piston rod must move smoothly over its complete length.

Refitting

10 Locate the components removed from the top of the shock absorber in their correct order, and screw on a new nut. Tighten the nut and fit the cap.

11 Locate the shock absorber in the rear wheel arch, then insert the new upper mounting bolts and tighten to the specified torque.

12 Extend the shock absorber if necessary, and fit the spacer and new lower mounting bolt. Do not tighten the lower mounting bolt at this stage.

13 Raise the suspension to the position recorded in paragraph 1. Take care not to lift the car off the axle stand as the suspension is being raised. With the suspension positioned at the normal vehicle ride height, tighten the shock absorber lower mounting bolt to the specified Stage 1 torque, then through the specified Stage 2 angle.

14 Refit the wheel arch liner.

15 Refit the roadwheel and lower the vehicle to the ground.

10 Rear coil spring – removal and refitting

 Warning: Before attempting to remove the coil spring, a suitable tool to hold the coil spring in compression must be obtained. Adjustable coil spring compressors are readily available, and are essential for this

10.2 Compress the coil spring

10.4 The pin on the base of the spring seat engages with a hole in the hub carrier

11.13 Right-hand rear subframe mounting bolt

operation. Any attempt to dismantle the strut without such a tool is likely to result in damage or personal injury.

Removal

1 Chock the front wheels, jack up the rear of the vehicle and support it securely on axle stands (see *Jacking and vehicle support*). Remove the rear roadwheel to improve access.

2 Fit the spring compressor, and compress the coil spring evenly and progressively until tension is relieved from the spring seats **(see illustration)**. Take care not to damage the hub carrier.

3 Continue compressing the spring until the stone deflector and lower spring seat can be taken out, then remove the compressed spring from the vehicle. Remove the upper spring seat.

Refitting

4 Refit the lower spring seat to the hub carrier. Note that the seat has a locating pin, which engages in a corresponding hole in the hub carrier **(see illustration)**.

5 Fit the upper spring seat, then place compressed spring into position Ensure the end of the spring contacts the limit stop in the lower seat.

6 Refit the stone deflector, then slowly decompress the spring. Guide the upper seat into place as the coil is released.

7 Refit the roadwheel, lower the vehicle to the ground, and tighten the wheel bolts to the specified torque.

11 Rear subframe –
removal and refitting

Note: *The following procedure details removal of the subframe complete with link arms and hub carriers. If required, remove these components as described elsewhere in this Chapter, then unbolt and remove the subframe using the relevant information from this Section.*

Removal

Note: *New retaining nuts and bolts will*

be required for all suspension component attachments, disturbed in this procedure.

1 Before commencing work, use a tape measure to measure the distance from the wheel centre to the lower edge of the rear wheel arch. Record this dimension as it will be used to position the suspension at the normal vehicle ride height when tightening the mounting bolts of any bonded rubber bush attachment.

2 Chock the front wheels, jack up the rear of the vehicle and support it securely on axle stands (see *Jacking and vehicle support*). Remove the rear roadwheels.

3 Release the fasteners and remove the rear and side underbody covers.

4 Remove the rear section of the exhaust system as described in Chapter 4B, Section 8.

5 Remove both rear coil springs (see Section 10).

6 Undo the retaining bolt and detach the brake hose and wiring loom support bracket from the hub carrier **(see illustration 8.6)**.

7 Disconnect the wiring connectors at the ABS wheel sensors, electronic handbrake actuators and, where fitted, from the vehicle level senders on each side.

8 Unclip the wiring harness from the subframe on both sides.

9 Unclip the stone deflector surround around the shock absorber lower mounting, then undo the lower mounting bolt **(see illustration 8.11)**. Collect the inner washer as the bolt is removed.

10 Undo the bolts and slide the brake caliper and mounting bracket from the hub carrier. Suspend the caliper from the vehicle body using string or wire, to prevent the brake hose from any strain.

11 Position a suitable workshop trolley jack with the necessary wooden blocks under the subframe, and take its weight.

12 Engage the help of an assistant and ensure that the subframe is well supported and stable on the trolley jack, then undo the three retaining bolts from the subframe front attachment on each side. Collect the support plates.

13 Undo the subframe rear mounting bolt on each side, then carefully lower the subframe **(see illustration)**.

14 Manoeuvre the assembly from under the vehicle.

15 If the subframe hydro-bushes are worn, they must be renewed. This task can only be performed with the help of special Audi tools. For this reason, we recommend the task be entrusted to an Audi dealer or suitably-equipped specialist.

Refitting

16 Refitting is a reversal of the removal procedure, noting the following points:

a) *Obtain new nuts and bolts for all disturbed fastenings.*

b) *Before tightening any retaining bolt at a bonded rubber bush mounting, position a trolley jack under the hub carrier and raise the suspension to the position recorded in paragraph 18. Take care not to lift the car off the axle stand as the suspension is being raised. With the suspension positioned at the normal vehicle ride height, tighten the mounting bolt to the specified Stage 1 torque, then through the specified Stage 2 angle.*

c) *On completion, have the rear wheel alignment checked at the earliest opportunity.*

12 Rear suspension link arms
– removal and refitting

Upper transverse link

Removal

Note: *New retaining nuts and bolts will be required for all suspension component attachments, disturbed in this procedure.*

1 In order to remove the transverse link inner mounting bolt, the subframe must be removed as described in Section 11.

2 Using a felt-tip pen or paint, mark the position of the upper transverse link eccentric bolt in relation to the hub carrier. Undo the nut, remove the eccentric washer, then remove the eccentric bolt.

3 Unscrew and remove the inner mounting bolt, and remove the transverse link.

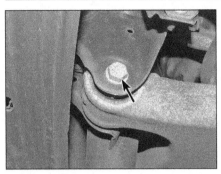

12.16 Lower transverse link rear mounting

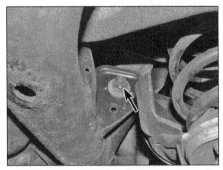

12.21 Track rod inner mounting nut and eccentric washer

Refitting

4 Bolt the transverse link loosely to the subframe using a new bolt and nut, then obtain a suitable straight-edge (such as a long strip of wood). Lay the straight edge on the transverse link inner mountings on each side so that the end of the wood is directly above the outboard mounting of the link being worked on.

5 Lift the transverse link so that a dimension of 8.0 mm is obtained between the underside of the straight edge and the upper surface of the link, directly above the outboard mounting. Hold the link in this position and tighten the inner mounting nut to the specified Stage 1 torque, then through the specified Stage 2 angle.

6 Transfer the alignment mark on the transverse link eccentric bolt to the new bolt. Reconnect the link to the hub carrier, aligning the previously-made marks, and tighten the nut to 20 Nm (15 lbf ft) only at this stage.

7 Refit the subframe as described in Section 11, but leave the vehicle raised and supported with the rear roadwheels removed.

8 With the subframe installed, raise the suspension to the position recorded prior to subframe removal. Take care not to lift the car off the axle stand as the suspension is being raised. With the suspension positioned at the normal vehicle ride height, slacken the transverse link-to-subframe retaining bolt nut, then tighten it to the specified Stage 1 torque, then through the specified Stage 2 angle.

9 On completion, refit the roadwheels and lower the vehicle to the ground. Tighten the wheel bolts to the specified torque.

10 Have the rear wheel alignment checked at the earliest opportunity.

Lower transverse link

Removal

Note: *New retaining nuts and bolts will be required for all suspension component attachments, disturbed in this procedure.*

11 Before commencing work, use a tape measure to measure the distance from the wheel centre to the lower edge of the rear wheel arch **(see illustration 3.1)**. Record this dimension as it will be used to position the

suspension at the normal vehicle ride height when tightening the transverse link mounting bolts.

12 Remove the rear suspension coil spring as described in Section 10.

13 Where applicable, undo the bolt securing the vehicle level sender bracket to the lower transverse link.

14 Undo the bolt securing the anti-roll bar drop link to the lower transverse link.

15 Undo the nut from the bolt securing the lower transverse link to the hub carrier **(see illustration 8.12)**. Remove the bolt and collect the spacer tube.

16 Undo the bolt securing the lower transverse link rear mounting to the subframe and the nut and bolt securing the front mounting to the subframe, then manoeuvre the link out from under the vehicle **(see illustration)**.

Refitting

17 Refitting is a reversal of removal, noting the following points:

a) *Obtain new nuts and bolts for all disturbed fastenings.*

b) *Initially tighten the lower transverse link mountings hand-tight only. Position a trolley jack under the hub carrier and raise the suspension to the position recorded in paragraph 11. Take care not to lift the car off the axle stand as the suspension is being raised. With the suspension positioned at the normal vehicle ride height, tighten the transverse link mountings to the specified Stage 1 torque, then through the specified Stage 2 angle.*

c) *On completion, have the rear wheel alignment checked at the earliest opportunity.*

Track rod

Removal

Note: *New retaining nuts and bolts will be required for all suspension component attachments, disturbed in this procedure.*

18 Before commencing work, use a tape measure to measure the distance from the wheel centre to the lower edge of the rear wheel arch **(see illustration 3.1)**. Record this dimension as it will be used to position the

suspension at the normal vehicle ride height when tightening the track rod mounting bolts.

19 Chock the rear wheels, firmly apply the handbrake, then jack up the front of the car and support it on axle stands (see *Jacking and vehicle support*). Remove the appropriate rear roadwheel.

20 Undo and remove the bolt securing the track rod to the hub carrier **(see illustration 8.10)**.

21 Using a felt-tip pen or paint, mark the position of the track rod eccentric bolt in relation to the subframe. Undo the nut, remove the eccentric washer, then remove the eccentric bolt **(see illustration)**.

22 Manipulate the track rod from its location and remove it from under the vehicle.

Refitting

a) *Obtain new nuts and bolts for all disturbed fastenings.*

b) *The track rod must be fitted with the triangular mark on the outside and with the tip of the marking pointing upward.*

c) *Transfer the alignment mark on the track rod eccentric bolt to the new bolt. Reconnect the track rod to the subframe and align the previously-made marks.*

d) *Initially tighten the track rod mountings hand-tight only. Position a trolley jack under the hub carrier and raise the suspension to the position recorded in paragraph 18. Take care not to lift the car off the axle stand as the suspension is being raised. With the suspension positioned at the normal vehicle ride height, tighten the track rod mountings to the specified Stage 1 torque, then through the specified Stage 2 angle.*

e) *On completion, have the rear wheel alignment checked at the earliest opportunity.*

---

13 Rear anti-roll bar – removal and refitting

Removal

Note: *New retaining nuts and bolts will be required for all suspension component attachments, disturbed in this procedure.*

1 Before commencing work, use a tape measure to measure the distance from the wheel centre to the lower edge of the rear wheel arch. Record this dimension as it will be used to position the suspension at the normal vehicle ride height when tightening the anti-roll bar and drop link retaining bolts bolts.

2 Chock the front wheels, then jack up the rear of the vehicle and support it securely on axle stands (see *Jacking and vehicle support*).

3 Release the fasteners and remove the rear underbody trim.

4 Undo the bolt securing the anti-roll bar drop link to the lower transverse link, and the nut and bolt securing the drop link to the anti-roll bar **(see illustration)**.

5 Undo the 2 bolts each side securing the anti-roll bar clamps to the subframe, and manoeuvre the anti-roll bar from under the vehicle **(see illustration)**.

6 Note that the clamps and rubber bushes must not be removed from the anti-roll bar. If any signs of wear or damage are evident, it will be necessary to obtain a new anti-roll bar assembly.

Refitting

7 Manoeuvre the bar into position, and refit the clamps and retaining bolts. Only hand-tighten these bolts at this stage.

8 Attach the drop links to the anti-roll bar, fit the upper and lower mounting bolts and hand-tighten them only.

9 Position a trolley jack under the hub carrier and raise the suspension to the position recorded in paragraph 1. Take care not to lift the car off the axle stand as the suspension is being raised. With the suspension positioned at the normal vehicle ride height, tighten the anti-roll bar clamp bolts and drop-link bolts to the specified Stage 1 torque, then through the specified Stage 2 angle.

10 The remainder of refitting is a reversal of removal.

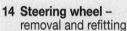 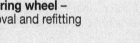
14 Steering wheel – removal and refitting

⚠️ **Warning: Refer to the precautions given in Chapter 12 Section 17 before handling airbag system components.**

Removal

1 Remove the airbag unit as described in Chapter 12 Section 18.

2 Position the front wheels in the straight-ahead position and engage the steering lock.

3 Slacken and remove the steering wheel securing bolt, then mark the steering wheel and steering column shaft in relation to each other **(see illustrations)**. Discard the securing bolt, a new one must be fitted.

4 Disconnect the wiring plug, and lift the

13.4 Anti-roll bar drop link attachments

steering wheel off the column splines, taking care not to damage the contact unit wiring. Do not rotate the contact unit whilst the wheel is removed.

Refitting

5 Refitting is a reversal of removal, noting the following points:
a) *Use the markings made during removal to ensure that the alignment between the steering wheel and column is correct.*
b) *Fit a new steering wheel securing bolt and tighten it to the specified torque, then through the specified angle.*
c) *On completion, refit the airbag unit as described in Chapter 12 Section 18.*

15 Steering gear assembly – removal, overhaul and refitting

Hydraulic steering gear

Removal

Note: *New retaining nuts and bolts will be required for all suspension and steering component attachments, disturbed in this procedure.*

1 Chock the rear wheels, firmly apply the handbrake, then jack up the front of the car and support it on axle stands (see *Jacking and vehicle support*). Remove the front roadwheels, then remove the engine undertrays.

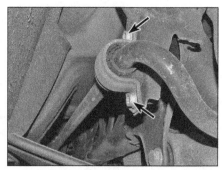
13.5 Undo the bolts and detach the anti-roll bar clamps

2 Set the steering in the straight-ahead position. To prevent unintentional turning, secure the steering wheel in the straight-ahead position using adhesive tape across the top of the airbag and onto the steering column upper shroud.

3 Using brake hose clamps, clamp both the supply and return hoses near the power steering fluid reservoir. This will minimise fluid loss during subsequent operations.

4 Working on one side at a time, loosen the nut securing the steering track rod balljoint to the hub carrier. To do this, fit a ring spanner to the nut, and then hold the balljoint pin stationary using an Allen key. With the nut removed, it may be possible to release the balljoint from the hub carrier by turning the balljoint pin with an Allen key. If not, leave the nut on by a few turns to protect the threads, then use a universal balljoint separator to release the balljoint. Remove the nut completely once the taper has been released noting that a new nut will be required for refitting.

5 Undo the nut securing the fluid supply pipe to the rubber mounting.

6 Remove the front anti-roll bar as described in Section 6.

7 Undo the retaining bolt and release the power steering fluid line from the left-hand side of the front subframe cross-brace.

8 Undo the six retaining bolts and remove the cross-brace from the front subframe **(see illustration)**.

9 Mark the unions to ensure that they are correctly positioned on reassembly, then

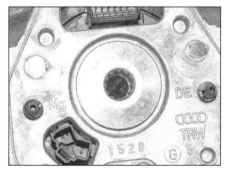
14.3a Undo the steering wheel retaining bolt

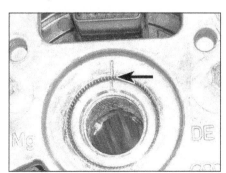
14.3b Make alignment marks between the wheel and the shaft

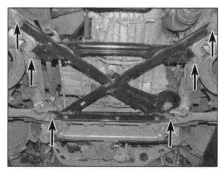
15.8 Undo the retaining bolts and remove the front subframe cross-brace

unscrew the feed and return pipe union bolts from the steering gear assembly; be prepared for fluid spillage, and position a suitable container beneath the pipes whilst unscrewing the union bolts. Disconnect both pipes and recover the sealing rings; discard the rings – new ones must be used on refitting. Plug the pipe ends and steering gear orifices, to prevent fluid leakage and to keep dirt out of the hydraulic system.
10 Disconnect the wiring connector from the solenoid valve on the steering gear housing.
11 Unscrew the pinch-bolt securing the universal joint at the base of the steering column shaft to the steering gear.
12 Pull the steering column universal joint off the steering gear pinion and move it to one side.
13 Undo the nut and bolt each side securing the steering gear to the subframe and withdraw the steering gear from under the car.

Refitting
14 Refitting is a reversal of the removal procedure, noting the following points:
a) *Obtain new nuts and bolts for all disturbed fastenings.*
b) *Tighten all nuts and bolts to the specified torque and, where applicable, through the specified angle.*
c) *Top-up the power steering fluid and bleed the hydraulic system as described in Section 17.*
d) *Have the front-wheel alignment checked at the earliest opportunity.*

Electro-mechanical steering gear

Removal
Note: *New retaining nuts and bolts will be required for all suspension and steering component attachments, disturbed in this procedure.*
15 Chock the rear wheels, firmly apply the handbrake, then jack up the front of the car and support it on axle stands (see *Jacking and vehicle support*). Remove the front roadwheels, then remove the engine undertrays.

16 Set the steering in the straight-ahead position. To prevent unintentional turning, secure the steering wheel in the straight-ahead position using adhesive tape across the top of the airbag and onto the steering column upper shroud.
17 Working on one side at a time, loosen the nut securing the steering track rod balljoint to the hub carrier. To do this, fit a ring spanner to the nut, and then hold the balljoint pin stationary using an Allen key. With the nut removed, it may be possible to release the balljoint from the hub carrier by turning the balljoint pin with an Allen key. If not, leave the nut on by a few turns to protect the threads, then use a universal balljoint separator to release the balljoint. Remove the nut completely once the taper has been released noting that a new nut will be required for refitting.
18 Slacken and remove the nuts securing both the anti-roll bar mounting clamps to the subframe and lower the anti-roll bar **(see illustration 6.4)**.
19 Undo the six retaining bolts and remove the cross-brace from the front subframe **(see illustration 15.8)**.
20 Unscrew the pinch-bolt securing the universal joint at the base of the steering column shaft to the steering gear.
21 Pull the steering column universal joint off the steering gear pinion and move it to one side.
22 Disconnect the two wiring connectors at the electronic control unit on the steering gear.
23 Undo the nut and bolt each side securing the steering gear to the subframe and withdraw the steering gear from under the car.

Refitting
24 Refitting is a reversal of the removal procedure, noting the following points:
a) *Obtain new nuts and bolts for all disturbed fastenings.*
b) *Tighten all nuts and bolts to the specified torque and, where applicable, through the specified angle.*
c) *Have the front wheel alignment checked at the earliest opportunity.*

16 Steering gear rubber gaiters – renewal

1 The steering gear gaiters can be removed and refitted with the steering gear unit in situ or removed from the vehicle.
2 Measure the exposed amount of adjustment thread showing on the inboard side of the track rod end balljoint locknut. This will act as a guide to the adjustment position when refitting the balljoint to the rod. Loosen off the locknut, and detach the track rod end from the track rod as described in Section 19.
3 Unscrew and remove the locking nut from the track rod.
4 Release the retaining clips and withdraw the gaiters from the steering gear and track rod **(see illustrations)**.
5 Refit in the reverse order of removal. Smear the inner bore of the gaiter with lubricant prior to fitting to ease its assembly. Renew the balljoint locknuts. Use new clips to retain the gaiters and ensure that the end of the gaiter locates correctly in the groove machined into the track rod, without twisting.
6 On completion, have the front wheel alignment checked and if necessary adjusted (see Section 21).

17 Power steering system – level check and bleeding

Level check
1 Position the vehicle on level ground with the front wheels straight-ahead and the engine stopped. The level check may be made with the hydraulic fluid cold or hot.
2 The power steering fluid reservoir is located on the left-hand side of the engine compartment. Slowly unscrew and remove the filler cap, which incorporates a fluid level dipstick **(see illustration)**.
3 Wipe clean the dipstick with a clean cloth, then screw it fully onto the reservoir and unscrew it again. Read off the fluid level on the dipstick.

16.4a Prise/cut off the inner gaiter clip

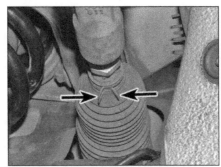
16.4b Use a pair of pliers to squeeze together the ends of the outer gaiter clip

17.2 Unscrew and remove the power steering fluid reservoir cap

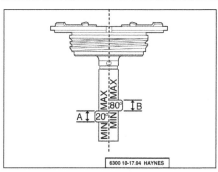

17.4 Power steering fluid dipstick marks.

4 If the fluid is cold (ambient temperature about 20° C), the level should be within the area 'A'. If the fluid is at operating temperature (above 80° C), the level should be within the area 'B' **(see illustration)**.
5 Where topping-up is required, add the specified type of fluid as necessary. On completion refit and tighten the cap.

Bleeding

6 The bleeding procedure varies depending on the extent of the work carried out to the steering hydraulic system.

If the steering gear has been removed

7 Check and if necessary top-up with the specified fluid with reference to the previous sub-Section.
8 Jack up the front of the vehicle and support it on axle stands to remove the weight from the front wheels (see *Jacking and vehicle support*).
9 With the engine switched off, turn the steering wheel from lock to lock 10 times.
10 Without turning the steering wheel, start the engine and allow it to idle for 2 seconds, then switch it off. Wait 30 seconds, then check the fluid level and top-up if necessary.
11 Repeat the procedure in paragraph 10, until the fluid level remains constant.
12 With the engine switched off, turn the steering wheel from lock-to-lock 10 times, then check the fluid level and top-up if necessary.
13 Start the engine and allow it to idle, then turn the steering wheel from lock to-lock 10 times, then switch off the engine.
14 Check the fluid level, and if necessary top-up.
15 Any remaining air in the system will dissipate after the vehicle has been driven 7 to 15 miles, so check the fluid level again after this distance.

If anything else has been removed

16 Check and if necessary top-up with the specified fluid with reference to paragraphs 1 to 5.
17 Start the engine and allow it to idle for 2 seconds, then switch it off. Wait 30 seconds, then check the fluid level and top-up if necessary.
18 Repeat the procedure in paragraph 17, until the fluid level remains constant.

19 Start the engine and leave it running for 2 to 3 minutes, without turning the steering wheel.
20 Check the fluid level, and if necessary top-up.
21 Any remaining air in the system will dissipate after the vehicle has been driven 7 to 15 miles, so check the fluid level again after this distance.

18 Power steering pump – removal and refitting

Removal

1 Firmly apply the handbrake then jack up the front of the vehicle and support it on axle stands (see *Jacking and vehicle support*).
2 Carefully pull the engine top cover off the four retaining pins, one after the other. Do not jerk the cover away and do not try to pull on one side only.
3 Undo the retaining fasteners and remove the undertray from beneath the engine.
4 Move the lock carrier at the front of the engine compartment to the service position as described in Chapter 11, Section 21.
5 Slacken the retaining clips and remove the air intake hose from the throttle housing. To give more access to the pump, also undo the retaining bolts and lower the plastic air ducting away from the rear of the alternator.
6 Using paint or a marker pen, make an alignment mark on the pump pulley and the pulley hub. This will be used to align the pulley with the retaining bolt holes in the hub when refitting. Due to the limited space, it is not possible to see the positions of the holes in the pulley relative to the holes in the hub during installation.
7 Slacken (but do not remove) the two accessible pump pulley retaining bolts. With reference to Chapter 1, Section 8, release the tension in the auxiliary drivebelt and turn the pulley so that the remaining retaining bolt is accessible. Slacken this bolt also.
8 Refer to Chapter 1 Section 8 and remove the auxiliary drivebelt.
9 Remove the three previously slackened pulley retaining bolts and take off the pump pulley.
10 Using brake hose clamps, clamp both the supply and return hoses near the power steering fluid reservoir. This will minimise fluid loss during subsequent operations.
11 Wipe clean the area around the power steering pump fluid pipe unions and hose connections.
12 Depending on pump type, either unscrew the union nut or undo the two retaining bolts and disconnect fluid pressure pipe from the pump; be prepared for fluid spillage, and position a suitable container beneath the pipe. Disconnect the pipe and recover the sealing ring; discard the ring, a new one must be used on refitting. Plug the pipe end and steering

pump orifice, to minimise fluid leakage and to keep dirt out of the hydraulic system.
13 Slacken the clip and disconnect the fluid supply hose from the rear of the power steering pump. Plug the end of the hose and cover the pump fluid port to prevent contamination.
14 Slacken and remove the three front mounting bolts and the rear mounting bolt and withdraw the pump from its bracket.
15 If the power steering pump is faulty it must be renewed. The pump is a sealed unit and cannot be overhauled.

Refitting

16 If a new pump is to be fitted, it must be primed with fluid prior to fitting, to ensure adequate lubrication during its initial stages of operation. Failure to do this could cause noisy operation and may lead to early pump failure. To prime the pump, pour the specified grade of hydraulic fluid (see *Lubricants and fluids* in *Weekly checks*) into the fluid supply port on the pump, and simultaneously rotate the pump pulley. When the fluid exits from the fluid delivery union, it is primed and ready for use.
17 Manoeuvre the pump into position, then refit its mounting bolts and tighten them to the specified torque.
18 Place the pulley on the pump, aligning the marks made on removal. Refit the three retaining bolts and tighten them to the specified torque.
19 Fit a new sealing ring to the hydraulic fluid pressure pipe end fitting, reconnect the pipe to the pump and screw in the union bolt or the two retaining bolts, as applicable. Ensure the pipe is correctly routed then tighten the fixings to the specified torque.
20 Reconnect the supply hose to the pump and secure it in position with the retaining clip. Remove the hose clamps used to minimise fluid loss.
21 Refit the auxiliary drivebelt as described in Chapter 1, Section 8.
22 Refit the air intake hose to the throttle housing.
23 Return the lock carrier to the normal position as described in Chapter 11, Section 21.
24 Refit the engine top cover.
25 Refit the engine compartment undertray, ensuring it is securely held by all its retaining bolts and fasteners.
26 On completion, top-up and bleed the hydraulic system as described in Section 17.

19 Track rod balljoint – removal and refitting

Removal

1 Apply the handbrake, then jack up the front of the vehicle and support it on axle stands (see *Jacking and vehicle support*). Remove the appropriate front roadwheel.

2 Measure the exposed amount of adjustment thread showing on the inboard side of the track rod balljoint locknut. This will act as a guide to the adjustment position when refitting the balljoint to the rod.

3 Loosen the nut securing the track rod balljoint to the hub carrier. To do this, fit a ring spanner to the nut, and then hold the balljoint pin stationary using an Allen key. With the nut removed, it may be possible to

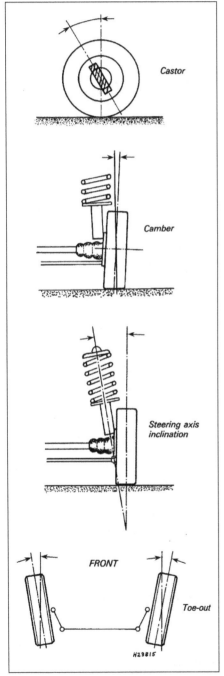

21.1 Wheel alignment and steering angle measurements

release the balljoint from the hub carrier by turning the balljoint pin with an Allen key. If not, leave the nut on by a few turns to protect the threads, then use a universal balljoint separator to release the balljoint. Remove the nut completely once the taper has been released noting that a new nut will be required for refitting.

4 Hold the track rod adjustment flats, and unscrew the balljoint locknut by a quarter of a turn. Do not move the locknut from this position, as it will serve as a handy reference mark on refitting.

5 Counting the exact number of turns necessary to do so, unscrew the balljoint assembly from the track rod.

6 Carefully clean the balljoint and the threads. Renew the balljoint if its movement is sloppy or too stiff, if excessively worn, or if damaged in any way; carefully check the stud taper and threads. If the balljoint gaiter is damaged, the complete balljoint assembly must be renewed; it is not possible to obtain the gaiter separately.

Refitting

7 Screw the balljoint onto the track rod by the number of turns noted on removal. This should bring the balljoint to within a quarter of a turn from the locknut, with the alignment marks that were made on removal (if applicable) lined up. Counter-hold the track rod adjustment flats and tighten the locknut securely.

8 Locate the balljoint shank in the hub carrier and fit the new locknut. Tighten the locknut to the specified torque.

9 Refit the roadwheel, then lower the vehicle to the ground and tighten the roadwheel bolts to the specified torque.

10 Have the front wheel alignment checked at the earliest opportunity.

20 Track rod – removal and refitting

Removal

1 Remove the track rod balljoint as described in Section 19.

2 Release the retaining clips and slide the rubber bellows towards the outboard end of the track rod; this will expose the large integral hex nut at the inner end of the track rod.

3 Hold the track rod hex nut securing using a large open-ended spanner, and unscrew the track rod from the end of the steering gear.

Refitting

4 Refitting is a reversal of removal noting the following points:

a) Tighten the track rod to the specified torque, using a suitable 'crow's foot' adapter.

b) Refit the track rod balljoint as described in Section 19.

c) Ensure that the rubber bellows is securely refitted, using new clips where necessary.

d) Have the front wheel alignment checked at the earliest opportunity.

21 Wheel alignment and steering angles – general information

Definitions

1 A car's steering and suspension geometry is defined in four basic settings – all angles are expressed in degrees; the steering axis is defined as an imaginary line drawn through the axis of the suspension strut, extended where necessary to contact the ground **(see illustration)**.

2 Camber is the angle between each roadwheel and a vertical line drawn through its centre and tyre contact patch, when viewed from the front or rear of the car. Positive camber is when the roadwheels are tilted outwards from the vertical at the top; negative camber is when they are tilted inwards. The front wheel camber cannot be adjusted. The rear wheel camber can be adjusted by altering the position of the eccentric bolt on the upper transverse link.

3 Castor is the angle between the steering axis and a vertical line drawn through each roadwheel's centre and tyre contact patch, when viewed from the side of the car. Positive castor is when the steering axis is tilted so that it contacts the ground ahead of the vertical; negative castor is when it contacts the ground behind the vertical. The castor angle is not adjustable.

4 Toe is the difference, viewed from above, between lines drawn through the roadwheel centres and the car's centre-line. Toe-in is when the roadwheels point inwards, towards each other at the front, while toe-out is when they splay outwards from each other at the front.

5 The front wheel toe setting is adjusted by screwing the track rods in or out of their balljoints, to alter the effective length of the track rod assembly. The rear wheel toe setting can be altered by repositioning the eccentric bolt on the track rod.

Checking and adjustment

6 Due to the fact that Audi insist that the alignment of all four wheels is checked at the same time, and special measuring equipment necessary to check the wheel alignment and steering angles, and the skill required to use it properly, the checking and adjustment of these settings is best left to an Audi dealer or similar expert. Note that most tyre-fitting shops now possess sophisticated checking equipment.

Chapter 11
Bodywork and fittings

Contents

Degrees of difficulty

Easy, suitable for novice with little experience	**Fairly easy,** suitable for beginner with some experience	**Fairly difficult,** suitable for competent DIY mechanic	**Difficult,** suitable for experienced DIY mechanic	**Very difficult,** suitable for expert DIY or professional

Specifications

Torque wrench settings	Nm	lbf ft
Bonnet hinge nuts	21	15
Bonnet lock bolts.	10	7
Boot lid (Saloon) mounting bolts	22	16
Door lock bolts.	20	15
Door mirror bolts	10	7
Seat belt anchor bolts	45	33
Seat belt front stalk mounting bolt.	33	24
Seat belt inertia reel bolt.	45	33
Seat retaining bolts	50	37
Tailgate (Avant) mounting bolts/nuts	22	16

1 General description

1 Two body types are covered by this manual – the four-door Saloon and the five-door Avant. The body is of all-steel construction, and incorporates calculated impact crumple zones at the front and rear, with a central safety cell passenger compartment.

2 During manufacture, the underbody is treated with underseal and, as a further anti-rust aid, some of the more exposed body panels are galvanised. The bumpers and wheel arch liners are plastic mouldings, for durability and strength.

2 Maintenance – bodywork and underframe

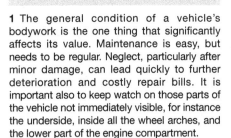

1 The general condition of a vehicle's bodywork is the one thing that significantly affects its value. Maintenance is easy, but needs to be regular. Neglect, particularly after minor damage, can lead quickly to further deterioration and costly repair bills. It is important also to keep watch on those parts of the vehicle not immediately visible, for instance the underside, inside all the wheel arches, and the lower part of the engine compartment.

2 The basic maintenance routine for the bodywork is washing – preferably with a lot of water, from a hose. This will remove all the loose solids which may have stuck to the vehicle. It is important to flush these off in such a way as to prevent grit from scratching the finish. The wheel arches and underframe need washing in the same way, to remove any accumulated mud which will retain moisture and tend to encourage rust. Paradoxically enough, the best time to clean the underframe and wheel arches is in wet weather, when the mud is thoroughly wet and soft. In very wet weather, the underframe is usually cleaned of large accumulations automatically, and this is a good time for inspection.

3 Periodically, except on vehicles with a wax-based underbody protective coating, it is a good idea to have the whole of the underframe of the vehicle steam-cleaned, engine compartment included, so that a thorough inspection can be carried out to see what minor repairs and renovations are necessary. Steam cleaning is available at many garages, and is necessary for the removal of the accumulation of oily grime, which sometimes is allowed to become thick in certain areas. If steam-cleaning facilities are not available, there are some excellent grease solvents available which can be brush-applied; the dirt can then be simply hosed off. Note that these methods should not be used on vehicles with wax-based underbody protective coating, or the coating will be removed. Such vehicles should be inspected annually, preferably just before Winter, when the underbody should be washed down, and any damage to the wax coating repaired. Ideally, a completely fresh coat should be applied. It would also be worth considering the use of wax-based protection for injection into door panels, sills, box sections, etc, as an additional safeguard against rust damage, where such protection is not provided by the vehicle manufacturer.

4 After washing paintwork, wipe off with a chamois leather to give an unspotted clear finish. A coat of clear protective wax polish will give added protection against chemical pollutants in the air. If the paintwork sheen has dulled or oxidised, use a cleaner/polisher combination to restore the brilliance of the shine. This requires a little effort, but such dulling is usually caused because regular washing has been neglected. Care needs to be taken with metallic paintwork, as special non-abrasive cleaner/polisher is required to avoid damage to the finish. Always check that the door and ventilator opening drain holes and pipes are completely clear, so that water can be drained out. Brightwork should be treated in the same way as paintwork. Windscreens and windows can be kept clear of the smeary film which often appears, by proprietary glass cleaner. Never use any form of wax or other body or chromium polish on glass.

3 Maintenance – upholstery and carpets

1 Mats and carpets should be brushed or vacuum-cleaned regularly, to keep them free of grit. If they are badly stained, remove them from the vehicle for scrubbing or sponging, and make quite sure they are dry before refitting. Seats and interior trim panels can be kept clean by wiping with a damp cloth. If they do become stained (which can be more apparent on light-coloured upholstery), use a little liquid detergent and a soft nail brush to scour the grime out of the grain of the material. Do not forget to keep the headlining clean in the same way as the upholstery. When using liquid cleaners inside the vehicle, do not over-wet the surfaces being cleaned. Excessive damp could get into the seams and padded interior, causing stains, offensive odours or even rot. If the inside of the vehicle gets wet accidentally, it is worthwhile taking some trouble to dry it out properly, particularly where carpets are involved. Do not leave oil or electric heaters inside the vehicle for this purpose.

4 Minor body damage – repair

Minor scratches

1 If the scratch is very superficial, and does not penetrate to the metal of the bodywork, repair is very simple. Lightly rub the area of the scratch with a paintwork renovator or a very fine cutting paste to remove loose paint from the scratch, and to clear the surrounding bodywork of wax polish. Rinse the area with clean water.

2 Apply touch-up paint to the scratch using a fine paint brush; continue to apply fine layers of paint until the surface of the paint in the scratch is level with the surrounding paintwork. Allow the new paint at least two weeks to harden, then blend it into the surrounding paintwork by rubbing the scratch area with a paintwork renovator or a very fine cutting paste. Finally, apply wax polish.

3 Where the scratch has penetrated right through to the metal of the bodywork, causing the metal to rust, a different repair technique is required. Remove any loose rust from the bottom of the scratch with a penknife, then apply rust-inhibiting paint to prevent the formation of rust in the future. Using a rubber or nylon applicator, fill the scratch with bodystopper paste. If required, this paste can be mixed with cellulose thinners to provide a very thin paste which is ideal for filling narrow scratches. Before the stopper-paste in the scratch hardens, wrap a piece of smooth cotton rag around the top of a finger. Dip the finger in cellulose thinners, and quickly sweep it across the surface of the stopper-paste in the scratch; this will ensure that the surface of the stopper-paste is slightly hollowed. The scratch can now be painted over as described earlier in this Section.

Dents

4 When deep denting of the vehicle's bodywork has taken place, the first task is to pull the dent out, until the affected bodywork almost attains its original shape. There is little point in trying to restore the original shape completely, as the metal in the damaged area will have stretched on impact, and cannot be reshaped fully to its original contour. It is better to bring the level of the dent up to a point which is about 3 mm below the level of the surrounding bodywork. In cases where the dent is very shallow anyway, it is not worth trying to pull it out at all. If the underside of the dent is accessible, it can be hammered out gently from behind, using a mallet with a wooden or plastic head. Whilst doing this, hold a suitable block of wood firmly against the outside of the panel, to absorb the impact from the hammer blows and thus prevent a large area of the bodywork from being 'belled-out'.

5 Should the dent be in a section of the bodywork which has a double skin, or some other factor making it inaccessible from behind, a different technique is called for. Drill several small holes through the metal inside the area – particularly in the deeper section. Then screw long self-tapping screws into the holes, just sufficiently for them to gain a good purchase in the metal. Now the dent can be pulled out by pulling on the protruding heads of the screws with a pair of pliers.

6 The next stage of the repair is the removal of the paint from the damaged area, and from an inch or so of the surrounding 'sound' bodywork. This is accomplished most easily by using a wire brush or abrasive pad on a power drill, although it can be done just as effectively by hand, using sheets of abrasive paper. To complete the preparation for filling, score the surface of the bare metal with a screwdriver or the tang of a file, or alternatively, drill small holes in the affected area. This will provide a good 'key' for the filler paste.

7 To complete the repair, see the Section on filling and respraying.

Rust holes or gashes

8 Remove all paint from the affected area, and from an inch or so of the surrounding 'sound' bodywork, using an abrasive pad or a wire brush on a power drill. If these are not available, a few sheets of abrasive paper will do the job most effectively. With the paint removed, you will be able to judge the severity of the corrosion, and therefore decide whether to renew the whole panel (if this is possible) or to repair the affected area. New body panels are not as expensive as most people think, and it is often quicker and more satisfactory to fit a new panel than to attempt to repair large areas of corrosion.

9 Remove all fittings from the affected area, except those which will act as a guide to the original shape of the damaged bodywork (eg headlight shells etc). Then, using tin snips or a hacksaw blade, remove all loose metal and any other metal badly affected by corrosion. Hammer the edges of the hole inwards, to create a slight depression for the filler paste.

10 Wire-brush the affected area to remove the powdery rust from the surface of the remaining metal. Paint the affected area with rust-inhibiting paint; if the back of the rusted area is accessible, treat this also.

11 Before filling can take place, it will be necessary to block the hole in some way. This can be achieved with aluminium or plastic mesh, or aluminium tape.

12 Aluminium or plastic mesh, or glass-fibre matting, is probably the best material to use for a large hole. Cut a piece to the approximate size and shape of the hole to be filled, then position it in the hole so that its edges are below the level of the surrounding bodywork. It can be retained in position by several blobs of filler paste around its periphery.

13 Aluminium tape should be used for small or very narrow holes. Pull a piece off the roll, trim it to the approximate size and shape required, then pull off the backing paper (if used) and stick the tape over the hole; it can be overlapped if the thickness of one piece is insufficient. Burnish down the edges of the tape with the handle of a screwdriver or similar, to ensure that the tape is securely attached to the metal underneath.

Filling and respraying

14 Before using this Section, see the Sections on dent, deep scratch, rust holes and gash repairs.

15 Many types of bodyfiller are available, but generally speaking, those proprietary kits which contain a tin of filler paste and a tube of resin hardener are best for this type of repair which can be used directly from the tube. A wide, flexible plastic or nylon applicator will be found invaluable for imparting a smooth and well-contoured finish to the surface of the filler.

16 Mix up a little filler on a clean piece of card or board – measure the hardener carefully (follow the maker's instructions on the pack), otherwise the filler will set too rapidly or too slowly. Using the applicator, apply the filler paste to the prepared area; draw the applicator across the surface of the filler to achieve the correct contour and to level the surface. When a contour that approximates to the correct one is achieved, stop working the paste – if you carry on too long, the paste will become sticky and begin to 'pick-up' on the applicator. Continue to add thin layers of filler paste at 20-minute intervals, until the level of the filler is just proud of the surrounding bodywork.

17 Once the filler has hardened, the excess can be removed using a metal plane or file. From then on, progressively-finer grades of abrasive paper should be used, starting with a 40-grade production paper, and finishing with a 400-grade wet-and-dry paper. Always wrap the abrasive paper around a flat rubber, cork, or wooden block – otherwise the surface of the filler will not be completely flat. During the smoothing of the filler surface, the wet-and-dry paper should be periodically rinsed in water. This will ensure that a very smooth finish is imparted to the filler at the final stage.

18 At this stage, the 'dent' should be surrounded by a ring of bare metal, which in turn should be encircled by the finely 'feathered' edge of the good paintwork. Rinse the repair area with clean water, until all the dust produced by the rubbing-down operation has gone.

19 Spray the whole area with a light coat of primer – this will show up any imperfections in the surface of the filler. Repair these imperfections with fresh filler paste or bodystopper, and again smooth the surface with abrasive paper. If bodystopper is used, it can be mixed with cellulose thinners, to form a thin paste which is ideal for filling small holes. Repeat this spray-and-repair procedure until you are satisfied that the surface of the filler, and the feathered edge of the paintwork, are perfect. Clean the repair area with clean water, and allow to dry fully.

20 The repair area is now ready for final spraying. Paint spraying must be carried out in a warm, dry, windless and dust-free atmosphere. This condition can be created artificially if you have access to a large indoor working area, but if you are forced to work in the open, you will have to pick your day very

carefully. If you are working indoors, dousing the floor in the work area with water will help to settle the dust which would otherwise be in the atmosphere. If the repair area is confined to one body panel, mask off the surrounding panels; this will help to minimise the effects of a slight mismatch in paint colours. Bodywork fittings (e.g. chrome strips, door handles etc) will also need to be masked off. Use genuine masking tape, and several thickness of newspaper, for the masking operations.

21 Before starting to spray, agitate the aerosol can thoroughly, then spray a test area (an old tin, or similar) until the technique is mastered. Cover the repair area with a thick coat of primer; the thickness should be built up using several thin layers of paint, rather than one thick one. Using 400 grade wet-and-dry paper, rub down the surface of the primer until it is smooth. While doing this, the work area should be thoroughly doused with water, and the wet-and-dry paper periodically rinsed in water. Allow to dry before spraying on more paint.

22 Spray on the top coat, again building up the thickness by using several thin layers of paint. Start spraying at one edge of the repair area, and then, using a side-to-side motion, work until the whole repair area and about 2 inches of the surrounding original paintwork is covered. Remove all masking material 10 to 15 minutes after spraying on the final coat of paint.

23 Allow the new paint at least two weeks to harden, then, using a paintwork renovator or a very fine cutting paste, blend the edges of the paint into the existing paintwork. Finally, apply wax polish.

Plastic components

24 With the use of more and more plastic body components by the vehicle manufacturers (e.g. bumpers, spoilers, and in some cases major body panels), rectification of more serious damage to such items has become a matter of either entrusting repair work to a specialist in this field, or renewing complete components. Repair of such damage by the DIY owner is not feasible, owing to the cost of the equipment and materials required for effecting such repairs. The basic technique involves making a groove along the line of the crack in the plastic, using a rotary burr in a power drill. The damaged part is then welded back together, using a hot air gun to heat up and fuse a plastic filler rod into the groove. Any excess plastic is then removed, and the area rubbed down to a smooth finish. It is important that a filler rod of the correct plastic is used, as body components can be made of a variety of different types (e.g. polycarbonate, ABS, polypropylene).

25 Damage of a less serious nature (abrasions, minor cracks etc) can be repaired by the DIY owner using a two-part epoxy filler repair material which can be used directly from the tube. Once mixed in equal proportions, this is used in similar fashion to the bodywork

filler used on metal panels. The filler is usually cured in twenty to thirty minutes, ready for sanding and painting.

26 If the owner is renewing a complete component himself, or if he has repaired it with epoxy filler, he will be left with the problem of finding a suitable paint for finishing which is compatible with the type of plastic used. At one time, the use of a universal paint was not possible, owing to the complex range of plastics met with in body component applications. Standard paints, generally speaking, will not bond to plastic or rubber satisfactorily, but professional matched paints, to match any plastic or rubber finish, can be obtained from some dealers. However, it is now possible to obtain a plastic body parts finishing kit which consists of a pre-primer treatment, a primer and coloured top coat. Full instructions are normally supplied with a kit, but basically the method of use is to first apply the pre-primer to the component concerned, and allow it to dry for up to 30 minutes. Then the primer is applied, and left to dry for about an hour before finally applying the special-coloured top coat. The result is a correctly coloured component, where the paint will flex with the plastic or rubber, a property that standard paint does not normally possess.

5 Major body damage – repair

1 Where serious damage has occurred, or large areas need renewal due to neglect, it means that complete new panels will need welding-in, and this is best left to professionals. If the damage is due to impact, it will also be necessary to check completely the alignment of the bodyshell, and this can only be carried out accurately by a Audi dealer using special jigs. If the body is left misaligned, it is primarily dangerous, as the car will not handle properly, and secondly, uneven stresses will be imposed on the steering, suspension and possibly transmission, causing abnormal wear, or complete failure, particularly to such items as the tyres.

6 Bonnet and support strut – removal, refitting and adjustment

Bonnet

Removal

1 Fully open the bonnet, then place some cardboard or rags beneath the corners by the hinges to protect the bodywork.

2 Prop the bonnet open using two stout lengths of wood, one positioned at each corner. Alternatively, enlist the help of an assistant to support the bonnet.

3 Disconnect the gas strut from the bonnet, with reference to the information given later in this Section.

4 Mark the location of the hinges with a pencil, then slacken the four hinge-to-bonnet retaining nuts (two each side) **(see illustration)**.

5 Support the bonnet as the retaining nuts are unscrewed, then withdraw the bonnet from the car.

Refitting and adjustment

6 Refitting is a reversal of removal. Ensure that the hinges are adjusted to their original positions. Close the bonnet very carefully initially; misalignment may cause the edges of the bonnet to damage the bodywork. If necessary, adjust the hinges to their original positions and check that the bonnet is level with the surrounding bodywork. If necessary, adjust the height of the bonnet front edge by screwing the rubber buffers in or out.

7 Check that the bonnet lock operates in a satisfactory manner. In particular, check that the safety catch holds the bonnet after the bonnet release cable has been pulled.

Support strut

Removal

8 Prop the bonnet open using two stout lengths of wood, one positioned at each corner. Alternatively, enlist the help of an assistant to support the bonnet.

9 Slightly lift the retaining clips in the mountings at each end of the strut, using a suitable screwdriver **(see illustration)**.

10 Pull the strut mounting from the pivot pin.

Refitting

11 Refitting is a reversal of removal.

7 Bonnet lock and release cable – removal and refitting

Bonnet lock

Removal

1 Extract the four plastic rivets, lift the lock carrier cover up at the rear, disengage it from the radiator grille at the front and remove it from the lock carrier **(see illustration)**.

2 Using a felt-tip pen or paint, make alignment marks around the bonnet lock to aid refitting.

3 Slacken and withdraw the three securing bolts and move the lock mechanism away from the lock carrier. Disconnect the wiring plug as the assembly is withdrawn.

4 Disengage the release cable end fitting and remove the bonnet lock.

Refitting

5 Reconnect the cable end fitting and wiring plug.

6 Position the lock mechanism on the lock carrier, aligning the previously-made marks, and tighten the retaining bolts to the specified torque.

7 Check the action of the release cable/lock, then refit the lock carrier cover.

Release cable

Removal

8 Using a small screwdriver, slightly pull out the retaining clip from the top of the front facing side of the release handle.

9 Pull the release handle to the rear (this releases the bonnet) and hold it in this position. Detach the release handle from its mounting by moving it towards the centre of the vehicle.

10 Remove the front side sill trim panel on the driver's side with reference to Section 25.

11 Undo the bolt and detach the release handle mounting, then disconnect the cable from the mounting.

6.4 Undo the bonnet retaining nuts each side

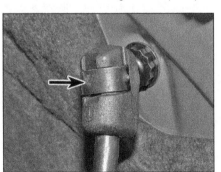

6.9 Lift the retaining clips and pull the end of the strut from the pivot pin

7.1 Remove the lock carrier cover

12 From within the engine compartment locate the cable connector near the bonnet lock assembly. Open the cable joiner and disengage the rear cable from the joiner.

13 Free the release cable from all its retaining clips in the engine compartment and vehicle interior.

14 Attach a suitable length of strong cord to the end of the release cable at the release handle end, then carefully draw the cable through into the engine compartment.

15 Undo the cord from the cable, and leave the cord ends exposed in the engine compartment and footwell.

Refitting

16 Refit in the reverse order of removal. Tie the inner end of the cable to the exposed cord in the engine compartment, carefully pull the cable through to the release handle, then untie the cord.

17 When positioning the cable in the engine compartment, ensure that it is re-routed correctly to avoid kinks, sharp bends and chafing. Check for satisfactory operation of the cable and the lock before closing the bonnet. Ensure that the bonnet locks properly when closed, and also that the safety catch operates correctly when the bonnet release cable is actuated.

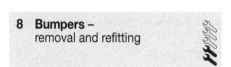

8 Bumpers –
removal and refitting

Front bumper

Removal

1 Jack up the front of the vehicle and support it securely on axle stands (see *Jacking and vehicle support*). Remove the front roadwheels. Undo the fasteners and remove the front section of the engine undertray.

2 Remove the front wheel arch liner on each side as described in Section 21.

3 Extract the four plastic rivets, lift the lock carrier cover up at the rear, disengage it from the radiator grille at the front and remove it from the lock carrier **(see illustration 7.1)**.

4 Disconnect the wiring connectors for the ambient temperature sensor, parking aid sensors and foglights, depending on equipment fitted **(see illustration)**.

5 Undo the bumper upper retaining bolt each side, adjacent to the headlights **(see illustration)**.

6 Undo the bumper lower retaining bolt and quick-release fastener on each side **(see illustration)**.

7 From under the wheel arch undo the two bolts each side securing the bumper to the lock carrier.

8 Disconnect the fog light wiring connectors.

9 With the help of an assistant, pull the ends of the bumper outwards from the guides on

8.4 Disconnect the wiring connectors for the bumper electrical attachments

8.6 Undo the bumper lower retaining bolt on each side

each side, and withdraw it from the front of the car **(see illustrations)**.

Refitting

10 Refitting is a reversal of removal. On completion, check for satisfactory operation of the accessory components as applicable.

Rear bumper

Removal

11 Remove the rear light cluster as described in Chapter 12 Section 8.

12 Where fitted, disconnect the parking sensors wiring plugs at the control unit and release the cable tie. Push the grommet and wiring through to the outside.

13 Working inside the luggage compartment, undo the nut each side.

8.9b...and withdraw it from the front of the car

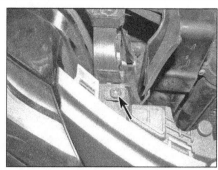

8.5 Undo the bumper upper retaining bolt each side

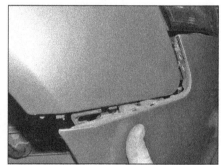

8.9a Pull the ends of the front bumper outwards from the guides on each side...

14 From under the bumper, undo the three central securing bolts **(see illustration)**.

15 Undo the fasteners and pull forwards the wheel arch liners where they contact the edges of the bumper.

16 From under the wheel arch, undo the three bolts each side securing the bumper edge.

17 Working in the rear light cluster aperture, pull out the pin each side securing the bumper to the bumper guide.

18 With the help of an assistant, release the ends of the rear bumper from the guides on each side, and withdraw it from the rear of the car.

Refitting

19 Refit in the reverse order of removal. Loosely fit all retaining bolts before fully tightening them.

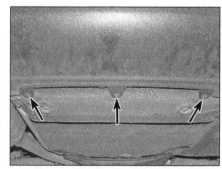

8.14 Retaining bolts on the underside of the bumper

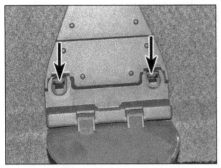

9.2 Release the clips and remove the warning triangle holder

9.3 Remove the lock latch cover

10.2a Pull away the plastic cover...

9 Boot lid – removal and refitting

Removal

1 Raise the boot lid, then remove warning triangle from its holder.
2 Release the two retaining clips and detach the warning triangle holder from the boot lid (see illustration).
3 Pull away the plastic cover over the lock catch mechanism (see illustration).
4 Undo the trim retaining bolt from the hand grip recess, then carefully pull away the trim. If necessary, use a wide-blade screwdriver to prise the clips from the boot lid.
5 Unplug the wiring connectors from the lock switch and number plate light units, then release the grommet and withdraw the wiring harness from the boot lid.
6 Mark the relationship between the boot lid and the hinges by drawing around the outside of each hinge with a marker pen.
7 Place cloths or pieces of cardboard over the surfaces of the rear wings, to prevent damage during removal.
8 Enlist the aid of an assistant to support the boot lid, then unscrew and remove the hinge-to-boot lid retaining nuts, and lift the lid clear.

Refitting

9 Refit in the reverse order of removal. Check the lid for correct alignment, and if necessary

10.2b...and detach the cable

loosen off the hinge bolts to adjust, then retighten them; there should be an even gap between the outside edge of the boot lid and the surrounding bodywork.

10 Boot lid lock – removal and refitting

Removal

1 Remove the trim from inside the boot lid, as described in Section 9.
2 Pull away the plastic cover, then pull the cable outer downwards, and disengage the cable end fitting from the lock (see illustrations).
3 Mark the fitted position of the lock with a marker pen, then unscrew the retaining nuts

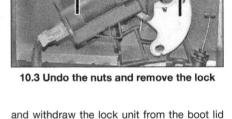

10.3 Undo the nuts and remove the lock

and withdraw the lock unit from the boot lid (see illustration). Disconnect the wiring plug as the lock is withdrawn.

Refitting

4 Refit in the reverse order of removal.

11 Tailgate and support struts (Avant models) – removal and refitting

Tailgate

Removal

1 Open the tailgate and remove the warning triangle (see illustrations).
2 Carefully prise out the luggage compartment light unit, disconnect the wiring connector and remove the light (see illustration).

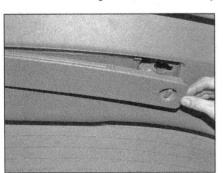

11.1a Remove the cover over the warning triangle...

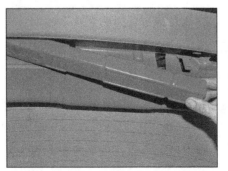

11.1b...then remove the warning triangle from the tailgate

11.2 Carefully prise out and remove the luggage compartment light unit

11.4 Unclip and remove the access covers from the tailgate trim panel

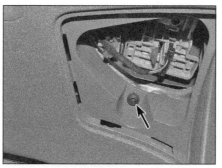
11.5a Undo the bolts in the rear light cluster aperture...

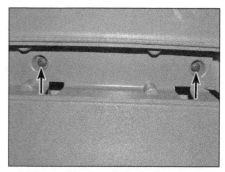
11.5b...and the two bolts in the warning triangle aperture

3 Where applicable, carefully prise out the switch for closure of the tailgate, disconnect the wiring connector and remove the switch.
4 Using a plastic spatula or similar tool, unclip and remove the rear bulb access covers from each side of the tailgate trim panel (see illustration).
5 Undo the retaining bolt in the rear light cluster aperture on each side, and the two bolts located in the warning triangle aperture (see illustrations).
6 Firmly pull the lower part of the trim panel away from the tailgate to release the lower retaining clips, then reach in with a large screwdriver and release the upper clips. Remove the trim panel from the tailgate (see illustrations).
7 Using a plastic spatula or similar tool release the tailgate upper trim starting at the sides, then releasing it at the top (see illustration).
8 Disconnect the wiring from all the tailgate components at their relevant connectors. Note the routing and attachment locations of the wires.
9 Disconnect the hose for the rear screen washer jet.
10 Mark the relationship between the tailgate and its hinges using a felt tip pen.
11 Enlist the aid of an assistant to help support the tailgate, then detach the tailgate struts as described later in this Section.
12 Unscrew and remove the tailgate-to-hinge securing bolts, and lift the tailgate clear of the vehicle (see illustration).

Refitting
13 Refit in the reverse order of removal. Check that the tailgate is correctly aligned before fully tightening the tailgate hinge bolts.
14 The fit and closing tension of the tailgate can be adjusted by altering the positions of the rubber buffers at the upper and lower edges of the tailgate.

Support struts
Removal
15 Open the tailgate and support it in its open position, or have an assistant hold it open.
16 Disconnect the strut(s) at the upper and lower balljoints by lifting (not removing) the spring clips, and prising the joint free (see illustration).
17 If a strut is defective in operation, it must

11.6a Pull the lower part of the trim panel away to release the lower clips...

be renewed. Do not attempt to dismantle and repair the strut. Note that the struts are filled with pressurised gas, and so should not be punctured or disposed of by incineration.
Refitting
18 Refit in the reverse order of removal. Ensure that the strut is engaged with the balljoints.

12 Tailgate lock and handle (Avant models) – removal and refitting

Lock unit
Removal
1 Remove the tailgate trim panel as described in Section 11.

11.6b...then use a large screwdriver to release the upper clips

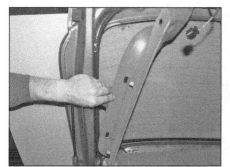
11.7 Release the tailgate upper trim starting at the sides, then at the top

11.12 Tailgate-to-hing securing bolts

11.16 Prise up the strut balljoint spring clip

12.3 Remove the plastic cover over the lock

12.4 Undo the lock retaining nuts

2 Disconnect the wiring connector from the lock.

3 Release the retaining clip and remove the cover over the lock unit **(see illustration)**.

4 Mark the fitted position of the lock with a marker pen, then unscrew the retaining nuts and withdraw the lock unit from the tailgate **(see illustration)**.

Refitting

5 Refitting is a reversal of removal.

Handle

Removal

6 Remove the tailgate trim panel as described in Section 11.

7 Disconnect the wiring connector from the handle.

8 Undo the retaining nuts, depress the clips and remove the handle.

Refitting

9 Refitting is a reversal of removal.

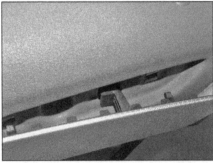

13.1 Carefully prise up the panel centre trim

13.2a Disengage the hooks on the panel centre trim...

13 Door trim panel –
removal and refitting

Removal

1 Using a plastic spatula or similar tool, carefully prise free the rear edge of the panel centre trim **(see illustration)**.

2 Release the remainder of the retaining clips, disengage the hooks, then move the panel to the rear to disengage the tabs at the front **(see illustrations)**.

3 Insert a screwdriver into the hole in the armrest trim and release the rear of the trim from the door **(see illustration)**.

4 Using a plastic spatula or similar tool, prise free the trim, then remove it from the door **(see illustrations)**.

5 Undo the five screws securing the trim panel to the door **(see illustrations)**.

6 Release the door trim panel studs, carefully

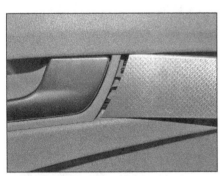

13.2b...then move the panel to the rear to disengage the tabs at the front

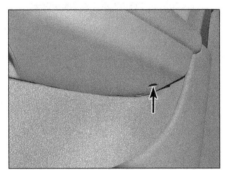

13.3 Insert a screwdriver into the hole and release the armrest trim at the rear

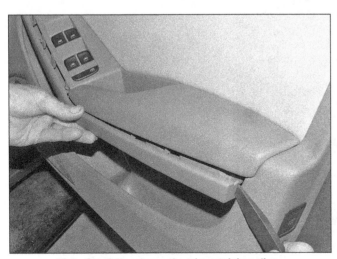

13.4a Carefully release the trim retaining clips...

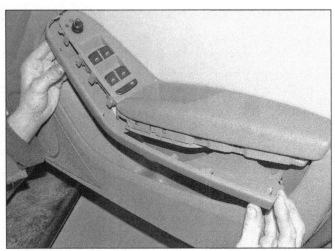

13.4b...and remove the trim from the door

13.5a Undo the retaining screw at the bottom of the trim panel...

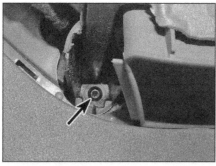

13.5b...the screw in the centre of the armrest...

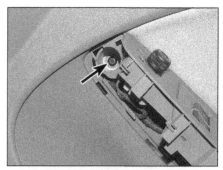

13.5c...the screw at the top of the armrest...

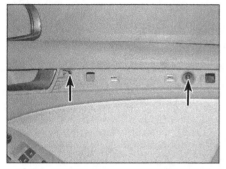

13.5d...and the two screws at the top of the panel

13.6a Carefully lever the trim panel...

13.6b...and remove it from the door

levering between the panel and door with a flat-bladed lever. Work around the outside of the panel, and when all the studs are released, lift the panel upwards and off the window slot.

13.7 Disconnect the wiring connector from the door electronics module

Support the panel away from the door (see illustrations).

7 Lift the locking lever and disconnect the wiring connector from the electronics module in the door (see illustration).

8 Release the interior handle operating cable from the trim panel, then disengage the inner cable end from the handle lever (see illustrations).

9 If removing a rear door trim panel, disconnect the wiring connector for the treble loudspeaker (where fitted).

Refitting

10 Refit in the reverse order of removal, noting the following point:

a) *Ensure that the wiring and connections are secure and correctly routed, clear of the window regulator and latch/lock components.*

b) *Renew any damaged retaining clips.*
c) *When reconnecting the interior handle operating cable, ensure the hook on the end of the cable is facing upwards.*

14 Door lock – removal and refitting

Removal

1 Remove the door trim panel as described in Section 13.

2 Remove the lock cylinder as described in Section 15.

3 Release the wiring from the clip on the door panel cover (see illustration).

4 Starting at the top disengage the door panel

13.8a Release the interior handle operating cable from the panel...

13.8b...then disengage the inner cable end from the handle lever

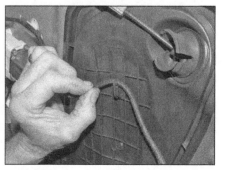

14.3 Release the wiring from the door panel cover

14.4a Disengage the door panel cover from the door...

14.4b...release the grommet from the cover...

14.7 Door lock retaining bolts

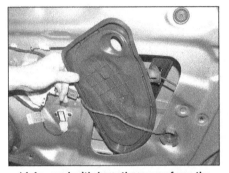

14.4c...and withdraw the cover from the operating cable

15.1 Prise out the blanking cap from the edge of the door

detached by prising up the outer cable fitting, rotating the inner cable fitting 90°, and lifting it from place.

Refitting

9 Refitting is a reversal of the removal procedure. Check that the door striker enters the lock centrally when the door is closed, and if necessary adjust the position of the striker.

15 Door handles and lock cylinder – removal and refitting

Lock cylinder

Removal

1 Open the door and carefully prise out the blanking cap from the rear edge of the door to gain access to the handle locking screw **(see illustration)**.
2 Insert a screwdriver into the hole and unscrew the handle locking screw as far as it will go **(see illustration)**.
3 Pull the exterior door handle outwards and hold it in the open position.
4 Press the retainer on the lock cylinder inwards. The door handle is now locked in the open position.
5 Pull the lock cylinder out of its mounting bracket.

Refitting

6 Refitting is a reversal of removal.

Interior handle

Removal

7 Remove the door trim panel as described in Section 13.
8 Disconnect the wiring from the central locking switch **(see illustration)**.
9 Where fitted, pull the illumination

cover from the door. Release the grommet and withdraw the door panel cover from the operating cable **(see illustrations)**.
5 Undo the bolt securing the door lock cover to the lock. Press the fastener together and detach the door lock cover from the lock, towards the rear.
6 Disconnect the lock operating cable from the door lock.
7 Undo the two retaining bolts at the edge of the door, and manoeuvre the lock from position **(see illustration)**. Disconnect the lock wiring plug as it's withdrawn.
8 If required, the interior handle cable can be

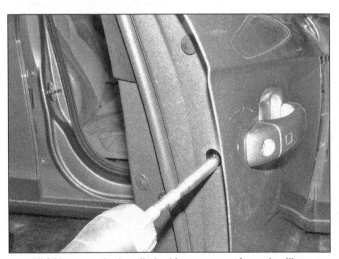

15.2 Unscrew the handle locking screw as far as it will go

15.8 Disconnect the wiring for the central locking switch

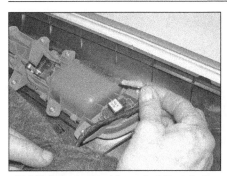

15.9 Pull the bulbholder out of the interior handle

15.10a Undo the retaining screws...

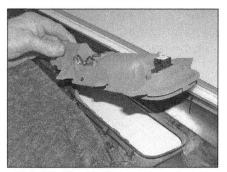

15.10b ...and remove the interior handle

bulbholder out of its location in the handle **(see illustration)**.

10 Undo the six retaining screws and remove the interior handle from the door trim panel **(see illustrations)**.

Refitting

11 Refitting is a reversal of removal.

Exterior handle

Removal

12 Remove the lock cylinder as described previously in this Section.

13 Move the exterior handle to the rear then swivel the rear portion of the handle outwards.

14 Disengage the front of the handle from the door and withdraw the handle. Where applicable, disconnect the wiring connector from the handle.

Refitting

15 Refitting is a reversal of removal.

---

16 Door window glass, regulator and motor – removal and refitting

Front door window glass

Removal

1 Remove the door trim panel as described in Section 13.

2 Remove the front door loudspeaker as described in Chapter 12 Section 15.

3 Remove the door panel cover as described in Section 14.

4 Temporarily reconnect the door trim panel wiring connector, then lower the window so that the window glass attachments to the regulator lifting channel are accessible through the holes in the regulator frame.

5 Insert a screwdriver or similar tool through one of the holes in the regulator frame and through the corresponding hole in the window glass to make contact with the window glass retainer **(see illustration)**.

6 Using the screwdriver, push back the window glass retainer while at the same time lifting the glass upward until it releases from the retainer. Hold the glass in that position and release the other retainer in the same way.

7 Once the glass has been released from both retainers, tilt it towards the front and lift it up and out from the outside of the door **(see illustration)**.

Refitting

8 Refitting is a reversal of removal, ensuring that the window glass positively engages with the retainers on the regulator.

Rear door window glass

Removal

Note: *Audi special tool T40231 will be required for this procedure.*

9 Remove the door trim panel as described in Section 13.

10 Remove the door panel cover as described in Section 14.

11 Using a plastic spatula or similar tool, carefully release the window frame inner trim from the door, starting at the bottom front corner.

12 Carefully prise off the door inner waist seal from the top of the door panel.

13 Insert tool T40231 on both sides of the glass at its attachment to the regulator. Press down on the tool to open the regulator mounting.

14 Lift the window glass out of the regulator and remove it from the door.

Refitting

15 Refitting is a reversal of removal, ensuring that the window glass positively engages with the retainers on the regulator.

Front door window regulator

Removal

16 Remove the front door window glass as described previously in this Section.

17 Remove the window regulator motor as described later in this Section.

18 Using an 11 mm socket bit fitted over the regulator motor threaded plugs in the door. Push on the socket to release the retaining tabs and remove the plugs from the door panel **(see illustration)**.

16.5 Use a screwdriver to release the window glass retainer

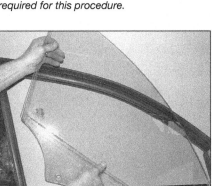

16.7 Lift the window glass up and out from the outside of the door

16.18 Use an 11 mm socket to release the retaining tabs and remove the threaded plugs from the door panel.

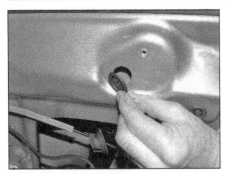

16.20 Remove the three sealing grommets from the door panel

16.21 Undo the regulator upper retaining nuts

16.22 Slacken the two lower regulator retaining bolts

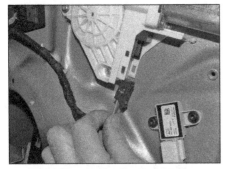

16.33 Disconnect the motor wiring connector

16.34a Undo the motor retaining bolts...

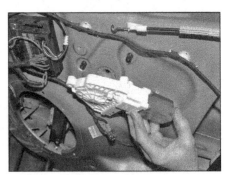

16.34b...and remove the motor from the door panel

19 Release the cable guide retaining clip from the upper part of the door panel.
20 Remove the three sealing grommets from the inner door panel **(see illustration)**.
21 Unscrew the two regulator retaining nuts at the top of the door panel **(see illustration)**.
22 Slacken the two lower regulator retaining bolts **(see illustration)**.
23 Lift the regulator up and out of the door.

Refitting

24 Refitting is a reversal of removal.

Rear door window regulator

Removal

25 Remove the rear door window glass as described previously in this Section.
26 Remove the window regulator motor as described later in this Section.

27 Using an 11 mm socket bit fitted over the regulator motor threaded plugs in the door. Push on the socket to release the retaining tabs and remove the plugs from the door panel **(see illustration 16.18)**.
28 Release the cable guide retaining clip from the upper part of the door panel.
29 Slacken the regulator upper retaining nut.
30 Undo the regulator lower retaining nut and remove the regulator from the door.

Refitting

31 Refitting is a reversal of removal.

Window regulator motor

Removal

32 Remove the door trim panel as described in Section 13.
33 Disconnect the motor wiring connector **(see illustration)**.

34 Undo the three retaining bolts and remove the motor from the door panel **(see illustrations)**.

Refitting

35 Refitting is a reversal of removal.

17 Doors – removal and refitting

Removal

1 Pull up the locking catch and disconnect the wiring connector from the door **(see illustration)**.
2 Undo the retaining bolt and release the door check strap from the door **(see illustration)**.
3 Detach the caps from the door hinge retaining studs **(see illustration)**.

17.1 Disconnect the door wiring connector

17.2 Undo the door check strap retaining bolt

17.3 Detach the caps from the door hinge retaining studs

4 Undo the retaining studs from the upper and lower hinges, then lift the door up and off the hinge pins.

Refitting

5 Refitting is a reversal of the removal procedure. On completion, shut the door and check it for closure and alignment. Check the depth at which the striker enters the lock. If adjustment is required, slacken the securing bolts and reposition the striker plate.

18 Windscreen, rear window glass and rear side window glass – general information

1 The windscreen, rear window glass, and rear side window glass are directly bonded to the metalwork. Their removal and refitting requires the use of special tools not readily available to the home mechanic. This work should therefore be left to an Audi dealer, or a specialist glass renewal company.

19 Sunroof – general

1 A sliding/tilting sunroof is fitted to some models. When fitted correctly, the roof panel in the fully closed position should be level with, or no more than 1.0 mm lower than, the roof panel at the leading edge. The rear edge must be level with, or no more than 1.0 mm higher than, the roof panel at the rear.
2 Removal and refitting, and adjustments to the roof panel, are best entrusted to an Audi garage, as specialised tools are required.
3 If the sunroof water drain hoses become blocked, they may be cleared by probing them with a length of suitable cable (an old speedometer drive cable is ideal), or it mat be worth trying a jet of air.
4 The front drain tubes terminate just below the A-pillars, between the pillar and the door – cable cleaning is carried out from the sunroof end. The rear drain tubes terminate in front of the rear wheel arch. Cable cleaning is carried out from the bottom end of the hose.

20 Exterior mirrors and associated components – removal and refitting

Removal

Exterior mirror

1 Remove the door trim panel as described in Section 13.
2 Disconnect the wiring for the exterior mirror at the door electronics module.
3 Using a small screwdriver carefully prise free the treble loudspeaker trim **(see illustration)**.
4 Release the treble loudspeaker retaining frame from the door seal, disconnect the speaker wiring connector and remove the frame **(see illustration)**.
5 Prise out the two blanking caps from the door to gain access to two of the three mirror retaining bolts **(see illustration)**.
6 Release the wiring grommet from the door and free the mirror wiring from any relevant cable ties **(see illustration)**.
7 Undo the three retaining bolts and remove the mirror from the door, guiding the wiring through the hole.

Mirror glass

Note: *The mirror glass is clipped into place. Removal of the glass without the Audi special forked tool is likely to result in breakage of the glass. Wear protective gloves and glasses to prevent personal injury.*
8 Press in the top of the mirror glass so that the bottom edge is furthest from the housing. Protect the edge of the housing with masking tape (or a cloth), then insert the special tool and lever the mirror glass from its mounting clips. Take great care when removing the glass; do not use excessive force, as the glass is easily broken. If the Audi special tool is not available, use a flat-bladed lever with tape around to prevent any damage to the mirror housing **(see illustration)**.
9 Disconnect the wiring connectors from the mirror heating element **(see illustration)**.

Mirror adjustment unit

10 Remove the mirror glass as described in paragraphs 8 and 9.

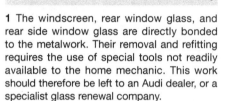

20.3 Carefully prise free the treble loudspeaker trim

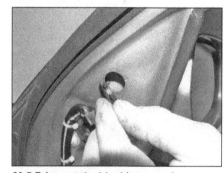
20.4 Release the loudspeaker frame from the door seal

20.5 Prise out the blanking caps for access to the mirror retaining bolts

20.6 Release the door mirror wiring grommet

20.8 Remove the exterior mirror glass...

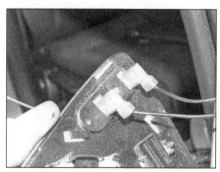
20.9...and disconnect the wiring

11 Undo the bolt in the centre of the adjustment unit.

12 Release the retaining tabs and remove the adjustment unit from the mirror body.

Mirror housing

13 Remove the mirror adjustment unit as described in paragraphs 10, 11 and 12.

14 Undo the two retaining screws and unclip the trim panel from the bottom of the mirror housing using a plastic spatula.

15 Using a plastic spatula carefully work round the housing to release the securing clips and withdraw it from its mounting.

Refitting

16 Refitting is the reverse of the relevant removal procedure. When refitting the mirror glass, press firmly at the centre taking care not to use excessive force, as the glass is easily broken.

---

21 Body exterior fittings – removal and refitting

Wheel arch liners and body under-panels

1 The various plastic covers fitted to the underside of the vehicle are secured in position by a mixture of screws, nuts and retaining clips and removal will be fairly obvious on inspection. Work methodically around the panel removing its retaining screws and releasing its retaining clips until the panel is free and can be removed from the underside of the vehicle (see illustration). Most clips used on the vehicle are simply prised out of position. Remove the wheels to ease the removal of the wheel arch liners.

2 On refitting, renew any retaining clips that may have been broken on removal, and ensure that the panel is securely retained by all the relevant clips and screws.

Body trim strips and badges

3 The various body trim strips and badges are held in position with a special adhesive tape and locating lugs. Removal requires the trim/badge to be heated, to soften the adhesive, and then carefully lifted away from

21.1 Removing a typical body under-panel

21.7 Release the retaining clips from the plenum chamber cover rear section

the surface. Due to the high risk of damage to the vehicle's paintwork during this operation, it is recommended that this task should be entrusted to an Audi dealer.

Plenum chamber cover

Removal

4 Remove the wiper arms as described in Chapter 12 Section 10.

5 Undo the retaining bolt at each end of the plenum chamber cover front section.

6 Release the central retaining clip and lift off the plenum chamber cover front section (see illustration).

7 Release the retaining clip at each end of the plenum chamber cover rear section (see illustration).

8 Apply a small quantity of soap solution to the transition between the windscreen and the plenum chamber cover rear section.

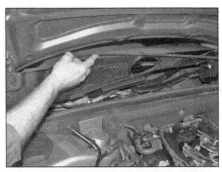

21.6 Lift off the plenum chamber cover front section

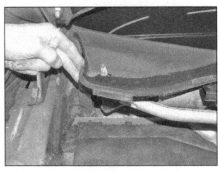

21.9 Removing the plenum chamber cover rear section

9 Starting at the edge of the windscreen, carefully pull the plenum chamber cover rear section vertically up and out of the retainer at the windscreen (see illustration).

Refitting

10 Refitting is a reversal of removal.

Plenum chamber partition panel

Removal

11 Drain the cooling system as described in Chapter 1, Section 31.

12 Remove the plenum chamber cover front section as described previously in this Section.

13 Remove the cover cap then unscrew the wiring junction box retaining bolt. Detach the wiring junction box from the body brace (see illustrations).

14 Release the wiring connector, located

21.13a Remove the cover cap...

21.13b ...unscrew the wiring junction box retaining bolt...

21.13c ...and detach the junction box from the body brace

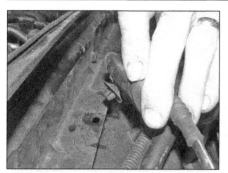

21.14 Release the wiring connector from the body brace, then disconnect the connector

21.15 Remove the rubber seal from the top of the body brace

21.16a Undo the body brace retaining nut on the left-hand side...

21.16b...and the two retaining nuts on the right-hand side

21.17 Undo the two bolts securing the partion panel to the body brace

21.18a Release the wiring harness cable ties...

adjacent to the junction box, from the body brace, then disconnect the connector **(see illustration)**.

15 Remove the bonnet seal from the top of the body brace **(see illustration)**.

16 Undo the body brace retaining nut on the left-hand side, and the two retaining nuts on the right-hand side **(see illustrations)**.

17 Undo the two bolts securing the plenum chamber partition panel to the body brace **(see illustration)**.

18 Release the cable ties securing the wiring harness to the body brace, then remove the brace from the engine compartment **(see illustrations)**.

19 Disconnect the vacuum hose from the rear of the plenum chamber partition panel, then detach the vacuum connection from the front of the panel **(see illustration)**.

20 Release the retaining clips and disconnect the two coolant hoses from the heater matrix pipe stubs **(see illustration)**.Pull the disconnected hoses out through the partition panel.

21 Undo the retaining nut on the right-hand side of the plenum chamber partition panel, then remove the partition panel from the engine compartment.

Refitting

22 Refitting is a reversal of removal. On completion, refill the cooling system as described in 1 Section 31.

Setting the lock carrier to the service position

Note: *To carry out this procedure, Audi special tools T10093 (or suitable alternatives)*

will be required. Alternatively, fabricate two home-made tools using two 8 mm diameter, 300 mm lengths of threaded rod and a selection of hex nuts.

23 The lock carrier is the name given to the section of bodywork that is mounted across the front of the engine compartment.A number of major components, including the bonnet lock mechanism, front bumper, radiator, condenser, intercooler and front light units are mounted on the lock carrier. The construction of the Audi A4 bodywork is such that the lock carrier can be moved forward several centimetres to a 'service position' without having to disconnect the various hoses, pipes and wiring harnesses that serve the components mounted on it. In this position, access to components at the front of the engine is greatly improved.

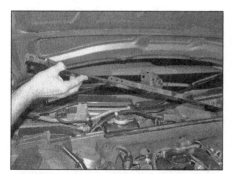

21.18b...then remove the body brace from the engine compartment

21.19 Detach the vacuum connection from the front of the partition panel

21.20 Disconnect the two coolant hoses from the heater matrix pipe stubs

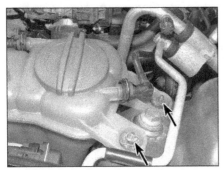

21.26 Undo the expansion tank retaining nuts

21.29 Audi special tools screwed into the longitudinal member

22.2 Carefully prise up the gear lever gaiter from the centre console

24 Remove the front bumper as described in Section 8.

25 From within the engine compartment locate the bonnet release cable connector near the bonnet lock assembly. Open the cable joiner and disengage the rear cable from the joiner.

26 Unscrew the cooling system expansion tank retaining nuts **(see illustration)**.Lift the expansion tank out of its lower mounting grommet.

27 Disconnect the wiring connectors at the headlight units.

28 Refering to Chapter 4B, Section 6, slacken the retaining clips and disconnect the air ducts from the elbows on each side of the intercooler.

29 Unscrew the bolts at the bottom left-hand and right-hand sides of the longitudinal member and screw in the Audi tools (guide pins) or home-made alternatives **(see illustration)**.

30 Undo the remaining bolts, then pull the lock carrier forwards on the guide pins. Take care not to overstretch hoses and wiring as you do this.

31 Returning the lock carrier to the fitted position is a reverse of this procedure, taking care not to trap any wiring as you do so.

22 Centre console – removal and refitting

Removal

1 Remove the heater/ventilation/air conditioning control panel as described in Chapter 3, Section 9.

2 Ensure the transmission is in the neutral position, then prise up the gear lever gaiter from the centre console using a plastic spatula or similar tool **(see illustration)**. Pull the gaiter up around the gear lever knob.

3 Reach through the gear lever gaiter aperture in the MMI control panel and pull the panel up at the rear to disengage the retaining clips. Lift the panel up and feed the gear lever gaiter through the panel aperture. Disconnect the wiring connectors and remove the MMI control panel **(see illustrations)**.

4 Undo the two bolts securing the front ashtray to the centre console. Move the ashtray rearwards to disengage the front mounting lugs, then disconnect the wiring connector and remove the ashtray **(see illustrations)**.

5 Remove the centre console air vents as described in Chapter 3, Section 9.

6 Working through the air vent aperture, undo the retaining bolt on the left-hand side of the centre console.

7 Starting at the bottom, use a plastic spatula

22.3a Pull the MMI control panel up at the rear to disengage the retaining clips...

22.3b...feed the gear lever gaiter through the panel aperture...

22.3c...then turn the panel over and disconnect the wiring connector

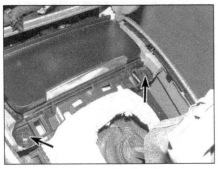

22.4a Undo the two bolts...

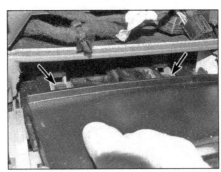

22.4b...disengage the front mounting lugs...

22.4c...then disconnect the wiring connector and remove the ashtray

22.7a Unclip the centre console rear trim...

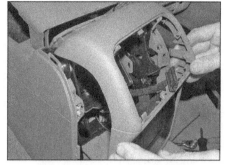

22.7b...then remove the trim and disconnect the wiring connector

22.8 Remove the air vent duct

or similar tool to unclip the centre console rear trim (see illustrations).

8 Remove the duct for the air vent from the rear of the centre console (see illustration).

9 Undo the two bolts securing the centre console to the armrest frame (see illustration).

10 Undo the four nuts securing the armrest frame to the floor (see illustration).

11 Undo the two nuts securing the top of the centre console to the armrest frame (see illustration).

12 Detach the wiring connectors from the base of the armrest frame (see illustration).

13 Lift the centre console up at the rear and take out the armrest frame (see illustration).

14 Lift the centre console up, move it to the rear to disengage the facia, then lift it over the gear/selector lever (see illustration).

Refitting

15 Refitting is the reversal of removal.

---

23 Facia panels and trim –
removal and refitting

Glovebox

Removal

1 Disconnect the battery negative lead as described in Chapter 5, Section 3.

2 On models with a storage box inside the glovebox, release the retaining hooks on each side using a screwdriver, and pull out the storage box.

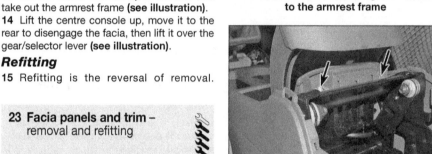

22.9 Undo the bolts securing the console to the armrest frame

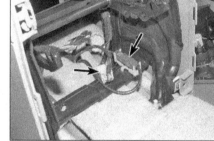

22.10 Armrest frame retaining nuts

22.11 Centre console upper rear retaining nuts

22.12 Detach the wiring connectors from the armrest frame

3 Where fitted, remove the CD/DVD changer as described in Chapter 12 Section 14.

4 Using a plastic spatula or similar tool,

remove the side panel from the left-hand end of the facia.

5 Undo the glovebox retaining bolt from the left-hand end of the facia (see illustration).

22.13 Lift the console up and take out the armrest frame

22.14 Lift the console up and over the gear/selector lever to remove

23.5 Undo the glovebox left-hand retaining bolt

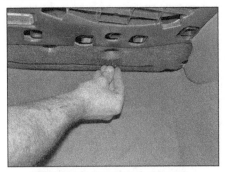

23.6a Undo the three fasteners...

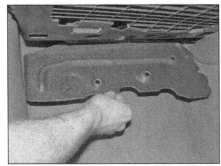

23.6b...and remove the insulation panel

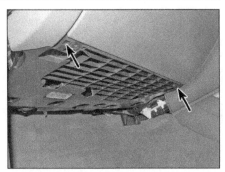

23.7 Undo the two lower retaining bolts

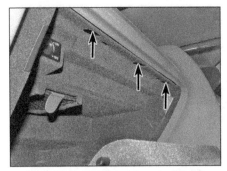

23.8a Undo the three upper retaining bolts...

23.8b...withdraw the glovebox...

23.8c...and disconnect the wiring connector

6 Undo the three fasteners and remove the insulation panel from beneath the glovebox **(see illustrations)**.
7 Undo the two glovebox lower retaining bolts **(see illustration)**.

8 Undo the three upper retaining bolts, withdraw the glovebox from the facia and disconnect the main wiring connector **(see illustrations)**.

Refitting

9 Refitting is the reverse sequence to removal.

Right-hand lower trim panel

Removal

10 Using a plastic spatula or similar tool, remove the side panel from the right-hand end of the facia **(see illustration)**.
11 Undo the panel upper retaining bolt from the right-hand end of the facia **(see illustration)**.
12 Undo the trim panel lower retaining bolts on the left-hand and right-hand side **(see illustrations)**.
13 Using a plastic spatula or similar tool carefully prise free the top edge of the panel and withdraw it from the facia **(see illustrations)**.

23.10 Remove the side panel from the end of the facia

23.11 Undo the trim panel upper retaining bolt

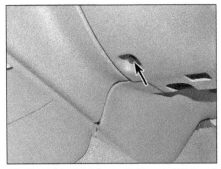

23.12a Undo the trim panel lower left-hand retaining bolt...

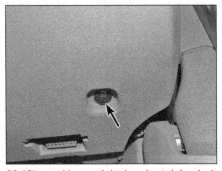

23.12b...and lower right-hand retaining bolt

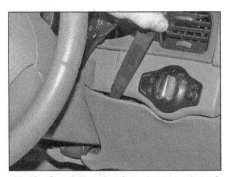

23.13a Carefully prise free the top edge of the panel...

23.13b...and withdraw the panel from the facia

23.14a Disconnect the wiring connector at the footwell illumination light...

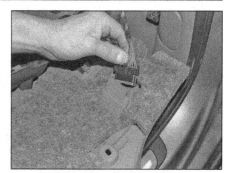

23.14b...and diagnostic socket

14 Disconnect the wiring connectors at the footwell illumination light and diagnostic socket, then remove the panel from the footwell **(see illustrations)**.

Refitting

15 Refitting is the reverse sequence to removal.

Steering column shrouds

Removal

16 Using the rake and reach adjuster, move the steering column down, and as far to the rear as possible.
17 Carefully unclip the trim cover for the instrument panel surround from the steering column upper shroud **(see illustration)**.
18 Turn the steering half a turn to the left or right from the straight-ahead position.
19 Using the plastic spatula, carefully prise the upper shroud off the lower shroud, then move it to the rear to disengage the lower shroud hooks **(see illustrations)**.
20 Undo the screw each side securing the lower steering column shroud to the multifunction switch **(see illustration)**.
21 Undo the lower bolt securing the shroud to the steering column and remove the shroud from the car **(see illustrations)**.

Refitting

22 Refitting is the reverse sequence to removal.

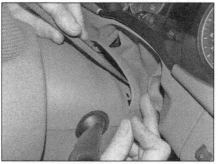

23.17 Unclip the instrument panel surround trim cover

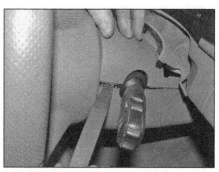

23.19a Carefully prise the steering column upper shroud off the lower shroud...

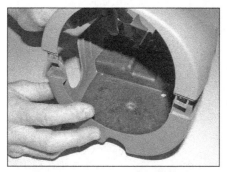

23.19b...to release the tabs at the rear...

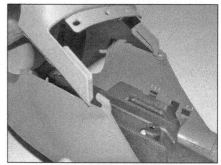

23.19c...and the hooks at the front (shown with shrouds removed)

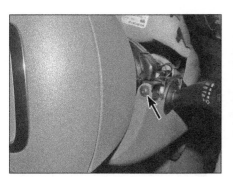

23.20 Undo the two screws securing the lower shroud to the multifunction switch

23.21a Undo the shroud lower bolt...

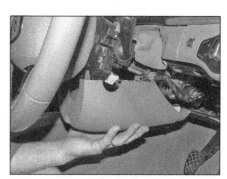

23.21b...and remove the shroud

24 Seats – removal and refitting

Front seat

 Warning: Both front seats are equipped with side airbags. Prior to disconnecting the airbag wiring plug, it is essential you are electrostatically discharged by touching a door lock or vehicle body briefly.

1 Move the seat rearwards to the extent of its travel.

2 Undo the multipoint bolt at the front of each seat rail securing the seat to the vehicle body **(see illustration)**.

3 Move the seat fully forwards.

4 Disconnect the battery negative lead (see Chapter 5, Section 3).

5 Undo the bolt at the rear of the each seat rail **(see illustration)**.

6 Lift up the cover in the floor then unplug the airbag wiring plug (see warning above), and where fitted, disconnect the wiring plugs for the seat heating and motor systems and remove the seat from the vehicle. If required, prise up the seat belt anchor plastic cover, lever out the retaining clip, and push the seat belt anchor downwards to disconnect it from the seat **(see illustrations)**. Due to the risk of injury or component failure, no further dismantling of the seats is recommended.

Note: *Whilst the seat is removed from the vehicle, Audi insist that the side airbag should still be earthed. This can be achieved with an Audi adapter/loom (VAG 6281) plugged into*

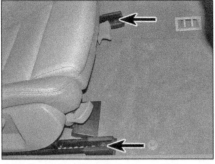
24.2 Undo the bolts at the front of the seat rails...

the connector on the seat and the connector to the airbag module. In the absence of the Audi adapter/loom, connect a cable from the yellow connector under the seat to a good chassis earth point.

7 Refit the seat in the reverse order of removal.

Note: *After refitting the seat(s), the airbag warning light on the dash may signal a fault. Take the vehicle to an Audi dealer or suitably-equipped specialist to have the self diagnosis system interrogated and the fault code erased.*

Rear seat bench

8 On models with rear seat side airbags, disconnect the battery negative lead (see Chapter 5, Section 3).

9 Grasp the front lower edge of the seat on one side and pull it upwards, to release the retaining pins from their plastic sockets. Pull the other side up in the same way. Note that the plastic sockets should be removed

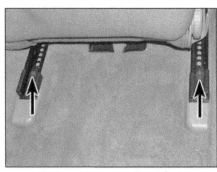
24.5...and the ones at the rear

from the floor during the seat removal and discarded – fit new ones before installing the seat bench **(see illustration)**.

10 Push the seat cushion rearwards firmly to detach the retainers, then slide the seat bench forward and remove it from the vehicle. Disconnect the airbag wiring plug as the seat is removed (where applicable).

11 Refit the seat bench in the reverse order of removal, using new seat plastic sockets.

Rear seat backrest

Folding rear seats

12 Remove the rear bench seat as described previously in this Section.

13 Undo the centre seat belt anchorage bolt.

14 Where applicable, disconnect the wiring connector for the backrest heating element.

15 Fold down both backrests, then prise up the trim from the centre hinge **(see illustration)**.

24.6a Lift up the cover and disconnect the seat wiring plugs

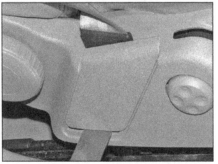
24.6b Prise up the cover...

24.6c...lever out the clip...

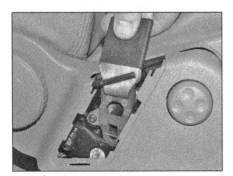
24.6d...and detach the seat belt from the seat

24.9 Renew the plastic sockets

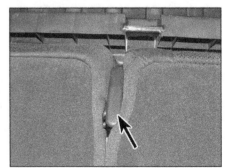
24.15 Prise up the trim from the centre hinge...

24.16...then undo the bolt and lift out the backrest

16 Undo the retaining bolt, lift out the clip and remove the backrest, disengaging the backrest from the locating pin on the vehicle body **(see illustration)**.
17 Refit the seat backrest in the reverse order of removal.

Fixed rear seats

18 Remove the rear bench seat as described previously in this Section.
19 Undo the three backrest retaining bolts in the luggage compartment, and the two retaining bolts at the base of the backrest in the passenger compartment.
20 Where applicable, disconnect the wiring connector for the backrest heating element.
21 Pull the backrest upwards and forwards at its bottom edge and remove it from the car.
22 Refit the seat backrest in the reverse order of removal.

---

25 Interior trim – removal and refitting

Interior trim panels

1 The interior trim panels are secured using either bolts or various types of trim fasteners, usually studs or clips.
2 Check that there are no other panels overlapping the one to be removed; usually there is a sequence that has to be followed, and this will only become obvious on close inspection.
3 Remove all obvious fasteners, such as bolts. If the panel will not come free, it is held by hidden clips or fasteners. These are usually situated around the edge of the panel and can be prised up to release them; note, however that they can break quite easily so new ones should be available. The best way of releasing such clips without the correct type of tool is to use a large flat-bladed screwdriver. Note in many cases that the adjacent sealing strip must be prised back to release a panel.
4 When removing a panel, never use excessive force or the panel may be damaged; always check carefully that all fasteners or other relevant components have

been removed or released before attempting to withdraw a panel.
5 Refitting is the reverse of the removal procedure; secure the fasteners by pressing them firmly into place and ensure that all disturbed components are correctly secured to prevent rattles.

Carpets

6 The passenger compartment floor carpet is in one piece and is secured at its edges by bolts or clips, usually the same fasteners used to secure the various adjoining trim panels.
7 Carpet removal and refitting is reasonably straightforward but very time-consuming because all adjoining trim panels must be removed first, as must components such as the seats, the centre console and seat belt lower anchorages.

Headlining

8 The headlining is clipped to the roof and can be withdrawn only once all fittings such as the grab handles, sunvisors, sunroof (if fitted), windscreen, rear quarter windows and related trim panels have been removed, and the door, tailgate and sunroof aperture sealing strips (as applicable) have been prised clear.
9 Note that headlining removal requires considerable skill and experience if it is to be carried out without damage and is therefore best entrusted to an expert.

---

26 Seat belt tensioning mechanism – general information

1 All models are fitted with seat belt pretensioners that are integrated into the airbag control system. The system is designed to instantaneously take up any slack in the seat belt in the case of a direct or oblique frontal impact, therefore reducing the possibility of injury to the occupants. Each front seat inertia reel is fitted with its own tensioner, which is triggered by a frontal impact above a predetermined force. Lesser impacts and impacts to the rear of the vehicle will not trigger the system.
2 When the system is triggered, the explosive gas in the tensioner mechanism retracts and locks the seat belt. This prevents the seat belt moving and keeps the occupant firmly in position in the seat. Once the tensioner has been triggered, the seat belt will be permanently locked, together with the impact sensors.
3 Always disconnect the battery negative lead (see Chapter 5, Section 3) before working on the pretensioners.
4 Note the following warnings before contemplating any work on the front seat belts.

 Warning: Do not expose the tensioner mechanism to temperatures in excess of 100°C.
 Warning: If the tensioner mechanism is dropped, it must be renewed, even it has suffered no apparent damage.
 Warning: Do not allow any solvents to come into contact with the tensioner mechanism.
 Warning: Do not attempt to open the tensioner mechanism as it contains explosive gas.
 Warning: Tensioners must be discharged before they are disposed of, but this task should be entrusted to an Audi dealer.

---

27 Seat belts – general information, removal and refitting

Note: *Refer to the warnings in Section 26 before working on the front seat belts.*

General

1 Periodically check the belts for fraying or other damage. If evident, renew the belt.
2 If the belts become dirty, wipe them with a damp cloth, using a little liquid detergent only.
3 Check the tightness of the anchor bolts, and if they are ever disconnected, make quite sure that the original sequence of fitting of washers, bushes, and anchor plate is retained.
4 Access to the front belt height adjuster and inertia reel units can be made by removing the trim from the B-pillar on the side concerned.
5 The rear seat belt anchorages can be checked by removing the rear seat bench. Access to the rear seat inertia reel units is made by removing the rear seat backrest, parcel shelf and luggage area side trim.
6 The torque wrench settings for the seat belt anchor bolts and other attachments are given in the Specifications at the start of this Chapter.
7 Never modify the seat belts, or alter the attachments to the body, in any way.

Removal

Front belt

8 Disconnect the battery negative lead as described in Chapter 5, Section 3.
9 Remove the upper and lower B-pillar trims with reference to Section 25.
10 Detach the outer seat belt anchorage point, and release the belt from the guide on the side of the seat **(see illustration 24.6d)**.
11 Undo the inertia reel mounting bolt and manoeuvre the reel from the pillar. Disconnect

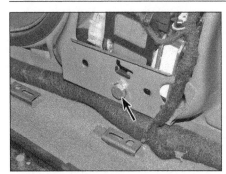

27.11 Undo the inertia reel mounting bolt

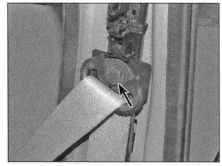

27.12 Undo the seat belt upper anchorage bolt

27.14 Seat belt stalk mounting bolt

27.16 Slacken the rear side seat belt inertia reel mounting bolt from the luggage compartment

the pretensioners wiring plug by prising up the locking element, and disconnecting the plug **(see illustration)**.
12 Undo the bolt at the upper seat belt anchorage point **(see illustration)**.

13 Undo the two bolts and remove the seat belt guide, then remove the belt from the car.
14 To remove the front seat belt stalk, first remove the front seat as described in Section 24. Unscrew the bolt, remove the washer, and withdraw the stalk from the seat. On models with a buckle sensor, disconnect the wiring plug and release the cable from the retaining clip **(see illustration)**.

Rear side belt

15 Remove the relevant trim panels as necessary for access with reference to Section 25.
16 Working in the luggage compartment, undo the bolt on the underside of the inertia reel **(see illustration)**.
17 Undo the lower seat belt anchorage point bolt and remove the belt.

Centre belt – parcel shelf-mounted

18 Remove the parcel shelf (where applicable).

19 Note the orientation of any spacers/washers, then undo the lower anchorage point bolt.
20 Working in the luggage compartment, undo the bolt on the underside of the inertia reel.
21 Remove the seat belt from the vehicle.

Centre belt – backrest-mounted

22 Where the inertia reel is located inside the seat backrest, the backrest trim must be removed and the backrest must be completely dismantled. This is a complex operation and considerable expertise is needed to remove and refit the seat upholstery and internal components without damage. Therefore, any problems with the seat belt and reel should be referred to an Audi dealer.

Refitting

23 Refitting is a reversal of removal, ensuring all bolts are tighten to their specified torque where given.

Chapter 12
Body electrical systems

Contents

Degrees of difficulty

Easy, suitable for novice with little experience 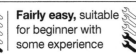	Fairly easy, suitable for beginner with some experience	Fairly difficult, suitable for competent DIY mechanic	Difficult, suitable for experienced DIY mechanic	Very difficult, suitable for expert DIY or professional

Specifications

System type	12 volt, negative earth

Bulbs	**Power rating (watts)**
Direction indicators	21
Foglight:	
Front	55 H11
Rear	21
Headlight:	
Dipped	55 H7
Main	55 H7
High-level brake light	LEDs
Number plate light	5
Luggage compartment light	5 capless
Reversing light	16
Sidelights	21
Stop-light	21
Tail light	21

Torque wrench settings	**Nm**	**lbf ft**
Rear window wiper arm nut	12	9
Windscreen wiper arm nuts	17	13
Windscreen wiper linkage bolts	8	6

1 General information and precautions

 Warning: Before carrying out any work on the electrical system, read through the precautions given in Safety first! and in Chapter 5.

1 The electrical system is of 12 volt negative earth type. Power for the lights and all electrical accessories is supplied by a lead-acid type battery which is charged by the alternator.

2 This Chapter covers repair and service procedures for the various electrical components not associated with the engine. Information on the battery, alternator and starter motor can be found in Chapter 5.

3 It should be noted that prior to working on any component in the electrical system, the ignition and all electrical consumers must be switched off. Additionally, where stated, the battery negative lead must be disconnected as described in Disconnecting the battery in Chapter 5, Section 3.

2 Electrical fault finding – general information

Note: *Refer to the precautions given in Safety first! and in Chapter 5 before starting work. The following tests relate to testing of the main electrical circuits, and should not be used to test delicate electronic circuits (such as anti-lock braking systems), particularly where an electronic control unit is used.*

Caution: The Audi A4 electrical system is extremely complex. Many of the ECUs are connected via a 'Databus' system, where they are able to share information from the various sensors, and communicate with each other. Due to the design of the Databus system, it is not advisable to backprobe the ECUs with a multimeter, in the traditional manner. Instead, the electrical systems are equipped with a sophisticated self-diagnosis system, which can interrogate the various ECUs to reveal stored fault codes, and help pin-point faults. In order to access the self-diagnosis system, specialist test equipment (fault code reader/scanner) is required.

General

1 Typically, electrical circuit consists of an electrical component, any switches, relays, motors, fuses, fusible links or circuit breakers related to that component, and the wiring and connectors which link the component to both the battery and the chassis. To help to pinpoint a problem in an electrical circuit, wiring diagrams are included at the end of this Chapter.

2 Have a good look at the appropriate wiring diagram, before attempting to diagnose an electrical fault, to obtain a complete understanding of the components included in the particular circuit concerned. The possible sources of a fault can be narrowed down by noting if other components related to the circuit are operating properly. If several components or circuits fail at one time, the problem is likely to be related to a shared fuse or earth connection.

3 An electrical problem will usually stem from a simple cause, such as loose or corroded connections, a faulty earth connection, a blown fuse, a melted fusible link, or a faulty relay (refer to Section 3 for details of testing relays). Visually inspect the condition of all fuses, wires and connections in a problem circuit before testing the components. Use the wiring diagrams to determine which terminal connections will need to be checked in order to pinpoint the trouble-spot.

4 The basic tools required for electrical fault finding include a circuit tester or voltmeter (a 12 volt bulb with a set of test leads can also be used for certain tests); a self-powered test light (sometimes known as a continuity tester); an ohmmeter (to measure resistance); a battery and set of test leads; and a jumper wire, preferably with a circuit breaker or fuse incorporated, which can be used to bypass suspect wires or electrical components. Before attempting to locate a problem with test instruments, use the wiring diagram to determine where to make the connections.

5 Sometimes, an intermittent wiring fault (usually caused to a poor or dirty connection, or damaged wiring insulation) can be pin-pointed by performing a wiggle test on the wiring. This involves wiggling the wiring by hand to see if the fault occurs as the wiring is moved. It should be possible to narrow down the source of the fault to a particular section of wiring. This method of testing can be used in conjunction with any of the tests described in the following sub-Sections.

6 Apart from problems due to poor connections, two basic types of fault can occur in an electrical circuit: open-circuit, or short-circuit.

7 Largely, open-circuit faults are caused by a break somewhere in the circuit, which prevents current from flowing. An open-circuit fault will prevent a component from working, but will not cause the relevant circuit fuse to blow.

8 Low resistance or short-circuit faults are caused by a 'short'; a failure point which allows the current flowing in the circuit to 'escape' along an alternative route somewhere in the circuit. This typically occurs when a positive supply wire touches either an earth wire, or an earthed component such as the bodyshell. Such faults are normally caused by a breakdown in wiring insulation, A short circuit fault will normally cause the relevant circuit fuse to blow.

9 Fuses are designed to protect a circuit from being overloaded. A blown fuse indicates that there may be problem in that particular circuit and it is important to identify and rectify the problem before renewing the fuse. Always renew a blown fuse with one of the correct current rating; fitting a fuse of a different rating may cause an overloaded circuit to overheat and even catch fire.

Finding an open-circuit

10 One of the most straightforward ways of finding an open-circuit fault is by using a circuit test meter or voltmeter. Connect one lead of the meter to either the negative battery terminal or a known good earth. Connect the other lead to a connector in the circuit being tested, preferably nearest to the battery or fuse. Switch on the circuit, bearing in mind that some circuits are live only when the ignition switch is moved to a particular position. If voltage is present (indicated either by the tester bulb lighting or a voltmeter reading, as applicable), this means that the section of the circuit between the relevant connector and the battery is problem-free. Continue to check the remainder of the circuit in the same fashion. When a point is reached at which no voltage is present, the problem must lie between that point and the previous test point with voltage. Most problems can be traced to a broken, corroded or loose connection.

 Warning: Under no circumstances may live measuring instruments such as ohmmeters, voltmeters or a bulb and test leads be used to test any of the airbag circuitry. Any testing of these components must be left to an Audi dealer or specialist, as there is a danger of activating the system if the correct procedures are not followed.

Finding a short-circuit

11 Loading the circuit during testing will produce false results and may damage your test equipment, so all electrical loads must be disconnected from the circuit before it can be checked for short circuits. Loads are the components which draw current from a circuit, such as bulbs, motors, heating elements, etc.

12 Keep both the ignition and the circuit under test switched off, then remove the relevant fuse from the circuit, and connect a circuit test meter or voltmeter to the fuse connections.

13 Switch on the circuit, bearing in mind that some circuits are live only when the ignition switch is moved to a particular position. If voltage is present (indicated either by the tester bulb lighting or a voltmeter reading, as applicable), this means that there is a short-circuit. If no voltage is present, but the fuse still blows with the load(s) connected, this indicates an internal fault in the load(s).

Finding an earth fault

14 The battery negative terminal is connected to 'earth': the metal of the engine/transmission and the car body – and most systems are wired so that they only receive a positive feed, the current returning through the metal of the car body. This means that the component mounting and the body form part of that circuit. Loose or corroded mountings can therefore cause a range of electrical faults, ranging from total failure of a circuit, to a puzzling partial fault. In particular, lights may shine dimly (especially when another circuit sharing the same earth point is in operation), motors (eg, wiper motors or the radiator cooling fan motor) may run slowly, and the operation of one circuit may have an apparently unrelated effect on another. Note that on many vehicles, earth straps are used between certain components, such as the engine/transmission and the body, usually where there is no metal-to-metal contact between components due to flexible rubber mountings, etc.

15 To check whether a component is properly earthed, disconnect the battery and connect one lead of an ohmmeter to a known good earth point. Connect the other lead to the wire or earth connection being tested. The resistance reading should be zero; if not, check the connection as follows.

16 If an earth connection is thought to be faulty, dismantle the connection and clean back to bare metal both the bodyshell and the wire terminal or the component earth connection mating surface. Be careful to remove all traces of dirt and corrosion, then use a knife to trim away any paint, so that a clean metal-to-metal joint is made. On reassembly, tighten the joint fasteners securely; if a wire terminal is being refitted, use serrated washers between the terminal and the bodyshell to ensure a clean and secure connection. When the connection is remade, prevent the onset of corrosion in the future by applying a coat of petroleum jelly or silicone-based grease or by spraying on (at regular intervals) a proprietary ignition sealer or a water dispersant lubricant.

3 Fuses and relays – general information

Fuses and fusible links

1 Fuses are designed to break a circuit when a predetermined current is reached, in order to protect the components and wiring, which could be damaged by excessive current flow. Any excessive current flow will be due to a fault in the circuit, usually a short-circuit (see Section 2).

2 The main fuseboxes are located behind a panel at each end of the facia and behind the trim panel on the right-hand side of the luggage compartment. To access a facia fusebox pull the panel from the end of the facia after releasing it using a plastic spatula or similar in the slot provided **(see illustration)**.Additional fuses are located in the engine compartment electronics box, and adjacent to the battery.

3 To remove a fuse, first switch off the circuit

3.2 Unclip the fusebox trim cover

concerned (or the ignition), and then pull the fuse out of its terminals **(see illustration)**.

4 The wire within the fuse should be visible; if the fuse has blown it will be broken or melted.

5 Always renew a fuse with one of the correct rating; never use a fuse with a different rating from that specified.

6 Refer to the wiring diagrams for details of the fuse ratings and the circuits protected. The fuse rating is stamped on the top of the fuse; the fuses are also colour-coded as follows.

Colour	Rating
Light brown	5A
Brown	7.5A
Red	10A
Blue	15A
Yellow	20A
White or clear	25A
Green	30A
Orange	40A

7 Never renew a fuse more than once without tracing the source of the trouble. If the new fuse blows immediately, find the cause before renewing it again; a short to earth as a result of faulty insulation is most likely. Where a fuse protects more than one circuit, try to isolate the fault by switching on each circuit in turn (where possible) until the fuse blows again. Always carry a supply of spare fuses of each relevant rating on the vehicle.

Relays

8 A relay is an electrically-operated switch, which is used for the following reasons:
a) *A relay can switch a heavy current remotely from the circuit in which the current is flowing, allowing the use of lighter-gauge wiring and switch contacts.*
b) *A relay can receive more than one control input, unlike a mechanical switch.*
c) *A relay can have a timer function – for example, the intermittent wiper relay.*

9 Most of the relays are located on the relay plate behind the driver's side facia; however, additional relays are located in the engine compartment electronics box, and on the right-hand side of the luggage compartment.

10 If a circuit or system controlled by a relay develops a fault, and the relay is suspect,

3.3 Removing a fuse from the facia fusebox

operate the system. If the relay is functioning, it should be possible to hear it click as it is energised. If this is the case, the fault lies with the components or wiring of the system. If the relay is not being energised, then either the relay is not receiving a main supply or a switching voltage, or the relay itself is faulty. Testing is by the substitution of a known good unit, but be careful – while some relays are identical in appearance and in operation, others look similar but perform different functions.

11 To remove a relay, first ensure that the relevant circuit is switched off. The relay can then simply be pulled out from the socket, and pushed back into position.

4 Steering column combination switch – removal and refitting

Removal

1 Disconnect the battery negative lead (see Disconnecting the battery in Chapter 5, Section 3).

2 Remove the steering wheel as described in Chapter 10, Section 14. Apply self-adhesive tape to the rotary contact unit to prevent accidental rotation.

3 Remove the steering column shrouds as described in Chapter 11, Section 23.

4 Prior to disconnecting the combination switch wiring connectors, it is essential you are electrostatically discharged by touching a door lock or vehicle body briefly.

5 Disconnect the two wiring connectors from the combination switch.

6 Remove the clamp bolt and remove the combination switch assembly from the steering column. Do not turn the spring contact assembly whilst the steering wheel is removed.

7 Undo the lower retaining bolt, release the two hooks and remove the rotary contact unit from the combination switch. If necessary, the direction indicator switch and wiper switch can now be detached from the combination switch.

Refitting

8 Refitting is a reversal of removal.

5.2a Release the retaining clip...

5.2b...and withdraw the fusebox

5 Switches –
removal and refitting

Facia-mounted light switch

1 Remove the trim panel from the right-hand end of the facia after releasing it using a plastic spatula or similar in the slot provided **(see illustration 3.2)**.
2 Release the retaining clip and withdraw the fusebox from the end of the facia **(see illustrations)**.
3 Reach in through the opening in the facia and push the light switch out from its location **(see illustration)**. Disconnect the wiring connector and remove the switch.
4 Refitting is a reversal of removal.

Glovebox light switch

5 Remove the trim panel from the left-hand end of the facia after releasing it using a plastic spatula or similar in the slot provided.
6 Working through the end of the facia, disconnect the switch wiring plug, and pull out the switch pivot pin.
7 Swivel the switch in an anti-clockwise direction, and remove it from position.
8 Refitting is a reversal of removal.

Door mirror adjuster

9 Remove the door trim panel, as described in Chapter 11, Section 13.

10 Detach the wiring connector, then carefully release the retaining clips and remove the switch from the door trim **(see illustrations)**.
11 Refitting is a reversal of removal.

Electric window switch/module

12 Remove the door trim panel as described in Chapter 11, Section 13.
13 Insert a small screwdriver between the switch and surround in the area of the retaining tabs and pull the switch out of the panel **(see illustrations)**.
14 Refitting is a reversal of removal.

Sunroof control

15 Open the sunglasses compartment in the roof console and undo the retaining screw **(see illustration)**.

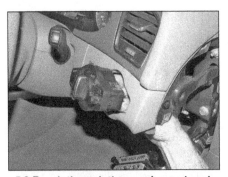

5.3 Reach through the opening and push the light switch out of the facia

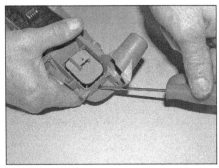

5.10a Release the clips retaining clips...

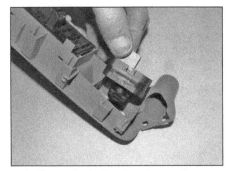

5.10b...and remove the mirror adjuster switch

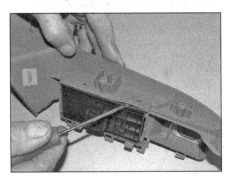

5.13a Release the switch retaining tabs...

5.13b...and pull the switch out of the panel

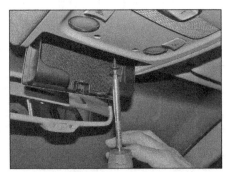

5.15 Undo the roof console retaining bolt

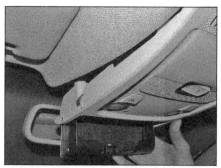

5.16a Pivot the console down at the front...

5.16b...to disengage the rear retaining tabs

5.20 Release the clip and press the central locking switch from the door trim panel

16 Pivot the console down at the front to disengage the rear retaining tabs **(see illustrations)**. Disconnect the wiring connectors and remove the console.

17 Undo the three retaining bolts and remove the control switch from the roof console.

18 Refitting is a reversal of removal.

Central locking switch

19 Remove the door trim panel as described in Chapter 11, Section 13.

20 Disconnect the wiring connector from the switch, release the retaining clip, then press the switch from the panel **(see illustration)**.

21 Refitting is a reversal of removal.

Courtesy light switches

22 The courtesy light are controlled by microswitches incorporated into the door locks. The switches are not available

separately. If defective, the door lock assembly must be renewed.

Centre console switches

23 Remove the MMI control panel as described in Chapter 11, Section 22.

24 From the underside of the panel undo the switch retaining screw (if fitted) **(see illustration)**.

25 Release the retaining tabs and remove the relevant switch from the control panel **(see illustrations)**.

26 Refitting is a reversal of removal.

Stop-light switch

27 Refer to Chapter 9, Section 15.

Steering column switches

28 Refer to Section 4.

Hazard warning switch

29 Using a plastic spatula or similar tool

carefully prise off the cover for the MMI screen **(see illustrations)**. Disconnect the hazard warning light switch wiring connector and remove the cover.

30 Depress the retaining tabs and remove the switch **(see illustration)**.

Seat heating switches

31 The front seat heating switches are integral with the heating/air conditioning control panel, and cannot be renewed separately. Removal of the panel is described in Chapter 3, Section 9.

32 To remove the rear seat switches, first remove the centre console rear trim as described in Chapter 11, Section 22.

33 Release the retaining clips and remove the relevant switch from the panel.

34 Refitting is a reversal of removal.

5.24 Where fitted, undo the switch retaining screw

5.25a Release the retaining tabs...

5.25b...and remove the relevant switch

5.29a Carefully prise free the cover for the MMI screen...

5.29b...then disconnect the wiring connector and remove the cover

5.30 Depress the tabs and remove the switch

6.3 Remove the cover from the headlight unit

6.4 Push the bulb sideways and remove it from the light unit

6.5 Disconnect the wiring connector from the bulb

6 Exterior light bulbs – renewal

1 Whenever a bulb is renewed, note the following points:
a) Remember that if the light has just been in use, the bulb may be extremely hot.
b) Do not touch the bulb glass with the fingers, as the small deposits can cause the bulb to cloud over.
c) Always check the bulb contacts and holder, ensuring that there is clean metal-to-metal contact. Clean off any corrosion or dirt before fitting a new bulb.
d) Wherever bayonet-type bulbs are fitted, ensure that the live contacts bear firmly against the bulb contact.
e) Always ensure that the new bulb is of the

6.11 Release the fasteners and remove the foglight surround

correct rating and that it is completely clean before fitting it.

Headlight dipped beam

2 Remove the headlight unit as described in Section 8.
3 Release the cover from the rear of the headlight **(see illustration)**.
4 Push the bulb sideways against spring pressure and pull it, together with the wiring connector out of the headlight unit **(see illustration)**. If the bulb is to be refitted, do not touch the glass with the fingers. If the glass is accidentally touched, clean it with methylated spirit.
5 Pull the wiring connector from the bulb **(see illustration)**.
6 Press the new bulb into the connector, then push the bulb into the light unit until it is retained by the spring clips.
7 Refit the cover to the rear of the headlight unit, then refit the headlight as described in Section 8.

Headlight main beam

8 The procedure for renewal of the headlight main beam bulb is identical to that for the dipped beam bulb described previously in this Section.

Gas discharge headlights (Xenon bulbs)

⚠️ **Warning: The headlight bulb contains gas at very high pressure, and it is recommended that gloves and eye protection be worn to prevent potential personal injury.**
9 Due to the high pressure of gas in this type of bulb, it is recommended that this

type of bulb be renewed by an Audi dealer or specialist workshop.
Caution: After refitting a gas discharge headlight, the basic setting of the automatic range control system should be checked. Because of the requirement for specialised equipment, this can only be carried out by an Audi dealer or suitably equipped specialist.

Sidelight and direction indicator

10 Renewal of the sidelight and direction indicator bulb modules entails cutting open the headlight unit for access to the bulbs. This carries a very great risk of irreparably damaging the headlight unit and wiring and for this reason it is recommended that this work is carried out by an Audi dealer.

Front foglight

11 Insert a thin screwdriver into the slots in the foglight surround and release the fasteners **(see illustration)**. Withdraw the inner edge of the surround, disengage the retaining tabs on the outer edge and remove the surround.
12 Undo the two bolts (three bolts on later models) and withdraw the foglight from the bumper **(see illustration)**. Disconnect the wiring connector and remove the foglight.
13 Rotate the bulbholder anti-clockwise and pull it from the foglight **(see illustration)**. Note that the bulb is integral with the bulbholder.
14 Fit the new bulb using a reversal of the removal procedure.

Tailgate/boot lid-mounted lights

15 Open the tailgate/boot lid and prise open the cover from the trim panel **(see illustration)**.

6.13 Rotate the bulbholder anti-clockwise to remove

6.15 Prise open the cover...

6.12 Undo the bolts and withdraw the foglight from the bumper

6.16a Press the retainer tab sideways and pull the bulbholder from the rear light

6.16b Disconnect the wiring connector and remove the bulbholder

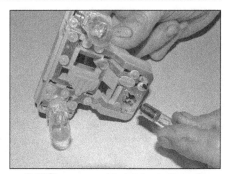

6.17 Depress and twist the bulb anti-clockwise

16 Press the retainer tab sideways and withdraw the bulbholder from the light unit. Disconnect the wiring connector and remove the bulbholder **(see illustrations)**.

17 Depending on model, either press and twist the relevant bulb anti-clockwise, and withdraw it from the bulbholder, or pull out the push-fit bulb **(see illustration)**.

18 Fit the new bulb using a reversal of the removal procedure.

Body-mounted rear lights

19 Prise open the cover and undo the nut retainer using the removal tool from the toolkit **(see illustration)**.

20 Swivel the light unit outward and disengage the retaining pins from the body **(see illustration)**.

21 Disconnect the wiring connector and remove the light unit.

22 Undo the three nuts and remove the bulbholder **(see illustrations)**.

23 Depending on model, either press and twist the relevant bulb anti-clockwise, and withdraw it from the bulbholder, or pull out the push-fit bulb **(see illustration)**.

24 Fit the new bulb using a reversal of the removal procedure.

Number plate light

25 Insert a screwdriver into the slot on the light unit and push it to the right **(see illustration)**.

26 Disconnect the wiring connector and remove the light unit **(see illustration)**.

6.19 Undo the light unit retaining nut using the removal tool from the tool kit

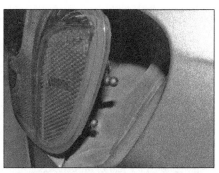

6.20 Swivel the light unit outward and disengage the retaining pins

6.22a Undo the three nuts...

6.22b...and remove the bulbholder

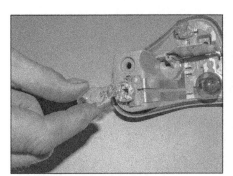

6.23 Removing a push-fit bulb from the bulbholder

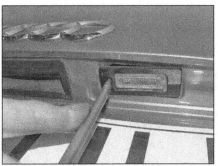

6.25 Use a screwdriver to release the number plate light

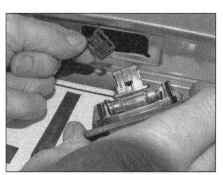

6.26 Disconnect the wiring connector and remove the light unit

6.27 Pull the festoon bulb from the contacts

27 Remove the festoon-type bulb from its holder **(see illustration)**.
28 Fit the new bulb using a reversal of the removal procedure.

High-level stop-light

Note: *The light is of LED design; therefore if faulty the complete unit must be renewed.*

Saloon models

29 Remove the D-pillar trim then detach the headlining from the body in the vicinity of the high-level stop-light.
30 Pull off the light unit by moving the cover evenly towards the rear of the vehicle.
31 Disconnect the wiring connector and remove the stop-light unit.
32 Refitting is a reversal of removal.

Avant models

33 Remove the tailgate trim panels as described in Chapter 11, Section 11.

7.3a Unclip the interior light lens...

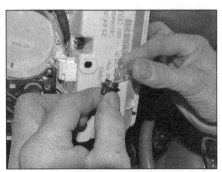

7.6b...then pull the bulb from the holder

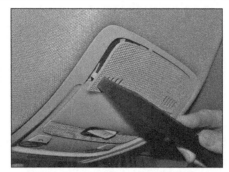

7.2 Unclip the trim for the hands-free microphone

34 Insert a screwdriver through the wiring hole in the tailgate, and slide the retaining rail to the right. Note that this will cause the five retaining clips, and the retaining rail to detach from the rear of the light unit.
35 Starting on the left-hand side, carefully prise the light unit from the outside of the tailgate, disconnecting the wiring plug as it's withdrawn.
36 Recover the retaining clips and rail, and reset them on the rear of the light unit. Reconnect the wiring plug, and refit the light unit into the tailgate. It should engage with an audible click.

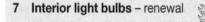

7   Interior light bulbs – renewal

1 Whenever a bulb is renewed, note the following points:

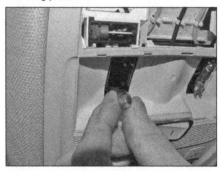

7.3b...and pull the festoon bulb(s) from the contacts

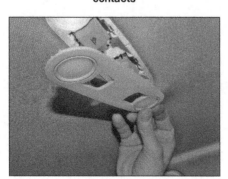

7.8a Prise free the lens from the rear light unit...

a) *Remember that if the light has just been in use, the bulb may be extremely hot.*
b) *Always check the bulb contacts and holder, ensuring that there is clean metal-to-metal contact between the bulb and its live and earth. Clean off any corrosion or dirt before fitting a new bulb.*
c) *Wherever bayonet-type bulbs are fitted, ensure that the live contact(s) bear firmly against the bulb contact.*
d) *Always ensure that the new bulb is of the correct rating and that it is completely clean before fitting it.*

Interior/reading lights

Front interior lights

2 Using a plastic spatula or similar tool, carefully unclip the trim for the hands-free microphone **(see illustration)**.
3 Unclip the lens, and pull the festoon bulb from the spring contacts **(see illustrations)**.
4 Fit the new bulb using a reversal of the removal procedure.

Front reading lights

5 Remove the roof console as described in paragraphs 15 and 16 of Section 5.
6 Twist the bulbholder anti-clockwise to remove it, then pull the bulb from the holder **(see illustrations)**.
7 Fit the new bulb using a reversal of the removal procedure.

Rear lights

8 Carefully prise free the lens from the light unit, then remove the relevant push-fit bulb **(see illustrations)**.

7.6a Twist the bulbholder anti-clockwise to remove...

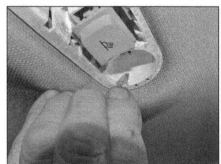

7.8b... then remove the relevant bulb

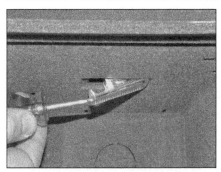

7.10 Prise out the end of the glovebox light lens

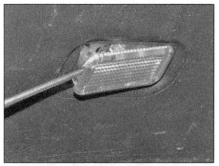

7.15 Prise the luggage compartment light from the panel...

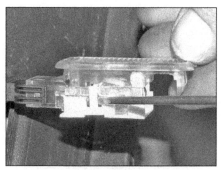

7.16 ...and prise free the reflector

9 Fit the new bulb using a reversal of the removal procedure.

Glovebox light

10 Insert a flat-bladed screwdriver behind the end of the lens, depress the retaining clip and prise free the light lens/unit **(see illustration)**. Pull the capless bulb from its holder.
11 Fit the new bulb using a reversal of the removal procedure.

Sunvisor/vanity mirror light

12 Insert a screwdriver into the slot in the lens, and prise free the lens from the headlining above the sunvisor. Detach the cover and the festoon bulb can be extracted from its holder.
13 Fit the new bulb using a reversal of the removal procedure.

Instrument panel bulbs

14 On all models covered by this Manual, it is not possible to renew the instrument panel bulbs individually as they are of LED design and soldered to a printed circuit board. Where an LED is not functioning, the complete instrument panel must be renewed.

Luggage compartment light

Saloon models

15 Insert a flat-bladed screwdriver behind the end of the lens, depress the retaining clip and prise free the light lens/unit **(see illustration)**.
16 Prise the reflector from place and

extract the capless bulb from its holder **(see illustration)**.
17 Fit the new bulb using a reversal of the removal procedure.

Avant models

18 To remove the tailgate mounted bulb, insert a screwdriver into the recess and carefully prise out the light unit **(see illustration)**.
19 Disconnect the wiring connector and remove the light unit.
20 Release the tab and lift off the cover **(see illustration)**.
21 Extract the push-fit bulb from the holder.
22 Fit the new bulb using a reversal of the removal procedure.
23 To remove the remainder of the luggage compartment bulbs, proceed as described previously for Saloon models.

Switch illumination

24 Switch illumination bulbs are usually built into the switch itself, and cannot be renewed separately. Refer to Section 5 and remove the switch – bulb renewal should then be self-evident, if it is possible; otherwise, renew the switch.

Heater/air conditioning control panel illumination

25 The control panel is illuminated by non-renewable LEDs. If defective, the control panel may need to be renewed.

Door handle illumination

26 Remove the door trim panel as described in Chapter 11, Section 13.
27 Pull the bulb from the holder.
28 Refitting is a reversal of removal.

Door courtesy light

29 Use a screwdriver to depress the retaining clip at the end of the lens, and prise the unit from the door.
30 Disconnect the wiring and remove the courtesy light unit.
31 Prise off the cover (where fitted) and pull the bulb from the contacts.
32 Fit the new bulb using a reversal of the removal procedure.

8 **Exterior light units** – removal, refitting and beam adjustment

Headlight unit

Caution: On models equipped with gas discharge headlights, disconnect the battery negative lead as described in Chapter 5, Section 3 prior to working on the headlights.
1 Extract the four plastic rivets, lift the lock carrier cover up at the rear, disengage it from the radiator grille at the front and remove it from the lock carrier **(see illustration)**.

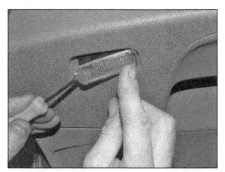

7.18 Carefully prise out the light unit

7.20 Release the tab and lift off the cover

8.1 Extract the plastic rivets and remove the lock carrier cover

8.2 Disconnect the headlight wiring connector

8.3 Remove the bolt at the top of the headlight

8.4 Withdraw the headlight from its mountings

2 Disconnect the headlight wiring connector **(see illustration)**.
3 Remove the bolt at the top of the headlight, and the two bolts at the rear of the headlight **(see illustration)**.
4 Slide the headlight unit forwards until the headlight guides have been guided out of mountings on mounting support. Swivel the headlight towards the wing and detach it from the mounting support **(see illustration)**.
5 Refitting is a reversal of the removal procedure. On completion check for satisfactory operation, and have the headlight beam adjustment checked as soon as possible.

Front foglight

6 The procedure is as described for bulb renewal in Section 6.

Tailgate/boot lid-mounted lights

7 Remove the bulbholder from the light unit as described in Section 6.
8 Undo the nut and remove the retainer **(see illustration)**.
9 Swivel the light unit outwards and remove it from the tailgate/boot lid **(see illustration)**.
10 Refitting is a reversal of removal, but tighten the mounting bolt securely, and ensure that the seal is correctly positioned.

Body-mounted rear lights

11 The procedure is as described for bulb renewal in Section 6.

Number plate light

12 The procedure is as described for bulb renewal in Section 6.

High-level stop-light

13 The procedure is as described for bulb renewal in Section 6.

Beam adjustment

Note: *On models with automatic (self-levelling) headlights, adjustment is only possible using dedicated Audi diagnostic equipment VAS 5051B. Entrust this task to an Audi dealer or suitably-equipped specialist.*
14 Accurate adjustment of the headlight beam is only possible using optical beam setting equipment, and this work should therefore be carried out by an Audi dealer or suitably-equipped workshop. Tyre pressures must correct, the car must be loaded with the driver (or equivalent of 75 kg), and the fuel tank should be at least 90% full. If the fuel tank is only half-full, an additional weight of 30 kg must be positioned in the luggage compartment.
15 Some models are equipped with an electrically-operated headlight beam adjustment system which is controlled through the switch in the facia. On these models, ensure that the switch is set to the basic O position before adjusting the headlight aim.

9 Instrument panel – removal and refitting

Note: *The instrument panel includes the immobiliser control module and its function is included in the vehicle's self-diagnosis program. If the instrument panel has a fault, it would be prudent to have the vehicle's fault code memory interrogated by an Audi dealer or specialist, prior to removing the panel.*
Note: *If the instrument panel is being substituted with a new or exchange module, the assistance of an Audi dealer or specialist is required to initialise/adapt the various instrument panel functions.*

Removal

1 Using the procedure described in Chapter 3, Section 9 remove the air vent on the driver's side.
2 Using a plastic spatula or similar tool carefully prise off the cover for the MMI screen **(see illustrations 5.29a and 5.29b)**. Disconnect the hazard warning light switch wiring connector and remove the cover.
3 Fully extend the steering column, and move it to its lowest position.
4 Using a plastic wedge or similar tool, carefully prise free the trim panel below the instrument panel and fold it back over the steering column shroud **(see illustration)**.

8.8 Undo the nut and remove the retainer

8.9 Swivel the light unit outwards

9.4 Prise free the trim panel below the instrument panel

9.5a Undo the instrument panel upper right-hand retaining bolt...

9.5b ...upper left-hand retaining bolt...

9.5c ...and lower centre retaining bolt

5 Undo the three bolts securing the instrument panel to the facia **(see illustrations)**.
6 Withdraw the instrument panel from the facia. As the panel is withdrawn, release the locking catches and disconnect the wiring plugs.

Refitting

7 Refitting is a reversal of removal, but see the notes at the beginning of this Section.

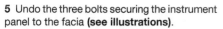

10 Windscreen wiper components – removal and refitting

Wiper blades

1 Refer to *Weekly checks*.

Wiper arms

2 If the wipers are not in their parked position, switch on the ignition, and allow the motor to automatically park.
3 Before removing an arm, mark its parked position on the glass with a strip of adhesive tape. Prise off the cover and unscrew the spindle nut **(see illustrations)**. Note that on Avant models with a tailgate wiper, prise apart the two cover sides slightly and pull the cover from place. Pull out the washer jet and undo the spindle nut **(see illustrations)**. Remove the washer and ease the arm from the spindle by rocking it slowly from side-to-side.
4 Refitting is a reversal of removal, but before tightening the spindle nuts, position the wiper blades as marked before removal.

Wiper motor and linkage

5 Remove the wiper arms as described in the previous sub-Section.
6 Remove the plenum chamber cover front section as described in Chapter 11, Section 21.
Note: *The following procedure describes removal of the wiper motor and linkage leaving the plenum chamber cover rear section in position. If difficulty is experienced manipulating the wiper motor and linkage from their location, remove the plenum chamber cover rear section as described in Chapter 11, Section 21.*
7 Pull the water drain channel off the linkage **(see illustration)**.
8 Undo the three linkage retaining bolts **(see illustrations)**.

10.3a Prise off the plastic cover...

10.3b ...and undo the spindle nut

10.3c Pull the two sides apart, and remove the cover

10.3d Prise the washer jet hose from the wiper spindle

10.7 Pull the water drain channel off the linkage

10.8a Undo the wiper linkage right-hand retaining bolt...

10.8b ...centre retaining bolt...

10.8c ...and left-hand retaining bolt

10.9 Disconnect the motor wiring connector

10.10a Lift the plenum chamber cover...

10.10b ...and manipulate out the motor and linkage

9 Disconnect the motor wiring connector **(see illustration)**.
10 Lift up the plenum chamber cover as much as possible and manipulate the motor and linkage out from the plenum chamber **(see illustrations)**.
11 Refitting is a reversal of removal.

11 Washer system – general

1 All models are fitted with a windscreen washer system. Avant models also have a tailgate washer, and some models are fitted with headlight washers.

2 The fluid reservoir for the windscreen/headlight washer is located under the wheel arch on the left-hand side. The windscreen washer fluid pump is attached to the side of the reservoir body, as is the level sensor **(see illustrations)** and where headlight washers are fitted, a lift cylinder/accumulator is located in the supply tube, behind the front bumper. Access to the reservoir, pump and lift cylinder is achieved by removing the roadwheel and the wheel arch liner.
3 The tailgate washer is fed by the same reservoir and pump, operating in the reverse direction.
4 The reservoir fluid level must be regularly topped-up with windscreen washer fluid

containing an antifreeze agent, but not cooling system antifreeze – see *Weekly checks*.
5 The supply hoses are attached by rubber couplings to their various connections, and if required, can be detached by simply pulling them free from the appropriate connector.
6 The windscreen washer jets can be adjusted by inserting a pin into the jet and altering the aim as required. To remove a washer jet, open the bonnet, and pull down the rear edge of the plastic cover under the jet.
7 Pull off the hose, disconnect the wiring plug, and remove the jet.
8 The headlight washer jets are best adjusted using the Audi tool, and should therefore be entrusted to an Audi garage to set.

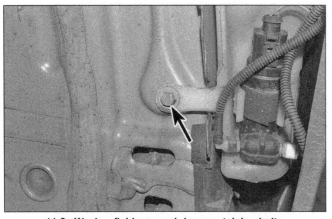

11.2a Washer fluid reservoir lower retaining bolt...

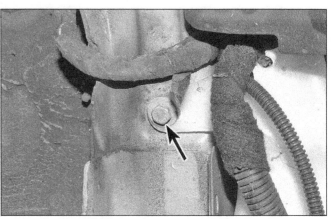

11.2b ...and upper retaining bolt

12.3a Detach the washer hose...

12.3b...then disconnect the wiring connector

12.4 Tailgate wiper motor retaining nuts

12 Tailgate wiper motor – removal and refitting

Removal

1 Make sure the tailgate wiper is switched off and in its rest position, then remove the tailgate trim panel as described in Chapter 11, Section 11.

2 Remove the wiper arm and blade as described in Section 10.

3 Detach the washer jet hose, then disconnect the wiring connector from the wiper motor **(see illustrations)**.

4 Undo the three wiper motor mounting nuts and remove the wiper motor from the tailgate **(see illustration)**. Check the condition of the spindle rubber grommet in the tailgate, and if necessary, renew it.

Refitting

5 Refit in the reverse order of removal. Refit the wiper arm and blade so that the arm is parked correctly.

13 Horns – removal and refitting

Removal

1 The horns are located at the front end of the

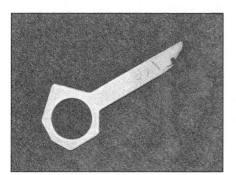

14.1 Audi unit removal tool

vehicle, behind the front bumper. Remove the bumper as described in Chapter 11, Section 8.

2 Disconnect the horn wiring plug, undo the mounting nut and remove the horn from the vehicle.

Refitting

3 Refit in the reverse order of removal. Check for satisfactory operation on completion.

14 Radio/CD player/ autochanger – removal and refitting

Note: *This Section applies only to standard-fit audio equipment.*

Removal

Radio/CD player

Note: *Numerous radio/CD player combinations may be fitted, according to model year and trim level. The following information applies to the more commonly encountered versions.*

1 The radio/CD player is fitted with special mounting clips, requiring the use of special removal tools (Audi T10057), which should be supplied with the vehicle, or may be obtained from an in-car entertainment specialist. Alternatively, it may be possible to make up some removal tools **(see illustration)**.

2 Insert the removal rods in the holes

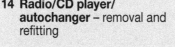

14.4 Fully insert the tools and pull the unit from the facia

provided on the lower, or upper and lower edges of the radio/CD player unit (depending on model).

3 Slide the removal tools fully into the slots until they locate.

4 Withdraw the radio/CD player from the facia **(see illustration)**, then disconnect the wiring plugs as the unit is withdrawn. Note that some radio units also have a fuse fitted on the rear face.

Autochanger

5 Open the passenger's glovebox, and insert the special Audi tools into the slots in the front face of the autochanger.

6 Pull the autochanger from position, then disconnect the wiring plugs.

Refitting

Radio/CD player

7 Refitting is a reversal of removal, but push the radio fully into its case until the spring clips are engaged. If the radio is of the security code type, it will be necessary to enter the code number before using the radio.

Autochanger

8 Reconnect the wiring plugs, and push the unit fully into position, until the retaining clips engage.

15 Speakers – removal and refitting

1 The audio system speakers are fitted in the front and rear doors, the facia panel, under the rear parcel shelf (Saloon models), and behind the luggage compartment side trim panel (Avant models). Separate mid-range and high frequency units are fitted in the front and rear door trim panels.

Door speakers

Low frequency speaker

2 To remove a door-mounted speaker, remove the appropriate door trim panel as described in Chapter 11, Section 13.

3 Disconnect the speaker wiring plugs, then

15.3 Removing a low frequency door speaker

15.7 Removing the treble speaker from the mounting panel

Warning: Do not allow any solvents or cleaning agents to contact the airbag assemblies. They must be cleaned using only a damp cloth.

Warning: The airbags and control unit are both sensitive to impact. If either is dropped or damaged they should be renewed.

Warning: Disconnect the airbag control unit wiring plug prior to using arc-welding equipment on the vehicle.

undo the retaining bolts and remove the speaker **(see illustration)**.
4 Refit in the reverse order of removal.

Front door high frequency (treble) speaker

5 Gain access to the speaker as described in Chapter 11, Section 13.
6 Starting at the front edge, carefully prise the speaker trim panel from the door trim.
7 Disconnect the wiring plug to the speaker, then release the retaining clips and detach the speaker from the mounting panel **(see illustration)**.
8 Refit in the reverse order of removal.

Rear door high frequency speaker

9 Remove the door trim panel as described in Chapter 11, Section 13.
10 Disconnect the wiring plug, then release the retaining lugs and turn the speaker anti-clockwise until it can be removed from the trim panel..
11 Refit in the reverse order of removal.

Facia speaker

12 Carefully prise up the loudspeaker trim from the facia.
13 Prise the sensor from the facia. Disconnect the wiring plug as the sensor is removed, and tape the wires to one side to prevent them disappearing into the facia recess.
14 Undo the two retaining bolts, and manoeuvre the speaker from the facia. Disconnect the speaker wiring plug as it's withdrawn.
15 Refitting is a reversal of removal.

Parcel shelf speaker

16 Remove the parcel shelf.
17 The speaker is secured by two bolts above the parcel shelf bracket, and one below. Undo the bolts, disconnect the wiring plug and remove the speaker.
18 Refitting is a reversal of removal.

Luggage compartment speaker

19 Remove the right-hand side luggage compartment side panel trim.
20 Disconnect the wiring plugs, then undo the four bolts and remove the speaker complete with the resonator box.

21 Undo the four bolts and detach the speaker from the resonator.
22 Refitting is a reversal of removal.

16 Engine compartment electronics box – removal and refitting

Removal

1 Remove the engine management ECU as described in Chapter 4A, Section 3. Note that it is not necessary to completely remove the ECU, just lift it out of the electronics box.
2 Note the locations of the wiring connections inside the electronics box and disconnect them.
3 Release the catches and detach the fuse holder from the electronics box.
4 Disengage the engine wiring harness from the electronics box and move it clear.
5 Undo the four electronics box retaining bolts.
6 Lift the electronics box from its location and disconnect the remaining wiring connectors.
7 Disengage the engine wiring harness from the electronics box, then release the retaining clips and press the engine management ECU retaining frame to one side.
8 Remove the electronics box from the plenum chamber.

Refitting

9 Refitting is the reversal of removal.

17 Airbag system – general information and precautions

1 Before carrying out any operations on the airbag system, disconnect the battery negative lead see (see Chapter 5, Section 3). When operations are complete, make sure no one is inside the vehicle when the battery is reconnected.

Warning: Note that the airbag(s) must not be subjected to temperatures in excess of 90°C. When the airbag is removed, ensure that it is stored with its padded surface uppermost to prevent possible inflation.

2 Both a driver's and passenger's airbag are fitted as standard equipment to models in the Audi A4 range. The driver's airbag is fitted to the centre of the steering wheel. The passenger's airbag is fitted to the upper surface of the facia, above the glovebox. The airbag system comprises the airbag unit(s) (complete with gas generators), an impact sensor, the control unit and a warning light in the instrument panel. Seat-mounted side airbags and overhead curtain airbags are also fitted on certain models, and seat belt tensioners are incorporated in the front seat belt reels.
3 The airbag system is triggered in the event of a direct or offset frontal impact above a predetermined force. The airbag is inflated within milliseconds, and forms a safety cushion between the driver and the steering wheel or (where applicable) the passenger and the facia. This prevents contact between the upper body and the steering wheel, column and facia, and therefore greatly reduces the risk of injury. The airbag then deflates almost immediately through vents in the side of the airbag.
4 Every time the ignition is switched on, the airbag control module performs a self-test. The self-test takes approximately 3 seconds, and during this time the airbag warning light on the facia is illuminated. After the self-test has been completed, the warning light should go out. If the warning light fails to come on, remains illuminated after the initial 3-second period, or comes on at any time when the vehicle is being driven, there is a fault in the airbag system. The vehicle should then be taken to an Audi dealer or specialist for examination at the earliest possible opportunity.

18 Airbag system components – removal and refitting

1 Refer to the warnings in Section 17 before carrying out the following operations.
2 Disconnect the battery negative terminal (see Disconnecting the battery in Chapter 5, Section 3.

Driver's airbag

Bolted on version – removal

3 Set the steering wheel to straight-ahead,

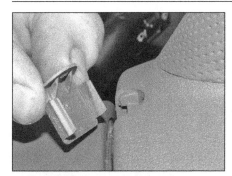

18.4a Prise out the plastic caps on the reverse side of the steering wheel...

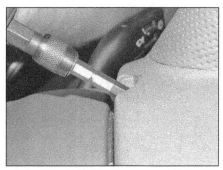

18.4b...and use a Torx bit to slacken the airbag retaining bolts

18.5a Lift the airbag from position...

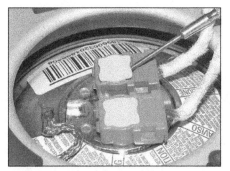

18.5b...prise up the yellow locking catches and disconnect the wiring plugs from the airbag...

18.5c...then disconnect the horn contact wiring plug from the right-hand side...

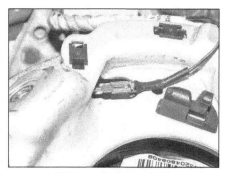

18.5d...and left-hand side

then turn it 90° to the left or right. Release the steering column adjustment lever, and pull the wheel out and down as far as possible.

4 Locate the access hole in the reverse side of the steering wheel (on some models, the hole is covered by a plastic cap), and slacken the Torx bolt securing the airbag to the steering wheel **(see illustrations)**. Turn the airbag 180° and slacken the second Torx bolt on the opposite side.

5 Temporarily touch the striker plate of the front door to discharge any electrostatic electricity. Return the steering wheel to the straight-ahead position, then carefully lift the airbag assembly away from the steering wheel and disconnect the wiring connector from the rear of the unit along with the horn button wiring plug **(see illustrations)**. Note that the airbag must not be knocked or dropped, and should be stored with its padded surface uppermost.

Pushed-on version – removal

6 The procedure is essentially the same as for the bolted-on version, but instead of retaining bolts, there are retaining clips. These are released by inserting a screwdriver into the holes in the rear of the steering wheel and releasing the clips.

All versions – refitting

7 On refitting, reconnect the wiring connectors and locate the airbag unit in the steering wheel, making sure the wire

does not become trapped, and tighten the retaining bolts (where applicable) securely. Switch on the ignition, then reconnect the battery negative lead (see Chapter 5, Section 3). Ensure no-one is in the vehicle when the battery is reconnected.

Passenger airbag

8 Remove the passenger's glovebox as described in Chapter 11, Section 23.
9 Slide back the locking catch, then disconnect the airbag wiring plug.
10 Undo the four airbag retaining nuts **(see illustration)**.
11 Lower the airbag from position. Note that the airbag must not be knocked or dropped, and should be stored with its hinged surface uppermost.
12 Refitting is a reversal of removal. Note that if the airbag unit has been triggered, the bolts should be renewed. Ensure that the wiring connector is securely reconnected. Ensure that no-one is inside the vehicle. Switch on the ignition, then reconnect the battery negative lead.

Airbag wiring contact unit

13 The airbag contact unit is part of the steering column combination switch. Refer to Section 4 for removal and refitting details.

All other airbag units and sensors

14 Further removal and refitting of the remaining airbag components should be

entrusted to an Audi dealer. Either extensive dismantling, or the use of specialist diagnostic equipment is required to calibrate and initiate all renewed components and this work is considered to be beyond the scope of this manual.

19 Anti-theft alarm system – general information

1 An anti-theft alarm and immobiliser system is fitted as standard equipment. Should the system become faulty, the vehicle should be taken to as Audi dealer or specialist for examination. They will have access to a special diagnostic tester which will quickly trace any fault present in the system.

18.10 Passenger's airbag location

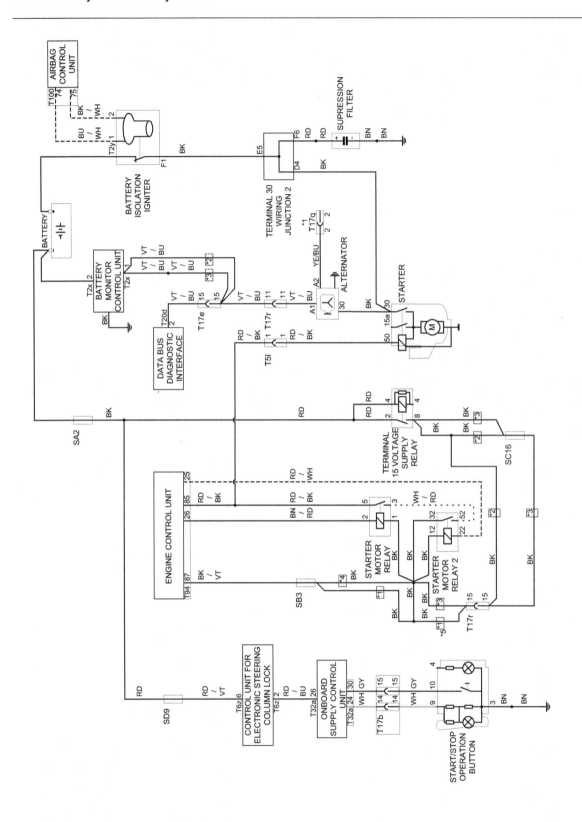

Starting and charging up to November 2011

*1 Gradually discontinued
*2 Up to April 2009
*3 From May 2009
*4 Gradual introduction
*5 Start/Stop

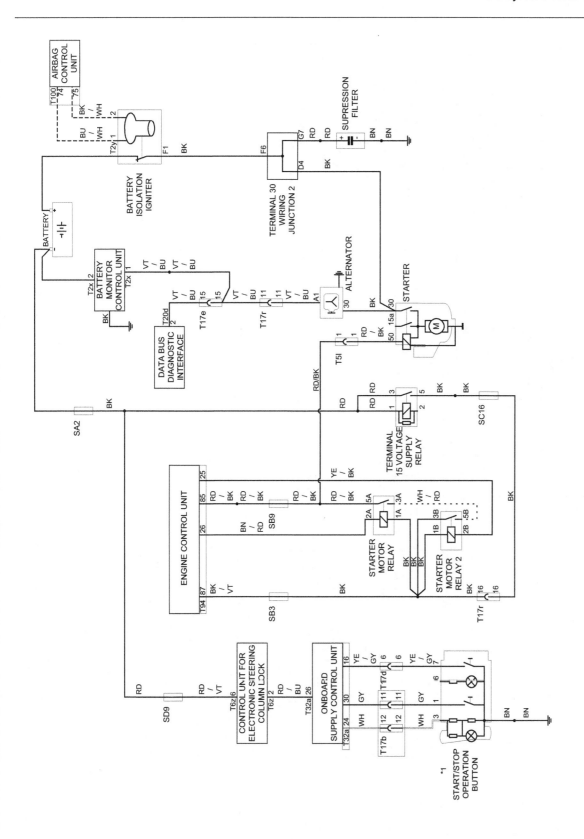

Starting and charging from November 2011

*1 Start/Stop

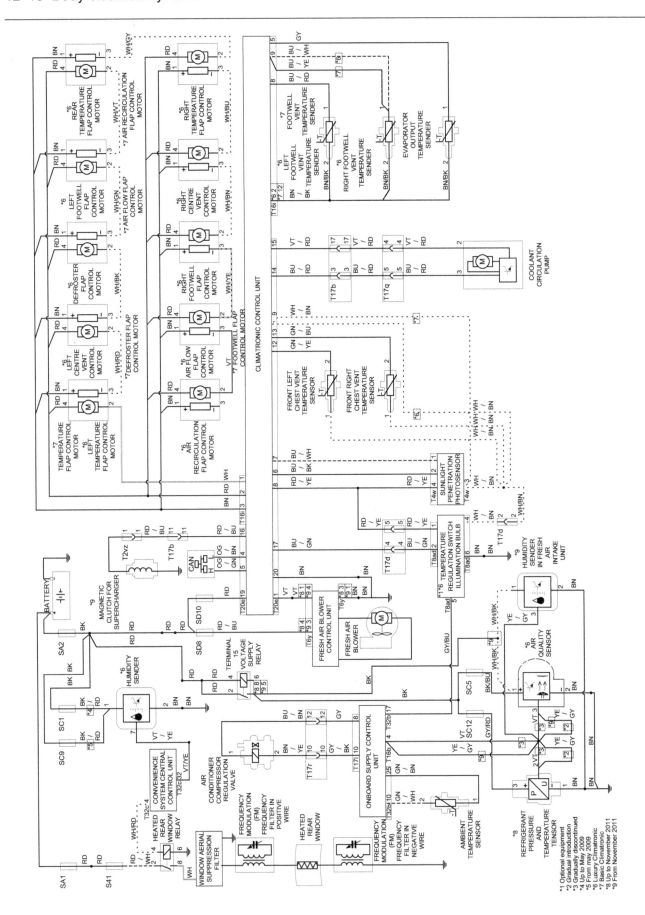

Air conditioning, heating and cooling – Basic and luxury Climatronic

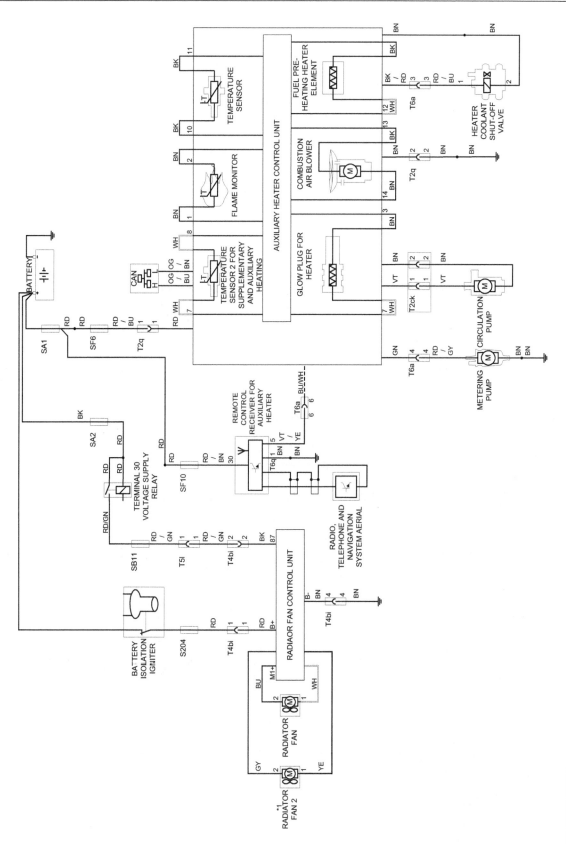

Air conditioning, heating and cooling - Circulation pump

*1 Used on 600W radiator fan

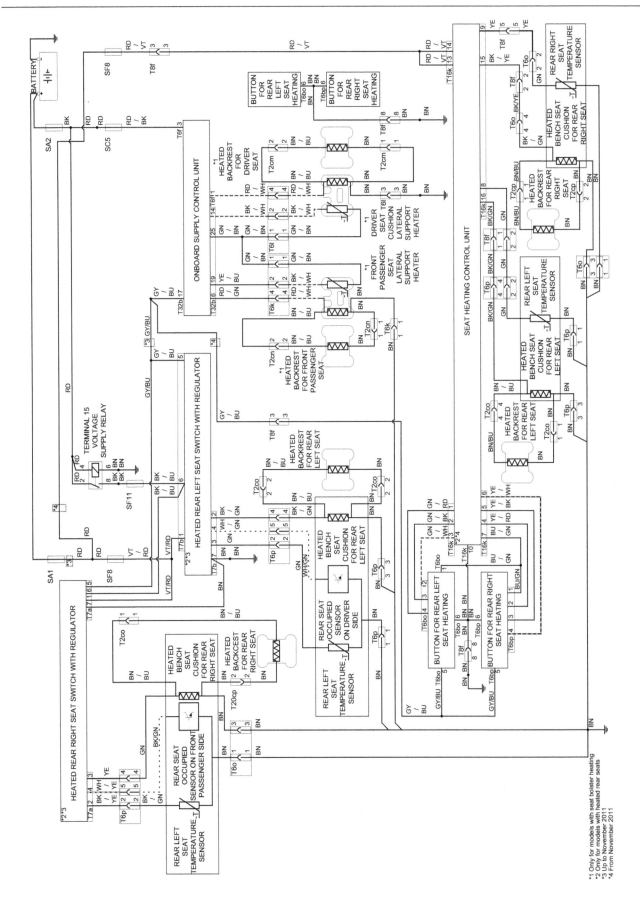

Air conditioning, heating and cooling - Seat heating

*1 Only for models with seat bolster heating
*2 Only for models with heated rear seats
*3 Up to November 2011
*4 From November 2011

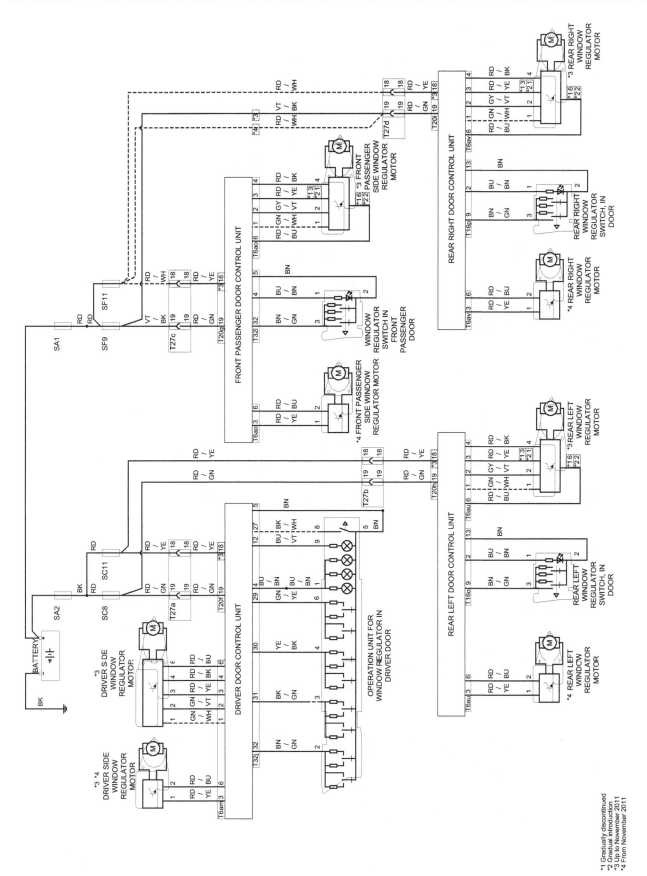

Power windows

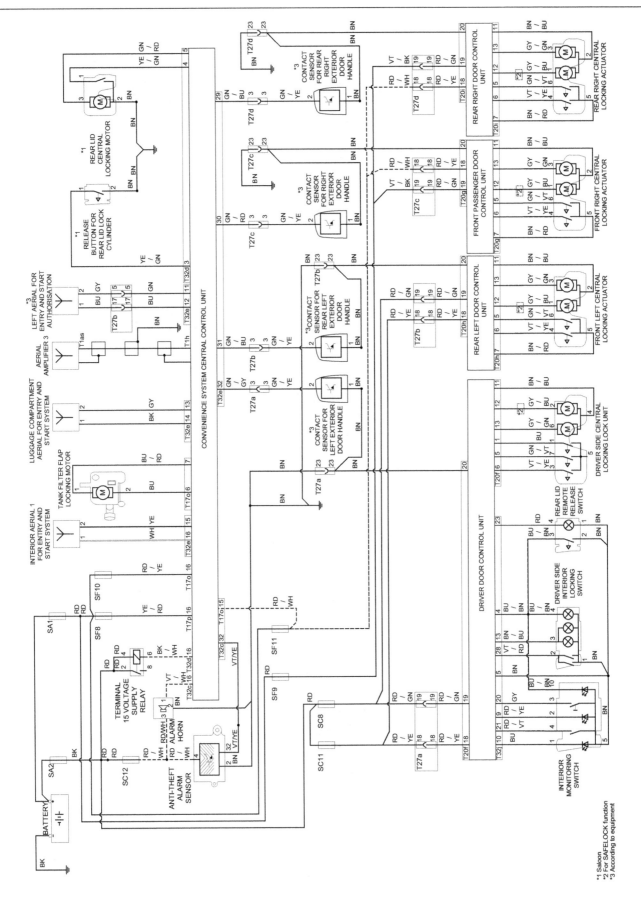

Power door locks

*1 Saloon
*2 For SAFELOCK function
*3 According to equipment

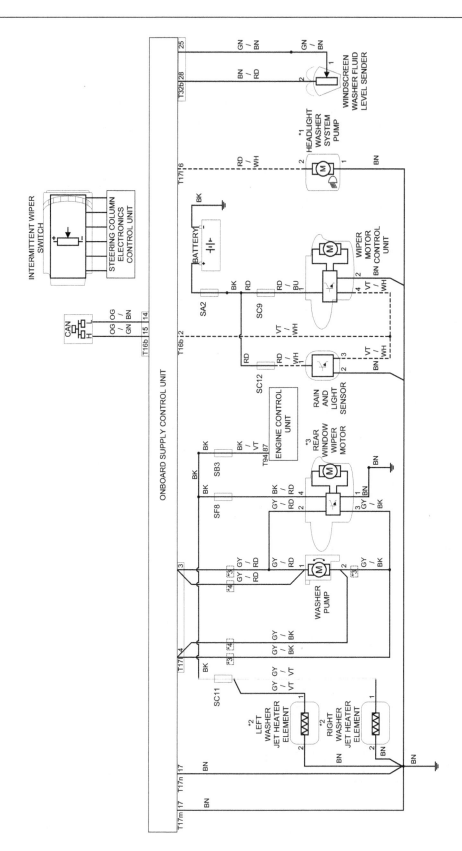

Wipers, washers

*1 Only models with headlight washer system
*2 Only models with heater elements for washer jets
*3 Avant
*4 Saloon

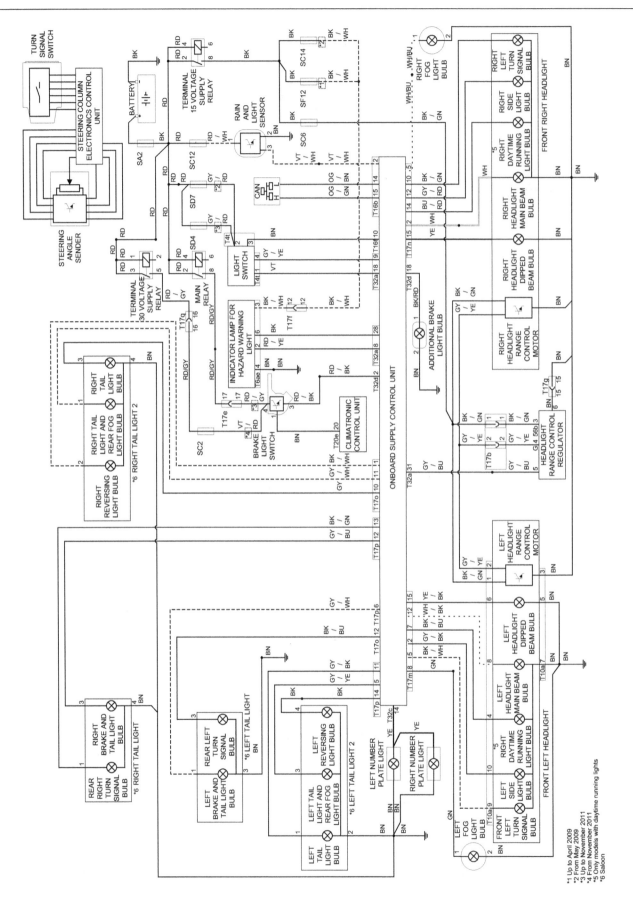

Exterior lights

Bi-Xenon lights up to November 2011

*1 According to equipment
*2 Only for models with daytime running lights
*3 Special equipment

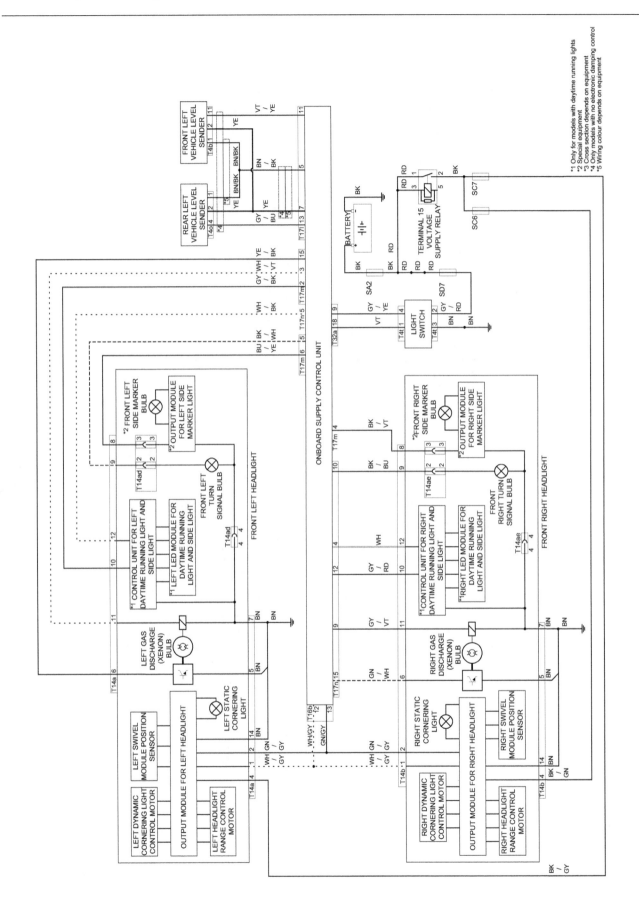

Bi-Xenon lights from November 2011

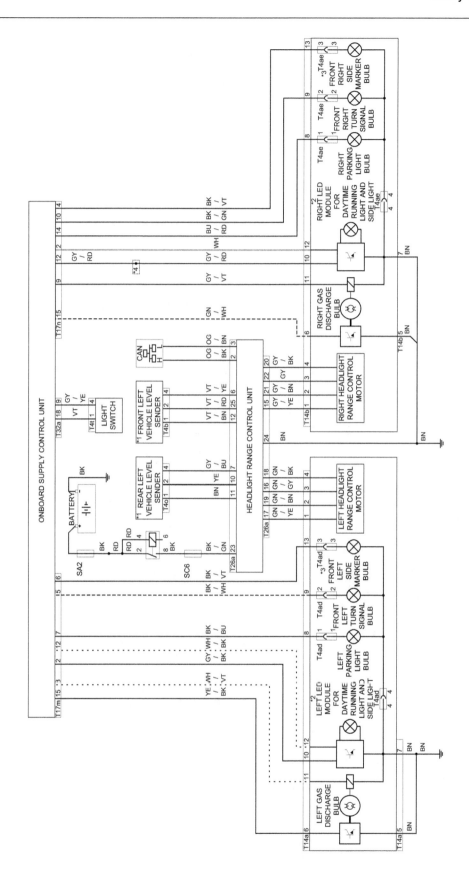

Xenon lights up to November 2011

*1 According to equipment
*2 Only for models with daytime running lights
*3 Special equipment
*4 Gradual introduction

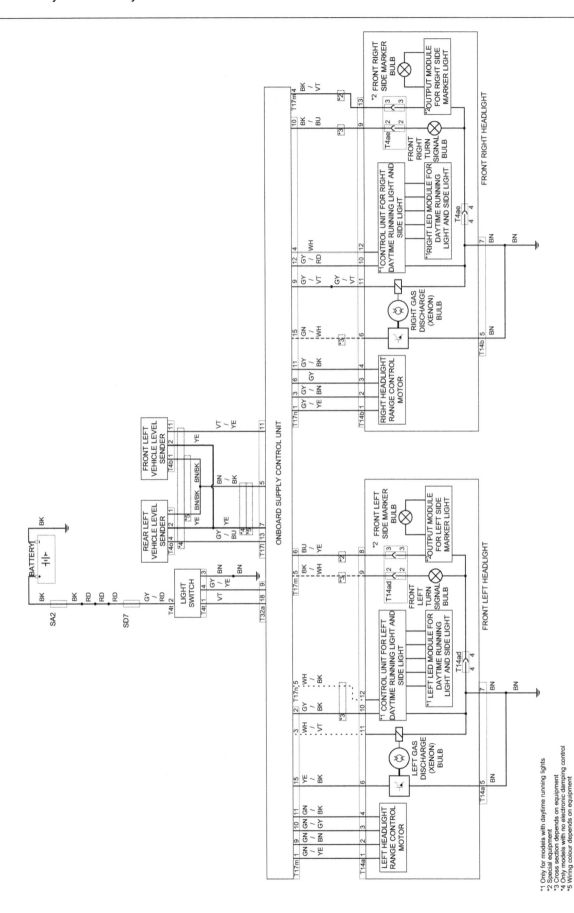

Xenon lights from November 2011

*1 Only for models with daytime running lights
*2 Special equipment
*3 Cross section depends on equipment
*4 Only models with no electronic damping control
*5 Wiring colour depends on equipment

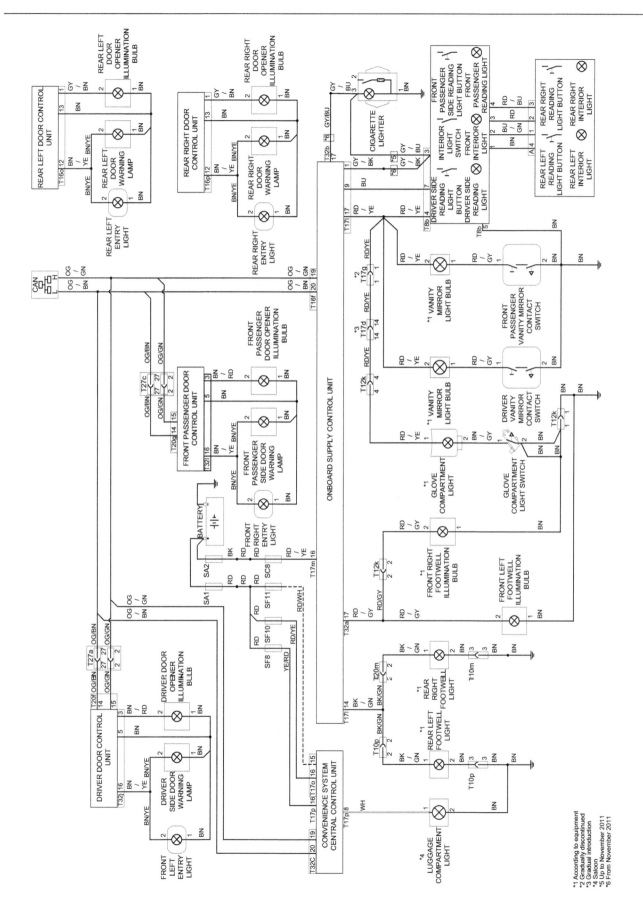

Interior lights

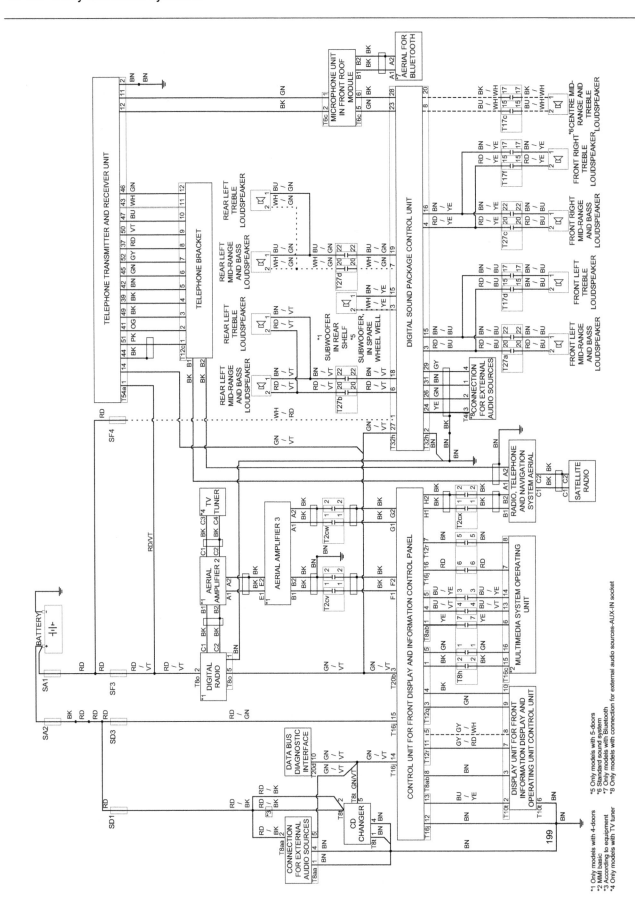

Sound system with MMI basic up to November 2011

*1 Only models with 4-doors
*2 MMI basic
*3 According to equipment
*4 Only models with TV tuner
*5 Only models with 5-doors
*6 Standard sound system
*7 Only models with Bluetooth
*8 Only models with connection for external audio sources-AUX-IN socket

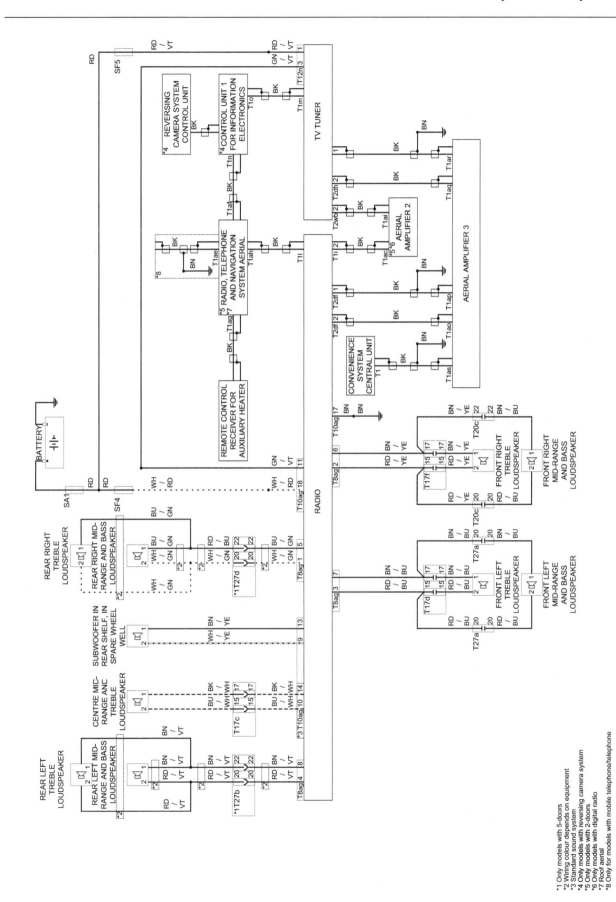

Sound system with MMI from November 2011

*1 Only models with 5-doors
*2 Wiring colour depends on equipment
*3 Standard sound system
*4 Only models with reversing camera system
*5 Only models with 2-doors
*6 Only models with digital radio
*7 Roof aerial
*8 Only for models with mobile telephone/telephone

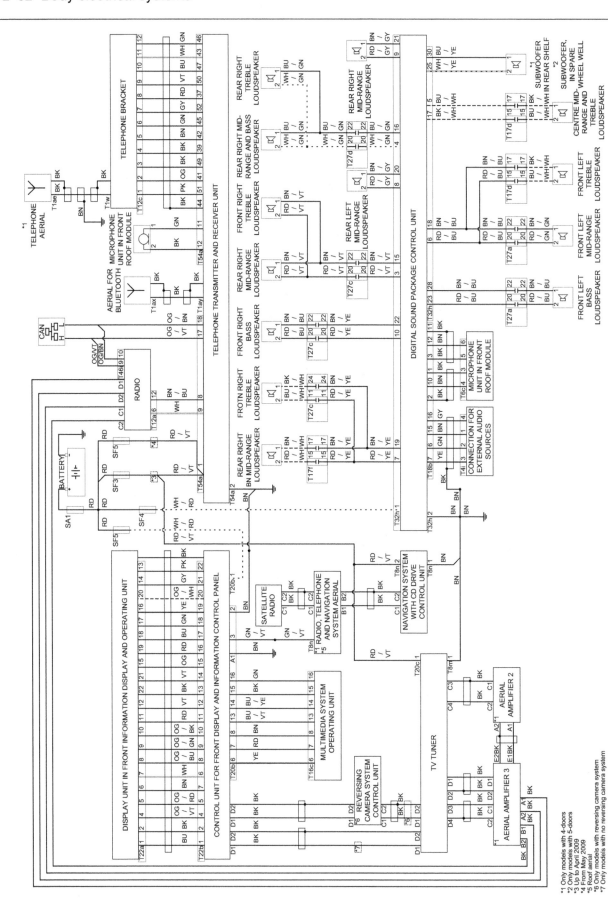

Sound system with MMI Bang & Olufsen up to November 2011

*1 Only models with 4-doors
*2 Only models with 5-doors
*3 Up to April 2009
*4 From May 2009
*5 Roof aerial
*6 Only models with reversing camera system
*7 Only models with no reversing camera system

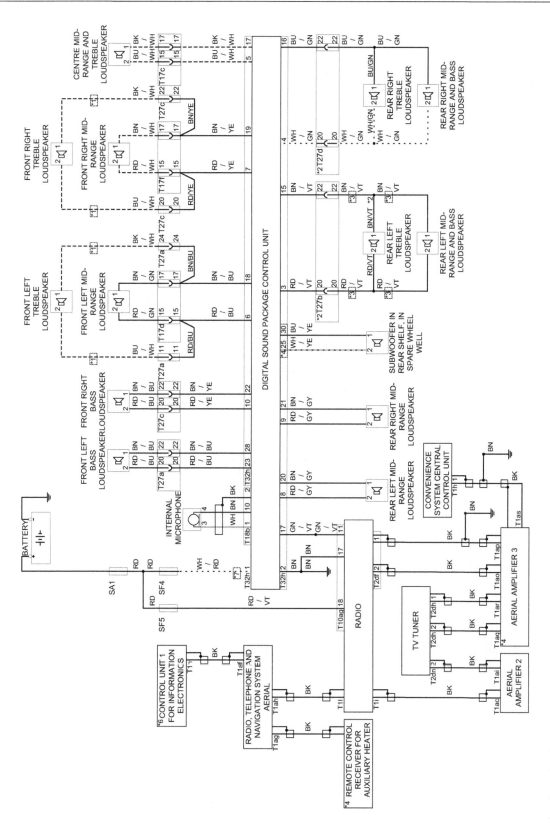

Sound system with MMI Bang & Olufsen from November 2011

*1 Cross section depends on equipment
*2 Only models with 5-doors
*3 Wiring colour depends on equipment
*4 According to equipment
*5 Only for models with TV tuner
*6 Optional equipment

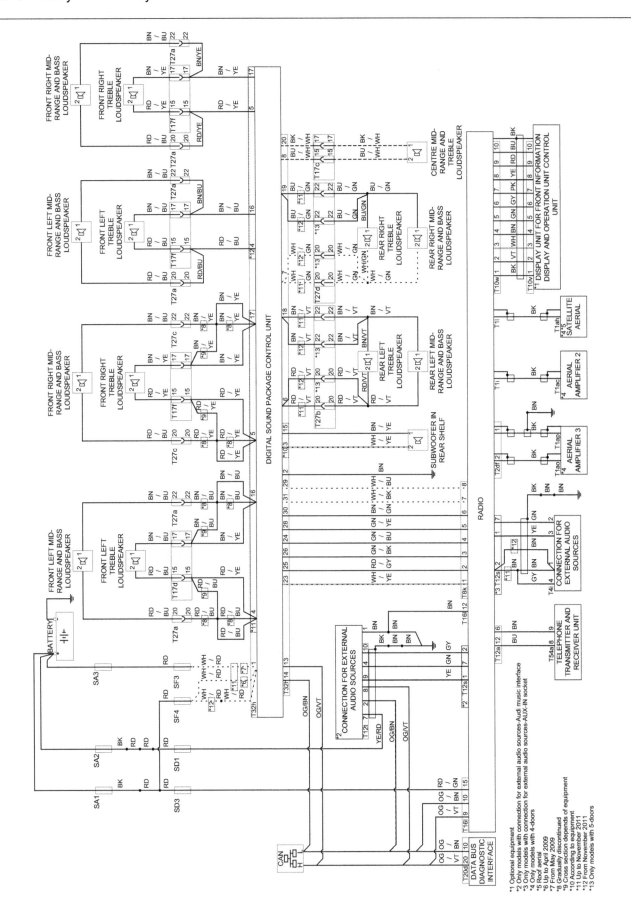

Radio and standard sound system

*1 Optional equipment
*2 Only models with connection for external audio sources-Audi music interface
*3 Only models with connection for external audio sources-AUX-IN socket
*4 Only models with 4-doors
*5 Roof aerial
*6 Up to April 2009
*7 From May 2009
*8 Gradually discontinued
*9 Cross section depends of equipment
*10 According to equipment
*11 Up to November 2011
*12 From November 2011
*13 Only models with 5-doors

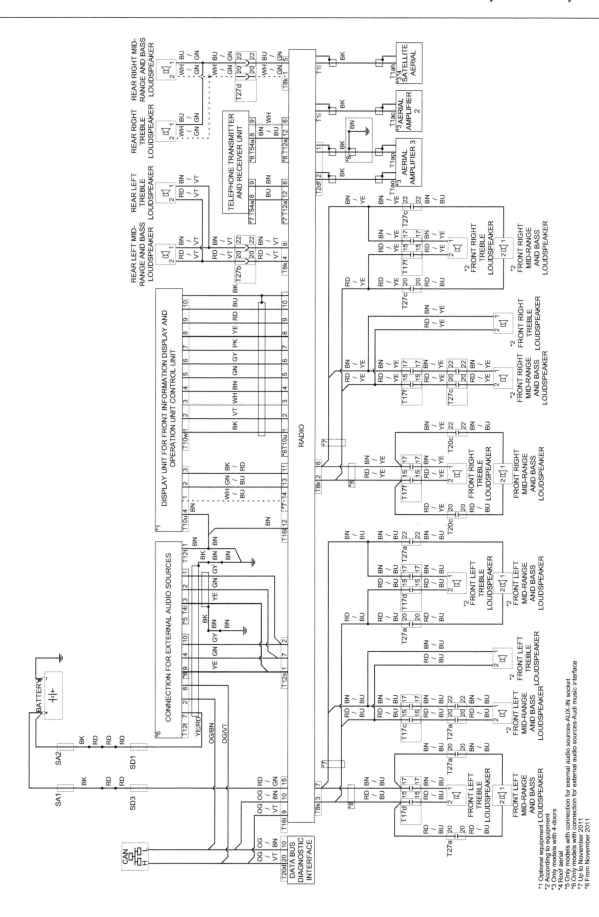

Radio with basic, and basic plus sound system

*1 Optional equipment
*2 According to equipment
*3 Only models with 4-doors
*4 Roof aerial
*5 Only models with connection for external audio sources-AUX-IN socket
*6 Only models with connection for external audio sources-Audi music interface
*7 Up to November 2011
*8 From November 2011

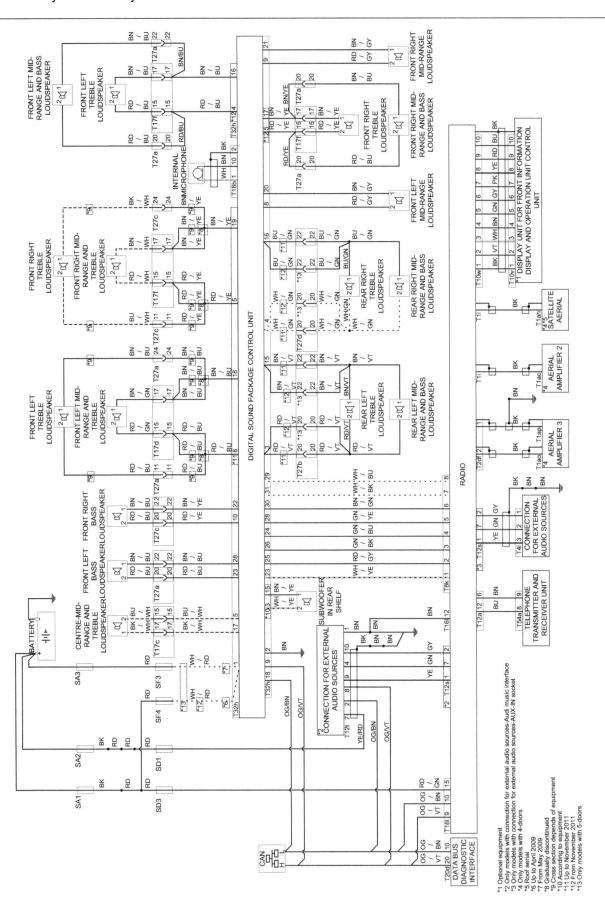

Radio with Bang & Olufsen sound system

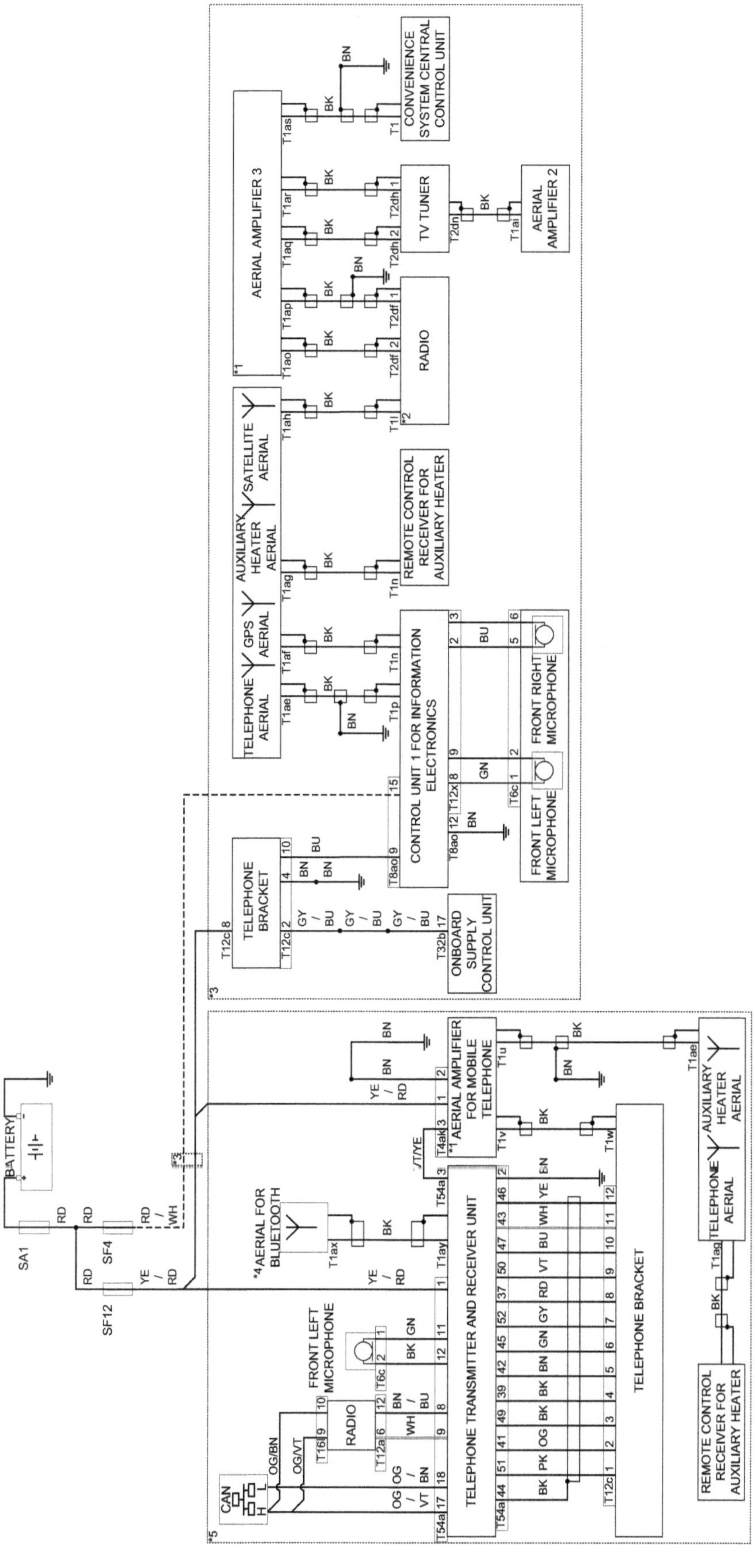

CONVENIENCE SYSTEM CENTRAL CONTROL UNIT

AERIAL AMPLIFIER 3

TV TUNER

AERIAL AMPLIFIER 2

RADIO

SATELLITE AERIAL

AUXILIARY HEATER AERIAL

REMOTE CONTROL RECEIVER FOR AUXILIARY HEATER

TELEPHONE AERIAL

GPS AERIAL

CONTROL UNIT 1 FOR INFORMATION ELECTRONICS

FRONT RIGHT MICROPHONE

FRONT LEFT MICROPHONE

TELEPHONE BRACKET

ONBOARD SUPPLY CONTROL UNIT

BATTERY

SA1

SF4

SF12

*4 AERIAL FOR BLUETOOTH

FRONT LEFT MICROPHONE

RADIO

CAN

TELEPHONE TRANSMITTER AND RECEIVER UNIT

*4 AERIAL AMPLIFIER FOR MOBILE TELEPHONE

TELEPHONE BRACKET

REMOTE CONTROL RECEIVER FOR AUXILIARY HEATER

TELEPHONE AERIAL

AUXILIARY HEATER AERIAL

*1 According to equipment
*2 Only models with radio
*3 Bluetooth car phone (MOST bus)
*4 Only models with Bluetooth
*5 Preparation for mobile telephone

Sound system with Bluetooth from November 2011

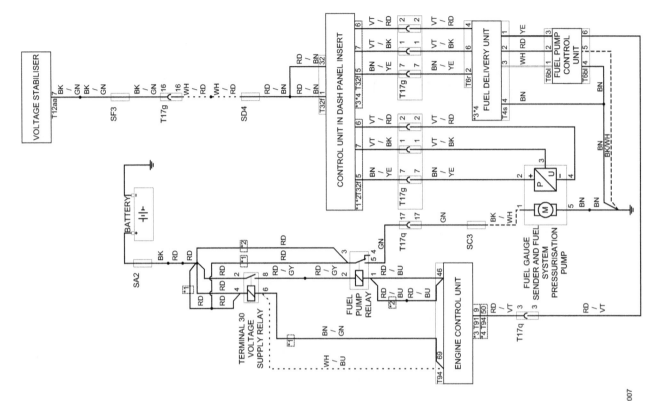

Fuel pump

*1 For engine codes CAFA, CAGA, CAGB, CAGC, CAHA, CAHB, CMEA from November 2007
*2 For engine codes CAGA, CAGC, CAGB, CAGC, CAHA, CAHB, CMEA, CJCB from May 2009
*3 From November 2011
*4 For engine codes CGLC, CGLD, CJCA, CJCB, CJCC, CJCD, CMFA

Fuse and relay box in engine compartment

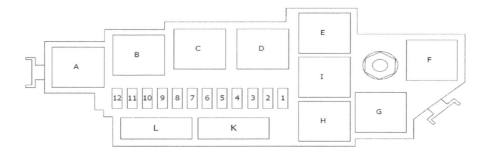

FUSE/RELAY	VALUE	DESCRIPTION
1	15 A	Automatic transmission control unit Mechatronic unit for the dual-clutch gearbox
2	5 A	Oil level and temperature sensor
3	5 A	Engine control unit Mass airflow meter
4	5 A	Engine control unit
5	5 A	Mass airflow meter Glow plug control unit Secondary air pump relay Throttle control motor with position sensor Inlet manifold valve control motor Low-output heating relay High-output heating relay Turbo pressure control solenoid Crankcase heater Canister
6	15 A	Engine control unit
7	10 A	Valve lift solenoid Continued coolant circulation relay Relay, additional coolant pump Turbo pressure control solenoid Canister purge solenoid Left electro-hydraulic engine mounting solenoid Right electro-hydraulic engine mounting solenoid Camshaft timing
8	5 A	Exhaust gas recirculation coolant pump Ignition coils 1 - 6 (5A also used) (10A also used)
9	5 A	Relay, additional fuel pump Oxygen sensor behind the catalytic converter Oxygen sensor 2 behind the catalytic converter (5A also used) (15A also used)
10	10 A	Primary heated oxygen sensor Secondary heated oxygen sensor Oxygen sensor behind the catalytic converter (10A also used)
11	5 A	Cooling fan control unit Cooling fan control unit 2
12	5 A	Mass airflow meter Automatic transmission control unit Mechatronic unit for the dual-clutch gearbox
A	NULL	Glow plug control unit Or Power supply relay
B	NULL	
C	NULL	Secondary air pump relay or not used
D	NULL	Terminal 30 voltage supply relay Or Motronic power supply relay
E	NULL	Fuel pump relay Relay , additional fuel pump Gearbox cooling relay Or Continued coolant circulation relay Relay, additional coolant pump Power supply relay 2 Brake servo relay
F	NULL	Secondary air pump relay 2 or not used
G	NULL	No information is available
H	NULL	No information is available
I	NULL	No information is available

Fuses and relays

Notes

Reference REF•1

Dimensions and weights

Note: *All figures are approximate, and may vary according to model. Refer to manufacturer's data for exact figures.*

Dimensions
Overall length	4703 mm
Overall width (including mirrors)	2006 mm
Overall height (unladen, including roof rails)	1427 mm
Turning circle	11.1 m

Weights
Kerb weight	1540 kg to 1635 kg
Maximum towing weight:	
Trailer without brakes	750 kg
Trailer with brakes	1800 kg
Maximum roof rack load	100 kg

Fuel economy

Although depreciation is still the biggest part of the cost of motoring for most car owners, the cost of fuel is more immediately noticeable. These pages give some tips on how to get the best fuel economy.

Working it out

Manufacturer's figures

Car manufacturers are required by law to provide fuel consumption information on all new vehicles sold. These 'official' figures are obtained by simulating various driving conditions on a rolling road or a test track. Real life conditions are different, so the fuel consumption actually achieved may not bear much resemblance to the quoted figures.

How to calculate it

Many cars now have trip computers which will

display fuel consumption, both instantaneous and average. Refer to the owner's handbook for details of how to use these.

To calculate consumption yourself (and maybe to check that the trip computer is accurate), proceed as follows.

1. Fill up with fuel and note the mileage, or zero the trip recorder.
2. Drive as usual until you need to fill up again.
3. Note the amount of fuel required to refill the tank, and the mileage covered since the previous fill-up.
4. Divide the mileage by the amount of fuel used to obtain the consumption figure.

For example:

Mileage at first fill-up (a) = 27,903
Mileage at second fill-up (b) = 28,346
Mileage covered (b - a) = 443
Fuel required at second fill-up = 48.6 litres

The half-completed changeover to metric units in the UK means that we buy our fuel

in litres, measure distances in miles and talk about fuel consumption in miles per gallon. There are two ways round this: the first is to convert the litres to gallons before doing the calculation (by dividing by 4.546, or see Table 1). So in the example:

48.6 litres ÷ 4.546 = 10.69 gallons
443 miles ÷ 10.69 gallons = 41.4 mpg

The second way is to calculate the consumption in miles per litre, then multiply that figure by 4.546 (or see Table 2).

So in the example, fuel consumption is:

443 miles ÷ 48.6 litres = 9.1 mpl
9.1 mpl x 4.546 = 41.4 mpg

The rest of Europe expresses fuel consumption in litres of fuel required to travel 100 km (l/100 km). For interest, the conversions are given in Table 3. In practice it doesn't matter what units you use, provided you know what your normal consumption is and can spot if it's getting better or worse.

Table 1: conversion of litres to Imperial gallons

litres	1	2	3	4	5	10	20	30	40	50	60	70
gallons	0.22	0.44	0.66	0.88	1.10	2.24	4.49	6.73	8.98	11.22	13.47	15.71

Table 2: conversion of miles per litre to miles per gallon

miles per litre	5	6	7	8	9	10	11	12	13	14
miles per gallon	23	27	32	36	41	46	50	55	59	64

Table 3: conversion of litres per 100 km to miles per gallon

litres per 100 km	4	4.5	5	5.5	6	6.5	7	8	9	10
miles per gallon	71	63	56	51	47	43	40	35	31	28

Maintenance

A well-maintained car uses less fuel and creates less pollution. In particular:

Filters

Change air and fuel filters at the specified intervals.

Oil

Use a good quality oil of the lowest viscosity specified by the vehicle manufacturer (see *Lubricants and fluids*). Check the level often and be careful not to overfill.

Spark plugs

When applicable, renew at the specified intervals.

Tyres

Check tyre pressures regularly. Under-inflated tyres have an increased rolling resistance. It is generally safe to use the higher pressures specified for full load conditions even when not fully laden, but keep an eye on the centre band of tread for signs of wear due to over-inflation.

When buying new tyres, consider the 'fuel saving' models which most manufacturers include in their ranges.

Driving style

Acceleration

Acceleration uses more fuel than driving at a steady speed. The best technique with modern cars is to accelerate reasonably briskly to the desired speed, changing up through the gears as soon as possible without making the engine labour.

Air conditioning

Air conditioning absorbs quite a bit of energy from the engine – typically 3 kW (4 hp) or so. The effect on fuel consumption is at its worst in slow traffic. Switch it off when not required.

Anticipation

Drive smoothly and try to read the traffic flow so as to avoid unnecessary acceleration and braking.

Automatic transmission

When accelerating in an automatic, avoid depressing the throttle so far as to make the transmission hold onto lower gears at higher speeds. Don't use the 'Sport' setting, if applicable.

When stationary with the engine running, select 'N' or 'P'. When moving, keep your left foot away from the brake.

Braking

Braking converts the car's energy of motion into heat – essentially, it is wasted. Obviously some braking is always going to be necessary, but with good anticipation it is surprising how much can be avoided, especially on routes that you know well.

Carshare

Consider sharing lifts to work or to the shops. Even once a week will make a difference.

Electrical loads

Electricity is 'fuel' too; the alternator which charges the battery does so by converting some of the engine's energy of motion into electrical energy. The more electrical accessories are in use, the greater the load on the alternator. Switch off big consumers like the heated rear window when not required.

Freewheeling

Freewheeling (coasting) in neutral with the engine switched off is dangerous. The effort required to operate power-assisted brakes and steering increases when the engine is not running, with a potential lack of control in emergency situations.

In any case, modern fuel injection systems automatically cut off the engine's fuel supply on the overrun (moving and in gear, but with the accelerator pedal released).

Gadgets

Bolt-on devices claiming to save fuel have been around for nearly as long as the motor car itself. Those which worked were rapidly adopted as standard equipment by the vehicle manufacturers. Others worked only in certain situations, or saved fuel only at the expense of unacceptable effects on performance, driveability or the life of engine components.

The most effective fuel saving gadget is the driver's right foot.

Journey planning

Combine (eg) a trip to the supermarket with a visit to the recycling centre and the DIY store, rather than making separate journeys.

When possible choose a travelling time outside rush hours.

Load

The more heavily a car is laden, the greater the energy required to accelerate it to a given speed. Remove heavy items which you don't need to carry.

One load which is often overlooked is the contents of the fuel tank. A tankful of fuel (55 litres / 12 gallons) weighs 45 kg (100 lb) or so. Just half filling it may be worthwhile.

Lost?

At the risk of stating the obvious, if you're going somewhere new, have details of the route to hand. There's not much point in achieving record mpg if you also go miles out of your way.

Parking

If possible, carry out any reversing or turning manoeuvres when you arrive at a parking space so that you can drive straight out when you leave. Manoeuvering when the engine is cold uses a lot more fuel.

Driving around looking for free on-street parking may cost more in fuel than buying a car park ticket.

Premium fuel

Most major oil companies (and some supermarkets) have premium grades of fuel which are several pence a litre dearer than the standard grades. Reports vary, but the consensus seems to be that if these fuels improve economy at all, they do not do so by enough to justify their extra cost.

Roof rack

When loading a roof rack, try to produce a wedge shape with the narrow end at the front. Any cover should be securely fastened – if it flaps it's creating turbulence and absorbing energy.

Remove roof racks and boxes when not in use – they increase air resistance and can create a surprising amount of noise.

Short journeys

The engine is at its least efficient, and wear is highest, during the first few miles after a cold start. Consider walking, cycling or using public transport.

Speed

The engine is at its most efficient when running at a steady speed and load at the rpm where it develops maximum torque. (You can find this figure in the car's handbook.) For most cars this corresponds to between 55 and 65 mph in top gear.

Above the optimum cruising speed, fuel consumption starts to rise quite sharply. A car travelling at 80 mph will typically be using 30% more fuel than at 60 mph.

Supermarket fuel

It may be cheap but is it any good? In the UK all supermarket fuel must meet the relevant British Standard. The major oil companies will say that their branded fuels have better additive packages which may stop carbon and other deposits building up. A reasonable compromise might be to use one tank of branded fuel to three or four from the supermarket.

Switch off when stationary

Switch off the engine if you look like being stationary for more than 30 seconds or so. This is good for the environment as well as for your pocket. Be aware though that frequent restarts are hard on the battery and the starter motor.

Windows

Driving with the windows open increases air turbulence around the vehicle. Closing the windows promotes smooth airflow and

reduced resistance. The faster you go, the more significant this is.

And finally . . .

Driving techniques associated with good fuel economy tend to involve moderate acceleration and low top speeds. Be considerate to the needs of other road users who may need to make brisker progress; even if you do not agree with them this is not an excuse to be obstructive.

Safety must always take precedence over economy, whether it is a question of accelerating hard to complete an overtaking manoeuvre, killing your speed when confronted with a potential hazard or switching the lights on when it starts to get dark.

Conversion factors

Length (distance)
Inches (in)	x 25.4	= Millimetres (mm)	x 0.0394	= Inches (in)
Feet (ft)	x 0.305	= Metres (m)	x 3.281	= Feet (ft)
Miles	x 1.609	= Kilometres (km)	x 0.621	= Miles

Volume (capacity)
Cubic inches (cu in; in³)	x 16.387	= Cubic centimetres (cc; cm³)	x 0.061	= Cubic inches (cu in; in³)
Imperial pints (Imp pt)	x 0.568	= Litres (l)	x 1.76	= Imperial pints (Imp pt)
Imperial quarts (Imp qt)	x 1.137	= Litres (l)	x 0.88	= Imperial quarts (Imp qt)
Imperial quarts (Imp qt)	x 1.201	= US quarts (US qt)	x 0.833	= Imperial quarts (Imp qt)
US quarts (US qt)	x 0.946	= Litres (l)	x 1.057	= US quarts (US qt)
Imperial gallons (Imp gal)	x 4.546	= Litres (l)	x 0.22	= Imperial gallons (Imp gal)
Imperial gallons (Imp gal)	x 1.201	= US gallons (US gal)	x 0.833	= Imperial gallons (Imp gal)
US gallons (US gal)	x 3.785	= Litres (l)	x 0.264	= US gallons (US gal)

Mass (weight)
Ounces (oz)	x 28.35	= Grams (g)	x 0.035	= Ounces (oz)
Pounds (lb)	x 0.454	= Kilograms (kg)	x 2.205	= Pounds (lb)

Force
Ounces-force (ozf; oz)	x 0.278	= Newtons (N)	x 3.6	= Ounces-force (ozf; oz)
Pounds-force (lbf; lb)	x 4.448	= Newtons (N)	x 0.225	= Pounds-force (lbf; lb)
Newtons (N)	x 0.1	= Kilograms-force (kgf; kg)	x 9.81	= Newtons (N)

Pressure
Pounds-force per square inch (psi; lbf/in²; lb/in²)	x 0.070	= Kilograms-force per square centimetre (kgf/cm²; kg/cm²)	x 14.223	= Pounds-force per square inch (psi; lbf/in²; lb/in²)
Pounds-force per square inch (psi; lbf/in²; lb/in²)	x 0.068	= Atmospheres (atm)	x 14.696	= Pounds-force per square inch (psi; lbf/in²; lb/in²)
Pounds-force per square inch (psi; lbf/in²; lb/in²)	x 0.069	= Bars	x 14.5	= Pounds-force per square inch (psi; lbf/in²; lb/in²)
Pounds-force per square inch (psi; lbf/in²; lb/in²)	x 6.895	= Kilopascals (kPa)	x 0.145	= Pounds-force per square inch (psi; lbf/in²; lb/in²)
Kilopascals (kPa)	x 0.01	= Kilograms-force per square centimetre (kgf/cm²; kg/cm²)	x 98.1	= Kilopascals (kPa)
Millibar (mbar)	x 100	= Pascals (Pa)	x 0.01	= Millibar (mbar)
Millibar (mbar)	x 0.0145	= Pounds-force per square inch (psi; lbf/in²; lb/in²)	x 68.947	= Millibar (mbar)
Millibar (mbar)	x 0.75	= Millimetres of mercury (mmHg)	x 1.333	= Millibar (mbar)
Millibar (mbar)	x 0.401	= Inches of water (inH₂O)	x 2.491	= Millibar (mbar)
Millimetres of mercury (mmHg)	x 0.535	= Inches of water (inH₂O)	x 1.868	= Millimetres of mercury (mmHg)
Inches of water (inH₂O)	x 0.036	= Pounds-force per square inch (psi; lbf/in²; lb/in²)	x 27.68	= Inches of water (inH₂O)

Torque (moment of force)
Pounds-force inches (lbf in; lb in)	x 1.152	= Kilograms-force centimetre (kgf cm; kg cm)	x 0.868	= Pounds-force inches (lbf in; lb in)
Pounds-force inches (lbf in; lb in)	x 0.113	= Newton metres (Nm)	x 8.85	= Pounds-force inches (lbf in; lb in)
Pounds-force inches (lbf in; lb in)	x 0.083	= Pounds-force feet (lbf ft; lb ft)	x 12	= Pounds-force inches (lbf in; lb in)
Pounds-force feet (lbf ft; lb ft)	x 0.138	= Kilograms-force metres (kgf m; kg m)	x 7.233	= Pounds-force feet (lbf ft; lb ft)
Pounds-force feet (lbf ft; lb ft)	x 1.356	= Newton metres (Nm)	x 0.738	= Pounds-force feet (lbf ft; lb ft)
Newton metres (Nm)	x 0.102	= Kilograms-force metres (kgf m; kg m)	x 9.804	= Newton metres (Nm)

Power
Horsepower (hp)	x 745.7	= Watts (W)	x 0.0013	= Horsepower (hp)

Velocity (speed)
Miles per hour (miles/hr; mph)	x 1.609	= Kilometres per hour (km/hr; kph)	x 0.621	= Miles per hour (miles/hr; mph)

Fuel consumption*
Miles per gallon, Imperial (mpg)	x 0.354	= Kilometres per litre (km/l)	x 2.825	= Miles per gallon, Imperial (mpg)
Miles per gallon, US (mpg)	x 0.425	= Kilometres per litre (km/l)	x 2.352	= Miles per gallon, US (mpg)

Temperature
Degrees Fahrenheit = (°C x 1.8) + 32   Degrees Celsius (Degrees Centigrade; °C) = (°F - 32) x 0.56

It is common practice to convert from miles per gallon (mpg) to litres/100 kilometres (l/100km), where mpg x l/100 km = 282

Spare parts are available from many sources, including maker's appointed garages, accessory shops, and motor factors. To be sure of obtaining the correct parts, it will sometimes be necessary to quote the vehicle identification number. If possible, it can also be useful to take the old parts along for positive identification. Items such as starter motors and alternators may be available under a service exchange scheme – any parts returned should be clean.

Our advice regarding spare parts is as follows.

Officially appointed garages

This is the best source of parts which are peculiar to your car, and which are not otherwise generally available (eg, badges, interior trim, certain body panels, etc). It is also the only place at which you should buy parts if the car is still under warranty.

Accessory shops

These are very good places to buy materials and components needed for the maintenance of your car (oil, air and fuel filters, light bulbs, drivebelts, greases, brake pads, touch-up paint, etc). Components of this nature sold by a reputable shop are usually of the same standard as those used by the car manufacturer.

Besides components, these shops also sell tools and general accessories, usually have convenient opening hours, charge lower prices, and can often be found close to home. Some accessory shops have parts counters where components needed for almost any repair job can be purchased or ordered.

Motor factors

Good factors will stock all the more important components which wear out comparatively quickly, and can sometimes supply individual components needed for the overhaul of a larger assembly (eg, brake seals and hydraulic parts, bearing shells, pistons, valves). They may also handle work such as cylinder block reboring, crankshaft regrinding, etc.

Engine reconditioners

These specialise in engine overhaul and can also supply components. It is recommended that the establishment is a member of the Federation of Engine Re-Manufacturers, or a similar society.

Tyre and exhaust specialists

These outlets may be independent, or members of a local or national chain. They frequently offer competitive prices when compared with a main dealer or local garage, but it will pay to obtain several quotes before making a decision. When researching prices, also ask what extras may be added – for instance fitting a new valve, balancing the wheel and tyre disposal all both commonly charged on top of the price of a new tyre.

Other sources

Beware of parts or materials obtained from market stalls, car boot sales, on-line auctions or similar outlets. Such items are not invariably sub-standard, but there is little chance of compensation if they do prove unsatisfactory. In the case of safety-critical components such as brake pads, there is the risk not only of financial loss, but also of an accident causing injury or death.

Second-hand components or assemblies obtained from a car breaker can be a good buy in some circumstances, but this sort of purchase is best made by the experienced DIY mechanic.

Vehicle identification numbers

Modifications are a continuing and unpublicised process in vehicle manufacture, quite apart from major model changes. Spare parts manuals and lists are compiled upon a numerical basis, the individual vehicle identification numbers being essential to correct identification of the component concerned.

When ordering spare parts, always give as much information as possible. Quote the car model, year of manufacture, body and engine numbers as appropriate.

The Vehicle Identification Number (VIN) is visible from the outside of the vehicle, through the left-hand lower corner of the windscreen and is also stamped on the top of the right-hand inner wing in the engine compartment.

The engine number is stamped on the left-hand side of the cylinder block. The engine code can also be found on the vehicle data sticker in the luggage compartment.

Other identification numbers or codes are stamped on major items such as the gearbox, etc. These numbers are also printed on the Vehicle data sticker located in the luggage compartment adjacent to the spare wheel **(see illustration)**.

Vehicle data sticker in the luggage compartment

Whenever servicing, repair or overhaul work is carried out on the car or its components, observe the following procedures and instructions. This will assist in carrying out the operation efficiently and to a professional standard of workmanship.

Joint mating faces and gaskets

When separating components at their mating faces, never insert screwdrivers or similar implements into the joint between the faces in order to prise them apart. This can cause severe damage which results in oil leaks, coolant leaks, etc upon reassembly. Separation is usually achieved by tapping along the joint with a soft-faced hammer in order to break the seal. However, note that this method may not be suitable where dowels are used for component location.

Where a gasket is used between the mating faces of two components, a new one must be fitted on reassembly; fit it dry unless otherwise stated in the repair procedure. Make sure that the mating faces are clean and dry, with all traces of old gasket removed. When cleaning a joint face, use a tool which is unlikely to score or damage the face, and remove any burrs or nicks with an oilstone or fine file.

Make sure that tapped holes are cleaned with a pipe cleaner, and keep them free of jointing compound, if this is being used, unless specifically instructed otherwise.

Ensure that all orifices, channels or pipes are clear, and blow through them, preferably using compressed air.

Oil seals

Oil seals can be removed by levering them out with a wide flat-bladed screwdriver or similar implement. Alternatively, a number of self-tapping screws may be screwed into the seal, and these used as a purchase for pliers or some similar device in order to pull the seal free.

Whenever an oil seal is removed from its working location, either individually or as part of an assembly, it should be renewed.

The very fine sealing lip of the seal is easily damaged, and will not seal if the surface it contacts is not completely clean and free from scratches, nicks or grooves. If the original sealing surface of the component cannot be restored, and the manufacturer has not made provision for slight relocation of the seal relative to the sealing surface, the component should be renewed.

Protect the lips of the seal from any surface which may damage them in the course of fitting. Use tape or a conical sleeve where possible. Where indicated, lubricate the seal lips with oil before fitting and, on dual-lipped seals, fill the space between the lips with grease.

Unless otherwise stated, oil seals must be fitted with their sealing lips toward the lubricant to be sealed.

Use a tubular drift or block of wood of the appropriate size to install the seal and, if the seal housing is shouldered, drive the seal down to the shoulder. If the seal housing is unshouldered, the seal should be fitted with its face flush with the housing top face (unless otherwise instructed).

Screw threads and fastenings

Seized nuts, bolts and screws are quite a common occurrence where corrosion has set in, and the use of penetrating oil or releasing fluid will often overcome this problem if the offending item is soaked for a while before attempting to release it. The use of an impact driver may also provide a means of releasing such stubborn fastening devices, when used in conjunction with the appropriate screwdriver bit or socket. If none of these methods works, it may be necessary to resort to the careful application of heat, or the use of a hacksaw or nut splitter device. Before resorting to extreme methods, check that you are not dealing with a left-hand thread!

Studs are usually removed by locking two nuts together on the threaded part, and then using a spanner on the lower nut to unscrew the stud. Studs or bolts which have broken off below the surface of the component in which they are mounted can sometimes be removed using a stud extractor.

Always ensure that a blind tapped hole is completely free from oil, grease, water or other fluid before installing the bolt or stud. Failure to do this could cause the housing to crack due to the hydraulic action of the bolt or stud as it is screwed in.

For some screw fastenings, notably cylinder head bolts or nuts, torque wrench settings are no longer specified for the latter stages of tightening, "angle-tightening" being called up instead. Typically, a fairly low torque wrench setting will be applied to the bolts/nuts in the correct sequence, followed by one or more stages of tightening through specified angles.

When checking or retightening a nut or bolt to a specified torque setting, slacken the nut or bolt by a quarter of a turn, and then retighten to the specified setting. However, this should not be attempted where angular tightening has been used.

Locknuts, locktabs and washers

Any fastening which will rotate against a component or housing during tightening should always have a washer between it and the relevant component or housing.

Spring or split washers should always be renewed when they are used to lock a critical component such as a big-end bearing retaining bolt or nut. Locktabs which are folded over to retain a nut or bolt should always be renewed.

Self-locking nuts can be re-used in non-critical areas, providing resistance can be felt when the locking portion passes over the bolt or stud thread. However, it should be noted that self-locking stiffnuts tend to lose their effectiveness after long periods of use, and should then be renewed as a matter of course.

Split pins must always be replaced with new ones of the correct size for the hole.

When thread-locking compound is found on the threads of a fastener which is to be re-used, it should be cleaned off with a wire brush and solvent, and fresh compound applied on reassembly.

Special tools

Some repair procedures in this manual entail the use of special tools such as a press, two or three-legged pullers, spring compressors, etc. Wherever possible, suitable readily-available alternatives to the manufacturer's special tools are described, and are shown in use. In some instances, where no alternative is possible, it has been necessary to resort to the use of a manufacturer's tool, and this has been done for reasons of safety as well as the efficient completion of the repair operation. Unless you are highly-skilled and have a thorough understanding of the procedures described, never attempt to bypass the use of any special tool when the procedure described specifies its use. Not only is there a very great risk of personal injury, but expensive damage could be caused to the components involved.

Environmental considerations

When disposing of used engine oil, brake fluid, antifreeze, etc, give due consideration to any detrimental environmental effects. Do not, for instance, pour any of the above liquids down drains into the general sewage system, or onto the ground to soak away, as this is likely to pollute your local environment. Many local council refuse tips provide a facility for waste oil disposal, as do some garages. You can find your nearest disposal point by calling the Environment Agency on 03708 506 506 or by visiting www.oilbankline.org.uk.

Note: It is illegal and anti-social to dump oil down the drain. To find the location of your local oil recycling bank, call 03708 506 506 or visit www.oilbankline.org.uk.

The jack supplied with the vehicle tool kit should only be used for changing the roadwheels – see *Wheel changing* in *Roadside Repairs*. When carrying out any other kind of work, raise the vehicle using a hydraulic trolley jack, and always supplement the jack with axle stands positioned under the vehicle jacking points.

Do not attempt to jack the vehicle under the front crossmember, the sump, or any of the suspension components.

 Warning: Never work under, around, or near a raised car unless it is adequately supported in at least two places.

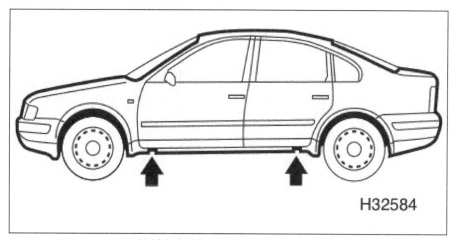

Vehicle jacking points under the sills

Audio unit anti-theft system – precaution

The audio unit fitted as standard equipment by Audi may be equipped with a built-in security code to deter thieves. If the power source to the unit is cut, the anti-theft system will activate. Even if the power source is immediately reconnected, the unit will not function until the correct security code has been entered. Therefore, if you do not know the correct security code for the unit, do not disconnect the battery negative lead, or remove the unit from the vehicle.

Introduction

A selection of good tools is a fundamental requirement for anyone contemplating the maintenance and repair of a motor vehicle. For the owner who does not possess any, their purchase will prove a considerable expense, offsetting some of the savings made by doing-it-yourself. However, provided that the tools purchased meet the relevant national safety standards and are of good quality, they will last for many years and prove an extremely worthwhile investment.

To help the average owner to decide which tools are needed to carry out the various tasks detailed in this manual, we have compiled three lists of tools under the following headings: *Maintenance and minor repair, Repair and overhaul,* and *Special.* Newcomers to practical mechanics should start off with the *Maintenance and minor repair* tool kit, and confine themselves to the simpler jobs around the vehicle. Then, as confidence and experience grow, more difficult tasks can be undertaken, with extra tools being purchased as, and when, they are needed. In this way, a *Maintenance and minor repair* tool kit can be built up into a *Repair and overhaul* tool kit over a considerable period of time, without any major cash outlays. The experienced do-it-yourselfer will have a tool kit good enough for most repair and overhaul procedures, and will add tools from the *Special* category when it is felt that the expense is justified by the amount of use to which these tools will be put.

Maintenance and minor repair tool kit

The tools given in this list should be considered as a minimum requirement if routine maintenance, servicing and minor repair operations are to be undertaken. We recommend the purchase of combination spanners (ring one end, open-ended the other); although more expensive than open-ended ones, they do give the advantages of both types of spanner.

- [ ] *Combination spanners:*
  Metric - 8 to 19 mm inclusive
- [ ] *Adjustable spanner - 35 mm jaw (approx.)*
- [ ] *Spark plug spanner (with rubber insert) - petrol models*
- [ ] *Spark plug gap adjustment tool - petrol models*
- [ ] *Set of feeler gauges*
- [ ] *Brake bleed nipple spanner*
- [ ] *Screwdrivers:*
  Flat blade - 100 mm long x 6 mm dia
  Cross blade - 100 mm long x 6 mm dia
  Torx - various sizes (not all vehicles)
- [ ] *Combination pliers*
- [ ] *Hacksaw (junior)*
- [ ] *Tyre pump*
- [ ] *Tyre pressure gauge*
- [ ] *Oil can*
- [ ] *Oil filter removal tool*
- [ ] *Fine emery cloth*
- [ ] *Wire brush (small)*
- [ ] *Funnel (medium size)*
- [ ] *Sump drain plug key (not all vehicles)*

Repair and overhaul tool kit

These tools are virtually essential for anyone undertaking any major repairs to a motor vehicle, and are additional to those given in the *Maintenance and minor repair* list. Included in this list is a comprehensive set of sockets. Although these are expensive, they will be found invaluable as they are so versatile - particularly if various drives are included in the set. We recommend the half-inch square-drive type, as this can be used with most proprietary torque wrenches.

The tools in this list will sometimes need to be supplemented by tools from the *Special* list:

- [ ] *Sockets (or box spanners) to cover range in previous list (including Torx sockets)*
- [ ] *Reversible ratchet drive (for use with sockets)*
- [ ] *Extension piece, 250 mm (for use with sockets)*
- [ ] *Universal joint (for use with sockets)*
- [ ] *Flexible handle or sliding T "breaker bar" (for use with sockets)*
- [ ] *Torque wrench (for use with sockets)*
- [ ] *Self-locking grips*
- [ ] *Ball pein hammer*
- [ ] *Soft-faced mallet (plastic or rubber)*
- [ ] *Screwdrivers:*
  Flat blade - long & sturdy, short (chubby), and narrow (electrician's) types
  Cross blade – long & sturdy, and short (chubby) types
- [ ] *Pliers:*
  Long-nosed
  Side cutters (electrician's)
  Circlip (internal and external)
- [ ] *Cold chisel - 25 mm*
- [ ] *Scriber*
- [ ] *Scraper*
- [ ] *Centre-punch*
- [ ] *Pin punch*
- [ ] *Hacksaw*
- [ ] *Brake hose clamp*
- [ ] *Brake/clutch bleeding kit*
- [ ] *Selection of twist drills*
- [ ] *Steel rule/straight-edge*
- [ ] *Allen keys (inc. splined/Torx type)*
- [ ] *Selection of files*
- [ ] *Wire brush*
- [ ] *Axle stands*
- [ ] *Jack (strong trolley or hydraulic type)*
- [ ] *Light with extension lead*
- [ ] *Universal electrical multi-meter*

Sockets and reversible ratchet drive

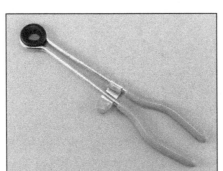

Brake bleeding kit

Torx key, socket and bit

Hose clamp

Angular-tightening gauge

Special tools

The tools in this list are those which are not used regularly, are expensive to buy, or which need to be used in accordance with their manufacturers' instructions. Unless relatively difficult mechanical jobs are undertaken frequently, it will not be economic to buy many of these tools. Where this is the case, you could consider clubbing together with friends (or joining a motorists' club) to make a joint purchase, or borrowing the tools against a deposit from a local garage or tool hire specialist. It is worth noting that many of the larger DIY superstores now carry a large range of special tools for hire at modest rates.

The following list contains only those tools and instruments freely available to the public, and not those special tools produced by the vehicle manufacturer specifically for its dealer network. You will find occasional references to these manufacturers' special tools in the text of this manual. Generally, an alternative method of doing the job without the vehicle manufacturers' special tool is given. However, sometimes there is no alternative to using them. Where this is the case and the relevant tool cannot be bought or borrowed, you will have to entrust the work to a dealer.

- ☐ Angular-tightening gauge
- ☐ Valve spring compressor
- ☐ Valve grinding tool
- ☐ Piston ring compressor
- ☐ Piston ring removal/installation tool
- ☐ Cylinder bore hone
- ☐ Balljoint separator
- ☐ Coil spring compressors (where applicable)
- ☐ Two/three-legged hub and bearing puller
- ☐ Impact screwdriver
- ☐ Micrometer and/or vernier calipers
- ☐ Dial gauge
- ☐ Stroboscopic timing light
- ☐ Dwell angle meter/tachometer
- ☐ Fault code reader
- ☐ Cylinder compression gauge
- ☐ Hand-operated vacuum pump and gauge
- ☐ Clutch plate alignment set
- ☐ Brake shoe steady spring cup removal tool
- ☐ Bush and bearing removal/installation set
- ☐ Stud extractors
- ☐ Tap and die set
- ☐ Lifting tackle
- ☐ Trolley jack

Buying tools

Reputable motor accessory shops and superstores often offer excellent quality tools at discount prices, so it pays to shop around.

Remember, you don't have to buy the most expensive items on the shelf, but it is always advisable to steer clear of the very cheap tools. Beware of 'bargains' offered on market stalls or at car boot sales. There are plenty of good tools around at reasonable prices, but always aim to purchase items which meet the relevant national safety standards. If in doubt, ask the proprietor or manager of the shop for advice before making a purchase.

Care and maintenance of tools

Having purchased a reasonable tool kit, it is necessary to keep the tools in a clean and serviceable condition. After use, always wipe off any dirt, grease and metal particles using a clean, dry cloth, before putting the tools away. Never leave them lying around after they have been used. A simple tool rack on the garage or workshop wall for items such as screwdrivers and pliers is a good idea. Store all normal spanners and sockets in a metal box. Any measuring instruments, gauges, meters, etc, must be carefully stored where they cannot be damaged or become rusty.

Take a little care when tools are used. Hammer heads inevitably become marked, and screwdrivers lose the keen edge on their blades from time to time. A little timely attention with emery cloth or a file will soon restore items like this to a good finish.

Working facilities

Not to be forgotten when discussing tools is the workshop itself. If anything more than routine maintenance is to be carried out, a suitable working area becomes essential.

It is appreciated that many an owner-mechanic is forced by circumstances to remove an engine or similar item without the benefit of a garage or workshop. Having done this, any repairs should always be done under the cover of a roof.

Wherever possible, any dismantling should be done on a clean, flat workbench or table at a suitable working height.

Any workbench needs a vice; one with a jaw opening of 100 mm is suitable for most jobs. As mentioned previously, some clean dry storage space is also required for tools, as well as for any lubricants, cleaning fluids, touch-up paints etc, which become necessary.

Another item which may be required, and which has a much more general usage, is an electric drill with a chuck capacity of at least 8 mm. This, together with a good range of twist drills, is virtually essential for fitting accessories.

Last, but not least, always keep a supply of old newspapers and clean, lint-free rags available, and try to keep any working area as clean as possible.

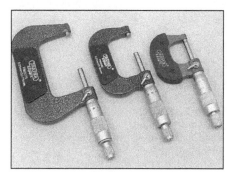

Micrometers

Dial test indicator ("dial gauge")

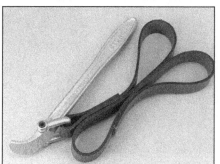

Strap wrench

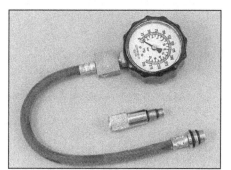

Compression tester

Fault code reader

This is a guide to getting your vehicle through the MOT test. Obviously it will not be possible to examine the vehicle to the same standard as the professional MOT tester. However, working through the following checks will enable you to identify any problem areas before submitting the vehicle for the test.

It has only been possible to summarise the test requirements here, based on the regulations in force at the time of printing. Test standards are becoming increasingly stringent, although there are some exemptions for older vehicles.

An assistant will be needed to help carry out some of these checks.

The checks have been sub-divided into four categories, as follows:

1 Checks carried out **FROM THE DRIVER'S SEAT**

2 Checks carried out **WITH THE VEHICLE ON THE GROUND**

3 Checks carried out **WITH THE VEHICLE RAISED AND THE WHEELS FREE TO TURN**

4 Checks carried out on **YOUR VEHICLE'S EXHAUST EMISSION SYSTEM**

---

1 Checks carried out **FROM THE DRIVER'S SEAT**

Handbrake

☐ Test the operation of the handbrake. Excessive travel (too many clicks) indicates incorrect brake or cable adjustment.
☐ Check that the handbrake cannot be released by tapping the lever sideways. Check the security of the lever mountings.

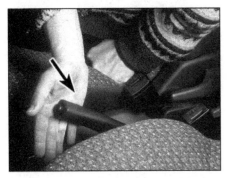

Footbrake

☐ Depress the brake pedal and check that it does not creep down to the floor, indicating a master cylinder fault. Release the pedal, wait a few seconds, then depress it again. If the pedal travels nearly to the floor before firm resistance is felt, brake adjustment or repair is necessary. If the pedal feels spongy, there is air in the hydraulic system which must be removed by bleeding.

☐ Check that the brake pedal is secure and in good condition. Check also for signs of fluid leaks on the pedal, floor or carpets, which would indicate failed seals in the brake master cylinder.
☐ Check the servo unit (when applicable) by operating the brake pedal several times, then keeping the pedal depressed and starting the engine. As the engine starts, the pedal will move down slightly. If not, the vacuum hose or the servo itself may be faulty.

Steering wheel and column

☐ Examine the steering wheel for fractures or looseness of the hub, spokes or rim.
☐ Move the steering wheel from side to side and then up and down. Check that the steering wheel is not loose on the column, indicating wear or a loose retaining nut. Continue moving the steering wheel as before, but also turn it slightly from left to right.
☐ Check that the steering wheel is not loose on the column, and that there is no abnormal

movement of the steering wheel, indicating wear in the column support bearings or couplings.

Windscreen, mirrors and sunvisor

☐ The windscreen must be free of cracks or other significant damage within the driver's field of view. (Small stone chips are acceptable.) Rear view mirrors must be secure, intact, and capable of being adjusted.

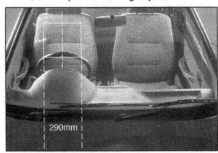

290mm

☐ The driver's sunvisor must be capable of being stored in the "up" position.

Seat belts and seats

Note: *The following checks are applicable to all seat belts, front and rear.*

☐ Examine the webbing of all the belts (including rear belts if fitted) for cuts, serious fraying or deterioration. Fasten and unfasten each belt to check the buckles. If applicable, check the retracting mechanism. Check the security of all seat belt mountings accessible from inside the vehicle.

☐ Seat belts with pre-tensioners, once activated, have a "flag" or similar showing on the seat belt stalk. This, in itself, is not a reason for test failure.

☐ The front seats themselves must be securely attached and the backrests must lock in the upright position.

Doors

☐ Both front doors must be able to be opened and closed from outside and inside, and must latch securely when closed.

2 Checks carried out WITH THE VEHICLE ON THE GROUND

Vehicle identification

☐ Number plates must be in good condition, secure and legible, with letters and numbers correctly spaced – spacing at (A) should be at least twice that at (B).

☐ The VIN plate and/or homologation plate must be legible.

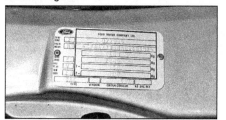

Electrical equipment

☐ Switch on the ignition and check the operation of the horn.

☐ Check the windscreen washers and wipers, examining the wiper blades; renew damaged or perished blades. Also check the operation of the stop-lights.

☐ Check the operation of the sidelights and number plate lights. The lenses and reflectors must be secure, clean and undamaged.

☐ Check the operation and alignment of the headlights. The headlight reflectors must not be tarnished and the lenses must be undamaged.

☐ Switch on the ignition and check the operation of the direction indicators (including the instrument panel tell-tale) and the hazard warning lights. Operation of the sidelights and stop-lights must not affect the indicators - if it does, the cause is usually a bad earth at the rear light cluster.

☐ Check the operation of the rear foglight(s), including the warning light on the instrument panel or in the switch.

☐ The ABS warning light must illuminate in accordance with the manufacturers' design. For most vehicles, the ABS warning light should illuminate when the ignition is switched on, and (if the system is operating properly) extinguish after a few seconds. Refer to the owner's handbook.

Footbrake

☐ Examine the master cylinder, brake pipes and servo unit for leaks, loose mountings, corrosion or other damage.

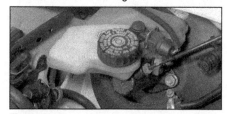

☐ The fluid reservoir must be secure and the fluid level must be between the upper (**A**) and lower (**B**) markings.

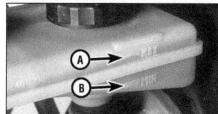

☐ Inspect both front brake flexible hoses for cracks or deterioration of the rubber. Turn the steering from lock to lock, and ensure that the hoses do not contact the wheel, tyre, or any part of the steering or suspension mechanism. With the brake pedal firmly depressed, check the hoses for bulges or leaks under pressure.

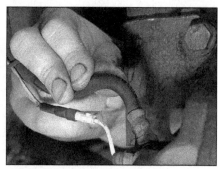

Steering and suspension

☐ Have your assistant turn the steering wheel from side to side slightly, up to the point where the steering gear just begins to transmit this movement to the roadwheels. Check for excessive free play between the steering wheel and the steering gear, indicating wear or insecurity of the steering column joints, the column-to-steering gear coupling, or the steering gear itself.

☐ Have your assistant turn the steering wheel more vigorously in each direction, so that the roadwheels just begin to turn. As this is done, examine all the steering joints, linkages, fittings and attachments. Renew any component that shows signs of wear or damage. On vehicles with power steering, check the security and condition of the steering pump, drivebelt and hoses.

☐ Check that the vehicle is standing level, and at approximately the correct ride height.

Shock absorbers

☐ Depress each corner of the vehicle in turn, then release it. The vehicle should rise and then settle in its normal position. If the vehicle continues to rise and fall, the shock absorber is defective. A shock absorber which has seized will also cause the vehicle to fail.

Exhaust system

☐ Start the engine. With your assistant holding a rag over the tailpipe, check the entire system for leaks. Repair or renew leaking sections.

3 Checks carried out
WITH THE VEHICLE RAISED AND THE WHEELS FREE TO TURN

Jack up the front and rear of the vehicle, and securely support it on axle stands. Position the stands clear of the suspension assemblies. Ensure that the wheels are clear of the ground and that the steering can be turned from lock to lock.

Steering mechanism

☐ Have your assistant turn the steering from lock to lock. Check that the steering turns smoothly, and that no part of the steering mechanism, including a wheel or tyre, fouls any brake hose or pipe or any part of the body structure.
☐ Examine the steering rack rubber gaiters for damage or insecurity of the retaining clips. If power steering is fitted, check for signs of damage or leakage of the fluid hoses, pipes or connections. Also check for excessive stiffness or binding of the steering, a missing split pin or locking device, or severe corrosion of the body structure within 30 cm of any steering component attachment point.

Front and rear suspension and wheel bearings

☐ Starting at the front right-hand side, grasp the roadwheel at the 3 o'clock and 9 o'clock positions and rock gently but firmly. Check for free play or insecurity at the wheel bearings, suspension balljoints, or suspension mountings, pivots and attachments.
☐ Now grasp the wheel at the 12 o'clock and 6 o'clock positions and repeat the previous inspection. Spin the wheel, and check for roughness or tightness of the front wheel bearing.

☐ If excess free play is suspected at a component pivot point, this can be confirmed by using a large screwdriver or similar tool and levering between the mounting and the component attachment. This will confirm whether the wear is in the pivot bush, its retaining bolt, or in the mounting itself (the bolt holes can often become elongated).

☐ Carry out all the above checks at the other front wheel, and then at both rear wheels.

Springs and shock absorbers

☐ Examine the suspension struts (when applicable) for serious fluid leakage, corrosion, or damage to the casing. Also check the security of the mounting points.
☐ If coil springs are fitted, check that the spring ends locate in their seats, and that the spring is not corroded, cracked or broken.
☐ If leaf springs are fitted, check that all leaves are intact, that the axle is securely attached to each spring, and that there is no deterioration of the spring eye mountings, bushes, and shackles.

☐ The same general checks apply to vehicles fitted with other suspension types, such as torsion bars, hydraulic displacer units, etc. Ensure that all mountings and attachments are secure, that there are no signs of excessive wear, corrosion or damage, and (on hydraulic types) that there are no fluid leaks or damaged pipes.
☐ Inspect the shock absorbers for signs of serious fluid leakage. Check for wear of the mounting bushes or attachments, or damage to the body of the unit.

Driveshafts (fwd vehicles only)

☐ Rotate each front wheel in turn and inspect the constant velocity joint gaiters for splits or damage. Also check that each driveshaft is straight and undamaged.

Braking system

☐ If possible without dismantling, check brake pad wear and disc condition. Ensure that the friction lining material has not worn excessively, (A) and that the discs are not fractured, pitted, scored or badly worn (B).

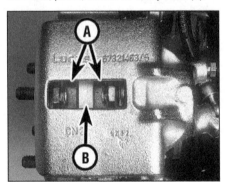

☐ Examine all the rigid brake pipes underneath the vehicle, and the flexible hose(s) at the rear. Look for corrosion, chafing or insecurity of the pipes, and for signs of bulging under pressure, chafing, splits or deterioration of the flexible hoses.
☐ Look for signs of fluid leaks at the brake calipers or on the brake backplates. Repair or renew leaking components.
☐ Slowly spin each wheel, while your assistant depresses and releases the footbrake. Ensure that each brake is operating and does not bind when the pedal is released.

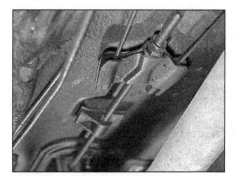

□ Examine the handbrake mechanism, checking for frayed or broken cables, excessive corrosion, or wear or insecurity of the linkage. Check that the mechanism works on each relevant wheel, and releases fully, without binding.

□ It is not possible to test brake efficiency without special equipment, but a road test can be carried out later to check that the vehicle pulls up in a straight line.

Fuel and exhaust systems

□ Inspect the fuel tank (including the filler cap), fuel pipes, hoses and unions. All components must be secure and free from leaks.

□ Examine the exhaust system over its entire length, checking for any damaged, broken or missing mountings, security of the retaining clamps and rust or corrosion.

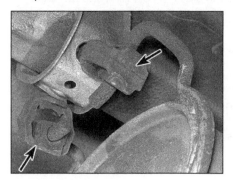

Wheels and tyres

□ Examine the sidewalls and tread area of each tyre in turn. Check for cuts, tears, lumps, bulges, separation of the tread, and exposure of the ply or cord due to wear or damage. Check that the tyre bead is correctly seated on the wheel rim, that the valve is sound and properly seated, and that the wheel is not distorted or damaged.

□ Check that the tyres are of the correct size for the vehicle, that they are of the same size and type on each axle, and that the pressures are correct.

□ Check the tyre tread depth. The legal minimum at the time of writing is 1.6 mm over at least three-quarters of the tread width. Abnormal tread wear may indicate incorrect front wheel alignment.

Body corrosion

□ Check the condition of the entire vehicle structure for signs of corrosion in load-bearing areas. (These include chassis box sections, side sills, cross-members, pillars, and all suspension, steering, braking system and seat belt mountings and anchorages.) Any corrosion which has seriously reduced the thickness of a load-bearing area is likely to cause the vehicle to fail. In this case professional repairs are likely to be needed.

□ Damage or corrosion which causes sharp or otherwise dangerous edges to be exposed will also cause the vehicle to fail.

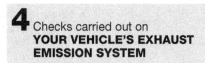

4 Checks carried out on **YOUR VEHICLE'S EXHAUST EMISSION SYSTEM**

Petrol models

□ The engine should be warmed up, and running well (ignition system in good order, air filter element clean, etc).

□ Before testing, run the engine at around 2500 rpm for 20 seconds. Let the engine drop to idle, and watch for smoke from the exhaust. If the idle speed is too high, or if dense blue or black smoke emerges for more than 5 seconds, the vehicle will fail. Typically, blue smoke signifies oil burning (engine wear); black smoke means unburnt fuel (dirty air cleaner element, or other fuel system fault).

□ An exhaust gas analyser for measuring carbon monoxide (CO) and hydrocarbons (HC) is now needed. If one cannot be hired or borrowed, have a local garage perform the check.

CO emissions (mixture)

□ The MOT tester has access to the CO limits for all vehicles. The CO level is measured at idle speed, and at 'fast idle' (2500 to 3000 rpm). The following limits are given as a general guide:

At idle speed – Less than 0.5% CO
At 'fast idle' – Less than 0.3% CO
Lambda reading – 0.97 to 1.03

□ If the CO level is too high, this may point to poor maintenance, a fuel injection system problem, faulty lambda (oxygen) sensor or catalytic converter. Try an injector cleaning treatment, and check the vehicle's ECU for fault codes.

HC emissions

□ The MOT tester has access to HC limits for all vehicles. The HC level is measured at 'fast idle' (2500 to 3000 rpm). The following limits are given as a general guide:

At 'fast idle' – Less then 200 ppm

□ Excessive HC emissions are typically caused by oil being burnt (worn engine), or by a blocked crankcase ventilation system ('breather'). If the engine oil is old and thin, an oil change may help. If the engine is running badly, check the vehicle's ECU for fault codes.

Diesel models

□ The only emission test for diesel engines is measuring exhaust smoke density, using a calibrated smoke meter. The test involves accelerating the engine at least 3 times to its maximum unloaded speed.

Note: *On engines with a timing belt, it is VITAL that the belt is in good condition before the test is carried out.*

□ With the engine warmed up, it is first purged by running at around 2500 rpm for 20 seconds. A governor check is then carried out, by slowly accelerating the engine to its maximum speed. After this, the smoke meter is connected, and the engine is accelerated quickly to maximum speed three times. If the smoke density is less than the limits given below, the vehicle will pass:

Non-turbo vehicles: 2.5m-1
Turbocharged vehicles: 3.0m-1

□ If excess smoke is produced, try fitting a new air cleaner element, or using an injector cleaning treatment. If the engine is running badly, where applicable, check the vehicle's ECU for fault codes. Also check the vehicle's EGR system, where applicable. At high mileages, the injectors may require professional attention.

Engine

- [ ] Engine fails to rotate when attempting to start
- [ ] Engine rotates, but will not start
- [ ] Engine difficult to start when cold
- [ ] Engine difficult to start when hot
- [ ] Starter motor noisy or excessively-rough in engagement
- [ ] Engine idles erratically
- [ ] Engine misfires at idle speed
- [ ] Engine misfires throughout the driving speed range
- [ ] Engine hesitates on acceleration
- [ ] Engine lacks power
- [ ] Oil pressure warning light illuminated with engine running
- [ ] Engine runs-on after switching off
- [ ] Engine noises

Fuel and exhaust systems

- [ ] Excessive fuel consumption
- [ ] Fuel leakage and/or fuel odour
- [ ] Excessive noise or fumes from exhaust system

Cooling system

- [ ] Overheating
- [ ] Overcooling
- [ ] External coolant leakage
- [ ] Internal coolant leakage
- [ ] Corrosion

Clutch

- [ ] Pedal travels to floor – no pressure or very little resistance
- [ ] Clutch fails to disengage (unable to select gears)
- [ ] Clutch slips (engine speed increases, with no increase in vehicle speed)
- [ ] Judder as clutch is engaged
- [ ] Noise when depressing or releasing clutch pedal

Manual transmission

- [ ] Noisy in neutral with engine running
- [ ] Noisy in one particular gear
- [ ] Difficulty engaging gears
- [ ] Jumps out of gear
- [ ] Vibration
- [ ] Lubricant leaks

Multitronic transmission

- [ ] Fluid leakage
- [ ] General gear selection problems
- [ ] Transmission will not downshift (kickdown) with accelerator pedal fully depressed
- [ ] Engine will not start in any gear, or starts in gears other than Park or Neutral
- [ ] Transmission slips, shifts roughly, is noisy, or has no drive in forward or reverse gears

Braking system

- [ ] Vehicle pulls to one side under braking
- [ ] Noise (grinding or high-pitched squeal) when brakes applied
- [ ] Excessive brake pedal travel
- [ ] Brake pedal feels spongy when depressed
- [ ] Excessive brake pedal effort required to stop vehicle
- [ ] Judder felt through brake pedal or steering wheel when braking
- [ ] Pedal pulsates when braking hard
- [ ] Brakes binding
- [ ] Rear wheels locking under normal braking

Driveshafts

- [ ] Vibration when accelerating or decelerating
- [ ] Clicking or knocking noise on turns (at slow speed on full-lock)

Steering and suspension

- [ ] Vehicle pulls to one side
- [ ] Wheel wobble and vibration
- [ ] Excessive pitching and/or rolling around corners, or during braking
- [ ] Wandering or general instability
- [ ] Excessively-stiff steering
- [ ] Excessive play in steering
- [ ] Lack of power assistance
- [ ] Tyre wear excessive

Electrical system

- [ ] Battery will not hold a charge more than a few days
- [ ] Ignition/no-charge warning light remains illuminated with engine running
- [ ] Ignition/no-charge warning light fails to come on
- [ ] Lights inoperative
- [ ] Instrument readings inaccurate or erratic
- [ ] Horn inoperative, or unsatisfactory in operation
- [ ] Windscreen/tailgate wipers inoperative, or unsatisfactory in operation
- [ ] Windscreen washers inoperative, or unsatisfactory in operation
- [ ] Electric windows inoperative, or unsatisfactory in operation
- [ ] Central locking system inoperative, or unsatisfactory in operation

Introduction

The vehicle owner who does his or her own maintenance according to the recommended service schedules should not have to use this, Section of the manual very often. Modern component reliability is such that, provided those items subject to wear or deterioration are inspected or renewed at the specified intervals, sudden failure is comparatively rare. Faults do not usually just happen as a result of sudden failure, but develop over a period of time. Major mechanical failures in particular are usually preceded by characteristic symptoms over hundreds or even thousands of miles. Those components which do occasionally fail without warning are often small and easily carried in the vehicle.

With any fault-finding, the first step is to decide where to begin investigations. Sometimes this is obvious, but on other occasions, a little detective work will be necessary. The owner who makes half a dozen haphazard adjustments or replacements may be successful in curing a fault (or its symptoms), but will be none the wiser if the fault recurs, and ultimately may have spent more time and money than was necessary. A calm and logical approach will be found to be more satisfactory in the long run. Always take into account any warning signs or abnormalities that may have been noticed in the period preceding the fault – power loss, high or low gauge readings, unusual smells, etc – and remember that failure of components such as fuses or spark plugs may only be pointers to some underlying fault.

The pages which follow provide an easy-reference guide to the more common problems which may occur during the operation of the vehicle. These problems and their possible causes are grouped under headings denoting various components or systems, such as Engine, Cooling system, etc. The general Chapter which deals with the problem is also shown in brackets; refer to the relevant part of that Chapter for system-specific information. Whatever the fault, certain basic principles apply. These are as follows:

Verify the fault. This is simply a matter of being sure that you know what the symptoms are before starting work. This is particularly important if you are investigating a fault for someone else, who may not have described it very accurately.

Don't overlook the obvious. For example, if the vehicle won't start, is there fuel in the tank? (Don't take anyone else's word on this particular point, and don't trust the fuel gauge either!) If an electrical fault is indicated, look for loose or broken wires before digging out the test gear.

Cure the disease, not the symptom. Substituting a flat battery with a fully-charged one will get you off the hard shoulder, but if the underlying cause is not attended to, the new battery will go the same way. Similarly, changing oil-fouled spark plugs for a new set will get you moving again, but remember that the reason for the fouling (if it wasn't simply an incorrect grade of plug) will have to be established and corrected.

Don't take anything for granted. Particularly, don't forget that a new component may itself be defective (especially if its been rattling around in the boot for months), and don't leave components out of a fault diagnosis sequence just because they are new or recently-fitted. When you do finally diagnose a difficult fault, you'll probably realise that all the evidence was there from the start.

Diesel fault diagnosis

The majority of starting problems on small diesel engines are electrical in origin. The mechanic who is familiar with petrol engines but less so with diesel may be inclined to view the diesel's injectors and pump in the same light as the spark plugs and distributor, but this is generally a mistake.

When investigating complaints of difficult starting for someone else, make sure that the correct starting procedure is understood and is being followed. Some drivers are unaware of the significance of the preheating warning light – many modern engines are sufficiently forgiving for this not to matter in mild weather, but with the onset of winter, problems begin. Glow plugs in particular are often neglected – just one faulty plug will make cold-weather starting very difficult.

As a rule of thumb, if the engine is difficult to start but runs well when it has finally got going, the problem is electrical (battery, starter motor or preheating system). If poor performance is combined with difficult starting, the problem is likely to be in the fuel system. The low-pressure (supply) side of the fuel system should be checked before suspecting the injectors and high-pressure pump. The most common fuel supply problem is air getting into the system, and any pipe from the fuel tank forwards must be scrutinised if air leakage is suspected.

Engine

Engine fails to rotate when attempting to start

☐ Battery terminal connections loose or corroded (see *Weekly checks*).
☐ Battery discharged or faulty (Chapter 5, Section 2).
☐ Broken, loose or disconnected wiring in the starting circuit (Chapter 5, Section 7).
☐ Defective starter solenoid or switch (Chapter 5, Section 7).
☐ Defective starter motor (Chapter 5, Section 8).
☐ Starter pinion or driveplate ring gear teeth loose or broken (Chapter 2A, Section 12).

Engine rotates, but will not start

☐ Fuel tank empty.
☐ Battery discharged (engine rotates slowly) (Chapter 5, Section 2).
☐ Battery terminal connections loose or corroded (see *Weekly checks*).
☐ Preheating system faulty (Chapter 5, Section 10).
☐ Air in fuel system (Chapter 4A, Section 10).
☐ Major mechanical failure (e.g. timing belt) (Chapter 2A).

Engine difficult to start when cold

☐ Battery discharged (Chapter 5, Section 2).
☐ Battery terminal connections loose or corroded (see *Weekly checks*).
☐ Preheating system faulty (Chapter 5, Section 10).
☐ Low cylinder compressions (Chapter 2A, Section 2).

Engine difficult to start when hot

☐ Air filter element dirty or clogged (Chapter 1, Section 27).
☐ Low cylinder compressions (Chapter 2A, Section 2).

Starter motor noisy or excessively-rough in engagement

☐ Starter pinion or driveplate ring gear teeth loose or broken (Chapter 5 and 2A).
☐ Starter motor mounting bolts loose or missing (Chapter 5, Section 8).
☐ Starter motor internal components worn or damaged (Chapter 5, Section 8).

Engine (continued)

Engine idles erratically
- ☐ Air filter element clogged (Chapter 1, Section 27).
- ☐ Uneven or low cylinder compressions (Chapter 2A, Section 2).
- ☐ Camshaft lobes worn (Chapter 2A, Section 9).
- ☐ Timing belt incorrectly fitted (Chapter 2A, Section 7).
- ☐ Faulty injector(s) (Chapter 4A, Section 4).

Engine misfires at idle speed
- ☐ Faulty injector(s) (Chapter 4A, Section 4).
- ☐ Uneven or low cylinder compressions (Chapter 2A, Section 2).
- ☐ Disconnected, leaking, or perished crankcase ventilation hoses (Chapter 4B, Section 2).

Engine misfires throughout the driving speed range
- ☐ Fuel filter choked (Chapter 1, Section 24).
- ☐ Faulty injector(s) (Chapter 4A, Section 4).
- ☐ Uneven or low cylinder compressions (Chapter 2A, Section 2).

Engine hesitates on acceleration
- ☐ Faulty injector(s) (Chapter 4A, Section 4).

Engine lacks power
- ☐ Timing belt incorrectly fitted or tensioned (Chapter 2A, Section 7).
- ☐ Fuel filter choked (Chapter 1, Section 24).
- ☐ Uneven or low cylinder compressions (Chapter 2A, Section 2).
- ☐ Faulty injector(s) (Chapter 4A, Section 4).
- ☐ Brakes binding (Chapter 1, Section 10 and Chapter 9, Section 1).
- ☐ Clutch slipping (Chapter 6, Section 6).
- ☐ Air filter element clogged (Chapter 1, Section 27).

Oil pressure warning light illuminated with engine running
- ☐ Low oil level, or incorrect oil grade (*Weekly checks*).
- ☐ Faulty oil pressure switch (Chapter 2A, Section 16).
- ☐ Worn engine bearings and/or oil pump (Chapter 2B, Section 16).
- ☐ High engine operating temperature (Chapter 3).
- ☐ Oil pressure relief valve defective (Chapter 2A, Section 15).
- ☐ Oil pick-up strainer clogged (Chapter 2B, Section 10).

Engine runs-on after switching off
- ☐ Excessive carbon build-up in engine (Chapter 2B, Section 7).
- ☐ High engine operating temperature (Chapter 3).

Engine noises

Whistling or wheezing noises
- ☐ Leaking exhaust manifold gasket or pipe-to-manifold joint (Chapter 4B).
- ☐ Leaking vacuum hose (Chapter 4A or Chapter 4B).
- ☐ Blowing cylinder head gasket (Chapter 2A, Section 11).

Tapping or rattling noises
- ☐ Worn valve gear or camshaft (Chapter 2A, Section 9).
- ☐ Ancillary component fault (coolant pump, alternator, etc).

Knocking or thumping noises
- ☐ Worn big-end bearings (regular heavy knocking, perhaps less under load) (Chapter 2B, Section 15).
- ☐ Worn main bearings (rumbling and knocking, perhaps worsening under load) (Chapter 2B, Section 16).
- ☐ Ancillary component fault (coolant pump, alternator, etc).

Fuel and exhaust systems

Excessive fuel consumption
- ☐ Air filter element dirty or clogged (Chapter 1, Section 27).
- ☐ Faulty injector(s) (Chapter 4A, Section 4).
- ☐ Tyres under-inflated (see *Weekly checks*).

Fuel leakage and/or fuel odour
- ☐ Damaged fuel tank, pipes or connections (Chapter 4A, Section 8).

Excessive noise or fumes from exhaust system
- ☐ Leaking exhaust system or manifold joints (Chapter 4B, Section 7).
- ☐ Leaking, corroded or damaged silencers or pipe (Chapter 4B, Section 8).
- ☐ Broken mountings causing body or suspension contact (Chapter 4B, Section 8).

Cooling system

Overheating

- [ ] nsufficient coolant in system (*Weekly checks*).
- [ ] Thermostat faulty (Chapter 3, Section 4).
- [ ] Radiator core blocked, or grille restricted (Chapter 3, Section 3).
- [ ] Electric cooling fan or thermostatic switch faulty (Chapter 3, Section 5, 6).
- [ ] Airlock in cooling system Chapter 1, Section 31.
- [ ] Expansion tank pressure cap faulty Chapter 3, Section 3.

Overcooling

- [ ] Thermostat faulty (Chapter 3, Section 4).
- [ ] Inaccurate temperature gauge sender unit (Chapter 3, Section 6).

External coolant leakage

- [ ] Deteriorated or damaged hoses or hose clips (Chapter 3, Section 2).

- [ ] Radiator core or heater matrix leaking (Chapter 3, Section 3 or 9).
- [ ] Pressure cap faulty (Chapter 3, Section 3).
- [ ] Coolant pump internal seal leaking (Chapter 3, Section 7).
- [ ] Coolant pump-to-housing seal leaking (Chapter 3, Section 7).
- [ ] Boiling due to overheating (Chapter 3, Section 1).
- [ ] Core plug leaking (Chapter 2B, Section 13).

Internal coolant leakage

- [ ] Leaking cylinder head gasket (Chapter 2A, Section 11).
- [ ] Cracked cylinder head or cylinder block (Chapter 2B, Section 7, 13).

Corrosion

- [ ] infrequent draining and flushing (Chapter 1, Section 31).
- [ ] Incorrect coolant mixture or inappropriate coolant type (Chapter 1, Section 31).

Clutch

Pedal travels to floor – no pressure or very little resistance

- [ ] Faulty master or slave cylinder (Chapter 6, Section 4, 5).
- [ ] Faulty hydraulic release system (Chapter 6, Section 1).
- [ ] Broken clutch release bearing or arm (Chapter 6, Section 8).
- [ ] Broken diaphragm spring in clutch pressure plate (Chapter 6, Section 7).

Clutch fails to disengage (unable to select gears)

- [ ] Faulty master or slave cylinder (Chapter 6, Section 4, 5).
- [ ] Faulty hydraulic release system (Chapter 6, Section 1).
- [ ] Clutch disc sticking on gearbox input shaft splines (Chapter 6, Section 7).
- [ ] Clutch disc sticking to driveplate or pressure plate (Chapter 6, Section 7).
- [ ] Faulty pressure plate assembly (Chapter 6, Section 7).
- [ ] Clutch release mechanism worn or incorrectly assembled (Chapter 6, Section 8).

Clutch slips (engine speed increases, with no increase in vehicle speed)

- [ ] Faulty hydraulic release system (Chapter 6, Section 1).
- [ ] Clutch disc linings excessively worn (Chapter 6, Section 7).

- [ ] Clutch disc linings contaminated with oil or grease (Chapter 6, Section 7).
- [ ] Faulty pressure plate or weak diaphragm spring (Chapter 6, Section 7).

Judder as clutch is engaged

- [ ] Clutch disc linings contaminated with oil or grease (Chapter 6, Section 7).
- [ ] Clutch disc linings excessively worn (Chapter 6, Section 7).
- [ ] Faulty or distorted pressure plate or diaphragm spring (Chapter 6, Section 7).
- [ ] Worn or loose engine or gearbox mountings (Chapter 2A, Section 14).
- [ ] Clutch disc hub or gearbox input shaft splines worn (Chapter 6, Section 7).

Noise when depressing or releasing clutch pedal

- [ ] Worn clutch release bearing (Chapter 6, Section 8).
- [ ] Worn or dry clutch pedal pivot (Chapter 6, Section 3).
- [ ] Faulty pressure plate assembly (Chapter 6, Section 7).
- [ ] Pressure plate diaphragm spring broken (Chapter 6, Section 7).
- [ ] Broken clutch friction plate cushioning springs (Chapter 6, Section 7).

Manual transmission

Noisy in neutral with engine running
- [ ] Input shaft bearings worn (noise apparent with clutch pedal released, but not when depressed) (Chapter 7A, Section 4).
- [ ] *Clutch release bearing worn (noise apparent with clutch pedal depressed, possibly less when released) (Chapter 6, Section 8).

Noisy in one particular gear
- [ ] Worn, damaged or chipped gear teeth (Chapter 7A, Section 4).*

Difficulty engaging gears
- [ ] Clutch fault (Chapter 6).
- [ ] Worn or damaged gear linkage (Chapter 7A, Section 2).
- [ ] Worn synchroniser units (Chapter 7A, Section 4).*

Jumps out of gear
- [ ] Worn or damaged gear linkage (Chapter 7A, Section 2).
- [ ] Worn synchroniser units (Chapter 7A, Section 4).
- [ ] *Worn selector forks (Chapter 7A, Section 4).*

Vibration
- [ ] Worn bearings (Chapter 7A, Section 4).*

Lubricant leaks
- [ ] Leaking oil seal (Chapter 7A, Section 6).
- [ ] Leaking housing joint (Chapter 7A, Section 4).
- [ ] *Leaking input shaft oil seal (Chapter 7A, Section 6).

Although the corrective action necessary to remedy the symptoms described is beyond the scope of the home mechanic, the above information should be helpful in isolating the cause of the condition, so that the owner can communicate clearly with a professional mechanic.

Multitronic transmission

Fluid leakage
- [ ] Note: Due to the complexity of the Multitronic transmission, it is difficult for the home mechanic to properly diagnose and service this unit.
- [ ] For problems other than the following, the vehicle should be taken to a dealer service department or automatic transmission specialist.
- [ ] Do not be too hasty in removing the transmission if a fault is suspected, as most of the testing is carried out with the unit still fitted.
- [ ] Automatic transmission fluid is usually dark in colour.
- [ ] Fluid leaks should not be confused with engine oil, which can easily be blown onto the transmission by airflow.
- [ ] To determine the source of a leak, first remove all built-up dirt and grime from the transmission housing and surrounding areas using a degreasing agent, or by steam-cleaning.
- [ ] Drive the vehicle at low speed, so airflow will not blow the leak far from its source.
- [ ] Raise and support the vehicle, and determine where the leak is coming from.

General gear selection problems
- [ ] Chapter 7B, Section 5 deals with checking and adjusting the selector mechanism on Multitronic transmissions.
- [ ] The following are common problems which may be caused by a poorly-adjusted mechanism:

a) Engine starting in gears other than Park or Neutral.
b) Indicator panel indicating a gear other than the one actually being used.
c) Vehicle moves when in Park or Neutral.
d) Poor gear shift quality or erratic gear changes.
Refer to Chapter 7B, Section 5 for the selector mechanism adjustment procedure.

Transmission will not downshift (kickdown) with accelerator pedal fully depressed
- [ ] Low transmission fluid level (Chapter 1, Section 28).
- [ ] Incorrect selector mechanism adjustment (Chapter 7B, Section 5).

Engine will not start in any gear, or starts in gears other than Park or Neutral
- [ ] Incorrect selector mechanism adjustment (Chapter 7B, Section 5).

Transmission slips, shifts roughly, is noisy, or has no drive in forward or reverse gears
- [ ] There are many probable causes for the above problems, but unless there is a very obvious reason (such as a loose or corroded wiring plug connection on or near the transmission), the car should be taken to a franchise dealer or specialist for the fault to be diagnosed.
- [ ] The transmission control unit incorporates a self-diagnosis facility, and any fault codes can quickly be read and interpreted by a dealer with the proper diagnostic equipment.

Braking system

Vehicle pulls to one side under braking

- ☐ Note: Before assuming that a brake problem exists, make sure that the tyres are in good condition and correctly inflated, that the front wheel alignment is correct, and that the vehicle is not loaded with weight in an unequal manner.
- ☐ Apart from checking the condition of all pipe and hose connections, any faults occurring on the anti-lock braking system should be referred to a Audi dealer for diagnosis.
- ☐ Worn, defective, damaged or contaminated front or rear brake pads on one side (Chapter 1, Section 4).
- ☐ Seized or partially-seized front or rear brake caliper (Chapter 9, Section 9 or 10).
- ☐ A mixture of brake pad lining materials fitted between sides (Chapter 9, Section 4 or 6).
- ☐ Brake caliper mounting bolts loose (Chapter 9, Section 9 or 10).
- ☐ Worn or damaged steering or suspension components (Chapter 1, Section 16).

Noise (grinding or high-pitched squeal) when brakes applied

- ☐ Brake pad friction lining material worn down to metal backing (Chapter 1, Section 4).
- ☐ Excessive corrosion of brake disc – may be apparent after the vehicle has been standing for somtime).
- ☐ Foreign object (stone chipping, etc) trapped between brake disc and shield.

Excessive brake pedal travel

- ☐ Faulty master cylinder (Chapter 9, Section 11).
- ☐ Air in hydraulic system (Chapter 9, Section 2).
- ☐ Faulty vacuum servo unit (Chapter 9, Section 13).
- ☐ Faulty vacuum pump, where fitted (Chapter 9, Section 18).

Brake pedal feels spongy when depressed

- ☐ Air in hydraulic system (Chapter 9, Section 2).

- ☐ Deteriorated flexible rubber brake hoses (Chapter 1, Section 10).
- ☐ Master cylinder mountings loose (Chapter 9, Section 11).
- ☐ Faulty master cylinder (Chapter 9, Section 11).

Excessive brake pedal effort required to stop vehicle

- ☐ Faulty vacuum servo unit (Chapter 9, Section 13).
- ☐ Disconnected, damaged or insecure brake servo vacuum hose (Chapter 9, Section 14).
- ☐ Faulty vacuum pump (Chapter 9, Section 18).
- ☐ Primary or secondary hydraulic circuit failure (Chapter 1, Section 10).
- ☐ Seized brake caliper (Chapter 9, Section 9 or 10).
- ☐ Brake pads incorrectly fitted (Chapter 9, Section 4 or 6).
- ☐ Incorrect grade of brake pads fitted (Chapter 9, Section 4 or 6).
- ☐ Brake pads contaminated (Chapter 9, Section 4 or 6).

Judder felt through brake pedal or steering wheel when braking

- ☐ Excessive run-out or distortion of brake disc(s) (Chapter 9, Section 7 or 8).
- ☐ Brake pad linings worn (Chapter 1, Section 4).
- ☐ Brake caliper mounting bolts loose (Chapter 9, Section 9 or 10).
- ☐ Wear in suspension or steering components or mountings (Chapter 1, Section 16).

Pedal pulsates when braking hard

- ☐ Normal feature of ABS – no fault

Brakes binding

- ☐ Seized brake caliper piston(s) (Chapter 9, Section 9 or 10).
- ☐ Faulty master cylinder (Chapter 9, Section 11).

Rear wheels locking under normal braking

- ☐ Rear brake pad linings contaminated (Chapter 9, Section 6).
- ☐ Rear brake discs warped (Chapter 9, Section 8).

Driveshafts

Vibration when accelerating or decelerating

- ☐ Worn inner constant velocity joint (Chapter 8, Section 3).
- ☐ Bent or distorted driveshaft (Chapter 8, Section 2).

Clicking or knocking noise on turns (at slow speed on full-lock)

- ☐ Worn outer constant velocity joint (Chapter 8, Section 3).
- ☐ Lack of constant velocity joint lubricant, possibly due to damaged gaiter (Chapter 8, Section 3).

Steering and suspension

Vehicle pulls to one side

- [ ] Note: Before diagnosing suspension or steering faults, be sure that the trouble is not due to incorrect tyre pressures, mixtures of tyre types, or binding brakes.
- [ ]
- [ ] Defective tyre (see *Weekly checks*).
- [ ] Excessive wear in suspension or steering components (Chapter 1, Section 16).
- [ ] Incorrect front wheel alignment (Chapter 10, Section 21).
- [ ] Accident damage to steering or suspension components (Chapter 1, Section 16).

Wheel wobble and vibration

- [ ] Front roadwheels out of balance (vibration felt mainly through the steering wheel) (Chapter 10).
- [ ] Rear roadwheels out of balance (vibration felt throughout the vehicle) (Chapter 10).
- [ ] Roadwheels damaged or distorted (Chapter 10).
- [ ] Faulty or damaged tyre (*Weekly checks*).
- [ ] Worn steering or suspension joints, bushes or components (Chapter 1, Section 16).
- [ ] Wheel bolts loose (Chapter 1).

Excessive pitching and/or rolling around corners, or during braking

- [ ] Defective shock absorbers (Chapter 1, Section 16).
- [ ] Broken or weak coil spring and/or suspension component (Chapter 10, Section 3, 10).
- [ ] Worn or damaged anti-roll bar or mountings (Chapter 10, Section 6).

Wandering or general instability

- [ ] Incorrect front wheel alignment (Chapter 10, Section 21).
- [ ] Worn steering or suspension joints, bushes or components (Chapter 1, Section 16).
- [ ] Roadwheels out of balance (Chapter 10).
- [ ] Faulty or damaged tyre (*Weekly checks*).
- [ ] Wheel bolts loose (Chapter 10).
- [ ] Defective shock absorbers (Chapter 10, Section 3, 9).

Excessively-stiff steering

- [ ] Seized track rod end balljoint or suspension balljoint (Chapter 10, Section 5, 19).

- [ ] Broken or incorrectly adjusted auxiliary drivebelt (Chapter 1, Section 8).
- [ ] Incorrect front wheel alignment (Chapter 10, Section 21).
- [ ] Steering gear damaged (Chapter 10, Section 15).

Excessive play in steering

- [ ] Worn steering column universal joint(s) (Chapter 10, Section 15).
- [ ] Worn steering track rod end balljoints (Chapter 10, Section 19).
- [ ] Worn steering gear (Chapter 10, Section 15).
- [ ] Worn steering or suspension joints, bushes or components (Chapter 1, Section 16).

Lack of power assistance

- [ ] Broken or incorrectly-adjusted auxiliary drivebelt (Chapter 1, Section 8).
- [ ] Incorrect power steering fluid level (*Weekly checks*).
- [ ] Restriction in power steering fluid hoses (Chapter 10, Section 17).
- [ ] Faulty power steering pump (Chapter 10, Section 18).
- [ ] Faulty steering gear (Chapter 10, Section 15).

Tyre wear excessive

Tyres worn on inside or outside edges

- [ ] Incorrect camber or castor angles (Chapter 10, Section 21).
- [ ] Worn steering or suspension joints, bushes or components (Chapter 1, Section 16).
- [ ] Excessively-hard cornering.
- [ ] Accident damage.

Tyre treads exhibit feathered edges

- [ ] Incorrect toe setting (Chapter 10, Section 21).

Tyres worn in centre of tread

- [ ] Tyres over-inflated (*Weekly checks*).

Tyres worn on inside and outside edges

- [ ] Tyres under-inflated (*Weekly checks*).
- [ ] Worn shock absorbers (Chapter 10, Section 3, 9).

Tyres worn unevenly

- [ ] Tyres/wheels out of balance (*Weekly checks*).
- [ ] Excessive wheel or tyre run-out (Chapter 10, Section 21).
- [ ] Worn shock absorbers (Chapters 1 and 10).
- [ ] Faulty tyre (*Weekly checks*).

Electrical system

Battery will not hold a charge more than a few days

- [ ] Note: For problems associated with the starting system, refer to the faults listed under Engine earlier in this, Section.
- [ ] Battery defective internally (Chapter 5, Section 2).
- [ ] Battery electrolyte level low – where applicable (*Weekly checks*).
- [ ] Battery terminal connections loose or corroded (*Weekly checks*).
- [ ] Auxiliary drivebelt worn – or incorrectly adjusted, where applicable (Chapter 1, Section 8).
- [ ] Alternator not charging at correct output (Chapter 5, Section 4).
- [ ] Alternator or voltage regulator faulty (Chapter 5, Section 4).
- [ ] Short-circuit causing continual battery drain (Chapter 5, Section 2).

Ignition/no-charge warning light remains illuminated with engine running

- [ ] Auxiliary drivebelt broken, worn, or incorrectly adjusted (Chapter 1, Section 8).
- [ ] Internal fault in alternator or voltage regulator (Chapter 5, Section 4).
- [ ] Broken, disconnected, or loose wiring in charging circuit (Chapter 5, Section 4).

Ignition/no-charge warning light fails to come on

- [ ] Broken, disconnected, or loose wiring in warning light circuit (Chapter 12, Section 2).
- [ ] Alternator faulty (Chapter 5, Section 4).

Lights inoperative

- [ ] Bulb blown (Chapter 12, Section 6).
- [ ] Corrosion of bulb or bulbholder contacts (Chapter 12, Section 6).
- [ ] Blown fuse (Chapter 12, Section 3).
- [ ] Faulty relay (Chapter 12, Section 3).
- [ ] Broken, loose, or disconnected wiring (Chapter 12, Section 2).
- [ ] Faulty switch (Chapter 12, Section 5).

Instrument readings inaccurate or erratic

Fuel or temperature gauges give no reading

- [ ] Faulty gauge sender unit (Chapter 4A, Section 7).
- [ ] Wiring open-circuit (Chapter 12, Section 2).
- [ ] Faulty gauge (Chapter 12, Section 9).

Fuel or temperature gauges give continuous maximum reading

- [ ] Faulty gauge sender unit (Chapter 4A, Section 7).
- [ ] Wiring short-circuit (Chapter 12, Section 2).
- [ ] Faulty gauge (Chapter 12, Section 9).

Horn inoperative, or unsatisfactory in operation

Horn operates all the time

- [ ] Horn contacts permanently bridged or horn push stuck down (Chapter 12, Section 5).

Horn fails to operate

- [ ] Blown fuse (Chapter 12, Section 3).
- [ ] Cable or cable connections loose, broken or disconnected (Chapter 12, Section 2).
- [ ] Faulty horn (Chapter 12, Section 13).

Horn emits intermittent or unsatisfactory sound

- [ ] Cable connections loose (Chapter 12, Section 2).
- [ ] Horn mountings loose (Chapter 12, Section 13).
- [ ] Faulty horn (Chapter 12, Section 13).

Windscreen/tailgate wipers inoperative, or unsatisfactory in operation

Wipers fail to operate, or operate very slowly

- [ ] Wiper blades stuck to screen, or linkage seized or binding (*Weekly checks* and Chapter 12, Section 10).
- [ ] Blown fuse (Chapter 12, Section 3).
- [ ] Cable or cable connections loose, broken or disconnected (Chapter 12, Section 2).
- [ ] Faulty relay (Chapter 12, Section 3).
- [ ] Faulty wiper motor (Chapter 12, Section 10).

Wiper blades sweep over too large or too small an area of the glass

- [ ] Wiper arms incorrectly positioned on spindles (Chapter 12, Section 10).
- [ ] Excessive wear of wiper linkage (Chapter 12, Section 10).
- [ ] Wiper motor or linkage mountings loose or insecure (Chapter 12, Section 10).

Electrical system (continued)

Wiper blades fail to clean the glass effectively

☐ Wiper blade rubbers worn or perished (*Weekly checks*).
☐ Wiper arm tension springs broken, or arm pivots seized (Chapter 12, Section 10).
☐ Insufficient windscreen washer additive to adequately remove road film (*Weekly checks*).

Windscreen washers inoperative, or unsatisfactory in operation

One or more washer jets inoperative

☐ Blocked washer jet (Chapter 12, Section 11).
☐ Disconnected, kinked or restricted fluid hose (Chapter 12, Section 11).
☐ Insufficient fluid in washer reservoir (*Weekly checks*).

Washer pump fails to operate

☐ Broken or disconnected wiring or connections (Chapter 12, Section 2).
☐ Blown fuse (Chapter 12, Section 3).
☐ Faulty washer switch (Chapter 12, Section 4).
☐ Faulty washer pump (Chapter 12, Section 11).

Electric windows inoperative, or unsatisfactory in operation

Window glass will only move in one direction

☐ Faulty switch (Chapter 12, Section 5).

Window glass slow to move

☐ Regulator seized or damaged, or in need of lubrication (Chapter 11, Section 16).
☐ Door internal components or trim fouling regulator (Chapter 11, Section 13).
☐ Faulty motor (Chapter 11, Section 16).

Window glass fails to move

☐ Blown fuse (Chapter 12, Section 3).
☐ Faulty relay (Chapter 12, Section 3).
☐ Broken or disconnected wiring or connections (Chapter 12, Section 2).
☐ Faulty motor (Chapter 11, Section 16).

Central locking system inoperative, or unsatisfactory in operation

Complete system failure

☐ Blown fuse (Chapter 12, Section 3).
☐ Faulty relay (Chapter 12, Section 3).
☐ Broken or disconnected wiring or connections (Chapter 12, Section 2).

Latch locks but will not unlock, or unlocks but will not lock

☐ Faulty switch (Chapter 12, Section 5).
☐ Broken or disconnected latch operating rods or levers (Chapter 11, Section 14).
☐ Faulty relay (Chapter 12, Section 3).

One lock fails to operate

☐ Broken or disconnected wiring or connections (Chapter 12, Section 2).
☐ Faulty motor (Chapter 11, Section 14).
☐ Broken, binding or disconnected lock operating rods or levers (Chapter 11, Section 14).
☐ Fault in door lock (Chapter 11, Section 14).

A

ABS (Anti-lock brake system) A system, usually electronically controlled, that senses incipient wheel lockup during braking and relieves hydraulic pressure at wheels that are about to skid.

Air bag An inflatable bag hidden in the steering wheel (driver's side) or the dash or glovebox (passenger side). In a head-on collision, the bags inflate, preventing the driver and front passenger from being thrown forward into the steering wheel or windscreen.

Air cleaner A metal or plastic housing, containing a filter element, which removes dust and dirt from the air being drawn into the engine.

Air filter element The actual filter in an air cleaner system, usually manufactured from pleated paper and requiring renewal at regular intervals.

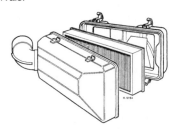

Air filter

Allen key A hexagonal wrench which fits into a recessed hexagonal hole.

Alligator clip A long-nosed spring-loaded metal clip with meshing teeth. Used to make temporary electrical connections.

Alternator A component in the electrical system which converts mechanical energy from a drivebelt into electrical energy to charge the battery and to operate the starting system, ignition system and electrical accessories.

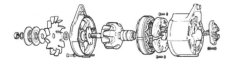

Alternator (exploded view)

Ampere (amp) A unit of measurement for the flow of electric current. One amp is the amount of current produced by one volt acting through a resistance of one ohm.

Anaerobic sealer A substance used to prevent bolts and screws from loosening. Anaerobic means that it does not require oxygen for activation. The Loctite brand is widely used.

Antifreeze A substance (usually ethylene glycol) mixed with water, and added to a vehicle's cooling system, to prevent freezing of the coolant in winter. Antifreeze also contains chemicals to inhibit corrosion and the formation of rust and other deposits that would tend to clog the radiator and coolant passages and reduce cooling efficiency.

Anti-seize compound A coating that reduces the risk of seizing on fasteners that are subjected to high temperatures, such as exhaust manifold bolts and nuts.

Anti-seize compound

Asbestos A natural fibrous mineral with great heat resistance, commonly used in the composition of brake friction materials. Asbestos is a health hazard and the dust created by brake systems should never be inhaled or ingested.

Axle A shaft on which a wheel revolves, or which revolves with a wheel. Also, a solid beam that connects the two wheels at one end of the vehicle. An axle which also transmits power to the wheels is known as a live axle.

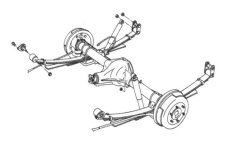

Axle assembly

Axleshaft A single rotating shaft, on either side of the differential, which delivers power from the final drive assembly to the drive wheels. Also called a driveshaft or a halfshaft.

B

Ball bearing An anti-friction bearing consisting of a hardened inner and outer race with hardened steel balls between two races.

Bearing

Bearing The curved surface on a shaft or in a bore, or the part assembled into either, that permits relative motion between them with minimum wear and friction.

Big-end bearing The bearing in the end of the connecting rod that's attached to the crankshaft.

Bleed nipple A valve on a brake wheel cylinder, caliper or other hydraulic component that is opened to purge the hydraulic system of air. Also called a bleed screw.

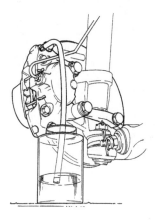

Brake bleeding

Brake bleeding Procedure for removing air from lines of a hydraulic brake system.

Brake disc The component of a disc brake that rotates with the wheels.

Brake drum The component of a drum brake that rotates with the wheels.

Brake linings The friction material which contacts the brake disc or drum to retard the vehicle's speed. The linings are bonded or riveted to the brake pads or shoes.

Brake pads The replaceable friction pads that pinch the brake disc when the brakes are applied. Brake pads consist of a friction material bonded or riveted to a rigid backing plate.

Brake shoe The crescent-shaped carrier to which the brake linings are mounted and which forces the lining against the rotating drum during braking.

Braking systems For more information on braking systems, consult the *Haynes Automotive Brake Manual*.

Breaker bar A long socket wrench handle providing greater leverage.

Bulkhead The insulated partition between the engine and the passenger compartment.

C

Caliper The non-rotating part of a disc-brake assembly that straddles the disc and carries the brake pads. The caliper also contains the hydraulic components that cause the pads to pinch the disc when the brakes are applied. A caliper is also a measuring tool that can be set to measure inside or outside dimensions of an object.

Camshaft A rotating shaft on which a series of cam lobes operate the valve mechanisms. The camshaft may be driven by gears, by sprockets and chain or by sprockets and a belt.

Canister A container in an evaporative emission control system; contains activated charcoal granules to trap vapours from the fuel system.

Canister

Carburettor A device which mixes fuel with air in the proper proportions to provide a desired power output from a spark ignition internal combustion engine.

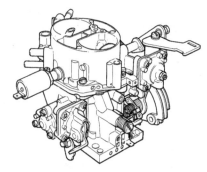

Carburettor

Castellated Resembling the parapets along the top of a castle wall. For example, a castellated balljoint stud nut.

Castellated nut

Castor In wheel alignment, the backward or forward tilt of the steering axis. Castor is positive when the steering axis is inclined rearward at the top.

Catalytic converter A silencer-like device in the exhaust system which converts certain pollutants in the exhaust gases into less harmful substances.

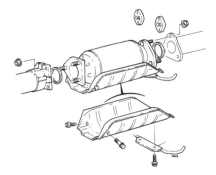

Catalytic converter

Circlip A ring-shaped clip used to prevent endwise movement of cylindrical parts and shafts. An internal circlip is installed in a groove in a housing; an external circlip fits into a groove on the outside of a cylindrical piece such as a shaft.

Clearance The amount of space between two parts. For example, between a piston and a cylinder, between a bearing and a journal, etc.

Coil spring A spiral of elastic steel found in various sizes throughout a vehicle, for example as a springing medium in the suspension and in the valve train.

Compression Reduction in volume, and increase in pressure and temperature, of a gas, caused by squeezing it into a smaller space.

Compression ratio The relationship between cylinder volume when the piston is at top dead centre and cylinder volume when the piston is at bottom dead centre.

Constant velocity (CV) joint A type of universal joint that cancels out vibrations caused by driving power being transmitted through an angle.

Core plug A disc or cup-shaped metal device inserted in a hole in a casting through which core was removed when the casting was formed. Also known as a freeze plug or expansion plug.

Crankcase The lower part of the engine block in which the crankshaft rotates.

Crankshaft The main rotating member, or shaft, running the length of the crankcase, with offset "throws" to which the connecting rods are attached.

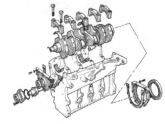

Crankshaft assembly

Crocodile clip See Alligator clip

D

Diagnostic code Code numbers obtained by accessing the diagnostic mode of an engine management computer. This code can be used to determine the area in the system where a malfunction may be located.

Disc brake A brake design incorporating a rotating disc onto which brake pads are squeezed. The resulting friction converts the energy of a moving vehicle into heat.

Double-overhead cam (DOHC) An engine that uses two overhead camshafts, usually one for the intake valves and one for the exhaust valves.

Drivebelt(s) The belt(s) used to drive accessories such as the alternator, water pump, power steering pump, air conditioning compressor, etc. off the crankshaft pulley.

Accessory drivebelts

Driveshaft Any shaft used to transmit motion. Commonly used when referring to the axleshafts on a front wheel drive vehicle.

Driveshaft

Drum brake A type of brake using a drum-shaped metal cylinder attached to the inner surface of the wheel. When the brake pedal is pressed, curved brake shoes with friction linings press against the inside of the drum to slow or stop the vehicle.

Drum brake assembly

E

EGR valve A valve used to introduce exhaust gases into the intake air stream.

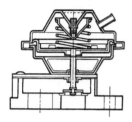

EGR valve

Electronic control unit (ECU) A computer which controls (for instance) ignition and fuel injection systems, or an anti-lock braking system. For more information refer to the *Haynes Automotive Electrical and Electronic Systems Manual*.

Electronic Fuel Injection (EFI) A computer controlled fuel system that distributes fuel through an injector located in each intake port of the engine.

Emergency brake A braking system, independent of the main hydraulic system, that can be used to slow or stop the vehicle if the primary brakes fail, or to hold the vehicle stationary even though the brake pedal isn't depressed. It usually consists of a hand lever that actuates either front or rear brakes mechanically through a series of cables and linkages. Also known as a handbrake or parking brake.

Endfloat The amount of lengthwise movement between two parts. As applied to a crankshaft, the distance that the crankshaft can move forward and back in the cylinder block.

Engine management system (EMS) A computer controlled system which manages the fuel injection and the ignition systems in an integrated fashion.

Exhaust manifold A part with several passages through which exhaust gases leave the engine combustion chambers and enter the exhaust pipe.

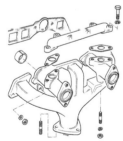

Exhaust manifold

F

Fan clutch A viscous (fluid) drive coupling device which permits variable engine fan speeds in relation to engine speeds.

Feeler blade A thin strip or blade of hardened steel, ground to an exact thickness, used to check or measure clearances between parts.

Feeler blade

Firing order The order in which the engine cylinders fire, or deliver their power strokes, beginning with the number one cylinder.

Flywheel A heavy spinning wheel in which energy is absorbed and stored by means of momentum. On cars, the flywheel is attached to the crankshaft to smooth out firing impulses.

Free play The amount of travel before any action takes place. The "looseness" in a linkage, or an assembly of parts, between the initial application of force and actual movement. For example, the distance the brake pedal moves before the pistons in the master cylinder are actuated.

Fuse An electrical device which protects a circuit against accidental overload. The typical fuse contains a soft piece of metal which is calibrated to melt at a predetermined current flow (expressed as amps) and break the circuit.

Fusible link A circuit protection device consisting of a conductor surrounded by heat-resistant insulation. The conductor is smaller than the wire it protects, so it acts as the weakest link in the circuit. Unlike a blown fuse, a failed fusible link must frequently be cut from the wire for replacement.

G

Gap The distance the spark must travel in jumping from the centre electrode to the side

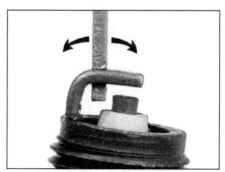

Adjusting spark plug gap

electrode in a spark plug. Also refers to the spacing between the points in a contact breaker assembly in a conventional points-type ignition, or to the distance between the reluctor or rotor and the pickup coil in an electronic ignition.

Gasket Any thin, soft material - usually cork, cardboard, asbestos or soft metal - installed between two metal surfaces to ensure a good seal. For instance, the cylinder head gasket seals the joint between the block and the cylinder head.

Gasket

Gauge An instrument panel display used to monitor engine conditions. A gauge with a movable pointer on a dial or a fixed scale is an analogue gauge. A gauge with a numerical readout is called a digital gauge.

H

Halfshaft A rotating shaft that transmits power from the final drive unit to a drive wheel, usually when referring to a live rear axle.

Harmonic balancer A device designed to reduce torsion or twisting vibration in the crankshaft. May be incorporated in the crankshaft pulley. Also known as a vibration damper.

Hone An abrasive tool for correcting small irregularities or differences in diameter in an engine cylinder, brake cylinder, etc.

Hydraulic tappet A tappet that utilises hydraulic pressure from the engine's lubrication system to maintain zero clearance (constant contact with both camshaft and valve stem). Automatically adjusts to variation in valve stem length. Hydraulic tappets also reduce valve noise.

I

Ignition timing The moment at which the spark plug fires, usually expressed in the number of crankshaft degrees before the piston reaches the top of its stroke.

Inlet manifold A tube or housing with passages through which flows the air-fuel mixture (carburettor vehicles and vehicles with throttle body injection) or air only (port fuel-injected vehicles) to the port openings in the cylinder head.

J

Jump start Starting the engine of a vehicle with a discharged or weak battery by attaching jump leads from the weak battery to a charged or helper battery.

L

Load Sensing Proportioning Valve (LSPV) A brake hydraulic system control valve that works like a proportioning valve, but also takes into consideration the amount of weight carried by the rear axle.
Locknut A nut used to lock an adjustment nut, or other threaded component, in place. For example, a locknut is employed to keep the adjusting nut on the rocker arm in position.
Lockwasher A form of washer designed to prevent an attaching nut from working loose.

M

MacPherson strut A type of front suspension system devised by Earle MacPherson at Ford of England. In its original form, a simple lateral link with the anti-roll bar creates the lower control arm. A long strut - an integral coil spring and shock absorber - is mounted between the body and the steering knuckle. Many modern so-called MacPherson strut systems use a conventional lower A-arm and don't rely on the anti-roll bar for location.
Multimeter An electrical test instrument with the capability to measure voltage, current and resistance.

N

NOx Oxides of Nitrogen. A common toxic pollutant emitted by petrol and diesel engines at higher temperatures.

O

Ohm The unit of electrical resistance. One volt applied to a resistance of one ohm will produce a current of one amp.
Ohmmeter An instrument for measuring electrical resistance.
O-ring A type of sealing ring made of a special rubber-like material; in use, the O-ring is compressed into a groove to provide the sealing action.

O-ring

Overhead cam (ohc) engine An engine with the camshaft(s) located on top of the cylinder head(s).
Overhead valve (ohv) engine An engine with the valves located in the cylinder head, but with the camshaft located in the engine block.
Oxygen sensor A device installed in the engine exhaust manifold, which senses the oxygen content in the exhaust and converts this information into an electric current. Also called a Lambda sensor.

P

Phillips screw A type of screw head having a cross instead of a slot for a corresponding type of screwdriver.
Plastigage A thin strip of plastic thread, available in different sizes, used for measuring clearances. For example, a strip of Plastigage is laid across a bearing journal. The parts are assembled and dismantled; the width of the crushed strip indicates the clearance between journal and bearing.

Plastigage

Propeller shaft The long hollow tube with universal joints at both ends that carries power from the transmission to the differential on front-engined rear wheel drive vehicles.
Proportioning valve A hydraulic control valve which limits the amount of pressure to the rear brakes during panic stops to prevent wheel lock-up.

R

Rack-and-pinion steering A steering system with a pinion gear on the end of the steering shaft that mates with a rack (think of a geared wheel opened up and laid flat). When the steering wheel is turned, the pinion turns, moving the rack to the left or right. This movement is transmitted through the track rods to the steering arms at the wheels.
Radiator A liquid-to-air heat transfer device designed to reduce the temperature of the coolant in an internal combustion engine cooling system.
Refrigerant Any substance used as a heat transfer agent in an air-conditioning system. R-12 has been the principle refrigerant for many years; recently, however, manufacturers have begun using R-134a, a non-CFC substance that is considered less harmful to the ozone in the upper atmosphere.

Rocker arm A lever arm that rocks on a shaft or pivots on a stud. In an overhead valve engine, the rocker arm converts the upward movement of the pushrod into a downward movement to open a valve.
Rotor In a distributor, the rotating device inside the cap that connects the centre electrode and the outer terminals as it turns, distributing the high voltage from the coil secondary winding to the proper spark plug. Also, that part of an alternator which rotates inside the stator. Also, the rotating assembly of a turbocharger, including the compressor wheel, shaft and turbine wheel.
Runout The amount of wobble (in-and-out movement) of a gear or wheel as it's rotated. The amount a shaft rotates "out-of-true." The out-of-round condition of a rotating part.

S

Sealant A liquid or paste used to prevent leakage at a joint. Sometimes used in conjunction with a gasket.
Sealed beam lamp An older headlight design which integrates the reflector, lens and filaments into a hermetically-sealed one-piece unit. When a filament burns out or the lens cracks, the entire unit is simply replaced.
Serpentine drivebelt A single, long, wide accessory drivebelt that's used on some newer vehicles to drive all the accessories, instead of a series of smaller, shorter belts. Serpentine drivebelts are usually tensioned by an automatic tensioner.

Serpentine drivebelt

Shim Thin spacer, commonly used to adjust the clearance or relative positions between two parts. For example, shims inserted into or under bucket tappets control valve clearances. Clearance is adjusted by changing the thickness of the shim.
Slide hammer A special puller that screws into or hooks onto a component such as a shaft or bearing; a heavy sliding handle on the shaft bottoms against the end of the shaft to knock the component free.
Sprocket A tooth or projection on the periphery of a wheel, shaped to engage with a chain or drivebelt. Commonly used to refer to the sprocket wheel itself.

Starter inhibitor switch On vehicles with an automatic transmission, a switch that prevents starting if the vehicle is not in Neutral or Park.

Strut See MacPherson strut.

T

Tappet A cylindrical component which transmits motion from the cam to the valve stem, either directly or via a pushrod and rocker arm. Also called a cam follower.

Thermostat A heat-controlled valve that regulates the flow of coolant between the cylinder block and the radiator, so maintaining optimum engine operating temperature. A thermostat is also used in some air cleaners in which the temperature is regulated.

Thrust bearing The bearing in the clutch assembly that is moved in to the release levers by clutch pedal action to disengage the clutch. Also referred to as a release bearing.

Timing belt A toothed belt which drives the camshaft. Serious engine damage may result if it breaks in service.

Timing chain A chain which drives the camshaft.

Toe-in The amount the front wheels are closer together at the front than at the rear. On rear wheel drive vehicles, a slight amount of toe-in is usually specified to keep the front wheels running parallel on the road by offsetting other forces that tend to spread the wheels apart.

Toe-out The amount the front wheels are closer together at the rear than at the front. On front wheel drive vehicles, a slight amount of toe-out is usually specified.

Tools For full information on choosing and using tools, refer to the *Haynes Automotive Tools Manual.*

Tracer A stripe of a second colour applied to a wire insulator to distinguish that wire from another one with the same colour insulator.

Tune-up A process of accurate and careful adjustments and parts replacement to obtain the best possible engine performance.

Turbocharger A centrifugal device, driven by exhaust gases, that pressurises the intake air. Normally used to increase the power output from a given engine displacement, but can also be used primarily to reduce exhaust emissions (as on VW's "Umwelt" Diesel engine).

U

Universal joint or U-joint A double-pivoted connection for transmitting power from a driving to a driven shaft through an angle. A U-joint consists of two Y-shaped yokes and a cross-shaped member called the spider.

V

Valve A device through which the flow of liquid, gas, vacuum, or loose material in bulk may be started, stopped, or regulated by a movable part that opens, shuts, or partially obstructs one or more ports or passageways. A valve is also the movable part of such a device.

Valve clearance The clearance between the valve tip (the end of the valve stem) and the rocker arm or tappet. The valve clearance is measured when the valve is closed.

Vernier caliper A precision measuring instrument that measures inside and outside dimensions. Not quite as accurate as a micrometer, but more convenient.

Viscosity The thickness of a liquid or its resistance to flow.

Volt A unit for expressing electrical "pressure" in a circuit. One volt that will produce a current of one ampere through a resistance of one ohm.

W

Welding Various processes used to join metal items by heating the areas to be joined to a molten state and fusing them together. For more information refer to the *Haynes Automotive Welding Manual.*

Wiring diagram A drawing portraying the components and wires in a vehicle's electrical system, using standardised symbols. For more information refer to the *Haynes Automotive Electrical and Electronic Systems Manual.*

*Note: References throughout this index are in the form "**Chapter number**" • "**Page number**". So, for example, 2C•15 refers to page 15 of Chapter 2C.*

Note: *References throughout this index are in the form* "**Chapter number**" • "**Page number**". *So, for example, 2C•15 refers to page 15 of Chapter 2C.*

Note: *References throughout this index are in the form* "**Chapter number**" • "**Page number**". *So, for example, 2C•15 refers to page 15 of Chapter 2C.*

Preserving Our Motoring Heritage

<

The Model J Duesenberg Derham Tourster. Only eight of these magnificent cars were ever built – this is the only example to be found outside the United States of America

Almost every car you've ever loved, loathed or desired is gathered under one roof at the Haynes Motor Museum. Over 300 immaculately presented cars and motorbikes represent every aspect of our motoring heritage, from elegant reminders of bygone days, such as the superb Model J Duesenberg to curiosities like the bug-eyed BMW Isetta. There are also many old friends and flames. Perhaps you remember the 1959 Ford Popular that you did your courting in? The magnificent 'Red Collection' is a spectacle of classic sports cars including AC, Alfa Romeo, Austin Healey, Ferrari, Lamborghini, Maserati, MG, Riley, Porsche and Triumph.

A Perfect Day Out

Each and every vehicle at the Haynes Motor Museum has played its part in the history and culture of Motoring. Today, they make a wonderful spectacle and a great day out for all the family. Bring the kids, bring Mum and Dad, but above all bring your camera to capture those golden memories for ever. You will also find an impressive array of motoring memorabilia, a comfortable 70 seat video cinema and one of the most extensive transport book shops in Britain. The Pit Stop Cafe serves everything from a cup of tea to wholesome, home-made meals or, if you prefer, you can enjoy the large picnic area nestled in the beautiful rural surroundings of Somerset.

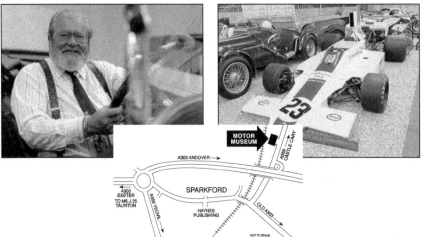

>

John Haynes O.B.E., Founder and Chairman of the museum at the wheel of a Haynes Light 12.

<

Graham Hill's Lola Cosworth Formula 1 car next to a 1934 Riley Sports.

The Museum is situated on the A359 Yeovil to Frome road at Sparkford, just off the A303 in Somerset. It is about 40 miles south of Bristol, and 25 minutes drive from the M5 intersection at Taunton.

Open 9.30am - 5.30pm (10.00am - 4.00pm Winter) 7 days a week, *except Christmas Day, Boxing Day and New Years Day*
Special rates available for schools, coach parties and outings Charitable Trust No. 292048